SHOPPING TOWN

1

2

3

SHOPPING TOWN

Designing the City in Suburban America

VICTOR GRUEN

Edited and Translated by
ANETTE BALDAUF

UNIVERSITY OF MINNESOTA PRESS
MINNEAPOLIS • LONDON

FRONTISPIECE. Victor Gruen in Seattle, circa 1941. Courtesy of Peggy Gruen.

The University of Minnesota Press is grateful for the contributions of Pat Blashill in the translation of this book.

A different version of *Shopping Town* appeared in German as *Shopping Town: Memoiren eines Stadtplaners (1903–1980)* by Victor Gruen, edited by Anette Baldauf, with essays in English by Michael Gruen and Peggy Gruen (Vienna: Böhlau Verlag, 2014).

Published by the University of Minnesota Press
111 Third Avenue South, Suite 290
Minneapolis, MN 55401-2520
http://www.upress.umn.edu

Printed in the United States of America on acid-free paper

The University of Minnesota is an equal-opportunity educator and employer.

22 21 20 19 18 17 10 9 8 7 6 5 4 3 2 1

Library of Congress Cataloging-in-Publication Data
Names: Gruen, Victor, 1903–1980, author. | Baldauf, Anette, editor, translator. | Gruen, Michael Stephen, writer of afterword.
Title: Shopping town : designing the city in suburban America / Victor Gruen ; edited and translated by Anette Baldauf.
Other titles: Shopping town. English
Description: Minneapolis : Univ Of Minnesota Press, 2017. | Includes bibliographical references.
Identifiers: LCCN 2017000440 | ISBN 978-1-5179-0209-4 (hc) | ISBN 978-1-5179-0210-0 (pb)
Subjects: LCSH: Gruen, Victor, 1903–1980. | Architects—Austria—Biography. | City planners—Austria—Biography. | BISAC: BIOGRAPHY & AUTOBIOGRAPHY / Artists, Architects, Photographers. | ARCHITECTURE / Individual Architects & Firms / General. | HISTORY / United States / State & Local / Midwest.
Classification: LCC NA1011.5.G76 A2 2017 | DDC 720.92 [B] —dc23
LC record available at https://lccn.loc.gov/2017000440

Contents

	Preface *Why Victor Gruen?* — ANETTE BALDAUF	vii
	Introduction	3
1	Vienna 1938	5
2	Flashback	25
3	Discovering America	59
4	The Big Breakthrough	101
5	Development of the Storm	137
6	Architectura	175
7	Environmental Planning	209
	Epilogue	231
	Afterword — MICHAEL GRUEN	235
	More about My Mother — PEGGY GRUEN	261
	Consumed? *The Heritage and Legacy of Victor Gruen* — ANETTE BALDAUF	265
	Notes	289
	Index	301

Promenade, Southdale Center, Edina, Minnesota, circa 1957. Courtesy of Gruen Associates.
Photograph by Warren Reynolds, Infinity Inc.

Preface

Why Victor Gruen?

ANETTE BALDAUF

In the spring of 1979, at the age of seventy-six, Victor Gruen asked his secretary to assist him in the reconstruction of his life. Over a period of seven months, Evelyn Neubauer and Gruen met regularly in his Schwarzenbergplatz apartment in the center of Vienna, then later at a nearby hospital. Together they recorded the milestones of his career, their efforts resulting in a 423-page manuscript titled "Buchplan. Ein Realistischer Träumer: Rückblicke, Einblicke, Ausblicke" (Book plan. A realistic dreamer: Hindsight, insights, and forecasts). It was dated December 20, 1979. Two months later, Victor Gruen died.

Twenty-five years later, I would read these pages for the first time in the Library of Congress in Washington, D.C. Drifting through the eighty folders and boxes marked "Victor Gruen," I remember feeling that it was somehow wrong for me to be peeking into the life of a stranger. There were scribbles on napkins, drawings from grandchildren, letters from his daughter along with the responses he drafted, lists of places formerly inhabited and of women married—the intimate remnants of a person I never met. Then there was a sheaf of several hundred typewritten pages whose historical significance I sensed immediately. Sifting through the pages, I saw a visionary power that was fired by both social criticism and a habit of thinking big. This was the long-overdue account of a man whose work had fundamentally altered the course of city development.

Since my first encounter with Gruen's papers, two relevant books on Gruen have been published. Alex Wall's *Victor Gruen: From Urban Shop to New City* (2005) gives a fascinating account of the continuities between Gruen's architectural work in Vienna and his understanding of urban planning as it developed in the United States.[1] M. Jeffrey Hardwick's *Mall Maker: Victor Gruen, Architect of an American*

Victor Gruen Box, Library of Congress. Photograph by Anette Baldauf.

Dream (2004) traces Gruen's vision for the shopping mall in U.S. postwar culture.[2] Both books embed Gruen's impact within the wider context of postwar urban development, but Gruen's personal writing offers a unique vantage point from which to trace the central forces that shaped the economic, political, and cultural transformations following World War II. His memoir supports an understanding of suburbanization as an expansive venture into unknown territory but also a means of large-scale economic restructuring, an attendant technology of Cold War politics, and a modality of race and gender politics. His account makes a corollary suggestion regarding consumerism as well: for Gruen, consumerism provided the ideological wing that carried the American Dream, and it formed the premise for a new model of economic production. Gruen's memoir serves as a magnifying glass through which to view the radical reorganization of the American landscape in the second half of the twentieth century. William Severini Kowinski argues that after the war, the shopping mall was "the culmination of all the American dreams, both decent and demented; the fulfillment . . . of the postwar paradise."[3] As material production was increasingly outsourced to low-wage countries and immaterial production started to prevail, the lines between consumption and production became increasingly blurry. Shopping turned into a form of labor, and the shopping mall into a variation on the factory.

Victor Gruen was born Viktor David Grünbaum in 1903 in the city of Vienna, where he grew up in a traditional upper-middle-class family. In the early twentieth century he was part of the Jewish cultural milieu that defined Vienna as a unique breeding ground for social criticism and radical visions of change. In the 1920s, he was a key figure in the socialist youth movement, and soon he pursued two careers: by day, the trained bricklayer and master builder was busy modernizing the flats and shops of Jewish friends and acquaintances; by night, he discussed politics, wrote sketches, and performed onstage with other members of a group called the Political Cabaret (1926–34). In the theater, Gruen countered censorship with the art of the pun. On one occasion he literally weighed words on a market scale after a policeman had warned him that in the future he should "weigh his words more carefully."

In 1938, four months after Nazi Germany's annexation of Austria, and after a series of life-threatening arrests, Gruen managed to flee to the United States. First he reunited the cabaret group on Broadway in New York. Despite the success of the Refugee Artists Group, he opted for a return to architecture. He began to promote his vision for a regional shopping center, and, referring back to his Viennese experience, he argued that all major European cities were built on solid combinations of commercial and civic space. But in postwar America, he criticized, the vast agglomerations of suburban developments consisted solely of individualized, private homes. In order to boost civic life in this barren sprawl Gruen suggested introducing what he called "shopping towns." A man of grand visions, the self-appointed "people's architect" promoted the construction of vast projects combining commercial and civic activities—and promising isolated housewives and roaming teenagers places where they could meet and mingle.

From his early work on store design in prewar Vienna to his later projects on city development in the United States as well as Europe, Gruen was driven by an intuitive understanding of the city as a stage and an unquestioned faith in the integrative power of commerce. Capitalizing on his excellent credentials in the art of staging and spatializing distraction, he set out to structure the amorphous agglomerations of American suburbs and, later, the neglected city centers. He built gigantic commercial machines in the expanding suburbscapes and large-scale pedestrian zones in neglected downtowns. His concept of the shopping town was meant to strengthen civic life in the atomized suburbs, and he hoped his pedestrian zones would nourish starving city centers.

In his memoir, while reviewing his career, Gruen recalls both the small and the grand events of his life and weighs them carefully with regard to gravity and impact. At the point in his life when he was writing, Gruen had become well known as the father of the shopping mall, and his innovation, developed together with his second wife, interior designer Elsie Krummeck, had been widely discussed as a highly ambiguous contribution to the fields of retail architecture and postwar city development. Gruen himself had come to see the shopping mall as a force of decentralization and fragmentation in Western cities; he repeatedly accused shopping mall developers of hollowing out his original vision. In the case of the Glatt Einkaufszentrum in Zurich, Gruen even sued the developer for using Gruen's name for promotional purposes while reducing the agreed-upon 51 percent of noncommercial mall spaces. He criticized developers for exacerbating damage to the environment by fueling the growing dependence on the automobile and for taking advantage of what he called monotheistic city administrations that worshipped the automobile as their one and only god. As an advocate of dense urban centers, he came to recognize that whatever radical vision he had for his shopping towns, they paradoxically facilitated the neglect of inner cities and even discriminated against existing, organically grown urban fabric. As an advocate of the pedestrian zone, he also saw that the rescaling of U.S. cities brought the white middle class back to the city centers—but, at this time in history, first and foremost as consumers.

Within architecture today, the term *Gruen effect* has come to refer to the quasi-magical ability of attractive store design to lure customers to abandon their intentions of purchasing specific items and instead lose themselves in aimless shopping and strolling. If transposed onto the scale of the city, the concept of the Gruen effect captures the central features of the condition of the postindustrial city, where goods produced elsewhere are sold in branded flagship stores, where *flânerie* is key and information a major currency—in other words, where the city itself has become a shopping mall. It is not surprising that in his later life, while fighting for an ecological and just city, Gruen rigorously distanced himself from the heritage of the mall.

In his memoir, Gruen offers numerous insider stories and reflects on the complex field of forces that sustained the postwar remaking of American cities. Even though he writes without the political vocabulary to name and contextualize these processes—or, more accurately, without the vocabulary we might use in our interpretation today—he clearly takes a critical stance. His outspokenness resurfaces in the later part of his life, when he devotes his focus to questions of energy policy and especially to the political struggle against nuclear power. Already in his youth, when he ridiculed the idiosyncrasies of Vienna's Socialist Party onstage, or when he projected the first regional shopping center in the midst of social isolation and

Altman & Kuhne, New York, 1940. Courtesy of Gruen Associates.

uprooting, his work was guided by strong humanistic ideals. Like some of his con temporaries (such as Reyner Banham, to mention one example), Gruen defined architecture as environmental planning: it was his contribution to the search for a peaceful coexistence of humans and nature.

Gruen's life story is not just that of a man who began as an interior designer, became an internationally renowned urban planner, and eventually ended up a visionary environmentalist. It is also the story of a Jewish emigrant who—unlike many of his acquaintances and relatives—narrowly escaped the Holocaust, together with his first wife, Alice (Lizzie) Kardos. At his first opportunity, Gruen returned to Vienna in 1948. Horrified to find that the city had been turned into a landscape of ruins, he visited as often as possible thereafter. He lectured at conferences and worked as an adviser on innumerable urban planning committees. In 1960, with his then wife Lazette van Houten, editor of a renowned retail magazine, Gruen bought an apartment at Schwarzenbergplatz in the center of Vienna. He founded Victor Gruen International based on the credo "Amerika darf man nicht kopieren, man muss es kapieren" (America must not be imitated, it must be understood). In 1968, he officially retired from Victor Gruen Associates in Los Angeles and moved to Vienna with his fourth wife, Kemija Salihefendic, to engage more deeply with the European market.

Thirty years after he fled the Nazi terror, Gruen was still not welcome in his hometown. His reception was cruelly symptomatic of the antipathy that continues to mark the relationship between official Austria and the nation's emigrants. In 1967, at the request of the ambitious but little-known architect Herbert Müller-Hartburg, the Federal Chambers of Architects and Engineers took Gruen to court.[4] The charge: when Gruen fled Austria in 1938, he had not acquired the certifications necessary to identify himself officially as an architect. The chambers preferred not to acknowledge that, as a persecuted Jew, socialist, and political satirist in Nazi Vienna, Gruen had been unable to finish his studies; further, he would have been summarily denied these certifications, or might simply have been killed. The plaintiffs never appeared in court, but Gruen did, choosing to represent himself. The judgment was a compromise typical of the Austrian legal system: the court grudgingly agreed to allow Austria's most successful urban planner to use the English title *architect,* but it denied him use of the German *Architekt.* In exchange, Gruen was required to make a private donation of 10,000 schillings to the chambers (an average month's salary in 1967 was 3,300 schillings). Faced with such pettiness and hatred, Gruen made use of what had always been his most powerful weapon: humor. He was respectful to the magistrates but said he couldn't promise that the waiter at Café Landtmann, his favorite coffeehouse, would now suddenly greet him with "Guten Morgen, Herr 'Architect.'"

Considering the atrocities and eventual genocide Gruen was forced to witness, it is remarkable that throughout his memoir he expresses a strong attachment to the city of Vienna and a deep admiration for its culture and history. For Gruen, Vienna was not just the city of his birth and early upbringing—it also continued to be his central reference point in defining his vision of a city. At the end of this book, my essay "Consumed? The Heritage and Legacy of Victor Gruen" traces features of Gruen's space-making strategies back to Vienna's modernism at the beginning of the twentieth century. In the interwar years Gruen learned the art of distraction by perforating the boundaries between life and theater, street and store, private and public space. It might have been these skills, taught to him by a city on the verge of social and material collapse, that allowed him, working on another continent a few decades later, to respond so successfully to shoppers' longing for imaginative escape and mobilization.

Following Gruen's autobiographical record, Michael Gruen supplements the memoir with an account of the links between his father's private life and his work.

This afterword reveals how Gruen's sense of humor organized both his business and his family affairs. In her contribution, "More about My Mother," Peggy Gruen asks careful questions about her father's representation of his second wife, Elsie Krummeck. As she points out, in addition to being crucial to Gruen's entry into the world of designers and architects in New York, Krummeck was one of the country's most well established designers. Krummeck created new store designs and regional shopping centers together with Gruen, and their daughter's essay here raises delicate questions about the erasure of women from dominant storytelling—and from history books.

This memoir is the result of a minimally invasive revision and expansion of Gruen's original text. The raw manuscript, written in German and stored at the Library of Congress, starts ambitiously, as Gruen recalls with great passion detailed stories of growing up in Vienna, fleeing to the United States, and developing a grand idea. But the manuscript reveals that in the course of dictating his recollections, Gruen increasingly lost focus and attention; the reader gets the sense that he recognized that he was running out of time. In an ongoing dialogue with his daughter, Peggy Gruen, and his son, Michael Gruen, I have carefully translated and edited Gruen's writing, especially the later sections of the original manuscript. For the sake of clarity, I have straightened out wayward passages and cut distracting story lines. I have also added notes, with the aim of contextualizing some of the central protagonists, especially those who fled Austrofascism and National Socialism. I owe special thanks to Ursula Seeber, of the Austrian Archive for Exile Studies, who convinced me not to fundamentally rework or fictionalize the manuscript (i.e., by constructing an autobiographical fiction and introducing the voices of the many absent women); she encouraged me instead to accept the occasionally brittle transition and the anachronistic tone as Gruen's signature and heritage. I thank her for this suggestion, and I hope that the final text succeeds in striking a balance among originality, clarity, and reconstruction.

This book was made possible through the dedication and help of several people. Peggy Gruen and Michael Gruen kindly provided me with the material; I thank them for their trust. At Gruen Associates, Ki Suh Park generously provided access to the firm's photograph archive. Margaret Crawford, Michael Sorkin, and Alex Wall supported the project in its early phase. I especially thank Katharina Weingartner and Dorit Margreiter, my coconspirators in many projects. Together with Katharina I made the television documentary *The Gruen Effect: Victor Gruen and the Shopping Mall.* With Dorit I revisited some of Gruen's sites, and we made the book *Der Gruen Effekt.* Pat Blashill, Tina Yagijan, and Helen Young Chang worked on the English translation, and Maria Messer contributed the much-needed fact-checking input of a historian. I thank the University of Minnesota Press, especially Pieter Martin and Anne Carter, for bringing this work to completion. My appreciation also goes to an anonymous reader at the Press for helpful feedback. Finally, for their generous support of this project, I thank the Dietrich W. Botstiber Foundation in Pennsylvania, the Hochschuljubiläumsstiftung of the City of Vienna, and MA 7 of the City of Vienna and the Academy of Fine Arts Vienna.

SHOPPING TOWN

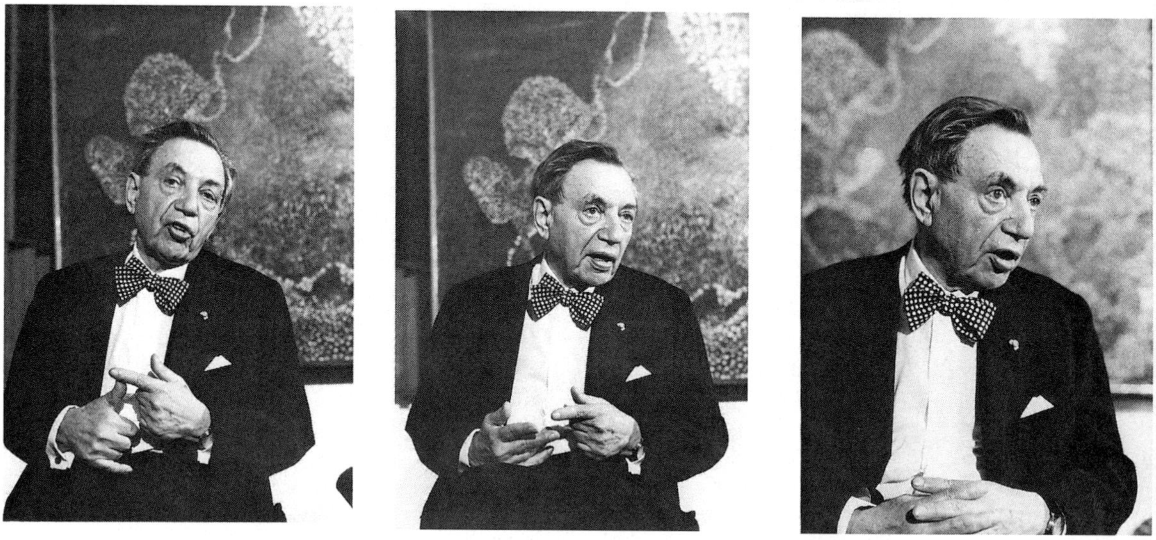

Victor Gruen, Vienna, 1978. Courtesy of Peggy Gruen. Photograph series by Peggy Gruen.

Introduction

I have been told that I should write my life story by thousands of my friends (or maybe just hundreds of them, but dozens for sure). For them, my life seems eventful but also quite long.

During the past five years I've made a number of attempts, but I always quit after about twenty pages. My keen interest in the present and the future has prevented me from dealing with the past. Now, on the occasion of my seventy-fifth birthday, I have decided at last to get to work. This decision was triggered by a comment from my highly esteemed doctor. When I complained about my various problems he suggested that by merely being alive I am flagrantly violating scientific statistics, which show that typically, today, men have a life span of seventy years. Since I am well aware that statistics determine all of human activity today (instead of, as you might think, vice versa), I summarily began seriously working on this book.

As a planner, I tend to approach every task by establishing certain goals. In this book I mean to relate some of the insights I have gained from flashbacks on my life, and then to deduce from them some outlooks for the future. It is very important to me to express my conviction that diversity and complexity not only enrich our own lives but also enable us to advocate for the universal interests of humanity. I am convinced that those who barricade themselves inside private rooms tend to block their hearts and minds from all other perspectives and even from a general worldview.

I have described only the highlights of my work and mentioned only those personal affairs that influenced my work. With the help of a dictionary, I discovered that such a biography is called ergography, because it is a report of the work (from the Greek *ergos*).

In retrospect, I think I can assert that I have succeeded as a jack-of-all-trades, partly by luck, partly by awareness of my luck, and partly by my willingness to accept all challenges. Since my work has not only been gratifying but also made me a useful member of human society, my objective with this book is to convince the reader that cosmopolitanism and breaking away from the boundaries of any specialization are joyful and useful attitudes toward life.

These stories—from a broad spectrum of events—are intended to represent how my concern with the confrontation between man and his environment was developed from a mosaic of different moments. But they may also open insights and outlooks for a more peaceful relationship between *Homo sapiens* and all other parts of creation.

For readers who hope to be entertained by a description of adventures, or for those who want to be enriched by reports of the success and various detours of a contemporary, I hope my story will suffice. After all, this contemporary was part of the first eight decades of the twentieth century.

—VIENNA, MARCH 8, 1979

1

Vienna 1938

THE GREAT FIRE

March 11, the fire burns and blazes from 11:00 p.m. until the early morning hours of the following day. I feed the flames and stare into the fire while I cower in front of our wood-burning stove. A passel of documents, offered up as a sacrifice, are spread out in a semicircle around me. My wife, Lizzie, digs into boxes and drawers, searching for new sacrificial material. The twenty-year record of a political past is bursting into flames. I'm burning everything that could be "combustible" in the near future. Actually, it would have been incriminating material four years ago already, but in that era of Austrofascism, known as "dictatorship tempered by sloppiness," we thought we could afford the risk.

The notes, manuscripts, programs, photographs, newspaper articles, and stage and costume designs consumed by the flames are documents from the Political Cabaret. From 1926 to 1934 I directed this group. I also supported it as an enthusiastic author, lecturer, actor, and singer. Every issue of our magazine, *The Political Stage*; the appeals and manifestos for the "Never Again War Movement" of the early twenties; all those writings against Austrofascism and Nazism penned since 1934—fall victim to the flames. I burn political speeches and articles for magazines and associations, political books and pamphlets, the names, addresses, and telephone numbers of all my friends and acquaintances.

But for all my haste, I also carefully set aside things that may be useful in the future. I keep my school reports, my charter as a journeyman bricklayer, a certificate from the master builder, my enrollment certificate from the Academy of Fine Arts Vienna, photographs of my architectural work, and articles about my professional activities published in national and international journals, as well as about fifty letters of appreciation from clients.

I sort through my numerous blue school notebooks filled with poems, aphorisms, and satirical sketches, mostly written on lonely nights when I was between twenty and twenty-five. I put these in a shoe box. The fact that a large portion of them will reappear on my seventieth birthday, in a book titled *Meine alte Schuhschachtel,* is not yet fathomable.[1] I keep the manuscripts of some small theater pieces, but hide them in editions of the Nazi newspaper the *People's Observer* to send on to a friend in Zurich.

At last, the bonfire is over. The fire burns out, the floor is swept, the room is smoky, my eyes burn. I need air.

I open the window wide and look outside. It is dawn. The view has been the same for the last thirty years, and it is completely unchanged this morning.

There is our tobacco shop, our convenience store, our mailbox, our café; there is also our security guard. He pulls a red armband with a swastika on a white circular background out of his coat pocket and puts it on purposefully.

The first day of the Millennial Empire has begun!

A VIENNESE SNACK

The hours before the cremation of my political past are dramatic. About twenty friends have gathered for refreshments in the largest room of the family home, where Lizzie and I have lived since our wedding in 1931. It's Friday. Most of the people present are younger than me, as I am approaching my thirty-fifth birthday. We share a passionate interest in human, social, and artistic issues. Many of us were involved in the Political Cabaret before it was banned in 1934—now many are working as writers, actors, and musicians at various Vienna cabarets. According to official regulations, these tiny theater companies, usually situated in the basements of coffeehouses, may host no more than forty-nine people, but between 1934 and 1938 they are important vehicles for freedom of expression.

I run a small architectural firm, but hardly anyone else works in such a bourgeois profession in these times of oppressive unemployment.

Our mood is cheerful and optimistic. We are expecting a change in the political landscape. Through secret conversations that have been going on for weeks, we feel justified in our hope that a relaxation of the dictatorship, a reauthorization of the Social Democratic Party (banned since 1934), and a restoration of democratic freedoms are all imminent.

A general amnesty for political prisoners has already been declared on February 15. Our gathering is a reunion with friends who have been imprisoned for their underground work. They tell us about their interrogations and we learn that we have all been spied upon. In the last few days, on the streets and in the public squares, and on the hiking trails in the Vienna Woods, we have all come across adolescents wearing socialist insignia, waving flags, and singing songs of liberation. In two days, on Sunday, March 13, a referendum will decide whether the continued independence of Austria is desirable. We are convinced that this question will be answered with a resounding yes. A new spring of political freedom will replace four years of oppression by a reactionary regime.

From time to time, as we nibble on cold cuts, cheese, and pastries and drink coffee, fruit juice, and wine, we turn on the radio to hear the latest news. Lizzie tries hard to keep the food and drink flowing. The radio tells us repeatedly that Chancellor Kurt Schuschnigg will make an important announcement soon.[2] Impatiently, we wait for his patriotic appeal to Austrians to stand together, to forget all our differences, to vote for a free Austria and, if necessary, to fight for it.

Finally, at 7:25 p.m., the voice of Dr. Schuschnigg comes out of the loudspeakers. The speech is as short as it is devastating. Schuschnigg says:

> The Federal President Miklas has asked me to inform the Austrian people that we are yielding to force. Because even in this serious hour, we are not disposed to spill German blood, we have ordered that in the event of an invasion, our armed forces are to offer no significant opposition—no resistance—but instead to withdraw and to await the decisions made in the next few hours. So in this hour, I take my leave of the Austrian people with the German word and my heart's desire: God protect Austria!

We are struck by lightning. There is silence for several minutes. Then a flood of questions: What should we do? Be patient and wait? Go underground? Should we flee abroad, and if so, where?

I briefly confer with Lizzie. The naive illusion that Austria can resist our big neighbor is destroyed at last. The Germans will invade Austria, and there will be war all across Europe. No country on this continent will be safe. Of this we are convinced. But how far away is far enough? Australia? China? Canada? The United States? We put all our hope in America. We want to go to America as fast as possible.

I immediately write two letters. The first is to my mother's brother, Herbert Levi, who has lived in America since 1914 and now calls himself Harry Lowry. The second is to the only other person we know in America, a New York actress named Ruth Yorke.[3] In both letters, I beg them to send an affidavit as soon as possible.[4] A few minutes later, I rush out to the street and put the letters in the mailbox in front of our house. I am afraid that the censorship of letters will begin within the next few days.

It is only then that I am able to worry about my friends. I tell them of our plans. They all want to do the same thing, but they say that the German language is the basis of their existence. "For you it is easy," they say. "As an architect, you can get a job without language skills. But for us writers and actors, we won't have a chance in a foreign language."

In this emotionally charged moment, I get carried away. I make a promise that I have no idea how I'll keep. Without knowing if and how we can get ourselves to America, or how we will survive there, I proclaim: "If we are able to reach New York, I will form a Viennese theater group, and we can do cabaret again. Let's try to smuggle our manuscripts abroad." Everybody is given the address of Ruth Yorke. But nobody really believes my words. Our joyous Viennese party has become a tragedy. We sadly say goodbye to each other, and no one knows when, or if, we will ever meet again.

NINETY DAYS IN THE THIRD REICH

The Nazification that had transformed the German Empire gradually, over a period of ten years, captured the city of Vienna almost overnight, in a climate of mass hysteria.

The explosion that erupted in the city included outbursts of enthusiasm and atrocities, especially against Jews, but also against the clergy and supporters of the Patriotic Front, and against communists and socialist officials. This intensity had never been seen in the Old Reich, and it surprised even our "liberators," the German troops, who were transported to Austria. It was a surprise to the bureaucrats as well, who arrived in droves to ensure a proper takeover of the newly annexed Ostmark (which was what Austria was now called). However, only part of the population responded with such enthusiasm. The vast majority of Austrians were either overwhelmed by the events or resigned to them. Many thought, "As bad as it is, it cannot get any worse." They acknowledged everything grudgingly, or timidly.

This mixture of enthusiasm, indifference, powerlessness, and fear may be explained historically. Since 1918, Austria had been "a state that nobody wanted." As the remnant of the great Austro-Hungarian Empire, it was considered an economic failure. The idea of an Anschluss to the Reich was as old as the republic itself. In November 1918, with the consent of all parties, the Republic of German-Austria had been declared part of the German Empire. But with the Treaty of Saint Germain, the victors of World War I (Britain, France, and the United States) insisted that the Republic of Austria become an independent state. Born from this pressure, the minor state was shaken by continual economic crises and mass unemployment, particularly of young people. There was constant strife between political parties, which led to civil war–like symptoms, corruption, and banking scandals.

In this atmosphere of crisis, paramilitary organizations began to form. These included the Socialist Schutzbund, a variety of *Heimatwehren,* or home defense forces, founded by adventurers and financed by Italian fascists, and the illegal *Sturmtruppler,* armed by Germany.[5]

The existence of these armed forces was a constant threat to democracy. The party in power was the Bürgerblock (a coalition of the Social Christian Party, the Agrarian League, and the Greater German Party), and its decisions were constantly opposed by the Social Democratic Party, which was nearly as large as the Bürgerblock.

By taking advantage of a parliamentary obscurity, in February 1934 the Bürgerblock used the methods of dictatorship to take total control of the country. The Social Democratic Party was banned, the parliamentary system was suspended, and all opposition was crushed with brute force by the combined power of the army and the various *Heimatwehren.* Only between 1924 and 1934, when the National Socialist Party shattered democracy in Germany, did the big political parties in Austria cease aiming for an Anschluss.

The dictatorship of Chancellor Engelbert Dollfuß, and, after his killing, of Chancellor Schuschnigg, asserted the formation of a "Patriotic Front" to spark Austrian patriotism, but this was doomed to failure. All these efforts came too late, and they were useless against the resentments of the masses of workers who had been bludgeoned. This corporate state could withstand neither the influence of fascism from Germany nor the dissatisfaction of its own people.

These chaotic conditions generated a vacuum that encouraged the violent occupation by Hitler's troops.

RED VIENNA

While the First Republic of Austria was mostly at odds with itself, there also existed islands of regional patriotism. These were the industrial cities administered by the Social Democratic Party, one example being Red Vienna (Rotes Wien). As the former capital of a multinational power, the Austro-Hungarian Empire, Vienna had grown into a city of almost two million people. Now that the rest of the republic had shrunk in size dramatically, critics, mostly entrepreneurs and the rural population, dismissed it as the hydrocephalus of Austria. Until 1934, all of the city's mayors and city council members were Social Democrats. Due to a qualitatively and quantitatively unique communal housing program and an exemplary health and social policy, Red Vienna was able to set new internationally recognized standards.

To finance the new social measures, the Social Democratic Party introduced higher taxes for the wealthy and prosperous. No wonder some critics called Red Vienna the red rag.

The population of Vienna was, and still is, as colorful as a rainbow, although over the decades, the hues of the rainbow have slowly changed. As the capital and home of the Habsburgs, the metropolis attracted many people of different nationalities. At the height of the Habsburgs' power in the sixteenth century, this meant an influx of immigrants from all parts of Europe, including France, Italy, Spain, and the Netherlands.

During World War I, the Austro-Hungarian Empire consisted of the "Kingdoms and Lands Represented in the Imperial Council," or about 52 million inhabitants. During the explosive growth of the Industrial Revolution in the nineteenth century, job seekers from all over the great empire moved to the city. By 1913, Vienna reached a peak population of 2.31 million people.

This population was a reflection of the ethnic groups existing under the monarchy. Czechs, Slovenes, Poles, Ruthenians, Croats, Serbs, Italians, Romanians, and Hungarians lived alongside a German-speaking Swabian-Alemannic and Bavarian-Austrian population.[6] Approximately 10 percent (5.5 million) lived in the territory known today as Austria, but this did not mean that they spoke German. The ethnic diversity of the city of Vienna was much remarked upon and praised, and it was reflected in the typical Viennese cuisine, culture, and language.

THE JEWS OF VIENNA

Similarly, the Jews living in Vienna had moved to the capital from all parts of the monarchy at various times. As Czechs or Hungarians, Germans or South Slavs, Poles or Ruthenians, they retained certain characteristics from their original cultures or lost them over generations as they assimilated into everyday Viennese life.

In the years between World Wars I and II, when Vienna was no longer a *kaiserlich und königlich* (k.u.k.; that is, Imperial and Royal) city but merely the capital of a small republic, the population decreased to about 1.87 million people. However, during this period, the number of Jewish immigrants from Eastern Europe rose in Vienna. In the Middle Ages, Jews had settled in Poland and Russia, but when they began to be persecuted in these countries, many sought refuge in the more liberal atmosphere of Vienna. These Russian and Polish Jews now returning to the West differed from those who had settled in Vienna earlier—they had remained very religious and conservative. As keepers of the German tradition, they spoke a modified Middle High German, enriched with flecks of Russian, Hebrew, and Yiddish. Because they dressed in caftans and wore their hair in *payot,* they were easy to spot. With their arrival, the proportion of the Jewish minority in Vienna rose by about 1 percent, from 8 to 9 percent of the city's population.

Throughout Europe, there were varied forms of anti-Semitism, some latent, some open. In Vienna, anti-Semitism formed part of a larger, overall hostility that pitted the many minority groups against each other. From time to time, the Czechs, Poles, Croats, Italians, and Protestants encountered this hostility, just as guest workers from Yugoslavia encounter it today.

Of the existing political parties, the Greater German or German National Party was openly racist and anti-Semitic, while the conservative Christian Social Party and the church took more subtly anti-Jewish positions. The only political party in which people of Jewish descent could occupy top positions was the Social Democratic Party.

Jews were not granted full civil rights until 1867. Politically, the Viennese Jewish community was just as fragmented as the rest of the population, with the bourgeoisie and wealthy Jews voting for the conservative Christian Social Party, while the intellectuals and those who were less well-off supported the Social Democratic Party.

As in earlier eras, the Jews in Vienna had limited professional options. It was extremely rare for Jews to find work in agriculture or forestry, in many types of crafts, or in the civil service. However, the number of those working in independent professions—as doctors, lawyers, journalists, writers, musicians, and merchants—in the city was relatively large. In high schools, Jews made up 40 percent of the population; at the university it was 30 percent. Artists and writers of the interwar period included many famous personalities of Jewish origin.

The Nazi battle cry "Jews out!" enjoyed great popularity for purely pragmatic reasons. The Aryanization of businesses made it possible for those who could provide Aryan identification cards to gain and enrich themselves. Others who owed money to Jewish merchants, doctors, and lawyers found themselves suddenly freed from these debts and could breathe a sigh of relief. Also, in terms of competition for scarce jobs, an entire minority group was suddenly disqualified.

So anti-Semitism was a popular prejudice, and the new rulers took advantage to the fullest extent.

THE PRACTICAL IMPLICATIONS

Whenever and wherever a new regime deprives a certain group of its rights, it can count on the unleashing of all kinds of aggression and base instincts. In the case of

National Socialism, the aggression was initially directed against the clearly recognizable Eastern European Jews, then later against all citizens of Jewish ancestry. It started with organized and often criminal youth gangs, which were financed by Germany and had already started to spread during Austrofascism.

Everyone who thought they had been mistreated by Jews joined the hunt. Denunciations of obnoxious neighbors, merchants, and intellectuals, usually on charges of being Jewish or communist, were the order of the day. Robbery, murder, and looting, if not instigated by the authorities, were passively accepted or treated with apathy. Though their duty should have been to preserve public order, the German police and Wehrmacht regarded the mistreatment of civilians as a sporting event.

The propaganda efforts of the new regime, communicated by the conformist mass media with posters, banners, party decorations, and street marches, had an overwhelming effect. The fear of being regarded as an opponent of the regime was so great that even those who had no sympathy for National Socialism were compelled to wear swastikas, give the Hitler salute, and join the "Heil!"

For the motley mixed minorities of Vienna, it was certainly thrilling to suddenly be considered as part of the "Germanic master race." Only gradually was this first wave of hysteria dispelled. But by the time the first forces of resistance were able to organize, it was too late. Austria was already in the middle of war.

ONLY NINETY DAYS

Though the ninety days I waited before fleeing were terrifying and deeply disturbing, I was lucky that I could leave soon enough. I narrowly escaped Austria before Kristallnacht descended in November 1938, with the ensuing "Final Solution of the Jewish Question." After that, there was hardly any escape from the gas chambers and other sophisticated methods of mass murder. I was fortunate because I had made an ironclad decision to leave as soon as possible, and because of a number of unusually lucky circumstances, which included bizarre conditions that could only be described as "illegal" legality. Above all, my ability to flee was attributable to the fact that the German propaganda, which claimed that the Viennese became loyal Nazis overnight, was just a fantasy.

"JEWS OUT!"

"Jews out!" the mob howls and screams from the walls and loudspeakers. But nothing is more difficult than carrying out this hostile disinvitation. At dozens of auditions and in endless waiting lines at police agencies and in front of other authorities, Jews have to prove that they have behaved decently, have no criminal record, and have no state, municipal, or private debt.

Anti-Semitic violence in Vienna, 1938. Austrian National Library, ÖNB/Hilscher H 4920/2.

People line up in front of the Swiss, French, and English consulates, hoping to get visas. After hours of waiting, one learns that only transit visas are being issued, and then only if one already holds an entry visa for an overseas country. I wait the longest in front of the U.S. consulate. Finally they register my application to immigrate. I am told that I can get an entry visa only if I can show an affidavit.

All this requires hundreds of trips across the city. On the streets, I feel like a hunted animal. I make wide arcs and even cross the street to avoid any uniformed person; I do not dare, even for a moment, to rest on a park bench or enter a coffeehouse. The fear does not diminish when I return home. Every ring of the doorbell or the phone makes me tremble. But somehow, in spite of all the danger, I manage to cautiously as well as prudently organize my escape plan.

EMERGENCY ASSISTANCE FOR REFUGEES

Early one morning, one of my best friends, the poet Jura Soyfer, shows up and asks for my help.[7] As a leftist activist, an antifascist author, and a Jew, he is thrice-threatened. He is an excellent athlete and wants to escape over the mountains into Switzerland. I hand over my ski equipment and give him a lift to the train station.

It is only much later, after we arrive in New York, that we receive the news that his escape attempt failed in the last moments. After an arduous mountain hike, he believed he had reached Swiss territory and stopped confidently at an illuminated mountain shelter. Unfortunately, he had judged the distances incorrectly. The cabin turned out to be the last German border guard station. He was arrested, interrogated in various jails, and, in June 1938, brought to the Dachau concentration camp. In September 1938, he was transferred to Buchenwald.

In New York, we set out to get him an American visa, and finally succeed at the end of 1938. He is formally released from the camp, but only on the condition that he first take care of a few prisoners who suffer from dysentery. He becomes infected himself and dies at the age of twenty-seven, on February 16, 1939.

MY CAR

In Vienna, due to my very successful architectural practice, I own a car: a Steyr 50, the direct forerunner of the Volkswagen. In these days, I use it for urgent trips. One day, I am stopped by a menacing gang of youths in uniform. I am asked to get out and my car is commandeered for the party. I timidly ask for a receipt and the boys burst with laughter. Yes, they say, that is possible if I accompany them to the barracks. I reject this dangerous offer—I'd rather go home on foot.

What follows is tragicomic. In the next few weeks, a polite policeman appears from time to time to notify me of traffic violations. When I tell him that my car has been commandeered, he does not believe it. He says, "Such a thing is illegal, and therefore impossible."

I see my car frequently because there are not many cars in Vienna. At first, it is apparently used by high-ranking German officers with drivers. Then one day, to my utter amazement, I see my old socialist friend Fritz Jahnel behind the wheel.[8]

Again, it is only later in America that I learn the facts. Since he was regarded as an Aryan of military age, my friend Jahnel was not allowed to leave the country. The National Socialist Party esteemed his services as a graphic designer and exhibition specialist. Eventually he was sent to Switzerland for a job. From there, he went to Paris, where his Jewish girlfriend, Judith Spindle, was waiting. They married and immigrated to New York. We saw each other there many times, until he died of multiple sclerosis. Thereafter, we enjoyed a most beautiful friendship with his widow and her second husband, Richard Kafka, who had also managed to escape from Vienna.

ON THE BUS

Another day, while I am on a bus, a uniformed man bumps into me. "Pardon," I say politely. He yells at me, "Wir Deutschen sagen 'Entschuldigung'!" (We Germans say "Forgive"!). On an impulse I stammer, "Je suis français." He becomes excessively polite and says, "Pardon, ich hab' ja net g'wußt, daß Sie dem Fremdenverkehr zug'hören" (Pardon me, I didn't know you were part of the tourism business).

ARREST

Despite all my cautions, I am stopped one day and arrested by two *Sturmtruppler.* I am marched a short distance to the Liebenberg Monument near the university, where I find about a hundred others who have already been detained. The line of captives, standing two by two, doubles within the next two hours. Everyone knows this is the end. From here we will probably be taken to barracks, and from there to a concentration camp. Rescue seems impossible. Suddenly, a man in uniform jumps up on a platform, and in pure Viennese dialect, says, "You have a *mazel.* We already have too many Jews for today. You can go home!"

The man has no idea that the word *mazel* is Yiddish. But as prisoners, we now know the true meaning of the word: it's an incredible stroke of luck! Without this *mazel,* I would have never written these lines.

MY HERR KARL

Helmut Qualtinger, a great satirist and comedian of the postwar period, created the now-classic character of the spineless Herr Karl. In Vienna in 1938, my very own

Herr Karl is actually named Franz. But otherwise he corresponds in every detail to the character sketched by Qualtinger.

Mr. Franz G. is one of two employees in my studio. His strength lies in producing compelling watercolors of indoor and outdoor spaces. Otherwise, he is charming and extremely lazy.

On the first working day after the Anschluss, Herr Karl greets me radiantly and says, "Herr Architect, I can give you the joyous news that because of my connections, we shall get many contracts. Since I have been an illegal Nazi for three years now, I will be the commissioner appointed to your company. From today onward, you are my employee. I will make sure that nothing happens to you, but only if you do not try to leave Vienna. I must insist on this, because without you, the work cannot be done." The loss of my office and all my equipment pains me, but my main worry is, how can I realize my plans to escape when Mr. G. will be watching my every move?

A fortunate circumstance solves this dilemma. Mr. G., because of his lovely laziness, celebrates the victory of his Führer day and night and appears in the office only rarely. His main job is to collect money from Jewish clients who are defaulting on their debts, and he lines his own pockets with great efficiency as he pursues this task. Occasionally he brings jobs to our firm, and these are usually for Kraft durch Freude events.[9] And so it happens that at night I find myself drawing the swastika that by day I avoid with all imaginable sophistication.

Finally, when it comes to sleeping, Herr Karl exhibits another unpleasant deceit. He enjoys tearing me from my sleep at two or three o'clock in the morning with phone calls. When I answer, he responds with "This is Gestapo headquarters." After a first terrible shock, I slowly recognize his voice and say, "Mr. G., are you drunk again?" Even today, phone calls in the middle of the night give me a similar shock.

The story of my Herr Karl would not be complete without a description of our reunion on the occasion of my first visit to postwar Vienna in 1948. After a heart-stirring march through my ruined hometown, I go to see a cabaret show on Liliengasse in the evening.[10] At the box office I suddenly spy Mr. G., looking shinier and even fatter than before the war. He welcomes me with open arms and cries, "Dear Herr Architect, welcome to Vienna, what a joy it is to see you again!" I have no desire to talk to him. But he says he has done me no wrong and instead wants to tell me about his suffering during the Third Reich. "What you probably want to tell me is that you were never a Nazi, correct?" I say. "How did you guess? That's just what I wanted to tell you," he exclaims. I am curious, and so we arrange a meeting in a café after the play.

There Mr. G. tells me that he was a *Märzveigerl* (a so-called March violet), like so many others who suddenly discovered their sympathy for the Nazi Party in March

1938. “Unfortunately,” he says, “they came after me and I was severely punished”—with the worst that one could do to him. “I had to work,” he moans.

In the Old Reich he was employed in an aircraft factory as a designer. There he did well because this strategically important industry was protected from air raids. At the end of the war the poor man was “liberated” by the Americans. But when they found out that he was an architect, he was again hired, this time as a designer of officers’ mess halls. Once again he demonstrated his flexibility. During times of extreme food shortage, his girth proved that he always fell on the buttered side.

Furthermore, he tells me, he would never again repeat his mistake of entering into a party too late. On the assumption that things would develop in Austria as they had in Czechoslovakia and in Hungary, he had already joined the Communist Party.

Despite his adaptability, he found himself in the district court a few years later, though not for political reasons but rather for the misappropriation of client funds. But this episode did not hurt him either. Some years later I would meet him again: blindingly handsome, he was a busy architect during the reconstruction.

BACK TO MARCH 14, 1938: THE MILITARY ENTRY OF HITLER

I use this day to visit the construction site of a ladies’ and men’s fashion store on Mariahilferstraße, as it lies directly on the military entry route of the Führer. Secretly, I am eager to see the parade. The building site is surrounded by wooden planks. There are twelve plasterers (*Gipsler,* as they are called in Vienna) working on an ornamental plaster ceiling located on the inner part of the scaffolding. As the “Heil!” cries keep coming closer, I turn to the workers and say, “Gentlemen, if you want to see the march of your Führer, I will give you some time off.” Nobody accepts this invitation. They work on the scaffolding with more enthusiasm than ever before. In light of this spontaneous refusal, I am also forced to stay behind at the site and miss the historic spectacle.

RUNNING THE OFFICE

As bizarre as it sounds, my office continues to run “normally.” Tradesmen, artisans, and vendors call on me. They all not only behave properly but also can hardly believe that I’ve encountered certain trouble. Many of them offer assistance. One client even energetically offers to get my car back for me. I strongly advise him not to do that.

The head of a big joinery company tells me, tear-choked, about his own family tragedy. His only daughter had been an illegal member of the Bund Deutscher Mädchen for several years, but an overzealous German discovered that her maternal grandmother is Jewish. His daughter has been expelled. She is inconsolable and considers suicide.

One day, when I open the office door, a *Sturmtruppler* faces me. He clicks his heels, his right arm shoots up, "Heil Hitler!" Then: "A dutiful servant of my leader, I am requested to forward our calculation. I ask you to kindly review it." Even for the usual tip, he thanks me with a brisk Hitler salute.

PURCHASE

Another time, two officers of the German Wehrmacht linger in front of my door. Politely, they ask if I intend to travel. Of course, they add, they are not looters, but would be very interested if I have anything to sell. They are particularly interested in my large leather armchairs. Their question about the price is a bad joke. Because I assume they will not pay at all, I tell them the paltry sum of twenty Reichsmarks. Immediately they agree, pay me, and ask me to keep a lookout in the stairways so that they don't surprise anyone with their "purchase." But what no one could know yet at the time is that twenty Reichsmarks is the exact sum that each emigrant is allowed to carry out of Austria.

A PIECE OF CHEESE

About two months after I send the letters to America I receive answers. Uncle Harry writes that he has tried everything but does not have the financial resources to invite us. However, Ruth Yorke's letter brings the wished-for result. She sends guardianship papers from Mr. Paul Gosman, who as director of a big oil company is entitled to issue an affidavit for Lizzie and me.

I can say without a doubt that I owe the opportunity to immigrate to America, and, most likely, to be alive, to Ruth Yorke and her good friend Gosman. I had met Ruth by chance. In the early thirties I had visited a great exhibition in Paris, Des Artes Decoratives.[11] On my return journey, I searched compartment after compartment on the train until I finally found one that was occupied only by a young couple. A very mature piece of cheese, which I had brought along with bread and fruit to eat, became the reason to strike up a conversation. The young woman politely inquired if she might open the window because of a strange odor she had noticed. I agreed, laughing, and explained the cause of the smell. From then on, we conversed splendidly in a mixture of English and German. I had picked up limited English-language skills in a course offered by Mrs. Annette Glass, a native Englishwoman and my mother's friend. The young woman, Ruth Yorke, was an actress taking German classes to attend the Max Reinhardt Seminar in Vienna.

Afterward in Vienna, we met each other almost daily. Thanks to my friends I was able to help Ruth and her husband. She was impressed by my architectural work and felt that my talents were wasted in tiny Austria. She insisted that I should move to America. After completing her studies she returned home, and we corresponded regularly.

That tiny piece of cheese proved to be a solid base for a lasting friendship. It enabled my immigration to the States and became the foundation of my career.

EMIGRATION LEGALITY

Despotism and terror against all unwanteds are in stark contrast to the plethora of bureaucratic emigration regulations. For example, Jews who have already obtained entry permits to foreign countries also have to get exit permits from Germany. That seems like a pure formality. They say you need only go to a certain counter, where a friendly official will stamp your exit permit. But even before you reach the counter, after a long wait, a rough SS man grabs your passport out of your hand and it is never to be seen again.

To avoid this fate, I speak to a lawyer who was recommended to me as a buyer of entry visas. Nobody knows through which illegal process he procures them. Certainly the business has its risks, but he does well. He asks me how much money I still have available. I tell him honestly the sum, whereupon he agrees to deliver my passport after I pay the quoted amount to his account in Switzerland. (He does not trust the German mark.) As soon as the Swiss bank certifies receipt of the money, I can pick up my passport with the entry visa. To my utter amazement he keeps his word. The exit visa stamped in my passport on May 28, 1938, states, "One-time departure to America via Switzerland, France, Great Britain and return to the German Reich allowed."

Furthermore, in Vienna, refugees are allowed to keep only enough money to buy the tickets to their destinations. Except for luggage (we have four cases) and a large wooden crate (a so-called liftvan) of prescribed dimensions, plus cash in the amount of twenty Reichsmarks, nothing may be exported. Exporting valuables is not allowed.

In my liftvan I pack a drafting table, drawing instruments, the self-designed furniture of my office, the art nouveau silver cutlery from my mother's dowry, hand-ground drinking glasses, which were a gift from my father to her, and a large amount of books, including the classic library I inherited from my father. These objects of great personal value will accompany me on my numerous travels throughout the United States and then, in 1972, return to their original location of Vienna.

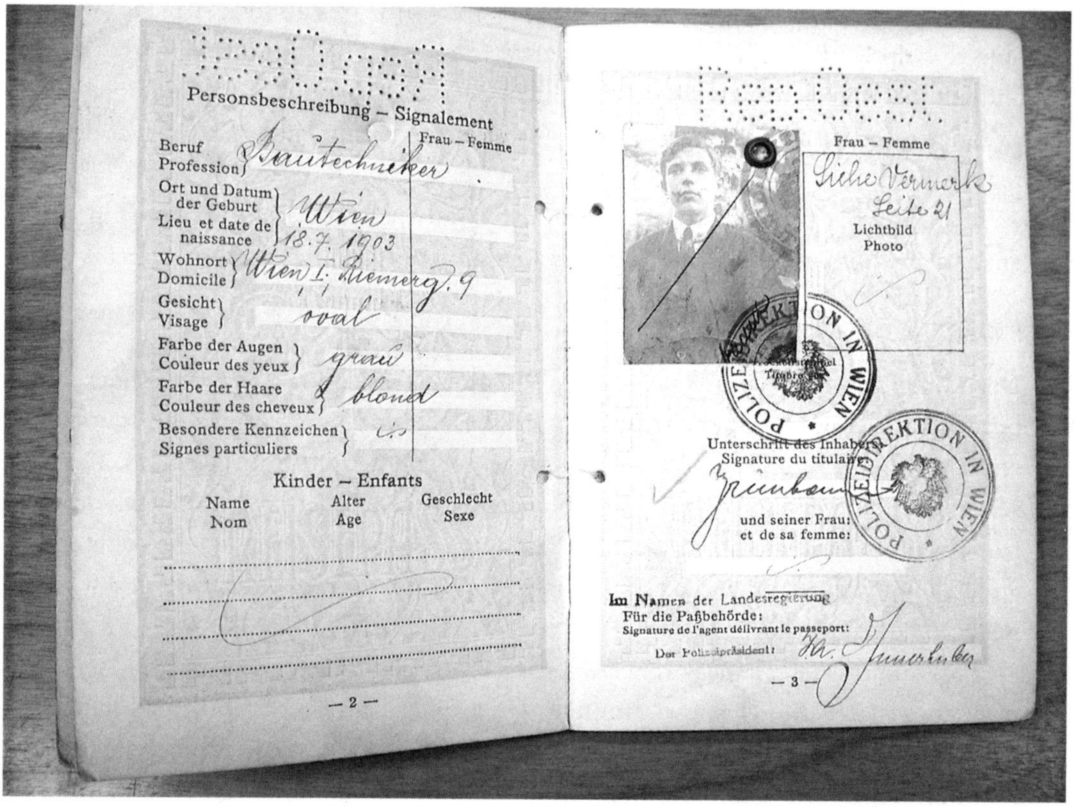

Austrian passport for Viktor David Grünbaum. Photograph by Anette Baldauf.

THE GESTAPO SHOWS UP

Finally, I pick up the travel tickets for Lizzie and me at the American Express office: for a plane from Vienna to Zurich, a train from Zurich via Paris to London, and finally a ship to New York (economy class on the *Statendam*). While waiting in line for my tickets, I am called to the telephone. Surprised that someone knows where I am, I take the handset and hear the excited voice of the young actress Illa Raudnitz.[12] Breathlessly she says, "Stay where you are. I'll be right there. Your apartment has been occupied by the Gestapo."

After ten minutes she arrives at the American Express office. She recounts her experience. She had wanted to visit us, and when she buzzed, Gestapo men opened our apartment door. As an Aryan she was able to question these people openly. She found out that they wanted to take me to jail because one of my suppliers with the old German name of Bogotay had pressed charges against me for not paying a small bill. In these final moments it seems my luck has run out. Helpless and desperate, I stand there, my tickets in hand.

Then, recovering from the initial shock, I call Bogotay's workshop to clarify this apparent misunderstanding, but I only get the supervisor on the phone. He is completely shocked, because he knows that I owe nothing to his shop. He offers to iron out the matter with Gestapo headquarters. I thank him for his good intentions, but I am also convinced that a meeting will not help. Everyone knows that if the Gestapo decide to intervene, no power on earth will stop them.

The only thing I can do is warn my wife, who is visiting her mother, not to go home under any circumstances. I beg my mother-in-law, who is an Aryan, to hide us. As a convinced antifascist she is immediately prepared to do this, although she risks her life. (Later, we also manage to arrange for her immigration to America.)

HIDDEN

So now we wait in the home of Lizzie's mother, hoping that it will take the Gestapo longer to find us. The problem is, how do we get our luggage? In this emergency, I call on Mr. Adolf Györgyfalvay, who has worked with me for many years as a furniture upholsterer and manufacturer. Shortly after the Anschluss, he visited me and told me that he was unfortunately forced to join the National Socialist Party, because otherwise it would be impossible for him to support his family. But he assured me that this would not change any of his Social Democratic convictions. He also told me he would be happy to help, should there be an emergency.

Such a plight exists now. Adolf Györgyfalvay agrees to do the job. Can I really trust him? I have no choice but tell him the address of our hiding place. Our lives are in his hands.

About three hours later, the doorbell rings. We answer and see a fully uniformed *Sturmtruppler* in front of us. It is Mr. Györgyfalvay, and he is carrying our luggage. He says that haste is necessary, he has a taxi waiting below and will take us to the airport. The leave-taking that we had planned for a few days from now has suddenly arrived. Hastily we bid farewell and take the taxi. Next to the chauffeur sits the *Sturmtruppler,* Adolf Györgyfalvay. Our destination: the Aspern airport. We fear that this ride will end at the headquarters of the secret police, in the Hotel Metropole at Franz-Josefs-Kai. Only after we pass Franz-Josefs-Kai, leave behind the Danube Canal of the Second District, and roar toward Aspern do we know that we are out of danger.

But at the airport, we are confronted with a few anxious hours of waiting. Strict body searches and luggage checks are performed. For this purpose, I am led into the men's room. There an Austrian policeman asks for my name and destination. When I tell him that we are immigrating to America, he sighs and says, "I congratulate you. I would like to be in your place." Nevertheless, he needs to make a detailed inspection of at least twenty minutes. But he explains that he has no intention of doing this. He would prefer to talk. In case someone enters, we agree that I will take off my jacket and pretend to undress. He reveals himself as an antifascist, and our conversation proceeds undisturbed. Without opening a single suitcase, he shakes my hand after twenty minutes and says, "I thank you very much and wish you good luck!"

We have plenty of luck. Not only is a plane ready to start, but there are also still seats available. On our last look back, we see Györgyfalvay, waiting on the flight ramp, waving warmly at us.

This episode has an epilogue. On one of my visits to Vienna after the war, I call on Mr. Györgyfalvay. He immediately comes to my hotel, visibly emotional and delighted to see me again. Now I ask the question that has plagued me since my departure from Vienna. "Mr. Györgyfalvay, you have explained to me why you were a party member, but why did you join the *Sturmtruppler*?" He replies, "I was never a *Sturmtruppler*."

"But Mr. Györgyfalvay, I saw you in the uniform myself when you arrived with our suitcases." He laughs: "How else do you imagine that I got the suitcases? I stole the uniform, then went to your apartment, cried 'Heil Hitler!' and said, 'The cases of the Jew Viktor Grünbaum are hereby confiscated.' Before the men from the Gestapo were able to recover, I raced down the stairs."

"Unfortunately," he continues, "they later discovered my deception. In my passport, I was identified as 'politically unreliable,' and so I had to enlist immediately. I never got beyond the rank of a common soldier. I was always sent to the most dangerous fronts, first to the Maginot Line in France, then to Stalingrad. By some miracle, I survived."

But fortune did not leave him! The written certification of his political unreliability helped him when the Russians occupied Vienna. Some of his business competitors pressed charges against him because of his alleged membership in the Nazi Party. When he assured the Russians that he had always been anti-Nazi, they wanted proof. The paper was stuck behind a picture in his apartment, which had been requisitioned by a Russian officer. The Russians marched to this apartment and found the picture and the certificate; after that, he was spared further harassment.

Years later, when we acquired an apartment in Vienna in 1960, the upholstered furniture, carpets, and curtains all came from the workshop of our dear friend Adolf Györgyfalvay.

FAREWELL TO EUROPE

Once we are on Swiss soil, we breathe a sigh of relief. The flight, which should have been a great experience since it was our first one, had been clouded by the fear of a possible emergency landing in German territory. Our near future is uncertain, but still we experience a feeling of freedom. The transformation from an oppressive dictatorship in Vienna to the free atmosphere in Switzerland is tangible, visible, and audible. On the ride from the airport into the city, we pass cheering people celebrating the victory of the Swiss football team against Germany. The sight of the white cross on a red background instead of the swastika is bliss.

In the seven weeks before our boat trip from England to America, we say goodbye to Europe and to the many friends who have fled Austria before us. This parting is very important to me. I can't shake the feeling that because the annexation of Austria turned out to be so easy, the appetite of the megalomaniac philistine from Braunau will grow, leading to a devastating war. As much as possible, I want to enjoy the European culture and lifestyle and store it all up because I assume I will find little of it in the New World. We visit museums and participate in what I will later in my writing call "urbanity." I want to meet, for one last time, all the loved ones I may never see again, so that I can remember these people forever.

We experience something new on this farewell journey through Zurich, Paris, and London: we live off the generosity of friends. We don't spend a penny of the twenty Reichsmarks. In Zurich, we are guests of the generous actress Mathilde Danegger, like so many other refugees from Hitler's Reich.[13]

We meet my childhood friend Leopold Lemberger, who now calls himself Lindtberg and is trying to get his theater career started. He will later become one of the most important directors in Germany. Poldi, as we call him, gives me all the manuscripts that I had sent him earlier, wrapped in copies of the *People's Observer.*

In Paris, Leopold's sisters, Hedi and Vally, receive us heartily. Vally and her husband, Willy Steiner, will later flee to Spain when Hitler invades France, and then to Mexico when the Franco dictatorship becomes unbearable.

In London, we are welcomed and entertained as guests of Dr. Friedrich and Herta Scheu.[14] Friedl had worked in Vienna for English newspapers, and on the day of Schuschnigg's speech, he left Austria. He was able to settle into London quickly. We also meet my mother, who had been able to leave Vienna just before us because of her close friendship with Annette Glass, an Englishwoman. We had to leave my sister in Vienna—she did not want to leave her beloved husband even though he was a Nazi. But eventually she grew disappointed, and through a series of lucky accidents, she made it to America months later.

OCEAN TRAVEL

The trip on the big steamer *Statendam* is a dreamlike experience. For seven days, we escape from harsh reality. With each rotation of the ship's propeller, we move farther away from our pain in Europe and closer to the uncertainty of a new land.

The endless sparkling waters of the Atlantic Ocean, the regular rhythm of the ship, the enjoyment of long missed, delicious meals tempt us to fully enjoy the present, and to push aside our fears about the past and the future.

Along with a group of fellow refugees, including Illa Raudnitz (the girl who warned me against the Gestapo), we imagine ourselves as leisure travelers. As we play games, drink tea, lounge in deck chairs, and dance in the evening, we forget the tragedies of our memories.

This first trip across the Atlantic remains unique and unmatched in my mind. I took dozens of others after the war, traveling first class or by jet plane, but not on any of them did I experience the same feeling of happiness.

Toward the end of the trip, a cloud of reality descends over our facade of insouciance. A passenger in luxury class, a genuine American, pulls me aside and into a conversation. "What will I do in America?" he asks. "I do not think it makes sense to worry about that. Some kind of work will be found, I guess. Perhaps washing dishes, cleaning shoes, or being a waiter," is my flippant answer. "Because I am not so optimistic to believe that I can continue my architectural profession in America."

"That's nonsense!" says my travel friend. "Millions of unemployed people in America want to wash dishes, shine shoes, or work as a waiter, but we do not have many good architects. If you think you are a reasonably good one, then stick with it."

Shortly before landing, our nervousness grows. Wild rumors about immigration controls begin to circulate. We hear that anyone with less than a hundred dollars will not be allowed to enter the United States. I worriedly beg my Viennese friend Dr. Rudolf Singer to loan me one hundred dollars for a few hours. I promise to return it right after the customs check. In fact, no one asks me for my money.

Twenty-five years later, this doctor will again prove to be very helpful. Even though it isn't his area of expertise, he will diagnose a mysterious poisoning of my blood (endocarditis) due to improper dental treatment. His intervention will save my life.

On the last night of the cruise, we are so excited that we cannot sleep. We go to the ship's bow and stare at the first lights of America. I then separate myself from the group. During these hours of expectant tension, I return to images of the past thirty-five years.

2

Flashback

CHILDHOOD

Memories are inevitably a mix of what one has experienced oneself and what one has heard so much about from others that one gradually comes to believe that one has experienced it as well.

A little red book titled *Unser Kind* that I have had for many years tells me that I was born on July 18, 1903, at 3:20 in the morning (a very inopportune hour for all involved), and that I received loving attention as a firstborn child. Also in this little red book, I find notes on my first funny ideas, attempts at walking, and early travels. My father, Dr. Adolf Grünbaum, was born in Vienna, the son of a miller from Lundenburg. My mother, Elly (Elizabeth Lea Levi), was about fifteen years younger than my father. The birth of my sister Luise, eighteen months after mine, is mentioned in the little red book as well. She was presented to me with the words, "This is your sister." At that time my language skills were not overwhelming. All I said was "Ischl." I used the same diminutive for my sister until our teenage years.

The apartment where we were born was at Marc-Aurel-Strasse 3 in the First District. The children's room was next to my father's law office. He tried to protect himself from our noise by placing a mattress against the double doors between the two rooms.

When I was about five years old, we moved to the second floor of a just-completed apartment building at Riemergasse 9, where I was to spend the next thirty years of my life. The house was next to the new district court, and it was designed specifically for lawyers. Our unit had two main entrance doors. One led through a small vestibule to the "k.u.k. Hof- und Gerichts-Advokaturskanzlei" of my father, the other to our apartment. The apartment consisted of a nursery that

Elly, Viktor David, and Luise Grünbaum, Vienna, 1906. Courtesy of Peggy Gruen.

also served as a living room, a master bedroom, and a large corner room that was reserved as a "salon" for guests and parties.

The apartment had the most up-to-date modern conveniences. It had a hall, a pantry, a tiny balcony, a bathroom with cold running water and a gas water heater, which was used once a week, and a toilet. Electric lighting was provided for each room. Since one could not quite yet trust this invention, there were also gas lighting fixtures, so-called Auer-stockings. (Years later, a descendant of the Austrian inventor Auer became my partner in America.) The tiny chamber where the cook and the maid slept had neither of these two advanced types of lighting. This was typical—it was assumed that service personnel had to content themselves with candles or kerosene lamps.

One of the three offices was equipped with a large library and had a dual purpose. During the day it was my father's study; in the evening, when we had guests, it was where the men smoked, drank, and talked politics, while the ladies in the salon continued their conversations about housewives' duties or fashions.

Although this may not seem very logical, I consider my childhood as those years before 1918, when my father died. I regard this era as a discrete period during which I lived in unclouded happiness, with loving parents who nurtured and cared for me. I lived unworried by anything until the war years.

What a perfect life of the aspiring middle class my parents led in that time before the outbreak of World War I! My father was a gifted, musical man who knew how to connect his career as a lawyer with his love for the arts, especially for the theater. His clients consisted mostly of friends and people he valued highly. He was not only the legal representative of a famous Viennese operetta theater, the Carltheater, but also an attorney for many composers, actors, and comedians. Among these clients were the composers Franz Lehár and Emmerich Kálmán, the violinist Fritz Kreisler, and actors such as Carl Treumann and Mizzi Zwerenz.[1] The famous cabaret artist Fritz Grünbaum, to whom we were not related, was both a friend and a client of my father.[2]

We were a typical Viennese family of the higher middle class. My father's family came from Moravia, and the Jewish patriarch of my mother's family came from Hamburg. Initially, Mama had some problems with the Viennese dialect. As a North German, "she stumbled over a sharp stone" and could barely adjust herself to the Viennese pronunciation of *schp* and *st.* When shopping for groceries on the Naschmarkt or in the wholesale market, my parents had to rely on the language skills of our faithful cook, Toni, since their requests for oranges, cauliflower, and tomatoes from the market women were met with incomprehension. Supported by a cook, a maid, a cleaning woman for the tougher work in the home, and a nanny and a tutor for the education of her children, my mother lived the life of an "elegant" lady. My father's large circle of friends and acquaintances soon turned her into a real *Wienerin.*

Despite the authoritarian methods of education, as children we were deeply connected with our parents. The most important meal, lunch, was eaten together in the nursery. Dad preferred typical Viennese cuisine; he ate *Tafelspitz* (boiled beef) almost daily, along with those pastries of Bohemian origin that were considered Viennese specialties. Good table manners were impressed upon us. My father believed that children should be seen but not heard, and that they should speak only when spoken to. So we listened attentively to the conversation of our parents, which revolved around art, literature, and world news. Everything that was not meant for our ears was expressed in French.

Much was also said about my father's enthusiastic involvement in the Schlaraffia union.[3] This German-speaking association, founded in Prague in 1865, devoted itself to the cultivation of friendship, brotherhood, art, and humor. As a men's association, it was of a liberal and progressive spirit in a time of monarchical-Christian class conceits; it had probably emerged from the Masonic movement and at the beginning of the twentieth century spread over the whole world. It had a peculiar rite: it imitated the language of chivalry, and each member had a Schlaraffen name. My father was called "Knight Pitaval on the bright side." Pitaval had been a famous French lawyer, and the nickname "on the bright side" referred to my father's sense of humor.

On extraordinary occasions, women and children were admitted to association events. When I first attended a festive gathering, my mother was introduced as "lady of the castle" and I as "Squire Pitaval." I had previously memorized the Schlaraff-style greeting "Lulu," but in my excitement, I confused this with another physical process and welcomed all with "Aa."

We often listened to my father's excellent piano playing and the many stories he made up on our Sunday walks, which we usually took to visit Grandma Grünbaum on Radetzkystraße. A series of unfortunate teachers and a specially hired "Madame" tried to teach me to play piano and speak the French language, but their efforts were not successful, which I regret to this day.

Our religious education stressed altruism and faith in God—but not in the specific god of one religion. Every night we said two prayers: "I am small, my heart is pure, no one dwells in it but God alone," and "I'm tired, go to sleep, close my eyes, Father, let your eyes be on my bed."

Otherwise, we celebrated the usual Catholic feasts and looked forward to a wonderful Christmas tree and many presents. At Easter, we held an Easter egg hunt. We had a passion for eating Jewish matzo, but we put ham on it.

Once or twice, my father insisted that we celebrate Passover, when he felt that the story of the liberation of the Jews from Egyptian slavery should be part of our education. I visited the beautiful Jewish temple on Seitenstettengasse, designed by the Victorian architect Josef Kornhäusel, only a few times, usually on the occasion of a wedding.

Because of the liberal lifestyle of my parents, who socialized with people from all faiths, as a child I was rarely aware of my own Judaism. One exception was in some of my interactions with our cook, Toni. She was a very devout Catholic who went to church each day at dawn. Facing an unspecified youthful folly, she was trying to find heavenly salvation by proselytizing me, a Jewish child. She scared and confused me with stories about the horrible torture of Jesus Christ by the wicked Jews. As a result, I concluded my evening prayer with an additional sentence: "Dear God, You who are always also the God of the Catholics, Protestants, Jews, and Muslims, please watch out and protect me so that nothing, but nothing happens."

Politically, my father was undoubtedly a liberal, but he was also an ardent Austria-Hungary patriot. In 1914, my parents were upset about the assassination of the Archduke Franz Ferdinand in Sarajevo. At the age of eleven, I went with my father to the newly established War Department and tested my knowledge of Latin reading the motto that adorns the facade of the building: "Si vis pacem para bellum" (If you want peace, prepare for war). Then came the historic moment in which Serbia rejected the Austrian ultimatum and Austria declared war. People shouted, "Long live Austria, Serbia must die!" And we were shouting enthusiastically along with everyone else.

When the war broke out, the comfortable lifestyle of my parents abruptly ended. Until then, my father and mother began their day with breakfast served in their bedroom. Then, also in the bedroom, they would wash up at a marble table, having been brought large jugs of hot and cold water. After that, they leisurely dressed (though the maid had to help my mother with her corset), and at about ten o'clock my father finally left the bedroom and went into his office. There he would begin his workday by placidly dictating some letters to his beautiful secretary, Betty Singer.

From our nursery window, we often watched our father give his speeches just opposite our apartment, in the courtroom of the Vienna Commercial Court (in the same courtroom where I would, in 1967, face charges of working as an architect without proper credentials). After lunch, father regularly went to the nearby Café de l'Europe on Stephansplatz to maintain his society relations. On the few occasions when he took me along, I discovered that he often played tarot and billiards. When he returned from the café, he completed correspondence or visited clients. I proudly accompanied this elegant gentleman—stiff black hat, collar, and walking stick—to meetings in the Carltheater. While Father was negotiating with director Siegmund Eibenschütz, I sat in the darkened auditorium and excitedly watched rehearsals of then-popular operettas such as *Der Rastelbinder* and *Ein Walzertraum.*

Undoubtedly, this is when my interest in theater awoke. I was introduced to famous artists. I once caused great laughter when I got a kiss from the very young soubrette Mizzi Zwerenz and cried, "I will not be kissed by an old lady!" My love for the theater was enhanced by visits to the opera, the Burgtheater, and the Volkstheater.

During the day, the maid or nanny usually supervised us children. Every day we took the short, safe walk across the wide Ringstrasse to the playground in the city park. We had so much more fun and many more friends in this park than did my own children in the isolated, well-manicured gardens and swimming pools of Los Angeles many years later.

Before falling asleep, my sister and I always played impromptu theater scenes with assigned roles. I was a designer and seller of lighting fixtures, and Ischl was a customer with extravagant desires. I described to her the most fantastic chandeliers, but she would always criticize them and want something different.

After our parents left us with our goodnight kisses, they went *drah'n,* as it was called back then (a word derived from the rotation of a waltz). This meant that they were out with friends, enjoying the nightlife of Vienna to the fullest: theater, concerts, and afterward a restaurant, café, or wine bar.

On Sundays and holidays in the warm months, we hiked with our father, who was an avid mountain climber, in the environs of Vienna. In the cold season, we visited the family Lemberger, with whom my parents were the closest friends. The adults would go out, while we five children—Poldi, Hedi, and Vally Lemberger and my sister and I—spent enjoyable afternoons together.

With assigned roles, we often played "state." We made money from slips of paper. Poldi was a theater director, Hedi the owner of a magazine store. I published a newspaper, which was sold by Hedi, and Luise and Vally took varying tasks. So-called tea was served: this was hot water sprinkled over chocolate powder. We then "drank" it with an old spoon that had a hole in it, so that the chocolate tea was able to run forever. (For my seventieth birthday, I received a replica of this perforated spoon in silver from Hedi.)

Later, we would all think back on this game from our childhood, especially since we were all scattered throughout various states of the world. To the dismay of her Jewish father, Vally married the goy (non-Jew) Willy Steiner; in New York, Hedi married Felix Salzer, the distinguished musicologist and relative of the philosopher Ludwig Wittgenstein; Luise died from cancer at the age of fifty-five, in Los Angeles, the city where I had opened a large architectural and planning firm. Luise never stopped her literary activities, and this may have stemmed from our childhood publishing game. As I have mentioned, Poldi, the theater director in our children's game, later became the great director Leopold Lindtberg.[4]

Part of our annual program was a summer trip to my mother's relatives in Germany. We were cost-conscious, traveling third class, but also class-conscious, wearing white gloves. Our trains usually went to Berlin, then to Hamburg, then to Eutin in Schleswig-Holstein, and finally to the North Sea.

In Berlin, we visited a cousin of my mother from the Fehr family. Selmar Fehr was general manager of Deutsche Bank. I was deeply impressed by the elegance of the Fehr family lifestyle, which included a driver and many servants. Of their three children, the only one I met later was Rudi, who became the black sheep of the family when he ran off early to Los Angeles because he was more interested in jazz tones than he was in banknotes. When he became a production manager for the Warner Bros. film company, the prodigal son proved to be the family savior. He retrieved his mother, Lucy, and his brother Gerd from Nazi Berlin. His father, Selmar, died in Berlin, shortly before the outbreak of war.

In Hamburg, we visited my mother's brothers: Richard, a serious doctor; John, a funny lawyer; and the youngest of them all, Herbert. Not long before World War I began, Herbert went to America, where he called himself Harry Lowry; he would later prove to be very helpful to me.

From Hamburg, we went to the Schleswig-Holstein town of Eutin, a picture-perfect small town in a landscape of lakes reminiscent of Switzerland. My mother's ancestral home in Eutin had a garden that stretched from the main road to the train station. There lived and reigned our Aunt Jenny, a lovable, funny, and stingy old maid. Her old-fashioned clothes and her habit of fishing in the last of her many underskirts for her wallet made her a comic figure for us.

In a way, Aunt Jenny anticipated the energy conservation ideas that became a movement in the late 1970s. Electric lights were not to be turned on as long as the illuminated sign of the cinema two hundred yards away was still burning. The modern bathroom, which cousin Selmar Fehr had built for her, was not to be used except during his brief visits. Instead, we had to use the six-seat latrine, so that Jenny would not lose valuable garden fertilizer.

For us children, this was very close to paradise. In the garden, there were chickens, berries, vegetables, and fruit of all kinds. Street vendors brought pastries and fresh fish. We had meadows to roam through, bushes to hide in, trees to climb. On warm summer nights, the adults promenaded in beautiful clothes along the boulevard on the main road, as we children carried colorful, brightly lit lanterns in front of us. Even today, the tune "Lantern, Lantern, Sun, Moon and Stars" sounds in my ear, and the candles of the lanterns flicker like a firefly parade before my eyes.

The Eutin house was built by my great-grandfather, Nathan, who was then mayor of the town. In summer, it became the gathering place of the Nathans of Paris, the Levis of Hamburg, the Fehrs of Berlin, and the Grünbaums of Vienna. For Father, this was a little too much family. He would arrive in the last few weeks, and then we would move on to Westerland, on the island of Sylt.

In Westerland, we roamed a wide, sandy beach, built sand castles, and watched as the hungry waves of the sea devoured them. We hunted for mussels and well-shaped stones; for lunch, we ate freshly caught lobsters. In order to reach a small hut, we rode the snowy white cars of a little railroad that crossed the island.

Wherever I was—Vienna, Eutin, or by the sea—these childhood years were exciting. Maybe this was because, unlike today, there was no radio or television, no cars and no airplanes. My father did not even allow a gramophone—he thought they were vulgar. Rather than being entertained, you were forced to come up with something yourself.

During my school days, my mind was apparently occupied with other matters, so I had to take additional private lessons in various subjects. My father was disappointed in me if I brought home bad grades. My mother scolded me by saying that my dad had always been a model student, but that discouraged me more than it inspired me. However, when Grandma Grünbaum once confided in me that her dear son had had to repeat one class, my feelings of inferiority lessened.

At for my career choice, my father said, "I will leave this completely to you. There is only one thing: I do not want you to become a lawyer. I disapprove of sons following in their fathers' footsteps." It's worth noting that thirty-five years later, I spoke the same words to my son Michael, and asked him not to become an architect. So he became a lawyer.

I will explain why I became an architect in a later chapter. My mother said that I showed a preference for architecture as a little child, because I played with building blocks so much, but this was completely wrong. As a child, if I did have a dream job, it was confectioner, because I was passionate about eating pie with *Schlagobers* (whipped cream), which I called *Oberschlag* (upper beat).

My first real impetus to study architecture came in grammar school during freehand drawing classes. Until then, all my teachers complained that I couldn't draw a straight line. I was warned not to pursue a profession in which I would need to draw. It was only my art teacher in secondary school, Professor Ludwig Rainer, an amiable genius (his son is the Austrian architect Professor Roland Rainer), who thought otherwise.

Professor Ludwig Rainer was a pioneer of modern music and art education. For example, he encouraged his students to translate sounds and rhythms into pictures. While a chamber music ensemble played on the podium of the classroom, we were told to paint what we heard. Then Rainer asked the musicians to play what we had imagined.

In the first class I took with him, we were asked to draw or paint what we had dreamed. I painted a pretty and wild abstract watercolor composition. His verdict: "Young man, you have imagination, you have talent, you should be an architect." From then on, drawing lessons were my favorite subject.

The outbreak of World War I darkened our lives. New restrictions brought limitations to our standard of living. For us children, the most emotional change was the loss of our holiday trips to northern Germany. Nevertheless, there were still vacations, though now at places closer to home, such as Seeboden, Attersee, Edlach an der Rax, and Weidling-Wurzbachtal an der Stadtbahn. Our parents grew worried by reports of the war.

My father put all his money into war bonds. My mother often went to the Hotel Imperial, where society ladies knitted socks and caps, prepared *Scharpie* for wound dressings, and rolled cigarettes for the soldiers at the front.[5] I wrote patriotic poems with titles like "Hooray, Hooray, for the Fatherland" and "We Need and Want to Win," which were printed in the local paper. Father wrote a play called "In the Trenches," which we staged during a family stay in Seeboden am Attersee at the Häuptel Inn. I played the role of an Austrian soldier.

Once, Father traveled to Hungary and brought back a piece of bread from that former part of the monarchy, which had obviously never suffered from a lack of food. We cut it ceremoniously, like a cake, and enjoyed the simple bun as a delicacy.

In 1916, from the windows of the office of Mr. Lemberger on Rotenturmstraße, we watched the funeral parade of Emperor Franz Joseph I. I was particularly moved by a little blond boy who marched obediently behind the coffin. It was Crown Prince Otto Habsburg, walking between Emperor Karl and Empress Zita.

At the end of the war, in the summer of 1918, the Spanish flu was rampant in Vienna, and among the victims were the painters Gustav Klimt and Egon Schiele. Poor nutrition in recent years had also severely weakened my father's health, so he had little resistance against the flu. He had also probably poisoned himself with the foul *Glimmstengeln* he had smoked for so long instead of his beloved Virginia cigars. He died at the age of fifty-nine.

They tried to force me to look at him in the coffin, but I refused. I wanted to keep him in my mind as he was when I saw him last: reading a book by Turgenev. After a routine funeral, which could not ease my pain, I did a pencil portrait of my father from a photograph and my memories.

COLLAPSE

With the death of my father in 1918, my childhood was finally over, but the entire political and social structure in Central and Eastern Europe had also collapsed. The vacuum created by this collapse of the Central Powers (the German Empire, Austria-Hungary, and all their smaller allies) unleashed a storm that shook all the structures of the past. The multination state—the Austro-Hungarian Empire—burst into independent small states. The hurricane swept away symbols of a social order as if they were withered leaves. Emperors, kings, and czars, the nobility, and dashing officers of the military were all blown away. The proud double eagle was gone from our flag. Regimes, democracies, counsel republics, and military dictatorships rose and fell through civil wars, coups, revolutions. The "ideal" world of the nineteenth century was now thought to have been "hypocritical."

Vienna, once a proud metropolis of the k.u.k. monarchy, became the capital of a torso state. Its streets and squares were flooded with the ragged figures of disintegrated, defeated armies. Wounded soldiers and returning prisoners mingled with civilians who were suffering from hunger and deprivation. Then there were those vultures who took advantage of every misery: speculators, profiteers, political adventurers.

In Austria, there was no bloody revolution; the changes took place under the dictatorship of the victorious powers. On November 12, 1918, when the Republic was proclaimed, I was wedged into a crowd in front of the parliament building. Two red-white-red flags of the Republic were meant to be hoisted, but protesters had cut out the white center sections of the flags as a way of calling into question the form of this new government and the social order itself. Because of this sort of questioning, the new Republic never found peace between the wars.

In this era of turmoil and uncertainty, at the age of fifteen, I took on the role of the head of the family. Our financial situation was bleak. My father's considerable savings—about two hundred thousand crowns—had been invested in war bonds and had become worthless overnight. For some years we counted on revenues from his law firm, which had been taken over by one of his former clerks, Dr. Theodore Mueller.

We clung to another glimmer of hope. My father had entrusted his allegedly wealthy friend, the architect Edmund Melcher, with our guardianship. Financially, he could not help us. But he was willing to employ me at his company if I attended a four-year college.

We made the following decisions: I would finish the fourth grade of grammar school and then attend the Higher State Vocational School, Department of Building Construction, in autumn of 1919. My sister went to a school for sewing and needlework. The house staff was immediately dismissed, and the office premises were subleased to Dr. Mueller, as were the salon and the servants' room.

The changes were most painful for my mother. She went from being a spoiled society lady to a careworn housewife. The food situation deteriorated steadily. With a handcart, we moved from freight stations to charitable dispensaries, only to find half-rotten potatoes, turnips, and dried herrings. We often ate in public kitchens.

The first postwar winter was the worst. We collected paper, wood chips, and waste in the streets, trying to find enough to heat two ovens—one for our tenant and the other a small iron stove (called "house friend") in the room where we lived all together. There was no money for the tram. Even long trips to my sister's school in the Eighth District had to be made on foot. Later, we children got cocoa and canned evaporated milk from an American relief operation.

Slowly, we got used to everything. An innate optimism helped my mother to forget her pain as she constantly toiled, in an admirable way, to master all our difficulties. After a few years, my sister established herself as a dressmaker and was very busy.

I alone had misgivings about my own future. The decision to attend a technical school in order to be hired later in a builder's business saved me from the agony of choice that young people of my age generally faced. On the other hand, it hardly seemed an inviting prospect. My chances of becoming a draftsman, structural engineer, or even a master builder seemed slight. With this plan, I thought, I would not get one inch closer to my goal of becoming an architect.

DEGRADATION

I hated the State Vocational School. How often I wished it would burn down or a terrible snowstorm would make the journey to school impossible, but nothing like that ever happened. I felt degraded and humiliated.

I had been torn out of the liberal and intellectual atmosphere of the secondary school, taken away from many intelligent friends, from the care of many strict but fair professors, and placed in an inferior environment. My classmates were the sons of petit bourgeois families with narrow intellectual interests. For the first time in my life, I felt like a despised outsider, because both teachers and classmates were rabid anti-Semites, which was something I had not experienced until then. They all sympathized with the nationalist Pan-German Party, one of the forerunners of the Nazis.

Bragging about drinking and heroic deeds to try to impress girls, cursing at socialists, and ranting against the Republic and democracy were standard operating procedure. The other students' ambitions were limited to becoming technical support staff in their fathers' businesses.

Besides me, there was only one other Jewish student, Rudolf Baumfeld, and he was to become a close lifelong friend, my assistant and partner. Both of us were beaten or mistreated in other ways nearly every day. "Planing," or sliding a classmate over two unequally high table edges, was a favorite bullying tactic. However, in this tribe of proud Germans, there was a special exception. The Aryan Karl Langer was by far our smartest and most educated classmate and, fortunately for us, also the biggest and strongest—and he was often our protector.

I never learned what became of the approximately thirty other students in my class. Only Rudi, Karl, and I applied for admission to the Academy of Fine Arts Vienna and passed the entrance exam. Another man who wanted to be an architect had taken this test some fifteen years before us, but had unfortunately failed: this was Adolf Hitler. Instead, he bitterly took revenge on the world.

We were the only three from the class to leave Austria in 1938, and we all became respected architects—Rudi and I in the United States, and Karl in Brisbane, Australia, where he had fled with his Jewish wife.

Even our professors treated Rudi and me as intruders. There were only two exceptions: one was Professor Stutterheim, who came from an old noble family and who taught design and architecture. From him I always received the grade "excellent," much to the dismay of his colleagues. "Excellent" was also the word Professor Olexinsky used to grade my skills with the German language. It gave him an almost devilish delight to show the "Lord Germans," as he called them, that none of them could actually write or speak German. He read my essays and poems to the class. This did not increase my popularity with my fellow students.

One minor class in bricklaying, carpentry, and joinery crafts was unpleasant for me. One of my problems was that because of my small hands, I couldn't cut a brick professionally without supporting it with my knee. My teacher, an outspoken anti-Semite, wanted me to fail.

Unhappy about my experiences at school, I turned to other pursuits in my spare time: politics, theater, and poetry. When one of my poems appeared in a major daily newspaper, there were unpleasant consequences.

Shortly after the start of the academic year of 1922, the rector announced a school assembly because of a serious problem. He explained that Viktor Grünbaum had published a poem that could be considered an example of the decay of youthful spirit. The poem that caused all this excitement read:

THE COLORED GLASS

"Why is there war on earth, father?
And why do people not love each other?"

"Come with me and I'll show you."

In the tower of the church, the two stood
in front of a brightly painted window.

"Look through this glass, my son,
what color are the trees?"

"Red, father!"

"And now through this?"

"The trees are blue, father!"

"People stand in front of colored glass, my son,
and they argue over
whether the trees are red or blue!"

To most people, this poem reads like the expression of a human mind. But in anticipation of Nazi censorship, the German nationalist, revanchist, and anti-Semitic clique viewed it as "destructive dirt and trash literature." Why? It was simply because blue was the color of the former Pan-German Party, and the poem dared to refuse the view through the blue glass as the only correct view of the world.

They considered immediately expelling me from school for this transgression, but decided that they would wait to see if such misbehaving would reoccur.

After this event, oddly enough, I got more respect from my colleagues. During a school reform, when the students were given the right to appoint lobbyists, I was elected as class representative of these curious anti-Semites, because they believed I was the one who could most eloquently represent them and how they felt. For my part, I now fought the feeling of degradation and concentrated fully on the dreaded exit exam, or *Matura,* which I passed in the summer of 1923. I was now confirmed in writing. In what context, I asked myself, was I now "mature"?

I knew about Greek and Roman style elements thoroughly. I had worked with my own hands on a cross vault made of bricks and on the necessary substructure. I now knew how to use a T square, triangles and circles, floor plans, elevations, sections, and perspectives drawn with pencil or ink.

I had strengthened my memory, and thus learned how to learn, even if what I learned would prove largely useless. School did not provide me with an education in the sense of the transmission of wide and deep knowledge. Perhaps this is not possible with institutionalized teaching, and only happens in later life.

In school, I learned absolutely nothing about architecture as an activity that could be responsible for the development of a community and creative life. I learned only about a few practical tools that could be useful in construction.

Occasionally, on my own, I attempted to come closer to that vision of architecture outside the school. For example, together with Rudi Baumfeld and Karl Langer, I took part in a competition to design a large municipal housing project on Lassallestraße.[6] We got one prize and good reviews in the newspapers. That one of our professors, who had also participated, went away empty-handed only increased our joy. I read technical books and journals and attended lectures and exhibitions about the new trends in architecture that were not being discussed in school: the German Bauhaus, the Wiener Werkstätte, the Secessionist style, and the works of the great architects Le Corbusier, Otto Wagner, and Adolf Loos.

In my *Matura* work in German, I tried to build a bridge between literary and sociological themes and architecture. For example, I wrote about Goethe's Faust, an unusual choice for an architecture student. I argued that Faust could have saved his soul with a grand vision of livable homes on land reclaimed from the sea. The idea was a little far-fetched, I now admit.

The fact that I was still dreaming of architecture manifested itself in a sketch I did for a letterhead design for a course in business correspondence. Rudi and I called ourselves "Grünbaumfeld, Architects," not yet anticipating that we would indeed become partners in an architectural firm thirty years later.

CIVIL ENGINEERING

Architect and town master mason Edmund Melcher kept his promise and hired me for his company in the Ninth District, Porzellangasse 2. I earned a salary that was initially low, but it grew gradually in the nine years that I worked for him (1923 to 1932), as did my responsibilities. This solved our financial problems, which had worsened when the modest income we had received from the law firm came to an end. My hope to come into real contact with architecture, however, was not fulfilled.

The haughty title of my guardian was completely meaningless. In fact, he led a small commercial business that probably had seen better times before 1914. Now the business existed within three rooms, as the appendix to a private apartment: one room for accounting, one for the general work area, and one for the engineer, Leo Steiner, who later married the daughter of the boss and in this way became co-owner. The staff consisted of master builder Mr. Melcher; engineer Mr. Steiner; a bookkeeper and kind soul named Erna; another master builder, Mr. Antalik, a

Viktor Grünbaum on a construction site, Vienna, 1924. Courtesy of Peggy Gruen.

choleric, very portly gentleman of the old school; and me. Later, a young man joined the company—his name was Kurt Singer, and we became close friends. From that moment on, together with Steiner, we actually did all the work.

The nonarchitectural character of this business very quickly inspired me to return to my training as an architect. I applied for admission to the master class of Professor Peter Behrens at the Academy of Fine Arts Vienna.[7] After I had submitted many drawings and passed the oral entrance exam, I asked my boss if I could use half a day to visit the academy.

During the academic year of 1924–25, I was a student at the academy. There I found an environment very different from that of the State Vocational School. Instead of anti-Semitism, here there was an atmosphere of happy bohemianism in artists' studios, where the sons of wealthy families were more or less eagerly playing at architecture, and where the main emphasis was on the aesthetic and the artistic. To my disappointment, there were no teaching courses.

Professor Behrens, who led a large studio in Germany, visited his class only a few times a year. Otherwise, he had his colorless assistant, a Mr. Alexander, represent him.

Among the important student activities were educational journeys. It was remarkable that these always headed for good wine regions. Without a doubt, I had neither the time nor the money for these fun trips. Instead, I'd usually be busy with a blueprint for a project that appealed to me because of its social task. One study project was to be the sports center for a union. I was attracted to it because it joined together different recreational activities as an expression of multifunctionality. In addition, I romantically imagined the center placed on top of a hill.

On the occasion of one of his rare visits, the "master" hunkered over my drawings and models, made some remarks, and gave me some critical comments. When he stopped by on his next round, even before I had a chance to correct anything, I was shocked to hear "Look, young man, now it is much better!"

In this master class, I also learned architectural jargon, drawing perspective, and model making. When, at the end of the second semester, my employer made the ultimate demand—that I should choose between my job and the academy—it was not hard to abandon my studies at the academy (which would have lasted six more semesters). Thus it is a fact that I never finished my academic study of architecture.

Since the team with master builder Melcher was so small, it had the advantage that there was no division of labor, as is common in larger offices. I got to know all facets of building and construction, including those for which larger companies use assistants. Facade renovations and rather complicated pillar replacements for shop fronts were the main jobs that we conducted on behalf of architects. Edmund Melcher also was a court-certified expert, and I assisted him in the inspection and evaluation of the conditions of many buildings as well as in the making of economic evaluations. With this insight into the poor conditions of many tenement houses of the Wilhelminian era, my understanding of social problems was aroused. Once I had the opportunity to design a villa in Grinzing, but because of the ultraconservative attitude of the owner, I accomplished nothing that could be called an architectural masterpiece.

One day, thanks to Melcher's connections at city hall, the company obtained an assignment for a large social housing project for about four hundred homes on Fendigasse, near the Margaretengürtel.[8] Our Mr. Antalik was the construction manager, and I was appointed to be his assistant and typist. We moved into a hut on the site. Mr. Antalik, who had considerable practical experience and a loud voice, hurried the Italian diggers, who worked with their horse-drawn carts on the excavation of the basement and the making of the foundations.

I was entrusted with the payroll, so every Saturday I handed out wages in paper bags. On paydays, both the *Mörtelweiber,*—the women who mixed sand, water, and lime for mortar—and many of the older male workers insisted on kissing my hand. This was somewhat embarrassing for me.

My field of activity, however, grew considerably larger after the basement and ground floor were completed and the building of the upper floors began. Since there were no cranes, it was necessary to reach each floor with ladders. Because of his corpulence, Mr. Antalik was not able to do this, so I had to take over this part of the management, which enhanced my practical knowledge considerably. Negotiating with the architect when he visited the construction site was now my job. He was mainly interested in the facade, especially the proper placement of small ceramic decorative elements above the windows.

After the obligatory period of three years, I was certified as a journeyman; after two more years, I was finally able to take the difficult exam to become a master builder. From then on, I could call myself "architect and master builder."

The performance of the company became more and more unsatisfactory. In 1932, Melcher told my friend Singer and me that he had to lay one of us off. The choice would be left to us. I took this opportunity to start my own business, for which I had already been preparing for years by taking on small independent projects, mostly interiors. At the time, I was transforming a large one-family villa close to the Prater into five medium-sized apartments. A few weeks after my discharge, in my capacity as an architect, it filled me with satisfaction to place an order with the company of Melcher and Steiner.

THE THIRD DIMENSION

During the sleepless night that preceded our arrival in New York, when I looked out from the bow of the ship to the first lights of the new continent, I felt gratitude for my life so far. I realized how much my childhood had been imbued with a fun-loving, liberal, and artistic spirit.

But it became clear to me that after the death of my father, this feeling was pulled away like a rug from under my feet. Neither the privations of life at home nor my slave training at the State Vocational School nor the routine of my existence as an employee in the years from 1918 to 1932 had been inspiring or had contributed significantly to my mental development. So I decided that night to reflect with joy and gratitude on a third dimension of my life that had filled my Sundays and holidays, all evenings and many nights, vacations, and idle school and evening hours.

At the age of thirteen, I became a Boy Scout. This brought comradeship, discipline, and love of nature, and also the romance of nights spent around campfires or sleeping in tents. In 1917, I joined a local Scout group, which was regarded as progressive and revolutionary. It was led by a classmate in secondary school, Edi Jahoda. In addition to the usual activities of tying knots and finding paths of virtue, there was a young revolutionary spirit in this group, with discussions of current affairs and criticism of the monarchy and an overall antiwar attitude. We were the only Scout group that declined to participate in a parade in front of Emperor Karl I.

We mingled anthems of socialist origin with cantatas, folk songs, and old mercenary soldiers' songs. We watched the Russian Revolution with enthusiasm, though our excitement subsided later, as inhumane show trials and cruel persecutions began in that land.

Eventually, we shed all the trappings of Scouting and joined the Wanderbund, which was a part of the socialist youth movement.[9] The so-called Jahoda circle was a small, core group. Unlike in the Boy Scouts, here there were boys and girls in complete equality.

We often spent lovely evenings in the house of the open-minded Jahoda family. The four Jahoda children—Edi, Rosi, Mitzi, and Fritz—were excellent musicians and played in a quartet.[10] We passionately discussed aesthetics as well as politics.

The ideas of Josef Popper-Lynkeus were another frequent topic.[11] This technician-philosopher pulled us under his spell. A visionary, he advocated the so-called general nutrition obligation instead of general conscription. His proposal was that all young citizens should be obligated to work for a few years for the common good, producing food, building shelter and health facilities, and providing other necessities to the community. For participating in this "nutrition service," all citizens would be given support for a subsistence-level existence for the rest of their lives. Thus freed from the necessity of earning a living, everyone could devote themselves to leisure, sport, or the arts. Those who did not want to settle for mere subsistence could earn additional money in a remaining free economy sector. As a technician and an economist, Popper-Lynkeus developed his vision of a socially just, peaceful society without poverty through careful research and planning. This "realistic dreamer," as he called himself, deeply influenced me for the rest of my life.[12] His idea was not realized until recently, but the modern welfare state can be viewed as an approximation of his vision.

At our meetings, I often gave speeches. I delivered lectures with titles such as "Art and Beauty" (in which I tried to prove that these expressions are not identical), "The House, the Apartment, the City," "The Building as a Molder of Men," and "City of the Future." Those evenings inspired me to write philosophical poems, short stories, and satires, many of which I would put down on paper the next night. In the poems, I tried to express my feelings about the omnipotence of nature. The satirical sketches were attacks against the even then much-vaunted idea of technological progress.

In "America in Vienna," a short story I wrote in 1922, Vienna is nightmarishly flooded with automobiles; in this story I predicted the construction site between the Secession and Karlsplatz that existed in the years 1970 to 1977. "Streamline Your Home—Science and Eggplant" is another prophetic story about a fully automated household. It does not have a happy ending.

In winter, we went skiing on simple wooden skis, and we spent the summers in camps—or, as we later would say, in colonies—of fifty to seventy young people living in mostly primitive conditions, usually sleeping in the barn on a farm.[13] Our colonies were healthy, even though I was often the cook. Today, one would call these camps communes. We dressed in an unorthodox, casual style, let our hair grow long, hated bourgeois "vices" like drinking and smoking, and otherwise had much in common with the later hippie movement.

While on one hand we stressed our closeness to nature, on the other we were enthusiastic admirers of the great satirist Karl Kraus, whose lectures in the central hall of the concert house we never missed.[14]

As a passionate reader, I devoured scientific works such as Friedrich Christoph Schlosser's twenty-volume *Weltgeschichte.* I was particularly interested in utopian literature, such as Friedrich Wilhelm Mader's *Distant Worlds: The Story of a Voyage to the Planets,* Ignatius Donnelly's *Caesar's Column: A Story of the Twentieth Century,* and the novels of Jules Verne.

From 1923 to 1926, my activities in the youth movement and my passion for the theater intermingled. Some of us came together to form an amateur drama group, and for hundreds of youngsters, we played scenes from the peasant wars and original skits of the "never again war" variety.[15] Chants, as they have been used in various celebrations as a dramatic medium, followed a series of outdoor performances that took place in an abandoned quarry called G'spöttgraben in Sievering that served as an amphitheater.

Due to the success of these open-air performances, I was invited by the Association of Socialist Students to participate as a consultant for the first night of a so-called political cabaret. The initiators of this cabaret were the then-prominent youth leaders Louis Wagner and Paul Lazarsfeld. (Wagner died relatively young, while Lazarsfeld would go on to become a leading social scientist in America.)

The cabaret event was due to take place on December 18, 1926, at the Czartoryskischlössel, which had a room with a miniature stage. Louis and Paul dreamed of

Viktor Grünbaum in the countryside, circa 1924. Courtesy of Peggy Gruen.

heroic and revolutionary scenes in which trucks with flag-waving proletarians would roll onto the stage. As a practical-minded technician, I convinced them that they would not even be able to do a cartwheel onstage, and that they would have to restrict the program to intimate satirical scenes with an emphasis on wit, irony, and spirit.

A program was developed that partly satirized characters and events within the socialist youth student movement and partly took aim at the Social Democratic Party leadership because of their reformist tendencies and inadequate willingness to revolt. I myself cannot remember many of the texts, but a few years ago, Chancellor Dr. Bruno Kreisky, who was then part of the audience, recalled one scene:

So goes the chorus of party leaders:
"And as a sign
that we reached the majority,
let's put on the town hall light!"

So answers a chorus of young people:
"And then what do you and then what do you?"
Choir of the party leaders:
"And then, you start all over again!"

The unique thing about this event was that many of the politicians criticized on the stage were sitting in the audience, amused and applauding. These included party leader Otto Bauer; Vienna's mayor, Karl Seitz; the city councilmen Julius Tandler and Hugo Breitner; national councilman Julius Deutsch; and other profiled party figures, of which there was no shortage back then.

I had directed, as far as that was possible with individualistic young people. During the show I was backstage to ensure the smooth running of the performance. An accident changed my role.

A young man named Becker was hired as master of ceremonies. At the beginning he started the performance in front of the curtain, in a funny style. Behind the curtain, we listened curiously to the response of the audience that filled the hall. When we heard giggling, we were highly delighted. But when it increased to uncontrollable guffaws of laughter, we were worried. Finally, we discovered the cause of this general hilarity: our friend Becker had forgotten to close his fly. To call his attention to this embarrassment, Helene Bauer, Otto Bauer's wife, who sat in the front row, handed him a note. Since everyone knew what was written on the paper, when Becker turned around and began moving strangely to fix his zipper, the hilarity grew to excess.

In this emergency, I was sent in front of the curtain to save Becker from his embarrassment. I told him that he was needed urgently behind the stage because of "reactionary activities," and I improvised a humorous introduction. I took over the presentation for the whole evening, and also for the next eight years, during which time our Political Cabaret became a permanent institution.

After this memorable performance, some party leaders admonished us not to aim the weapon of satire so much against our own party, but rather to use it against the threat of fascism.

Joyfully, we took on this proposal and founded the Socialist Event Group. Thereafter, part of the SEG performed with the Political Cabaret from 1926 to 1934, while another part of the group became the Red Players, who moved from place to place, provided with lyrics and stage directions by the magazine *The Political Stage.*[16]

THE POLITICAL CABARET

In the period from 1926 to 1934, the Political Cabaret was the focus of my creative life. In those eight years we produced fourteen different programs, performed more than four hundred sold-out performances for a total of about two hundred thousand audience members, and, with "wit, satire, and deeper meaning," taught, inspired, and influenced their political and social thinking.

But our impact went far beyond the audience. Scene clips and song lyrics were reproduced in magazines. Some of the songs, such as the "Schober song," which criticized the police chief Johann Schober, became popular hits and were sung by crowds at events and demonstrations.[17]

Our troupe consisted of twenty-five to thirty freedom-loving, progressive, pacifist, and antifascist theater enthusiasts. Enthusiasm was the only motive for our commitment. There was no pay, no quest for individual glory, no career aspirations—the group was a true collective.

Viktor Grünbaum, Political Cabaret, Vienna, 1926–34. Library of Congress.

Depending on our special talents, all of us had particular tasks as actors, house composers, pianists, authors, stage designers, dancers, costume designers, or manufacturers, but everyone also had to work as stagehands, ticket sellers, ushers, prop masters, scene painters, and, if necessary, brawlers, in skirmishes with troublemakers like the *Heimatwehr* gangs and the illegal but powerful and organized Nazis.

My duties were varied and challenging, and they filled me with pleasure and pride. I was director, organizer, coauthor, emcee, singer, and actor.

My labor was significant, and it claimed Sundays and holidays, along with many nights. But how refreshing it was to get the spontaneous reaction of an audience, to hear the roar of laughter or applause, or the contemplative silence after a serious, challenging scene.

In the early years, the programs consisted of series of short scenes, solos, songs, chants, and dances, all connected by the emcee. Later, the programs evoked continuous themes—we called these revues. They integrated theater, music, and dance, and they could be seen as forerunners to early musicals.

For example, in the thirteenth program, titled *MM 1* (for Machine Man 1), a character named Professor Electron invents a robot, MM 1, that is the ideal worker for an employer. It does not ask for payment, does not organize, and does not strike or think. MM 1 is offered to a fascist dictator, who wears a Hitler mask, and he shows delight. In the mind of the dictator, all people should be robots without brains who automatically stretch out their right arms, caw "Heil!" and march in lockstep to the slaughter. Our presentation of this program coincided with the rise to power of Hitler in Germany. It was not only a satire on the *Kadavergehorsam* of the Nazis but also a stern warning against the dehumanization of mankind by the machine cult.

For me, three places are particularly associated with the cabaret. The café in the City Park was the birthplace of the most dramatic pieces. There we sat—Robert Ehrenzweig, Jura Soyfer, Charles Sable, and myself—to the point of curfew on many an evening.[18] We would each consume a single cup of coffee, and if any of us had any money, we would order a couple of frankfurters or a bacon roll. We drank countless glasses of Vienna's springwater. What a wonderful institution the Viennese coffeehouse was. Alfred Polgar sang its praises: "You are not at home, and still not in the fresh air!"[19] With a cup of coffee you could sit there for hours, reading copies of foreign and domestic newspapers and illustrated magazines; you could have business talks or play cards, chess, or billiards. Students around us were reading, politicizing, and making plans for a revolution; we wrote plays.

The songs were written in another place, our apartment, because we had a piano. Besides the authors, the musicians Fritz Jahoda and Hermann Zimbelius were always there. We borrowed the tunes from old Viennese songs that we found in a scrapbook, or from folk songs or modern hits. If necessary, we changed them a little bit. For some skits, we created new background music.

In the house next door on Riemergasse, there was a theater hall, the Pan-Künstlerspiele, with a capacity of three hundred.[20] It was not only our place for rehearsals but also the place where we played the first three to four performances after each program's premiere.

Lizzie and I remember a special performance that was given there for our wedding on March 22, 1930.

From the Pan-Künstlerspiele, our shows would move to the large theaters in the outer boroughs and to inns, hotels, union houses, and workers' homes. The larger venues often held more than a thousand people, and here we were greeted by the same waves of enthusiasm we received from the intellectual audiences at the premieres. There were also performances in front of the workers and city employees of industrial cities such as St. Pölten, Wiener Neustadt, and Neunkirchen.

Our set decorations were created by the painters Arnold Meiselmann and Walter Harnisch in their studio, with the help of numerous volunteers. We designed, sewed, and and tried on our costumes in my sister Luise's sewing room.

The premieres were hailed as top events of the socialist intelligentsia, especially in leftist newspapers such as *Arbeiter Zeitung, Kleines Blatt,* and *Der Abend* and the weekly magazine *Der Kuckuck.* We were less flattered in parliament, where the Christian Social Party deputy Leopold Kunschak condemned us as politically dangerous elements.[21]

Of course, both the Political Cabaret and the Red Players suffered from conflicts with police, censorship, the *Heimwehr,* and the Nazis. One night, when I was tearing down posters that read "Jews out," I was attacked and beaten by two Nazis. The police intervened. They took all three of us to the next police station and then released the two hooligans; I was put into a *Grüne Heinrich* and taken to jail.[22]

I spent a most uncomfortable night with drunks, pickpockets, and prostitutes. The next morning, I was released due to the intervention of Deputy Julius Deutsch. (He had been one of the commanders of the International Brigade in the Spanish Civil War.) His daughter was involved in the cabaret.

That night onstage I recounted the amusing story of my involuntary stay in prison. I complained about the numerous bugs that had plagued me while I was at the police department. After my performance, the police served me a subpoena. I was accused of insulting an official because I had obviously used the term "bugs" to mean the police. I denied this accusation vigorously, explaining I had spoken only of six-legged insects. I demanded that the police inspect their own jail for insects.

When they actually found lots of bugs, I was discharged with a warning to weigh my words.

At my next performance I appeared onstage holding a market scale. I explained to the audience its relevance as decreed by the police. Whenever I made a risky political statement, I briefly presented the scale going up, implying regret that unfortunately I could not finish the sentence. This always got a laugh, since everyone knew what I meant to say anyway.

When Hitler became chancellor, the terrified Austrian government prohibited the pictorial representation of all leading foreign politicians. Until this moment it had been easy to portray Hitler onstage using a glued-on mustache—the unmistakable shape provided a clear reference. But doing that was now forbidden. Fortunately, we had a man in the ensemble (Stiassny) with a real Hitler mustache. At appropriate occasions, we asked him to simply appear onstage.

At the end of one show, he was promptly arrested. Protesting that we had never intended to portray the German chancellor, we accompanied him to the police station. All attempts by the police to remove the allegedly fake facial hair were in vain, and they had to release Stiassny. It was not illegal to wear such a male ornament under one's nose.

Nevertheless, in early 1934, pressure from the Austrofascist dictatorship shut down the Political Cabaret and the Red Players. This was not the end of my theatrical activities, however. I wrote a nonpolitical folk song cycle that was successfully performed in the major halls of the suburbs. It was comic and retold the old story of a tyrannical guardian who tried to thwart the marriage of his pretty ward. The guardian was equipped with all the bad qualities of a reactionary petit bourgeois, and the young man who courted the beautiful ward possessed all the virtues of an upright young worker. At the climax of the show, the lovers sang a duet to the tune of the famous song "Das Glück ist ein Vogerl," whose refrain chimes, "In the end you do what's forbidden anyway." The censors had no complaints against the text, but a politically sensitive audience usually realized the deeper meaning—namely, the call for resistance against any dictatorship—and burst into tumultuous applause.

During the next four years, I also contributed intensively to all the various small theaters that sprouted like mushrooms after a rain. Despite the ridiculously low fees these small theaters paid, they were the refuge of talented young artists of liberal thinking. One of the most successful authors was my friend Jura Soyfer, whom I assisted with advice and action.

It required enormous skill to circumvent the strict censorship rules, but audiences came expecting to hear the forbidden. At that time the entire socialist leadership had fled to Prague, and from there they supported the underground movement through secret channels. There, for example, an illegal issue of the *Arbeiter Zeitung* was printed that could be found in all the coffeehouses, hidden among the legal newspapers. Our audience was very amused by our revision of one Viennese folk song. The new lyrics: "My mom she was Viennese; that's why I like Prague so much."

In early 1938, I was busy trying to organize the relocation of one small theater group to an auditorium with several hundred seats. With great success, this group staged the play *The Lost Melody,* translated from Danish. Perhaps this explained the confidence our guests had in me on that night in March 1938 when I promised to re-create our Viennese theater group in New York.

In the years after the war I found out the true importance of the Political Cabaret and the small theaters. In Geneva, for example, I had a conversation with my old friend the nuclear physicist Professor Victor Weisskopf, who then led the European Organization for Nuclear Research, or CERN.[23] I congratulated him for having reached this peak in his life. He replied, "The peak of my life was truly the time when I played piano at the Political Cabaret." "But Viki," I reminded him, "the piano players were Fritz Jahoda and Hermann Zimbelius." "That's right," he answered. "But whenever one of them was ill, I got to play the piano accompaniment." And he was absolutely right.

A book about the cabaret theater was published by Rudolf Weys, *Cabaret und Kabarett in Wien*. Another about the Political Cabaret was commissioned by the Federal Ministry for Science and Research; written by Dr. Friedrich Scheu, it was published in 1977 by Europa Verlag. Its three hundred pages contain many of the cabaret's scenes and song lyrics. Dr. Scheu had saved and systematically collected material that had been scattered by refugees throughout the world.

What happened to the participants of the Political Cabaret? I know the ongoing stories of some of them.

Jura Soyfer, as already reported, died in a concentration camp. His works are now experiencing a renaissance. Many of his pieces are produced in the theater and also on radio and television. A book about his life and work has been written by Dr. Horst Jarka.

Robert Ehrenzweig immigrated to England and worked there as a writer under the name of Robert Lucas. During the war, he worked for the BBC on a radio program that was broadcast to Germany and the territories occupied by the Germans, about the adventures of Corporal Adolf Hirnschal. This iconic character was a version of a Svejk, a standard figure of the Political Cabaret. The scripts from the program were published in book form right after the war in 1945 by Europa Verlag.

Karl Zobel married the Political Cabaret actress Mary Mayerhofer. He immigrated with her to Australia, where he lived under the name Karl Bittman and organized a Sydney theater group modeled on the Political Cabaret. They are still performing.

Fritz Jahoda became an orchestra conductor in New York.

Fritz and Liese Halpern ended up in London, where they now live after an odyssey that began in Shanghai.

Arnold Meiselmann became a respected painter and graphic artist in Israel, and he died there several years ago. His colleague Walter Harnisch survived the war in Austria and is still working as a graphic designer.

Monette Schober was one of the dancers; she now lives in Vorarlberg and is in constant contact with me.

Harry Horner began as an actor in the Political Cabaret, although this had been strictly forbidden by his father. He later became a set designer. He immigrated to the United States, became famous as a stage designer on Broadway and as a film director, and he now lives in Los Angeles. We continue to correspond.

Illa Raudnitz-Roden was not only my savior from the Gestapo in Vienna but also in 1939 the star of the New York theater production of *From Vienna*. She now runs a rhythmic dancing school for children with physical disabilities in Los Angeles. Her efforts to receive compensation from the Austrian government as a victim of fascism have failed thus far, she has been told, due to the fact that as an Aryan, she did not have to emigrate.

Manfred Inger and Liesl Neumann-Viertel both took part in our New York shows. They returned to Vienna soon after the war and continue to practice their acting careers successfully.

Occasionally, I hear from many others from distant countries. From still others, nobody will ever hear anything again, because those people perished in concentration camps.

ARCHITECT

Architecture in general was a strange story in the interwar period in Austria. Outside the public works of the city government, hardly any new buildings were erected. Hundreds of talented architects dealt with the adaptation and redecoration of worn-down homes that were taken over by new owners. Many designed furnishings and utensils as employees of the Wiener Werkstätte.

The field of work was surprisingly wide. Many young people who laid special emphasis on home decor, whose tastes could not be satisfied by ready-made objects, would hire architects to decorate single rooms or even entire homes. They spent proportionally more than what is spent on this today, which is understandable when one considers that the current temptations are cars, TVs, audio and home appliances, and travel. In the thirties, these temptations hardly existed.

Between 1920 and 1938, a Viennese interior style emerged. But after the Anschluss, both architects and clients disappeared. Some architects continued working after immigrating to various other countries. The architects Josef Frank and Oskar Wlach were particularly successful in the Scandinavian countries.[24] There they laid the foundation for what has today become famous as Danish, Swedish, and Finnish residential housing culture.

My own work as an architect began slowly, with small projects. Often it was just one bedroom or a small council flat. One of my first assignments was the conversion of a horse barn in the Tenth District to a low-budget but attractively furnished "school for rhythmic dance" for Karla Suschitzky (now Karla Zerner of Paris).[25]

Another job was to set up a room for the couple Friedrich and Herta Scheu in one of the few houses that was built by the famous architect Adolf Loos in Vienna.[26] This work was particularly important for me for two reasons: it gave me the opportunity to explore the nature of the architecture of Adolf Loos, and it gave me access to the intellectual and political circles around the Scheu family.

The fees from such projects were small, but they were sufficient to improve my income. After my marriage to Lizzie Kardos in 1930, I was able to renovate our alcove, which I changed exclusively for us. By cleverly exploiting the space, I transformed it into a combination living, sleeping, dining, and study area, and I was able to set up my drawing table. The built-in furniture was painted in green and white, with a lacquered finish, and was accented by natural-colored oak. I had specially designed the beds, tables, chairs, and lighting fixtures according to our taste and had them manufactured by skilled craftsmen, who were then abundant.

This four-purpose room was the ideal solution to the housing problems of the times. It was even depicted in the illustrated weekly magazine *Der Kuckuck* (The cuckoo).[27] From among the magazine's admiring readers, I found clients for new projects, one of which was the conversion of that large villa to five single homes that I mentioned earlier as a reason for leaving my employment.

When I was able to devote myself to designing full-time, my orders got larger. Soon I was so busy that I stopped subletting that room in my father's former office and turned it into my studio. I outfitted it with three drawing boards, a small desk, and a sofa table for meetings. (This sofa combination, made up of two armchairs covered with horsehair fabric, moved to New York with us, then ended up in Vienna again in 1972. It is still in the bedroom of my home.)

I designed every detail of a large apartment—with a new bathroom, new kitchen, and heating system—for the young couple Felix and Lilly Reichmann.[28] They also

Alice (Lizzie) Kardos, Vienna apartment, circa 1933. Library of Congress.

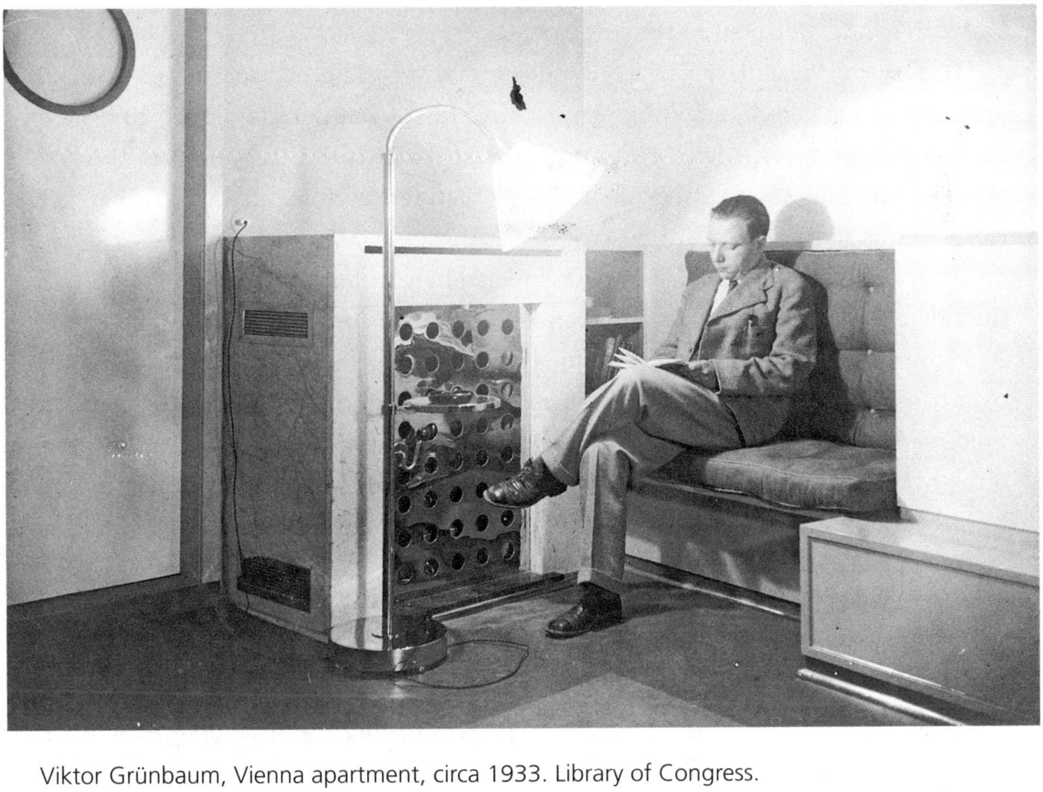

Viktor Grünbaum, Vienna apartment, circa 1933. Library of Congress.

had asked me to act as a consultant for their wedding gifts. Thus, every ornament, every vase and piece of tableware, was chosen by me. Everything was a unit. Since the Reichmanns held big parties, they turned out to be my best advertisement. Commissions for about fifty homes of this kind followed.

Furnishings that I designed back then were later taken all over the world by those who were fortunate enough to escape the Holocaust. Years later, the Reichmanns showed me photos of their present home in Ithaca, New York, where much of the furniture I designed still holds a place of honor.

After 1934 and the end of the Political Cabaret, I expanded my field of work to shop fronts and commercial interiors. The first job of this sort I owed to the acquaintance of the family Ulanowsky. The mother was an opera singer, and the son Paul was a concert pianist and a constant companion of the soprano Lotte Lehmann in America. The Ulanowskys' beautiful daughter Lilian, who was close friends with Robert Ehrenzweig, was entrusted with the management of a small perfume store, the Bristol-Parfumerie, which had belonged to her grandfather. The store, a tiny shop with a facade of two and a half meters, needed to be completely redesigned. I used a typical stage trick, putting mirrors on the ceiling and the back wall; this optically doubled the small interior space. I also dropped the usual separation between window display and customer area.

The Bristol-Parfumerie attracted much attention and was discussed in national and international architectural journals. After this, I was commissioned to design several fashion shops, a large perfumery, several candy shops, a bookstore, a travel agency, and a glove shop. All evidence of my Viennese architectural work no longer exists. It was all destroyed during World War II.

By 1937, I was a well-established architect. Then, unfortunately, a law to protect the title of "architect" was adopted. Since I had never completed my studies at the Academy of Fine Arts, I had to apply for special permission to use the title. In March 1938, based on my training, documents, photographs, and publications of my work, I received word that my request for an architecture license had been accepted. I had only to pick up the license at the ministry, and I would be sworn in as a graduate architect. At that time, after the Anschluss, I had no desire to report to any ministry. I reluctantly abandoned my chance to hold a diploma as an Austrian architect.

I had become modestly prosperous—I had a car and a moderate-sized savings account. All the rooms of the family home had been modernized. We no longer needed to rent to a lodger, and my mother was considerably relieved. My ambition was to get back the two other rooms of my father's former law firm and use them for the enlargement of my studio. Then came the annexation of Austria.

Bristol-Parfumerie, Vienna, 1935. Library of Congress.

FUSION

In retrospect, it seems as if from 1918 to 1938, I had led not only a double life but several lives simultaneously. This all suggests a certain confusion and fragmentation, and yet all my activities complemented and blended with one another, so that each of the activities influenced the others, and it all contributed to a wholeness.

An anecdote may illustrate this: In 1933 I was redesigning a penthouse apartment for the famous British writer John Lehmann.[29] As engaged in politics as we were, we discussed his extreme leftist political attitude, and he told me about his desire to learn the Russian language. Since I was a member of the Political Cabaret, I was friends with the Russian-born Jura Soyfer, whom I recommended as a Russian teacher. I was also still friends with my former colleague Kurt Singer. From this diversity in my life emerged a story that doesn't lack for comedy, but might have had tragic consequences.

As it happened, Singer knew the manager of Lehmann's building. He found out that the police had learned that dozens of communists met regularly at Lehmann's apartment. Through another friend of a friend, whose boyfriend was a policeman, Singer learned a police raid on Lehmann's place was in the works. Under the pretext of uncovering a nest of homosexuals, all those present in the apartment would be arrested. Lehmann had to be warned. Since I did not dare to warn him by telephone (the interception of telephone conversations, especially in the case of Lehmann and Soyfer, was likely), I asked both of them to visit me. I warned Jura not to meet with his political friends in Lehmann's apartment any longer, and I told Lehmann to be careful. The raid took place as planned, but the police were deeply disappointed. John Lehmann had a single guest: His Excellency, the ambassador of Great Britain. With long faces, the police withdrew.

Furthermore, because of my involvement with both the youth movement and the Political Cabaret, I had attained an unusually large amount of notoriety, one might even say popularity, and had won a wide circle of friends.

To the classic question of how to become a freelance architect, there are two answers: either one takes the fast lane and marries the boss's daughter, or one takes the slow lane, works five or ten years for the boss, then marries his daughter. A third possibility does not normally exist. The acquisition of a first client is impossible, because any prospective client will insist on seeing completed works that have been built for others.

In my case, the solution was that my friends and admirers naively thought that such a famous comedian as I was would also be an excellent architect. The first orders were small, but once the ice was broken, whenever I completed a project, several new commissions would result, and the sizes of these projects increased gradually.

Without my keen interest in architecture, which led me to various cities, I would never have gone to that decorative arts exhibition in Paris. I would never have met Ruth Yorke, we would never have become friends, and I would not have received the necessary documents for entry into the United States at that critical moment in 1938. What I learned at the vocational school and as a technical employee would have barely been enough to allow me to become a building technician. But my creativity, imagination, organizational skills, skills of persuasion, social understanding, and human empathy were fired by my other activities.

Whether these skills would have any value in the new world toward which we were heading on the *Statendam* was as mysterious as the mist of dawn.

3

Discovering America

ARRIVAL

The dawning of a new day, July 13, 1938, brings dreams of my past life to an end. In the pale light of morning it seems that we are approaching steep mountain cliffs. Only the sun's rays reveal these mountains as the skyscrapers of Manhattan. Suddenly on the left appears the Statue of Liberty. In our excitement she seems much more than a monument to us—it is as if she is holding out her arms to welcome us.

So now we have succeeded! In front of us lies America! The land of unlimited opportunity—the new world and its bizarre skyscraper-studded, million-metropolis of New York.

A kaleidoscope of constantly changing colors and shapes. The foaming waters of the harbor, fluted by ocean liners, cargo ships, puffing tugboats. A jazz concert of sirens, dark and light ships' bells, screeching seagulls.

Our ship is slowly towed to the dock. From there, a torrent of handkerchiefs waves at us. Thousands of welcome cries are combined into a single fanfare of jubilation. Over the ramp and down we go to the mainland of our new home. We get warm hugs from Uncle Harry and Ruth Yorke, then it's a thunderous, deafening ride on an express subway, which stops only at every tenth station. As Europeans, we find the variety of skin colors of the other passengers unusual.

And then the sudden silence at Ruth's home. A nice, cozy apartment in a four-story building in a quiet residential area on Sixty-eighth Street in Manhattan, it is in no way different from a home in a European city. Just around the corner is the lush green of romantic Central Park.

On the first day, we explore the surrounding area. We walk alone and ask directions in our clumsy English. Passersby try their best to understand us. On bustling

Ruth Yorke, New York, date unknown. Courtesy of Peggy Gruen.

Fifth Avenue, we admire the luxury goods on the shelves of major department stores. Crowds, noise, roaring traffic, vitality. Breathtaking views from the two tallest skyscrapers. Everything is a little numbing—but all without Nazi decoration!

At dinner with Ruth, we smile at each other. Here we are strangers in a strange land, but the really strange thing is that we feel at home.

CAFETERIA

For two weeks, we try desperately to learn the new language. We discipline ourselves to speak only English to each other. I guess at American newspapers, read English books. Gradually we are able to get something across. Now I want to work, but Ruth says this is nonsense. As a star of a radio soap opera, she makes enough money to support all of us. But I'm intent on being active.

My first job is in a small architecture office at Columbus Circle, a short walk from the apartment. "Are you able to design a cafeteria?" asks my boss, Selig Winston. "Absolutely!" I cry, remembering the countless hours I spent in Vienna coffeehouses. He hands me the plans for a big, empty street restaurant.

Finally I'm back at a drawing table. The work is fun, but I do have difficulties with the wretched system of feet and inches. I can think only in meters and have to convert everything. In a few days, I design a modern, really cozy, authentic Viennese coffeehouse. My boss is totally amazed. "Something like this has never existed in New York before!" he joyfully exclaims. He can hardly wait to present the project to his client.

The big day arrives. The client views the plans, sections, and perspectives, and then, his face flaming red, he jumps up: "You have gone completely crazy! You want to ruin me! In such a place, people would sit around for hours! I want them to eat quickly and then beat it!" My boss is flabbergasted when he hears that the order has been canceled. I am equally dismayed, and I fear that I will be fired.

My English was obviously not good enough. I did not understand the profound difference between "cafeteria" and "coffeehouse."

EXHIBITION EMPLOYMENT

Two days later, I am hired as a designer at a big organization called Ivel. They do not really want me, but they are obligated to give me a job. My sponsor, Paul Gosman, is director of the publicity department at the powerful Socony Oil Company, one of their most important customers. The company is engaged in design, construction, and installation of exhibition booths at promotional fairs and conferences. The name of the company's founder is Levi (the same as my mother's maiden name); read backward, it becomes Ivel. His partner's name is Berthel.

The organization is divided into three parts that are in constant warfare with each other: the sales department, unimaginative contact people; the construction department, practical men; and the design department, cheerful idea incubators who do not give a damn about the concerns of the other two departments. It is the task of the well-paid but always stressed bosses to establish a kind of "policy of détente" among the three hostile camps. When I join the staff, business as usual has been noticeably enlivened by the preparations for the first New York World's Fair.

The staff of the design department consists of about fifteen young, talented people who have studied in art and art-business schools. From the beginning, I'm included as a comrade in this carefree, bohemian community. Because they all call each other by their first names, including the bosses, I'm just "Vic." For a long while, I do not know who the real bosses are. I initially confuse them with two intelligent-looking errand boys. We "artists" present an acceptable front against the "bourgeois" tendencies of the others.

I'm quite useful to them in two ways, neither of which has much to do with my architectural skills. Because of my agitating with the Political Cabaret, I know a lot about advertising. For me it is fun and easy to develop effective ways to communicate ideas to the public. As a trained structural engineer, I also know how these ideas can be implemented at a reasonable cost. When we have linguistic misunderstandings, my new friends help me, often amid much laughter.

There is only one difficulty. Realistic graphics are usually needed for presentations, and creating them involves using an airbrush technique that requires the greatest dexterity and precision. This is not my strong suit. I tend to be sloppy. But with angelic patience, I dedicate myself to learning the finer points of airbrushing. Soon I have passably mastered this boring activity. But this is the only dull thing in my job. Otherwise, we have brilliant talks during work and daily picnics on an abandoned dock on the Hudson River, from which we watch the boat traffic and thousands of seagulls.

I get the most help from my work colleague Elsie Krummeck. As the most talented member of the department, she draws a salary of one hundred U.S. dollars per week, while I make only thirty dollars. Also, she is young and beautiful. Soon we go out together in the evening. The language instruction continues in her artist studio in Greenwich Village. This kind of linguistic study has proved to be the most effective in human history.

At the same time, Lizzie has fallen in love with a young Italian named Ben LaRosa. We agree that one day we will get a divorce, when we possess the means to do so. Years later, she married LaRosa, and she now lives with him and their son John in San Francisco.

Once I start to earn a steady income, we rent a new apartment on Sixty-fourth Street, but this place never gets too crowded. The only furnishings are our possessions from Vienna, which have finally arrived. We sublet one room to a lodger who is a likable man with a good income from a stock exchange job, as well as an admirer of Ruth Yorke. He pays us so generously for the sublet that the apartment is not a financial burden. Years later, my mother will live there.

A LITTLE OUTING

One Sunday in August, Lizzie, Ruth, and I are invited by our tenant, Heinz, to go for a ride in the countryside in his brand-new, elegant convertible. This seems like a brilliant idea, because it is one of those typical New York days when you do not know if you suffer more from the heat or the humidity.

Sweating and exhausted, we climb into the car, and Heinz drives us to the Hudson River highway. There we find out that all of New York has had the same idea. For three hours we crawl in a solid column; from time to time, Heinz encourages us to note the beautiful river views. I protest. "Let us go somewhere where we can stroll in the cool shade and then dine on the terrace of a small guesthouse and drink something!" I suggest. "You must have been stung by a wasp from the Vienna Woods!" says Heinz. "You cannot find something like that around New York, you can only take a little 'spin' to feel the breeze and surrender to the pleasure of driving."

RELATIVITY

Everything is relative. With a little more time, you can take the train to get out of New York. So one day, I find myself walking through the shady deserted alleys of the parklike realm of Princeton University, chatting with a small, white-haired man by my side. My interlocutor is a kindly, humorous, and wise man: Professor Albert Einstein. The day will remain unforgettable to me.

The meeting occurs thanks to some mysterious circumstances. Before I left Vienna, a young and not very important actor in the cabaret handed me a sealed envelope and urgently asked me to deliver it to the addressee personally. The actor hoped Einstein would give him the necessary affidavit to allow him to immigrate to the United States, perhaps even support the establishment of a Viennese theater group in America.

When I unpacked my bags much later, I came across the envelope. I was amazed when I read the address for the first time. Probably a bad joke! But later, in New York, when I called Princeton, I was connected with the professor surprisingly quickly. After I mentioned the name of the sender, he reacted right away: "Come to see me as soon as possible! I am at your complete disposal on Sunday."

The next Sunday finds us in deep conversation. I can hardly believe that I am speaking with the most famous scientist of our time. He reads the letter immediately and promises to take the necessary steps in order for Mr. M. to immigrate. Then he wants to know what I experienced in Vienna and what my plans are now. How can he help to found the theater group?

Suddenly our privacy is disrupted. A car that has been following us slowly for a long time finally stops. A man jumps out and pulls me aside, saying, "I'll pay any price, if you allow me to talk with the professor for a few minutes!" "Thanks," I reply, "but I cannot command the time of Professor Einstein."

The professor turns to the intruder and says, "I have no time now. Sign up by phone or in writing with my secretary." He apologizes for the disturbance and tries to explain. "He was probably one of the annoying representatives of a publisher who wants to publish a book of mine."

We sit down on a bench. Einstein says we are both newcomers with miserable English, but together we can write a semi-useful letter. He takes notes on a legal pad, which I later receive as a typewritten letter. It is on Princeton letterhead, dated September 28, 1938, and reads:

> I am convinced that such an opportunity to open a rich new field for the American theater and on the other side to promote this development of these artists, who would otherwise be lost to the world, should not be missed. I have complete confidence in the capabilities and reliability of Mr. Grünbaum, who I know personally and also in his practical judgment. I would certainly be more than delighted if the excellent plan of this group could get the help of all persons to whom this letter is presented.
>
> ALBERT EINSTEIN

The informality and friendliness of our conversation encourages me. "Professor, I've heard a lot about your theory of relativity," I start, "but frankly I do not quite understand it. Can you give me an example of relativity?"

The great man smiles. "I will give you a simple example. Until a few years ago, I was heralded as a major German physicist. In some years, I will be known as a distinguished American physicist, and even more distantly in time, the Germans will reclaim me as a famous German physicist. You see, that is relativity."

The mystery of the letter from actor M. to Professor Einstein remains unsolved. Rumors that it bargained on behalf of an illegitimate son were never confirmed.

I should mention an anecdote I heard from good friends that illuminates the human greatness of Professor Einstein. My friends had a young son, who would ask his mother for a package of bread from the Vienna Bakery every day, then disappear for some hours. One day, the mother followed her boy, then found him on a garden bench with Professor Einstein. She apologized a thousand times that her naughty son was pestering the professor. He said: "Madam, we have an equitable friendship. I help him with his math exercises, and he feeds me from your excellent bakery."

FUTURAMA

After working for Ivel for about three months, I thought that the rising value of my output should be rewarded with a salary increase. I talked to the boss. To his question "How much do you want to earn per week?" I replied, "Fifty dollars." He asked, "What would you do if I refuse?" In that case, I said, I will have to leave the place, to my regret. He patted me on the shoulder and said gently, "Thank you, it has been a great pleasure to have had you with us."

The sentence was too complicated for me. I asked my friends what Mr. Levi had meant. Somewhat worriedly, they told me that I had just been fired. This did not bother me so much, because as an experienced "Yankee," I had already found another job that would pay me fifty dollars a week.

So now I was working in a huge, factorylike building in a rundown neighborhood on the east side of 125th Street. The company was commissioned to design and build a giant detailed model for the General Motors pavilion at the New York World's Fair, which was based on the ideas of the designer Norman Bel Geddes. The name of this model: Futurama. Subtitle: The Streets of the Future.

Bel Geddes had a wonderful idea. He knew that all the car companies would be exhibiting their future models at the fair, but he understood that streets give birth to cars, and not, as most believe, that greater car traffic requires new streets. He persuaded General Motors to spend a small fortune on advertising the building of a national highway network. In his view, if America was crisscrossed with a network of highways, General Motors would never have to worry about selling cars again.

Bel Geddes's employers recognized the correctness of this idea and made impressive funds available for the construction of the model, which would form the center and summit of the exhibition. Fair attendees would be able to admire the model of a new road system that would link the East Coast to the Midwest to the West Coast.

Since money didn't matter, two hundred designers were hired. They were almost all refugees—Hitler had chased them out of half of Europe. The only common language was English. Without any limits to our imagination, we developed the most amazing ideas for underpasses and overpasses, for multistory sections of roads, for traffic cloverleafs and automatic signals. We could not foresee that this would become real. At the same time, we designed magnificent snow-white cities and metropolises of the future, which were like glistening jewels surrounded by woods and fields, mountain valleys, streams, lakes, and oceans. These, unfortunately, would not become reality.

The task force was cosmopolitan. My group included both a blond giant who sympathized with the Nazis and a black-haired Zionist. They had to mathematically calculate which parts of the model could be seen by onlookers under any circumstances and then incorporate this into their design. At work, they were of one heart and one soul; at lunch, they insulted each other in the wildest ways.

For me, this job was ideal. The discipline was very loose, and if you wanted a break, you could always excuse yourself by saying you needed to study details of the model in the great hall. On these breaks, I made many phone calls about the newly established Viennese Theatre Group. This interesting work on the Futurama model might have continued forever, but unfortunately, the opening date of the world's fair soon approached. When the directors of General Motors visited, there was a quarrel. The pace of work had to be accelerated so that the model would be finished by early January 1939. We succeeded, and immediately afterward, we were all unemployed and standing in the cold street.

Bel Geddes's idea was a hit. A federal commission was formed for the establishment of a national highway network. The financing came from taxes on the sales of cars and gasoline. The more roads were built, the more rapidly the traffic swelled, and the higher the tax revenues grew, and then still more roads were built.

Finally, some years after the war, this motorway network was so extensive that the railroad companies were forced into bankruptcy. Passenger travel by rail had fallen sharply, and now the wonderful luxury express trains, which I had used regularly, were discontinued. This increased air pollution, noise, and the number of auto fatalities and injuries. Urban sprawl, urban decay, and wastage of oil and gas were further consequences. It wasn't until the oil crisis of 1973, thirty-five years after Futurama, that work on the national highway network had to stop, or at least be slowed down. The funds were reallocated to build new or improved public transportation.

Of all of this I had not the slightest premonition. At the time, I made my modest contribution to the development of American automobile traffic for just fifty dollars a week.

THE ACTORS ARRIVE

Nor had I foreseen the consequences of the words I had spoken to my friends on March 11, 1938, in Vienna. In those emotional hours, I had promised to found a theater group with all those from our small troupe who made it to New York. Now they began to report, one by one, and remind me of my promise. So we created the Viennese Refugee Artists Group and began a series of preparations.

The goal should have been to perform in English, but the majority of the Viennese refugees had the opposite opinion. Within a few months, a sort of ghetto of Viennese immigrants had formed in New York. They separated themselves completely from the German residents of Yorkville, and also from the Jewish, Russian, and Polish immigrants who were all part of a community that had long existed in the Lower East Side. Now it turned out that Vienna was in fact not *verjudet* (too Jewish), as the Nazis claimed; rather, the Jews were *verwienert* (too Viennese).

The Jews of Vienna did not want anything to do with the Germans, the Jews, and even the Americans in New York. They settled close together in the middle West Side and founded true Viennese pastry shops and guesthouses, where they spent their time feeling sorry for each other, whining about the lost good old days, and waxing nostalgic about Wiener schnitzel, fine coffee with whipped cream, and all the other glories that they were unable to obtain in this barbaric America.

They organized Viennese evenings, with Viennese songs and Viennese jokes performed by Viennese actors (including Karl Farkas).[1] In their districts, they refused to speak English.

The most pitiable seemed to me those who had risked their lives to smuggle jewelry and money out of Austria yet now resigned themselves to waiting for the perfect business opportunity, until there was not a penny of their fortune left.

We did not behave like that. After long discussions, the decision was made: we would enact Viennese theater in the style of the *Kleinkunstbühnen,* but in English for an American audience.

What we had were gifts of various kinds: young actors, writers, musicians, and set designers and the smuggled texts of scenes and songs. What we did not have was money. Somehow all of the artists managed to earn livings as waiters, dishwashers, servants, or nannies.

Our texts were translated by night by young American writers. I worked on the Jura Soyfer satirical play *The Lechner Edi Looks into Paradise (Journey to Paradise),* which I translated into lousy English. Then a friend of Ruth Yorke, John Latouche, made an American adaptation. He was highly talented, but still completely unknown. Later he gained fame with his play *Opera for Americans,* but unfortunately died at a young age.

An excellent linguist, Arthur Lessack, was available to teach us English, but he also used complicated tongue exercises to eradicate any traces of an accent. There were rehearsals every night, which lasted until everyone was physically exhausted.

Unfortunately, I could not participate because of my work commitments. Therefore, I was never completely rid of my Viennese accent, in contrast with the others.

Intensive rehearsals began with the arrival of director Herbert Berghof. Soon we had a small repertoire of scenes, songs, and solos rehearsed in English.

Now armed with the letter from Professor Einstein, we appealed to wealthy Jewish families for help. We were invited to big parties, where we introduced ourselves with scenes and musical interludes. At one of these receptions, Mrs. Beatrice Kaufman, the wife of the famous playwright George S. Kaufman, was in attendance.[2] She was impressed by the group and called her husband. We all loaded into taxis and went to perform for Mr. Kaufman at his apartment. The audition seemed to please him, but he was less thrilled with our idea of performing in small venues. He suggested that instead we should prepare an intimate revue, which could be staged in one of the major Broadway theaters. He would try to win over as many members of the New York theater scene as possible to support us. But for this, it would be necessary for us to fill out the program by adding new scenes, continue our language training, and use the help of a few American theater professionals to raise our show to meet the high standards that New York audiences expected. We agreed with great enthusiasm.

Mr. Kaufman worked wonders. An American aid organization came into existence—its members included Irving Berlin, Eddie Cantor, Edna Ferber, Moss Hart, Al Jolson, Fredric March, Harpo and Zeppo Marx, Richard Rodgers, and our friend Ruth Yorke. As the only non-American, I was elected to the board of this group. The help we received was overwhelming. We were given the stages of various large theaters to use for our rehearsals. Enough money was collected to pay each member of the group a small stipend. George Kaufman personally helped as a director, Irving Berlin sat down at the piano to rehearse musical numbers with us, Donald Oenslager designed stage sets, Irene Sharaff created the costumes, and Charles Friedman served as a production assistant.[3]

In my role, I was the link between the Viennese and the Americans. I insisted that we all receive the same salary and secured a pledge of loyalty from all members as long as the group existed.

Our friends on Broadway also made sure that we saw lots of shows. We were able to attend performances of all the most successful shows. I was particularly impressed by the satirical revue *Pins and Needles,* which was highly reminiscent of the Political Cabaret.[4]

Even as I made these preparations, which sometimes swallowed up entire nights, I continued working on Futurama and freelance design projects. It was a hectic time, but unforgettably interesting, because all these experiences introduced me to many brilliant and talented American artists.

THE FIRST ASSIGNMENT

After nearly six months of working, I was unemployed for the first time. A little dejected, and deep in thought, I walked dreamily up Fifth Avenue. Suddenly, I heard my name being called. A well-dressed, middle-aged man said to me, "You are the architect Grünbaum from Vienna, aren't you?" When I assented, he said, "I finally found you. I was looking for you for weeks and also tried to reach you by phone." (Of course he could not, because I had no phone.) He introduced himself as Mr. Ludwig Lederer. In my mind, I immediately pictured all his shops in Vienna and other European cities. They were leather goods shops, and all of them had characteristic light-gray glass facades.

He explained that he had lost all his European shops, but that he had enough capital to begin again. We walked a few steps farther, and he showed me a bar that he had rented in a prime location, close to Fifty-fifth Street on Fifth Avenue. "I have always admired your stores in Vienna," he announced. "I want you to design my new store." We visited the premises. Afterward, in a nearby restaurant, we discussed his wishes, the budget, and all other conditions. At the end of this conversation, I had my first architectural commission in America in my pocket.

I happily hurried home to our apartment and sat down at my drawing table from Vienna. Now I could take advantage of all the drawing tools that I had brought along when I fled Austria. I started my layout. I drew only what already had been formed in my mind's eye in raw outlines. Whenever I felt challenged by a task, whether it was a literary or architectural one, the first draft would follow a creative moment of vision, as if it had just come to me.

As I sat down in front of the white paper on the drawing board, the next step was to try to match the physical form of the ground plan, the elevation, and the section to the layout in my head—an exciting activity.

My trained eye and the experience I had gained through the years rarely led me astray, and they did not do so here. After three days of diligent work, I was certain: the idea and the reality fit together. I could invite Mr. Lederer over to take a look at the sketches.

The vision: Create an atrium open to the sidewalk along Fifth Avenue, where pedestrians could collect like water in a reservoir. Here they would be protected from the weather as well as from the crush of passersby. The two side walls and the back wall of the atrium would be studded with six small individual glass cases; on the back wall, a glass door would allow a view into the store as well as entry. The exhibition showcases at both sides would be located at right angles to the entrance and would therefore attract more attention as shopwindows, which are usually located parallel to the walking direction. The areas between, above, and below the glass cabinets would be made of the same solid-gray glass that was typical for the European stores of the client. The ceiling of the atrium would consist of diaphanous glass, and invisible light sources above would illuminate the open forecourt evenly, but not too strongly. In front of me, in the middle of this newly created outdoor space, I imagined a glass exhibit case, like those used in museums, that would serve for the presentation of special goods. Like the items in the other glass cases, these would be illuminated by small, very powerful lights, like those used in theaters. The company's name would be placed in silver letters on the back wall above the entrance.

Mr. Lederer was thrilled. The six wall cases and the additional central exhibit space offered him the opportunity to present a large assortment of his goods. It was immediately clear to him that the new wind- and weather-protected space would provide a welcome escape from the crowds of pedestrian traffic. I assured him that this concept, along with a slightly simpler design of the interior space, could be realized within the proposed construction budget of about ten thousand dollars.

However, the building's owner, whose consent we needed, received us coolly. This very conservative man paid little attention to the drawings and stated, "I do not know Mr. Grünbaum, I've never heard of him. I cannot allow an unknown refugee to work on my building." But Mr. Lederer persisted. He explained that he couldn't entrust this assignment to anyone else. Finally we reached a compromise. The owner mentioned a young American architect who was currently in charge of the conversion of the neighboring store Ciro, which sold costume jewelry. He assumed that this not particularly busy young architect would be willing to cooperate with Mr. Grünbaum.

We sought out this architect, Mr. Morris Ketchum, immediately.

Arriving at the specified address, I was shocked. It was the most elegant new office building in New York, known as the "Cathedral of the Business World" at Rockefeller Center. I thought that this had to be a very famous and wealthy architect who could afford to maintain a studio in this palace. But it emerged that Mr. Ketchum only used a drafting table that he sublet from the offices of the very famous architect Edward Stone.

I showed Morris Ketchum the photos of my Viennese commercial buildings and the preliminary designs for the Lederer store. Mr. Lederer pointed out that he expected nothing more than that Mr. Ketchum would put his stamp and signature on my plans. Mr. Ketchum was in agreement. He would sign the plans for the Lederer store as an architect and support me in negotiations with construction companies. In exchange, I would help him with the adjoining Ciro store. This was acceptable to all of us. Then, more in jest than in earnest, we agreed that if there should be new contracts due to these two projects, we would continue in the same way, he as the architect and I the designer.

I also introduced myself to Edward Stone, whose works were well known to me. I told him about the agreement with Morris, and he liked that. When I showed him the photos of my work in Vienna, he asked permission to keep them. He assured me that they would appear alongside articles about me in American architectural journals (a promise he absolutely kept). I thanked him for his generosity and asked myself if something like that would have been possible in a similar case in Vienna.

The following months I worked side by side with Morris Ketchum. I contributed to the Ciro store considerably but concentrated more on the detailed design and supervision of the Lederer store.

Both stores opened in July 1939. Mr. Lederer was content and happy. I was even happier because the public response triggered by this small store exceeded my

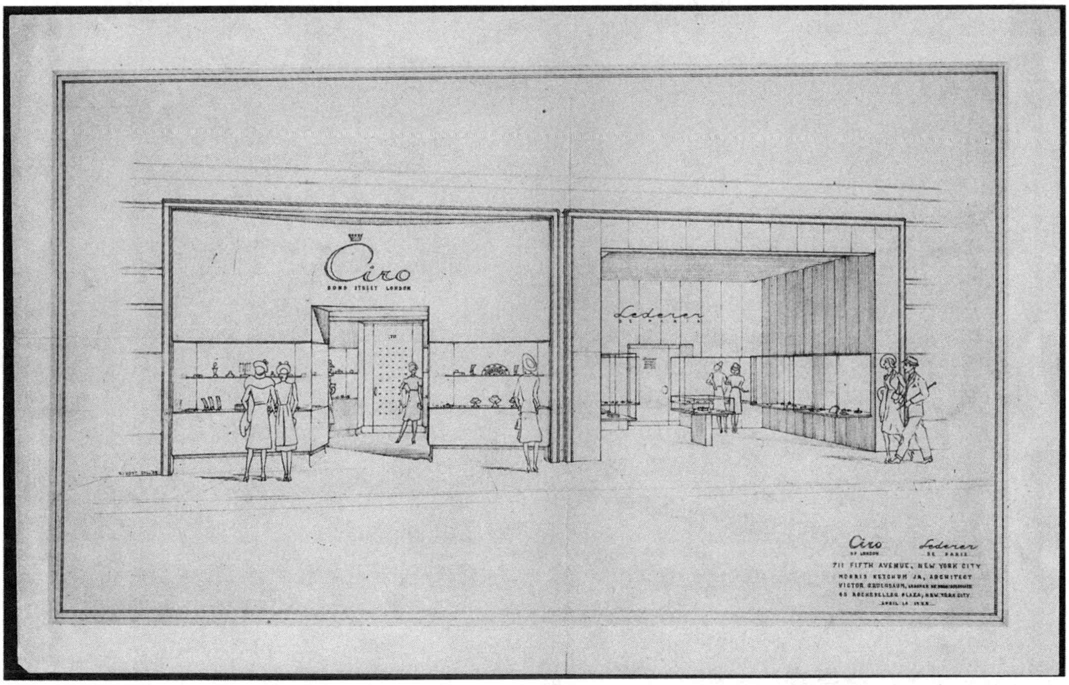

Drawing of Ciro and Lederer de Paris, New York, 1939. American Heritage Museum, Victor Gruen Collection.

wildest expectations. Not just architecture and trade press but also newspapers and weeklies published laudatory articles. They always remarked: "The Lederer store is the first important expression of contemporary architecture in this domain in America."

I was well satisfied with this result, but I could not fully explain the sensational reception. I found out the reason for that later: in fact, American architects had hardly dealt with retail and commercial construction so far. This activity was entirely

Lederer de Paris, New York, 1939. Courtesy of Gruen Associates. Photograph by Ezra Stoller.

left to large commercial builders, which provided all services from design to construction. Due to the monopoly of some of these large companies, there was a lack of individuality, originality, and inventiveness in the field of retail and commercial construction.

The Lederer store remained unchanged for a long time. It was discussed in detail in all relevant architecture books. Even when it burned down in 1963, a new owner commissioned me to restore the original design. But in the summer of 1976, I was witness to its demolition; it was replaced by a new store for a shoe store chain.

A PARTNERSHIP

Morris Ketchum and I were highly delighted with the success of both stores. The situation that we had jokingly mentioned at our first meeting now arrived. We received a number of orders for stores and shops of various categories. Encouraged by this success, Morris made me an offer one day to try to create an architecture firm in which we would be equal partners. I said yes.

A few days later, Morris invited me out for a walk in the oldest part of New York, the Wall Street district. He seemed to be very serious and somewhat confused. Finally, in front of the old Trinity Church, which is wedged between the skyscrapers of financial institutions, he told me that the parents of his wife, Isabel, had been married in this relic of the past. His wife had told him that it would not be proper for him, whose family had arrived in America as Pilgrims on the very first ship, the *Mayflower*, to associate with a newly arrived refugee. (Incidentally, over time, I heard about so many families claiming to have come to America on the *Mayflower* that I believe it must have been the largest ship in the world.)

Morris stammered that, to his chagrin, he would have to withdraw his original offer, but he could offer me a well-paid job as chief designer. I replied: "The Trinity Church is fairly old and venerable, but the synagogue where my parents were married is older. I consider my career as an employee in America to be finished. Therefore, I must refuse your offer. I'll try my luck as a freelance designer." With that, we decided to divide our current and prospective clients equitably. We parted as good friends.

Morris was a very capable architect. Given that fact, combined with our common good reputation, he was able, later in his career, to create a successful partnership with two Americans. His ambition (or perhaps that of his wife) also drove him to run for the presidency of the American Institute of Architects, a position that he achieved. So I felt some satisfaction, twenty years later, when he placed the AIA Grand Cordon of Fellowship, one of the greatest honors of the architects' institutes, around my neck.

SELF-EMPLOYED

To work as a freelance designer in New York, I had to make a big decision. I could not be successful if I limited myself to a drafting table rented from Edward Stone or in my apartment. I had to rent a studio.

I found it in a so-called loft building built for commercial purposes: each floor, from the frontage to the courtyard facade, consisted of a single room plus a bathroom. It was on the third floor, with no elevator, and it was very shabby and dirty. It had been empty for years and had formerly served as a milliners' salon—a faded wall painting of great ostrich feathers was the only trace of this history.

When Elsie Krummeck heard of my decision, she instantly decided to give up her lucrative job at Ivel to form a common cause. We founded the design firm Gruenbaum & Krummeck.[5] The furniture was sparse: my old drafting table from Vienna and sofas and a desk that we bought in a junk store, along with a few chairs. Otherwise, the space was just yawning emptiness. We worked on some projects that I had taken from the collaboration with Morris Ketchum, and we waited for our first new clients. Elsie and I lived in an ugly furnished room near the studio. Although our expenses and rents were low, I still had financial problems.

THE UNCLE IN AMERICA

Filled with confidence, I appealed to my Uncle Harry for financing. He was aghast at my audacity, but he lent me one thousand dollars, which I promised to pay back in three years, a promise that I was able to keep.

This was one of my rare meetings with Uncle Harry, who was a strange man, tormented by many problems. He had left Germany in 1914 and felt (not without reason) threatened by anti-Semitism. He had Americanized his name to Harry Lowry. He didn't want me to visit often, because it would have been noticed that he associated with a Jewish refugee. As long as we were in Europe, he had written long letters to my mother regularly. Because he almost always included a five- or ten-dollar bill in his letters, he was our "rich uncle in America." It wasn't until my arrival I found out that he worked—at the age of forty-three—as a baggage porter in a second-rate hotel. Later, he quit this position because it seemed to him too responsible. Then he lived in a cheap hotel room and swam daily in the Hudson River, until he died in 1974 at the age of eighty-three. Despite all his problems, he was a lovable man, warmhearted, generous, and devoted to the opera. Even in old age, he had an immense attraction to women, but I never got to know his many girlfriends, who devotedly nursed him and cared for him.

He was interested in everything I did, but he was horrified by my "crazy life," as he called it. I was moved to tears when I found out after his death that he had bequeathed five hundred dollars to the Center for Environmental Planning, which he knew was very important to me. With the thousand dollars that he lent me, I hired a secretary who was quite efficient, but who tyrannized Elsie and me.

A REMARKABLE CHARACTER

The first new client who climbed up our steep stairs was a Mr. Stefan Klein. He was one of the most remarkable characters that I ever met.

Mr. Klein had come from Poland and had spent several years in Vienna, where he was, as a representative of Carlsbad Wafers, in close contact with the candy shops. He had learned a lot about the production and sale of chocolate pralines. He came to me because he had known and admired the shops in Vienna that I designed. Whether he was speaking German or English, he used many Yiddish words and the tone and the diction of this German-Russian-Hebrew language mixture.

He began the conversation with this memorable phrase: "Under how much, Mr. Architect, can you not design a small candy store?" My answer: "Such a store cannot be set up for under $2,500." He looked at me innocently and asked if it would not be possible for $2,000. I said no, whereupon he left our studio in disappointment. After half an hour, he struggled to climb up the steep steps to us for a second time and made an offer of $2,200. I said, "You cannot haggle over this—in my experience $2,500 would be the minimum." With intense gestures, he reproached me by saying that I would lose a great opportunity; namely, he intended to set up a large chain of such stores, and he suggested that I should calculate what that would mean for my future. I repeated the first sum. Not until his third visit did he agree to the estimate of $2,500. Then came the negotiations about our fee. I asked for the usual 10 percent, he offered 5. It took some time until we reached consensus. Then, somewhat concerned, I asked if he would ever have the necessary capital. I should leave that to him, he said.

Mr. Klein's rented store was on upper Broadway near Eighty-second Street, in a middle-class Jewish residential area. What Mr. Klein received from us exceeded this fee easily: we not only created the inside of the store and the portal but also invented the name, Barton's Bonbonniere, and designed the trademark, the stationery, the wrapping paper, and the signage.[6]

A wooden screen prefabricated in Sweden delimited the storage space from the small sales space in a semicircular form. Mirrors created the illusion of a circular room. This impression was reinforced by overhead lights, which consisted of several semicircles of small individual bulbs. From the outside, through a single large pane of glass, you could see the entire sales space, which was designed with decorative glass cabinets and equipped with a counter embellished with a hand-painted pattern designed by Elsie.

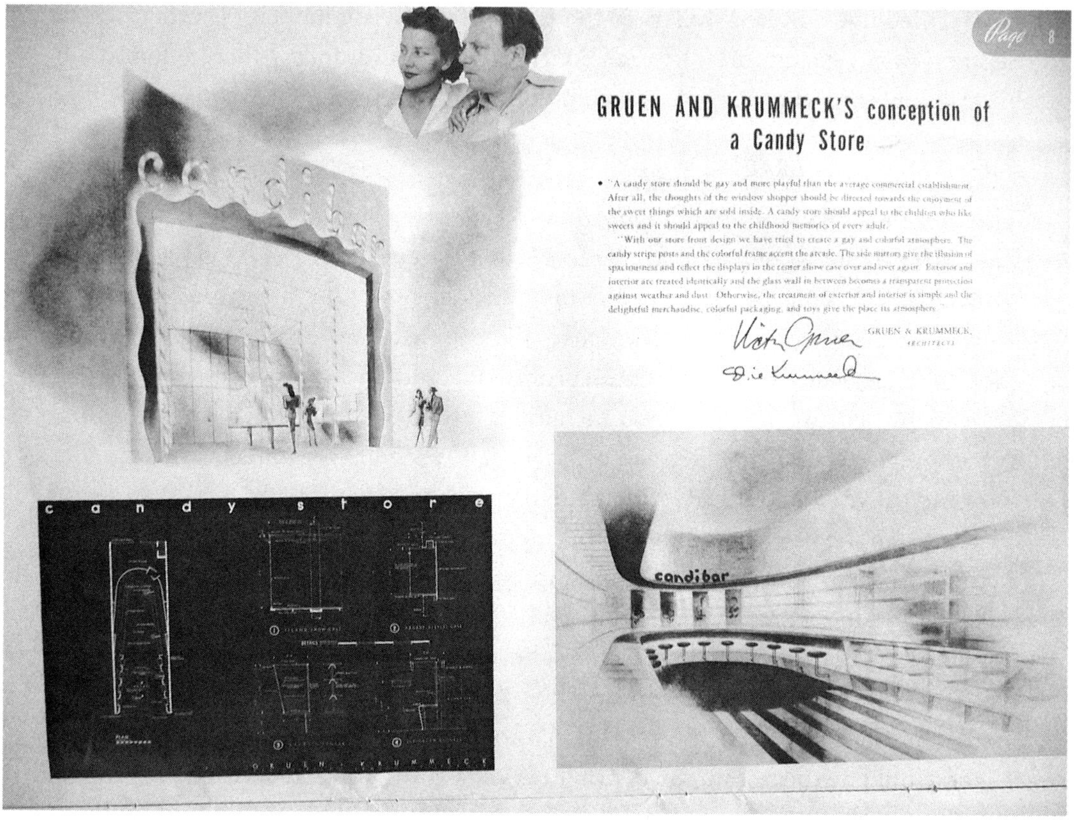

Design for Barton's Bonbonniere, New York, 1941. Courtesy of Peggy Gruen.

The store brought Mr. Klein resounding success. He offered something that bridged a gap in the U.S. market: small, typical Viennese chocolates, handmade by Mr. Klein and his six brothers in a common kitchen. Until then, there had only been mass-produced, oversized candies, sold lovelessly and tastelessly packaged in drugstores. A European-style candy store had never existed in the United States before the opening of Barton Bonbonniere.

Soon I discovered that when he gave us the assignment, Stefan (as we called him later) had possessed neither the money for the building nor our fee. But now began a success story that might be called the "Stefan Klein Saga," which proves that the United States was, at least for the brave, the country of unlimited possibilities.

Within a few weeks, Mr. Klein was able to pay us, and he also engaged us to design five more stores. After the sixth store, he said he could save on architects' fees, because the stores now just needed to be copied. From that point, he worked only with construction companies, whereupon the appearance of his stores steadily declined.

He employed Lizzie as a window dresser. Later, she was executive window designer and worked for him for a long time in the San Francisco area.

About twelve years after my first meeting with him, I was back in New York when I received a telegram forwarded to me from Los Angeles, where I had moved my office. It said that Mr. Klein wanted to talk to me. He was surprised and flattered by my immediate return call. I let him believe that I came to New York only for him. He proudly declared that he was now opening his fiftieth store. For this purpose, he had purchased a small building across from New York's largest department store, Macy's. In grateful remembrance that I had been the key to his success, he insisted that I should design this brilliant new store. I congratulated him on his success but expressed to him my concerns about a good working relationship, because I remembered him to be an unpleasant "chiseler." Mr. Klein protested vehemently. It was probably true that he once was a chiseler, but now as the owner of a large candy factory, forty-nine stores, and two Cadillacs, he would have no reason to haggle anymore. He would prove that to me by accepting any price.

I wanted to test him, so I pointed out that because of inflation, and because he wanted the design of a whole building, I estimated the costs at about seventy thousand dollars, and therefore I would have to require a fee of seven thousand dollars. After several minutes of total silence, there was a very meek question: "Could it not be six thousand dollars?"

"But Stefan," I exclaimed, "you just promised never to haggle again!" Again there was a long silence and then a very timid "Just this one time again, please!" I had to laugh uncontrollably. This laugh was worth a thousand dollars for me.

So began the construction of the fiftieth Barton's Bonbonniere. A new image for these stores seemed to be in order, so I consulted one of the most talented artists in America, Alvin Lustig, to redesign the labels and logos. The overall impression of the new store was sensational, fresh, and alive. Architecture magazines especially praised the playful and colorful composition.

It was another ten years before I heard from Stefan Klein again. In the meantime, the Barton empire experienced fantastic growth. In every city of the West and Midwest, in every shopping mall, Barton's stores sprang up like mushrooms. Barton's candies were in everyone's mouths.

By the time he called me in the early sixties, he had placed the management of the stores in the hands of his six brothers and was now active in the real estate business. His question this time was "Victor, how much less you cannot build a sixty-story office building?" I replied that I would rather have a good friendship with him than argue about costs and fees.

DESIGNERS IN NEW YORK

In the first months of our independence, Elsie and I received some interesting small assignments, including designs for an elegant apartment, exhibition spaces, and a significant number of stores. For example, we designed the Scandinavian delicacy shop Old Denmark, which enjoyed great popularity and still operates successfully. We were very busy, but the financial rewards were quite modest.

One day, we got a surprising visit. Mr. Berthel, the managing director of our former employer Ivel, made us an offer to become partners. He wanted to leave his own company. He admired our work and had come to the conclusion that we deserved more success. He suggested that if we would have him as a capable businessman by our side, we could make a lot of money. For Elsie and me, the proposal sounded a bit fishy. We asked what he really meant by "a lot of money." "At least three hundred dollars a week" was his answer. This seemed to be irresponsible boasting, so we rejected his proposal.

Soon after, we received a prestigious assignment. It concerned a candy store again and once more it was connected to Viennese refugees. In Vienna, the gentlemen Emil Altmann and Ernst Kühne had operated a renowned candy store that was designed by the famous architect Josef Hoffmann.[7] Now they wanted to open a very special confectionary in a restaurant on Fifth Avenue, directly across from the Lederer store.

This was a big challenge. We had the idea to present chocolates as jewels. The available space had high ceilings and was equipped with a balcony in the rear, which was reached by a spiral staircase with a glass balustrade. The premises were done up in eye-catching white and gold. Pink accents gave the space the charm you would expect in an exquisite confectionery parlor.

The construction barricades were removed in early December 1939, and the opening of the store was like a Broadway premiere. The store was praised as the most beautiful confectionery in the world. In the way that works of arts were usually discussed, the event was featured in major newspaper articles. In a book by Emrich Nicholson about store architecture in America, one passage in the preface mentioned that on both sides of Fifth Avenue in New York, exactly across from each other, there were two stores that could well be described as the finest of America, Lederer and Altmann & Kühne.[8]

Again, we received a tantalizing offer to give up our independence. This time it came from the construction company that had carried out the work for the Altmann & Kühne store. They wanted to make us their chief architects. We refused. We could have built a nice career in New York on this sensational success, but

Victor Gruen and Elsie Krummeck at work, New York, 1939. Courtesy of Peggy Gruen.

the price would have been that we would have been labeled as store design specialists. Once again it was serendipity that influenced my life. It also saved me from specialization.

THE PREMIERE

But even before this random event arrived, there had been another event that we had planned many months ahead. The premiere of the first production of the Viennese Theatre Group took place on June 20, 1939, at the Music Box Theatre, which had been one of the most beautiful theaters on Broadway. The musical revue was titled *From Vienna.* Our mission was clear in our minds: most of the young actresses and actors would at last stand in a real theater on a real stage—on Broadway, no less. For me, it meant even more. In the morning, my mother had arrived from England. Now she sat in the audience to see a show that was produced by her son.

Through a peephole in the curtain, I checked to see if there was an audience. It was summer and a dead season for theater, but the Music Box was crammed full. After a musical overture by an American orchestra we had engaged because of union rules, the curtain finally rose.

To open, the entire ensemble sang the song "Dear Parents," a wistful letter to "the parents at home." Then followed a skit by Hans Weigel, "Musical Day," which parodied classical music and had been translated into English by Werner Michel.[9] The main act of the first part was Jura Soyfer's play *Journey to Paradise* in six scenes. After the intermission there was a skit on the Salzburg Marionette Theater, a solo song-and-dance number by Illa Roden (text by Peter Hammerschlag), and the humorous skit "English in Six Easy Lessons," in which we parodied our language difficulties.[10] The conclusion featured a selection of Vienna choir songs in both German and English. The performance went smoothly, in spite of our excitement and nervousness, with abundant applause after each scene.

After the show, we all waited excitedly until dawn for the appearance of the reviews. We were nervous because we knew that bad reviews, especially in the *New York Times,* could abruptly put an end to the show. Even before the day dawned, we breathed a sigh of relief: the newspapers ran unusually long reviews that ranged from warmly sympathetic to enthusiastic. The long *Journey to Paradise* was praised a little less than the short scenes. Equally acknowledged with full admiration was the fact that a group of refugees were able to create a respectable Broadway show with such good English so soon after their arrival.

I quote from one of three major articles in the *New York Times*:

> No one can doubt that we must be grateful for their presence, because the "Refugee Artists" are cheerful and charming people with a lot of artistic talent and a winning

Announcement: The Refugee Artists Group, New York, 1939. Library of Congress.

> attitude.... There was a lot of emotion on both sides of the footlights, an emotion that could be shared without restriction.... The enthusiasm with which these actors approach each role is admirable itself, a "Revue-Technique" which is unknown in this country.... One of the obvious truths is that these "Refugees'" talents and ideas... will enrich our culture.

The article concludes with the words "Hitler's loss: our gain!"

The reviews were so good that they endangered the cohesion of the group. Individual actors were singled out as stars, especially Illa Roden. They said she deserved to be in a great show immediately. In fact, shortly after the premiere, she was offered a leading role in a Broadway show, but she declined out of loyalty to the group.

For the total run of three months, we were in the public eye with interviews, photo reports, and broadcasting reviews. One great joy was the visit from Eleanor Roosevelt, who came up onstage and thanked all those involved personally.

Due to the success of *From Vienna,* we created a second revue called *Reunion in New York.* It premiered on February 21, 1940, and also ran for about three months. It was already much more American, more experienced. Among other things, it featured the serious poem "The Dachau Song," which had been smuggled out of the concentration camp where Jura Soyfer had written it.

This time, the stage sets were designed by the Viennese Harry Horner, who had already participated in the Political Cabaret, and whose American Dream career I have already mentioned.

Although the show was a tremendous success for all those three months, we disbanded the group at its end. My promise on March 11, 1938, was fulfilled. Almost all the members of the team now had the chance to work in the American theater and film business. Some were very successful in the United States after that, and some returned to Europe after the war.

Working with the Viennese Theatre Group not only gave me great personal satisfaction, but it also enabled collaborations with leading American artists and intellectuals, which probably further accelerated and deepened my Americanization.

Our director Herbert Berghof married the German actress Uta Hagen and still leads a successful theater school, which also gives performances. One strange parallel to my first commission of a dance school in Vienna was that I designed the conversion of a four-story horse barn into a theater school and performance venue. Recently, I received a program from the Herbert Berghof Players. The cast list included my twelve-year-old granddaughter, Madeleine Gruen, in the supporting role of the Fourth Mouse.

THE CALL OF THE WEST

Upon successful completion of my time in the theater, I wanted to devote myself completely to architecture. The call of the West reached me in the form of an insignificant telephone call. Phil Harris introduced himself as vice president of a women's clothing house and asked me a favor. One of his employees, Mr. Zwarowsky (the brother of Ruth Yorke), had given him my name and phone number. He asked if I could send one of my technical illustrators to his office for a few hours. The matter concerned a small revision to the plans for the changing rooms of a large store on the West Coast. He knew exactly what he wanted, but he was not able to scale it down. Of course, I would be paid enough for the transfer of my employee. I explained that I would do a favor for anyone acquainted with Ruth Yorke.

As the only technical draftsman in my office, I went myself to the Grayson's company on Seventh Avenue, in the garment district.

Mr. Harris was very flattered. He explained the changes he wanted, which I sketched in an hour. He told me that these plans were for a store in Seattle, Washington, which would constitute the first major Grayson's branch on the West Coast. Thereafter, a number of branches would be built in other cities in the region. He proudly presented the entire plan package, done by an architect in Seattle. Then he asked me what I thought of it.

I thought the work was below average, and I decided I would lose nothing by telling him my honest opinion. So I criticized the plan relentlessly and, in particular, pointed out that the layout totally disregarded the fact that this was meant to be a four-story building. The upper floors were completely unused. In my opinion, this should have been reflected at the very least by the design of the facade. The current plan, which provided only a conventional, high-parterre front disbursement, was a missed opportunity that would not be useful for the establishment of future stores.

Mr. Harris was very upset. He asked me to wait a moment, then left. He came back with the news that the company's director general, Mr. Heiman Kouschai, wanted to talk to me.

In the executive office, I found something I'd seen only in American movies—a large corner room, an impressive desk in the farthest corner, and in the oversized fauteuil behind it, Mr. Heiman Kouschai, leaning back with a fat cigar, feet on desk. Without taking the cigar out of his mouth, he muttered condescendingly, "Young man, I am astonished that the plan for our big store in Seattle did not get your applause. Tell me, clearly and briefly, what you do not like."

I put forward my views, with which he seemed totally unimpressed. He merely responded with an ironic smile, "It is already too late to change anything in the plan. But I would like to see how you might imagine the design of the exterior."

Striking a professional pose, I answered that I would not lift a finger for a joke. Would he pay me for a simple sketch? Then I named what I thought of as an exorbitant sum: one hundred dollars. He grinned: "Today is Friday. If you submit me your draft Monday morning, I'll pay double." With pleasure I agreed.

My promise was neither reckless nor outrageous, because I was already pretty sure of my concept. I had already developed the basic idea of the facade during the conversation with Mr. Harris: much of the front four-story, ugly, and totally useless part of the building should be torn down twenty yards away from the street, leaving only the two roof-supporting pillars. This would create an imposing portico of about the same width, height, and depth along the walking street. This could be delineated by a parabolic curved ceiling that would reach from the height of the fourth floor down to the selling space on the ground floor. A twenty-meter-deep arcade would arise with two large side windows and two freestanding showcases around two support pillars. The rear glass wall would have two full glass doors into the building.

I showed Elsie the plans of the other architect, described my vision, and proposed a work schedule for the weekend. Now we had to look at the drawings to find out if the idea was feasible. Then we had the most important task: Elsie did a colored perspective drawing that expressed the idea for a layman in a convincing and easily understandable way. We worked like crazy on footprints, sections, and elevations, and were finished Sunday evening.

Punctually on Monday morning at ten o'clock, we presented our work. Mr. Kouschai was impressed by the effective drawing. "This design is probably the craziest thing I've ever seen," he said, "but it shows some talent and maybe we can give you the opportunity to work for Grayson's in the future." He handed us a check for two hundred dollars, smiled, and expressed the hope that his California partner would never see our drawings.

Then the door opened, and, like a deus ex machina, the California partner appeared. He was tall and slender, with a wide-brimmed hat over his tanned face; he was dressed entirely in white, with snow-white riding boots. This was Walter Kirschner. He had an aquiline nose and darkly shining eyes.

Although Mr. Kouschai tried to usher us out in a hurry, Mr. Kirschner wanted to know who we were and why we were there. He spotted the drawings, and, despite all the protests of his partner, he insisted on seeing them. He studied them gravely for a few minutes, then he turned to Elsie and me, asking in a sonorous voice, "What do you children have in mind for lunch?" "Nothing urgent," we replied. "Then we will have a small, intimate meeting during lunch, just the three of us."

The intimate lunch was in the swanky, spacious dining room of the Hotel New Yorker, where we were entertained by a raucous ice-skating show. All that noise made it difficult to communicate, but we finally understood that Kirschner was asking us what we were planning for tomorrow. I bluffed that I'd have to consult my calendar (even though I knew I had no plans for the next day), and he waved his hand: "I know exactly what you're doing tomorrow. You are flying to Seattle to make new plans for the store to be built there which will be based on the ideas that you have just presented."

After that, things got exciting. On Tuesday afternoon, Elsie and I sat in first class on an evening flight from New York to Seattle. In the era of propeller aircraft, flying was slower, but in many ways it was more pleasant than it would be in the later jet age. After takeoff, cocktails and an excellent dinner were served, then the seats were transformed into upper and lower beds, as in a railroad sleeping car. After a good sleep, breakfast was served in bed, and when we'd had enough time for washing and dressing, we landed in Seattle on the West Coast.

Mr. Kirschner had devised a careful itinerary for us. This included a visit to the store in Seattle and discussions with local general contractors, but also, for the next ten days, visits to a number of other cities. There we were to inspect store locations to form an opinion of position and structural properties. The whirlwind tour took us to Portland, San Francisco, Los Angeles, Santa Monica, San Diego, Omaha, and Chicago.

We barely had enough time to make all of our different air connections. But then the work at the various locations proceeded more easily than we thought it would. Soon we knew the truth of the dictum "If you've seen one American Main Street, you've seen them all!" In each town, there was a so-called hot corner where the main road crossed with the best side street. The closer a business was to this corner, the higher its value. Everywhere were branch stores of national chains, all with identical storefronts, shopwindows, and interiors. The exception to this rule was actually the place we had come from, Manhattan, which, in spite of all its skyscrapers, was the most European city in America.

In the short time that was available, we had to rely more on intuition than on thorough research for our structural and spatial assessments. After our return to New York, we submitted a detailed, exhaustive report, which was well received. We could now consider ourselves the "house and court architects" for both the Grayson's chain and the affiliated Robinson chain. This status would set us crisscrossing America for many years.

The first project was the big store in Seattle, where we had to go immediately to make all necessary plans in the office of the contractor, with the help of his technical staff. For several months, we also tried to maintain the New York studio. For that, we appointed Michael Auer, an old friend of Elsie, to be a partner. (The firm

Gruen and Krummeck on their first air trip to Los Angeles, 1940. Courtesy of Peggy Gruen.

was for a short time called Gruenbaum, Krummeck and Auer.) Unfortunately, the New York activity subsided without our constant presence. We continued to commute between New York and the West Coast, but before long it became apparent that our continued presence in Southern California would be necessary, as the main decisions were all made by the dynamic Mr. Kirschner, who resided on a ranch in Indio, near Palm Springs, in the desert east of Los Angeles. We rented a run-down furnished apartment on Irolo Street in Los Angeles, near Wilshire Boulevard, a main artery.

Kirschner was born in Russia, where he was destined to become a rabbi. He fled that country and stowed away on a ship to New York. There he spent some time working at a butcher shop named Grayson's and then in the New York textile district. Through luck and skill, he managed to become part owner of a chain of women's clothing stores, which he called Grayson's in memory of the butcher shop.

In Portland, I learned his method of establishing new branch stores. First, he would appear in town in a snow-white Cadillac, accompanied by a beautiful young lady, whom he would introduce as his nurse. He would rent the most elegant suite in the best hotel. Once we had chosen a building, Kirschner would send a large basket of fruit from his ranch (oranges, tangerines, grapefruits, and dates) and a huge bouquet of flowers to the wife of the owner of the building. Then he would visit the landlord. With winning charm, he negotiated the lease. Then he hurried to the largest local bank, where he invited the bankers to provide him with a loan. He would convince the bankers that they did not want to miss this opportunity, whereupon their wives also received fruit baskets and flowers.

He was thoroughly extroverted. He loved to sit in the limelight and to win over his contemporaries with his generosity and charm. He gladly arranged visits to his ranch for clients and liked to impress them with his enormous Spanish-style villa and his two large swimming pools. The huge windows of his oversized living room were reminiscent of the windows of a furniture store. The house had a rich library, which looked richer because Kirschner had purchased handsome, leather-bound books in bulk. In an annex, there was an art gallery with velvet-covered walls and lights above each painting. Among the paintings were mounted labels, framed in bronze. One read, for example: "Madonna by Raphael (copy), frame fourteen carat gold." Kirschner had purchased a carload of copies of oil paintings and then hired a graphic designer to create the labels.

Kirschner explained the often strikingly pretty nurses by saying that he had a serious heart condition. He also used this highly exaggerated or perhaps completely fictitious disease as a business advantage. If anyone objected or otherwise caused difficulties during negotiations, he would clutch his chest in pain, as if he were close to a heart attack. During the war, when the use of private cars was very limited, he visited his far-flung stores in an ambulance with wailing sirens.

Kirschner did much of his business while he was in one of his swimming pools. He had phones installed all around them and would swim back and forth between calls. Our discussions about the design of various stores usually took place around the pool, though only Walter was swimming, while we wore bathing suits and sat at the edge. If a sensitive issue such as our fee was being discussed, Walter dived a lot, in order to be able to claim later that he had never heard anything about the matter. Then when we eventually raised this point at picnics on dry land, he was in the habit of offering us half of our fee. We neutralized this unpleasant habit by demanding dual-fee deals, which stipulate that any negotiations that are not to the satisfaction of all parties may be terminated.

To close associates, like us, he was a very benevolent tyrant. He was interested in the private lives and the welfare of his subjects; on the other hand, he expected you to be at his command anytime and anyplace.

He called me at any hour, day or night. In one night call, he asked me to visit him in his shop in San Francisco as soon as possible. I took the next plane, but when I arrived, I was told that Kirschner had left for Hawaii a few hours before and expected me to follow.

He was also unscrupulous enough to take advantage of my ignorance of local laws. Once he invited us to be guests at a fiesta at his ranch. The festival was meant to benefit a charitable cause, namely, the establishment of a church in Indio. He asked me first to make a detour from Los Angeles through Las Vegas, Nevada, in order to acquire half a dozen used slot machines. I took the job, hoping to help the charity, not knowing that I was guilty of a crime: the importation of slot machines to California was strictly forbidden. In my ignorance, I was able to say no when authorities at the California border asked if I was bringing any prohibited goods into the state. Had I been caught, this would have destroyed my chances of ever obtaining U.S. citizenship. In the end, the slot machines did nothing for the charity. Because of a faulty mechanism, the players won every time they played.

With boundless energy, political tactics, and commercial ruthlessness, Kirschner built an extensive empire of Grayson's-Robinson stores within a few years; sales grew by six million dollars annually in 1940, to thirty-one million dollars in 1946.

Grayson's also owned the most famous New York discount clothing store chain, Klein on the Square. These shabby outlets were paradise for bargain hunters, even affluent ones. When we were entrusted with the design of a discount store in Newark, New Jersey, we had to learn how to artificially create an atmosphere of shabbiness, which was essential for such a store. For example, the cleaning people had to scatter trash around the store's stalls every morning, to suggest to customers that

Gruen and Krummeck in front of Grayson's, Los Angeles, circa 1940. Courtesy of Peggy Gruen.

the rooting for cheap goods had already taken place. The Newark store did have two escalators and air-conditioning, but the premises had to be arranged as uncomfortably and appear as disorderly as possible.

Walter Kirschner was a unique and curious mix of charm and very good business instincts. Similar to a gangland boss, he ran a tightly organized gang; the members of his gang probably committed no crimes, but they had to be ready for minor offenses at any time.

In the postwar period, when we no longer worked for Grayson's, Kirschner's artificially inflated organization collapsed and failed. But his shareholders had saved millions in assets. Walter retired to Florida, where he lived in an excellent financial position and finally married one of his nurses. Tragically, she died soon afterward, while Walter, with his alleged heart condition, outlived her for quite a while.

The last time I heard from him was in the late fifties, when he woke me up with a phone call at two in the morning. Half asleep, I heard Walter's warm voice: "How are you Victor? I'm calling you because I could not sleep and wanted to chat with someone." We spoke for about an hour, and our conversation covered politics, global issues, pain, and health. Then Walter said he could sleep now, and he hung up.

BECOMING SOUTHERN CALIFORNIANS

Sometime in the fall of 1941, everything changed completely. A year before, we had thought we could continue to live free and unattached. We had not even thought about marriage seriously. We would establish ourselves somewhere eventually, we felt. We liked New York by far the best. We also liked San Francisco: a city with a refreshing climate and the vital atmosphere of a concentrated, refined center. But we also struck a deal with our friend Walter Kirschner. He had recognized that we would be essential for the future of his organization (or his gang) after the triumphant success of the store opening in Seattle. With all his charm and talent for organization, he proceeded to bind and integrate us into his organization. His plan for us? First, we would get married. Second, we would settle down as close as possible to his headquarters in Indio, and that could only mean living in Los Angeles. Third, we would be integrated as shareholders and an executive team in the organization.

The third point he never reached, because of our will toward independence. But the first two he pursued tirelessly and with great success. So it happened that we settled down in Los Angeles, a city that we would not have chosen voluntarily.

COWBOY IN NEVADA

At the time, I was separated but not divorced from Lizzie. Walter arranged a three-week stay in the divorce paradise of Las Vegas. That was how I got my first holiday in the United States.

We stayed at a dude ranch in Las Vegas. A touch of the Wild West surrounded us. We lived in primitive cabins. Staff and guests wore cowboy clothes. We rode mustangs. As a completely inexperienced rider, I requested a good-natured horse. I got a huge one, which seemed to be tired. Horse and rider felt very uncomfortable on their slow rides in the desert, equally unhappy. Nevertheless, I enjoyed the unique beauty of this landscape: undulating sand dunes garnished with Joshua trees and cacti.

After the strain of riding, I recovered at barbecues or western saloons or by admiring the popular tradition of rodeo. Wherever you went—the supermarket, the hairdresser, in all stores and gas stations—you saw hungry slot machines. Some diligent people worked the one-armed bandits for hours. That strengthened the arm muscles enormously but weakened the wallet even more.

At nightfall, Las Vegas was the real city of skyscrapers. Its millions of colorful, dazzling, rotating advertising lights surpassed the bright, garish Times Square in New York by far. Everyone went to the sumptuously kitschy casinos on the Las Vegas Strip. We were also caught in the undertow of this Babylon. In addition to excellent restaurants where you could eat very well and cheaply, there were excellent and inexpensive musicals and variety shows. The money that you saved in the low-cost restaurants and shows got spent on roulette and baccarat in the gaming rooms.

At dawn, you left the palaces of happiness tired and broke. Then the lights went off, and the skyscrapers became shabby low-rises, bedecked with ghostly scaffoldings of advertising lights.

The inclination to be a cowboy or a player never quite took hold of me. But we had gotten something out of it: a divorce, plus driver's licenses. For the driver's test, we had to answer only two questions: "Are you crazy?" and "Are you blind?" We were able to truthfully answer no, and after paying a fee of five dollars, we had learners' permits to drive. In Los Angeles, these permits unfortunately lasted only three months, but we were able to practice within this period and then passed California's stricter driving tests.

WEDDING ON THE ISLAND OF MAGIC

Right after our return, Walter began the preparations for our wedding. Elsie's mother and mine were flown to L.A. in first class and put up in an elegant hotel. Walter's bouquets were already waiting for them. Even Elsie's mother, a typical German housewife who had never had anything to do with Jews, or wanted to, was overwhelmed: to her, this Kirschner seemed to be a real gentleman. And since I was one of his minions, she concluded that her daughter had hit the jackpot.

A chartered seaplane took the wedding party—Walter, his nurse, both mothers, and the bridal couple—to the island of Santa Catalina in the Pacific Ocean. Santa

Catalina must have once been a wonderfully secluded subtropical island, but it had recently been bought by the king of Wrigley's chewing gum and transformed into a cross between a South Sea Island and Disneyland.

Elsie, dressed elegantly for the first time, was enchanting. Our patron designed the wedding with generosity and warmth. Our mothers were particularly overwhelmed and amazed by the lavish celebration.

HOUSE HUNTING

The newlyweds needed two houses: a larger one for themselves and a smaller one for their mothers. That we had no money was irrelevant to Walter. He would lend us the necessary sums at the usual long-term interest rates. But where would we find a place to live in this never-ending Los Angeles?

Hollywood was the magic word, but where was Hollywood? There were the Hollywood Hills, characterized by a sign on a rocky hillside. There was Hollywood Boulevard, but on closer inspection, it turned out to be a pretty ordinary, cheap commercial street, featuring only one cinema, Grauman's Chinese Theatre, as a tourist destination. Nobody was able to say where the residential area began or ended.

Houses were recommended en masse by our real estate agents. We inspected a few dozen in every size, price range, and architectural style: colonial, French-Provence, Georgian, Spanish, Moorish, Chinese, Renaissance, country, and anything else your heart desired. Hollywood is part of the agglomeration called West Los Angeles, which comprises a number of areas with fancy names and a few independent cities like Beverly Hills. Furthermore, there were neighborhoods like Brentwood (for the wealthy), Bel Air (for mere millionaires), the various canyons (for individuals and artists), and others that did not belong to the city of Los Angeles.

Beyond the Hollywood Hills was the San Fernando Valley, which was a part of Los Angeles. At the time of our house hunting, this was a sparsely populated area. A few years later it was a district with more than a million inhabitants.

SUNNY SOUTHLAND

As two of the hundreds of thousands of easterners (meaning anyone who had moved from the eastern United States to some part of California), we settled down in the sunny Southland, in a two-story house enthroned proudly on a hill on Kings Road, a steep side street off the famous Sunset Boulevard. Sunset Boulevard is a broad band about twenty miles long; it snakes past stores, insurance firms, the former luxury villas of long-gone movie stars, shabby houses, and even vacant land. Sunset stretches from downtown to the Pacific Ocean, where it realizes, somewhat embarrassedly, that it cannot continue.

In our view, our house was not too far away. The question was, not too far away from what? We made our choice because the house was close—about five minutes' driving time—to some urban activities. We were particularly drawn to Schwab's Drugstore, a haunt of artists and intellectuals. It was a kind of literary café where we sat at a long counter and consumed sandwiches, hot dogs, or ice cream sodas and Coca-Cola. Nearby were two supermarkets, several restaurants, and a dry cleaning establishment—for us, who longed for a touch of big-city life, this area seemed like a slice of New York. For these nostalgic reasons, we bought the house at Kings Road. With this purchase, our dog Susi's problems were also solved. She breakfasted at Schwab's Drugstore and lunched and dined at other restaurants.

We owned not only a house and an undisciplined dog but also a large, red secondhand car, plus various pieces of ragtag furniture and household items; of these, the relics of my Viennese past were always the most cherished pieces. We had two goldfish swimming in a fountain, which made one part of the living space completely unusable. Elsie brought our first child into this home in the spring of 1942.

Gruen and Krummeck at Café de la Pay (and pay and pay) in front of the Santa Monica Boulevard office, Los Angeles, 1948. Courtesy of Peggy Gruen.

As newcomers, we also wanted to assimilate into the manners and customs of the natives (meaning anyone who had spent more than one year in Southern California). This was difficult, because there was a tremendous gap between appearance and reality in Los Angeles. On the surface, life in Los Angeles seems like a vacation paradise. Everyone wears casual, colorful, and scanty clothing. Many wear only bikinis, even though evening temperatures are close to zero. Sunglasses are mandatory. They serve as eye protection, and they also mask the tears that the pervasive smog causes. Feet are no longer used for anything except to put pressure on the accelerator. Sidewalks are unknown. For ordinary people, the car serves not only as a means of transportation but also as an actual home. People take meals in cars, served by girls in short skirts at drive-in restaurants. Entertainment is offered at drive-in movie theaters, mental relaxation at drive-in churches, and financial services at drive-in banks. Of course, the car is also frequently used as a love nest.

Traffic jams are not side dishes as they are elsewhere, but the main course, served several times a day. During these times, the natives resign themselves to sitting behind the wheel, smiling happily. They continue taking the car when they go to work, go shopping, visit friends, go to school, or look for entertainment. For a family to have two or three cars is not only a status symbol but also a means of survival. To possess no car is a sign of poverty and unemployment.

Outside the car, millions of single-family homes provide housing in large, medium, and small boxes surrounded by gardens on all sides. This arrangement wastes valuable land. Automatic sprinkler systems and pesticides maintain these gardens.

Los Angeles seems to be an Eden of the wealthy, with hundreds of thousands of swimming pools, giant supermarkets, elegant department stores and restaurants, and avenues lined with palm trees and tropical flower gardens. The wide beaches along the Pacific Ocean are stunning, and on clear days, one can see the snowcapped mountains of the Sierras in the east and the islands of the Pacific Ocean in the west.

But behind the cinematic facade hides a less pleasant reality. The exhaust fumes of millions of cars pollute the air and darken the sky. The drinking water, rivers, and sea are all contaminated. Termites gnaw at the foundations of even the most elegant houses. Millions of rats harass the residents.

Slums, racial discrimination, and increased crime rates are part of everyday life in Los Angeles. The urban sins here are perhaps not much worse than in other cities, but they hide behind a mask of cheerfulness that covers the entire territory. The official size of Los Angeles is about 80 times 190 kilometers. The settlement has created a loose, almost continuous pattern over the plains, hills, and valleys, from Santa Barbara in the north to the Mexican border in the south. This covers nearly 400 kilometers—in other words, the distance from Vienna to Munich.

Santa Monica Boulevard office, Los Angeles, 1948. Courtesy of Peggy Gruen.

Despite everything, millions swear that they would live nowhere else than in the sunny Southland. They delightedly praise the virtues of Los Angeles's way of life. Even we, who were now Los Angelenos, wanted to discover the beauty of this new environment.

WORLD WAR II

We had just begun to settle down in Los Angeles and to enjoy its pleasant climate. Grayson's kept us so busy that we had to hire technical staff. Our first employee was Karl Van Leuven. He had probably studied architecture, but later he worked for years at Walt Disney Studios in the production of famous cartoons.[11] That he had little architectural experience did not bother us. He was imaginative, talented, and very endearing.

The messages about Europe that we received from the radio and newspapers were becoming increasingly worrying. We listened with horror as Hitler's armies rolled over one country after another. We heard about the terrible persecution of the Jews, but we had no details. The apparent mood of America was divided. Most believed that America should not meddle in these European hostilities. Yet others felt that only an American entry into the war would bring a victory over Hitler. Even though I thought of myself as a pacifist, under these circumstances, I started to become a war agitator.

The sympathies of almost all Americans were with the democratic antifascist forces. When the Japanese air raid on Pearl Harbor destroyed the greater part of the American fleet in December 1942, America entered the war at last. The country was not prepared for war, but with tremendous verve and a surprising amount of voluntary forces, the nation mobilized.

We were concerned both professionally and personally. I received an "enemy alien card" and was officially classified as an Austrian, and therefore an enemy alien. My movements were severely restricted. I was allowed to take the main road between our home and our four sites in Southern California only once a week. But this lasted only a few weeks; then all the refugees displaced by Hitler were freed from these restrictions. I was even put on the draft rolls and told to be ready for military service, though I was never called! The Japanese of the West Coast fared poorly, however—they were placed in internment camps.

Shortly after the U.S. entry into the war in March 1942, our son Michael was born. After his birth he suffered from heart problems and had to go to a children's hospital, which Elsie and I regarded as a precautionary measure. The doctor told me there was little hope for his survival, but the next day, I learned that Michael's heart valve defect had been corrected and he was perfectly healthy.

EMERGENCY-RELATED ACTIVITIES

Everyone wanted to help with the preparations for war. The aircraft and munitions industries grew, the unemployment that had existed since the Depression disappeared overnight, and millions of women suddenly had to work in factories. Elsie and I attended a course for aircraft design and passed the examination with distinction. But as foreigners, we could not obtain employment in war industries. That was disappointing, because the building profession was at a standstill due to prohibitions on the use of strategically important materials for anything other than preparation for war. Still, Grayson's wanted to exploit the unprecedented economic boom. Now that so many more people were earning money, Kirschner believed consumer demand would increase immeasurably.

We invented a method of building temporary stores without the use of strategic materials. We called them "victory stores." They were created from wood and fireproof textiles. The cardboard signage bore not only the company name but also the words "Buy War Bonds." Grayson's built about twenty such stores. The surprising thing was that even these stores got recognition in the architectural press.

All Americans were convinced of a final victory. Except for those who lost family members on the battlefields of Europe and Japan, the population saw very little of the war. Certain luxury goods such as nylon stockings and steaks grew rare. Gasoline was rationed. Here and there, one was alarmed by rumors of Japanese submarines on the Pacific coast, but these rumors were never true. What did halt completely, though, was the construction of apartments and houses.

FATHER OF THE SHOPPING CENTER

Now I had more time to lecture and write articles. One of these articles proved to be vital for my future. It was written for the architecture magazine *Architectural Forum* and was published in the May 1943 special issue called "New Buildings for 194X" (a number meant to designate the year in which the war would end). The magazine had invited renowned architects to present their visions for the future in words and pictures. The words were mine, the illustrations Elsie's. I first considered the idea of a "mall" because of my daily confrontations with a problem particular to Los Angeles: though there were endless shops on both sides of the main thoroughfares, shoppers could reach them only by car. Shopping was not only time-consuming, but it also added to traffic problems. In addition, because of the parking spaces, the areas in front of most shops were decreased, leading to additional conflicts among all road users, including buses, trucks, cars, and pedestrians. This was how I got my idea for a neighborhood center that would be located off a main road.

194X. Drawing by Elsie Krummeck in "Drug Store and Dining Terrace," *Architectural Forum* (May 1943): 101.

The shops and businesses would be housed in a single building that would surround a landscaped, pedestrian-only courtyard. The facade of the building would be of a pleasant and modest design, without logos, and would not disrupt the residential character of the surroundings. Only one wide main entrance would lead into the center. For the delivery and removal of goods, and for car parking, there would be designated zones. The buyers would not enter the individual shops from the street side, but go through the parking area to the courtyard, where they would see the storefronts. Along these shops would be an open portico that would protect against wind and weather. So the buyers would be able to stroll along past the shops, enjoy the parklike atmosphere of the patio, and otherwise pursue their business, all the while completely separate from automobile traffic. This center would also include a post office, public library, doctors' offices, meeting rooms, and community centers. I particularly stressed that the individual stores would be allowed to design their own facades along the garden side. I pointed out that this neighborhood center could be executed on a larger scale as a regional center.

This article is why, even during World War II, I became known as the "Father of the Shopping Mall."

END OF THE WAR

I enjoyed the pleasure of becoming a father for the second time in 1944, when our daughter Margaret (Peggy) was born. We were proud parents and never got tired. We made endless home movies of our offspring. Michael was a very handsome, blond, helpful little boy, but he needed a long time to learn how to walk and to speak. Peggy was bright from the start and tried again and again to compete against her older brother. She was sometimes successful.

Although the war brought no particular hardships for many Americans at home, the nation rejoiced when the war was over, as one should with any war. The general population of the United States initially favored the atomic bombing of Hiroshima and Nagasaki, because this accelerated the end of a terrible war. Most did not realize until much later that this terrible end was also the beginning of a terror without end.

4

The Big Breakthrough

NEW PASTURES

At the end of World War II, Americans were euphoric. All restrictions on movement and construction activities had been lifted, revealing a great demand that led to a rapid economic upswing. I felt that I had to use this opportunity to broaden my professional activity and to break free from the design of Grayson's shops. Our work for Grayson's continued for a few more years nonetheless, but the projects were routine. We eventually ended our collaboration because we could not agree on new planning issues as they arose in new situations. *Architectural Forum* wrote about this under the headline "Architect Bites Client."

The prospect of competing with long-established business architects for contracts for conventional building design was for me neither attractive nor promising. In such cases, the architect becomes a technical henchman—a drawing slave—executing preset programs for client-focused, short-term returns.

It seemed much more promising to me to create and propagate new construction techniques, new building types, new architectural thinking. I wanted to attract clients who would turn trustingly toward the creators of new concepts. My basic idea was that instead of snatching clients in competition with conventional architects, I would create new clients with new concepts.

PUBLIC RELATIONS

I continued giving lectures, writing articles and brochures, and giving interviews on television and radio. I did this not only in Southern California but also in the Midwest and on the East Coast. New York, which was the intellectual, cultural, economic, and journalistic center of the United States, appeared to me to be particularly important. From there, projects in all parts of the country were developed and funded. The headquarters of the major newspapers and magazines, the major architecture magazines, and the large corporations and construction companies were all in New York.

In the meantime, I had acquired a good reputation, and this opened many doors. I was an invited lecturer at numerous national conferences, association meetings, and other events. Above all, I wrote and spoke about the special trust relationship between client and architect. My lecture "How to Live with Your Architect" was published as a book (with humorous drawings by Karl Van Leuven) and attracted considerable attention.[1]

I developed other themes as well, including flexibility in the construction of large department stores (which is now taken for granted internationally), improved isolation and weather protection for the purpose of energy savings, the building of city centers in suburbs (based on the article on shopping malls), and the revitalization of inner cities.

One of the many interviews I gave proved to be an important personal experience and decisive for my future. Lazette van Houten, a senior editor of the daily section of the trade magazine *Retailing Daily,* asked to interview me about new ideas for shop furnishings. She came to my New York hotel. Our conversation was extensive and interesting, and a series of articles emerged. I was fascinated by her personality. When I noticed that she had forgotten her gloves (whether intentionally or not, I never found out) after she had departed from our first meeting, I called her and asked her out to dinner. She accepted. We developed a close friendship. In order to be with Lazette, I flew from Los Angeles to New York more often than necessary, until I gradually spent almost every weekend with her.

That was not the only result of my New York public relations effort, although it was the happiest. I was called to the planning department of the largest department store in America, R. H. Macy's, and commissioned to design the interiors of two large retail stores, one in San Francisco and one in Kansas City.

NEW CONTACTS

I also had successful talks with the Tishman Realty company in their main offices: they wanted to expand their activities to the West Coast. After the talks, my studio did work on offices and residential projects for Tishman for many years.

After our work for Macy's in San Francisco, orders came in from the elegant women's clothing company Joseph Magnin. The boss, Cyril Magnin, planned to build the company's first branch store in Palo Alto, a fashionable suburb of San

Francisco. He asked me to design this medium-sized building, inside and out, in an unprecedented manner that would appeal to young customers. When I presented him with the plans, he was enthusiastic, but he stated that he was not ready to commit to such a revolutionary project unless I could show him similar stores that had been completed. It took some effort to convince him that creating an unprecedented store would be impossible if one like it already existed. Finally, he decided to take the risk.

This design—consisting of a number of boutiques clustered around a spiral staircase—aroused unusual attention. Its success was so great that we would go on to build a series of branch operations for Magnin over the next twenty years. We also got so many orders in and around San Francisco that we were able to open a branch office in that city.

THE DEPARTMENT STORE OF THE FUTURE

By happy coincidence, I also met the owner of Milliron's, a large department store in Los Angeles. The connection came about because the owner's son, Tom, was a friend of my longtime employee Karl Van Leuven. They had known each other since high school and were now engaged in creating that epochal invention, the strapless bra. (Unfortunately, the two failed to patent their invention, which later captivated ladies' worlds.) Through Karl I learned that Milliron senior wanted to abandon his downtown business for a new department store in the suburb of Westchester, near the Los Angeles airport. A meeting with Mr. Milliron was arranged.

When we met, I did not suggest building the usual imitation of an inner-city department store; instead, I described to him an entirely new concept for a suburban department store. This impressed him so much that he decided to abandon his previous plans and contracted with us to design our first large-scale building. The idea was essentially to focus all sales activities on the ground floor. The roof of the one-floor building was reached by two ramps for cars and served as a parking lot. We proposed the extension of one side of the roof, which was facing the main street, to include a meeting space, stage, and restaurant, which would be open in the evenings and on Sundays and holidays.

This single-story department store was unusual for its design as well as for its merchandising displays. The usual showcases were dispensed with completely because of the lack of pedestrian traffic. In order to attract the attention of motorists, large display cases were placed amid the greenery beyond the front of the main building, which was set slightly back from the street. The store was not only a great commercial success but also proved to be very economical in construction and

Victor Gruen in front of the architectural model for Milliron's, Los Angeles, 1946. Courtesy of Gruen Associates.

Construction site of Milliron's, Los Angeles, 1948. Courtesy of Peggy Gruen.

Gruen on the construction site of Milliron's, Los Angeles, 1948. Courtesy of Peggy Gruen.

operation. It was thoroughly discussed by the national architectural journals and hailed as "The Store of the Future."

NEW WORK AREAS

At the same time, we designed the Mid-Wilshire Medical Building. Here, a complicated static problem had to be solved. While the basement was to serve as a parking garage, and therefore needed to be kept open, the aboveground floors required pillars. I turned for advice to two consulting engineers, one of whom was Hungarian and the other Italian. The Italian, Edgardo Contini, impressed me with a brilliant and elegant solution. He had previously worked for the Detroit architect Albert Kahn, and he now became my partner in this project. The Mid-Wilshire Medical Building, of which I was both an owner and executive architect, was regarded as a building of a new kind. However, because of a lack of sufficient seed capital, we sold it at a loss.

A new area of work opened up when we were hired to design an urban housing project for Mexican guest workers. At the same time, we continued building shops and stores in other parts of the United States.

SEPARATING WORK FROM HOME

Our staff increased in size steadily. We were fortunate enough to engage very qualified personnel—perhaps our creative, unusual approach stood out in contrast to the dull routine of other architecture offices, and people may have found this particularly desirable.

Our house on Kings Road, though once idyllic, had become a chaotic mix of T squares, diapers, and toys. In that condition, it was impossible to use as a studio. We decided to separate our work area from our living area by renting space in a small building near our house. When this soon proved to be too small, we rented two additional workplaces. When even this turned out to be inefficient, we moved the entire office and staff, which had grown to about forty people, to a spacious former factory site. The new place was a bit shabby, but it had enough space to accommodate future growth. Our revenues increased, but so did our expenses, and the remaining profits were relatively modest.

In addition to my busy career, I crammed for exams to obtain architecture licenses in other U.S. states. Since I became a U.S. citizen in 1943 I had taken the opportunity to shorten Gruenbaum to Gruen. I got my first license in 1948 in the state of California and later acquired twenty-five additional state licenses. After my admission to the American Institute of Architects, I was entitled to place the letters AIA after my name. After 1948, our company was no longer known as Gruen & Krummeck Designers, but as Victor Gruen Architect AIA.

MARRIAGE CRISIS

These successful professional developments had an effect on my marriage to Elsie. Shortly after the birth of our daughter, Peggy, our relationship cooled down; this was when we began talking of a divorce, once the children were older.

I believe that I was attracted to Elsie in 1939, when we learned to love each other, partly because of her willingness to come to the aid of a helpless refugee. She contributed to an important part of my Americanization, but also to my work activities. But the more my career prospects brightened, the more my personal conditions seemed to darken. The more at home I felt in America, the more alienated I felt in our marriage.

Another thread between us that had now been cut was the cooperation of our early years. Partly because of her new duties as a mother and partly because the amount of work was greater and more technical, Elsie felt that her contribution as a graphic artist rapidly declined in importance. She gradually and then completely withdrew from the world of work. This was accelerated by the separation of our living and working spaces. On the other hand, I must admit that in my zeal for work, and through my many trips, I neglected my marital and family obligations.

In 1948—Michael was six years old, Peggy was four—we came to the conclusion that we should get a divorce. We discussed this during a walk in a romantic little forest in Griffith Park. Elsie assured me that she didn't want to make any financial claims for herself, but that she expected that I would pay for the living expenses and education of the children, which I promised to do. Then she expressed her worries about my future loneliness. Touched by this concern, I made the foolish mistake of telling her that I had met a woman in New York.

This imprudent remark had fierce consequences the next morning. Elsie told me she had reconsidered the whole matter thoroughly. She did not want to get divorced after all, because she still loved me. But if I insisted on a divorce, she would set conditions that would make me a pauper and prevent me from ever taking a new wife. When I suggested that we stick with our agreement from the previous day, she said I would hear from her lawyer.

I did not take this threat very seriously, because I knew Elsie's generous nature and knew that she had never laid any special emphasis on money. In any case, I left our home. I slept in the office, where I had a couch and a small washroom with a shower. A few days later I received a visit from Elsie's lawyer, who was a very capable man. The financial demands, as he put it, were so high that they seemed to me impossible. They were a multiple of what I could hope to earn, and I saw myself heading for financial ruin. The lawyer said with a smile that he had heard so many good things about my ability that he did not doubt that I would be able to meet these demands in the foreseeable future.

THORN IN MY SIDE

This remark felt like a thorn in my flesh. I began to ponder how I could carry out his prophecy, because for the present and near future I saw no solution. I left the children, our house, the furnishings, our dog, and our car to Elsie. I transferred reasonable amounts monthly for her and the children's living expenses.

I worked harder than ever before and traveled more often, especially to New York to be with Lazette. But in the long run, this gypsy life in hotels was unbearable. We finally rented an apartment on Twelfth Street in Greenwich Village—large enough even to accommodate Lazette's mother, who was very traditional and viewed our relationship negatively. The apartment had a large attic space, including adjoining rooms that were connected by internal stairs, which I wanted to use as a studio.

As luck would have it, on the day we moved in, a telegram came from my old client Stefan Klein. This concerned the design of his fiftieth shop (which I previously mentioned in connection with the "Klein Saga"). So I immediately had an opportunity to work in the new New York apartment.

Lazette and I agreed that we would get married as soon as I could obtain a divorce. She continued her professional career with great devotion. I began making plans for building a great organization that would put me in an economic situation that could bear the financial burden of the divorce claims.

RISE TO A VISION

The strong desire for financial flexibility, however, was just a new impetus behind visions I had been dreaming of since my youth. At that time, I had admired towering figures who had not confined themselves solely to designing individual buildings but had made significant contributions to the design of the human-made environment. One of my role models was Leonardo da Vinci, who saw himself as an artist, engineer, inventor, and architect simultaneously. Another was the Swiss French builder-artist Le Corbusier, who developed a new urban design based on the idea of social baselines (La Ville Radieuse) and whose writings impressed me so much that I wrote an article about the city's future for a Viennese newspaper.[2] Finally, I admired the Viennese architect Otto Wagner, who as a member of the Secession broke with the prevailing nineteenth-century eclecticism and instead pushed for an ingenious city plan for the explosive growth of Vienna. He created a series of public transport facilities, station buildings, and bridges, including the still-standing Stadtbahn rail system.

These three men, whom I idealized, were all intent on the integration of engineering, planning, and architecture with the fine arts. This fusion was intended as an overall environment-architecture. Today, I no longer agree with many of the urban design concepts of Le Corbusier and Wagner, but this has more to do with new developments in the second half of the twentieth century. I am still convinced that a general and integrated overall view is admirable and worth emulating.

I thought about how an all-encompassing city plan could be designed in our era of pluralistic technical, economic, and social structures. I came to the realization that, unlike in the past, this couldn't be achieved by one individual but only by a team within which architects, planners, painters, sculptors, graphic artists, business professionals, and engineers of all disciplines would work together.

To use such a team effectively would require a large, exceptional organization. In an optimistic way, I felt that I could build such a team from within the ranks of my current employees. But what was missing were extraordinary customers with projects that would make such a universal commitment possible, and even necessary.

EMERGENCY LANDING

Interviewers all over the world are in the habit of asking profound questions, and they expect answers of a few words. They have often tried to figure out where I develop most of my work: in my homes or my studios? My answer has always been "on planes." In fact, I have logged hundreds of thousands of miles as an air commuter, which is why some airlines have bestowed on me the VIP rank of "admiral."

In the pre-jet age, my weekly flights from Los Angeles to New York were time-consuming and far more dependent on the weather than they are today. I therefore made it a habit not to let the time in the air pass uselessly but to be productive by using a dictation machine, sketchbooks, and notepads.

On a flight one Saturday in the autumn of 1948, I focused closely on my work in order to overcome the anxiety caused by the rocking of the plane due to a storm. It was announced that all airports along the East Coast were closing due to dense fog, and that we must make an emergency landing in Detroit. This message struck me as fate. Instead of sitting around in the waiting room of the airport, I decided to pay a visit to the city of Detroit. There were several reasons for this: for one thing, I had been invited to visit the manager of a large local chain store there; also, Detroit was one of the few major U.S. cities I had not yet seen over the course of working for Grayson's. In addition, I wanted to see the fabled second-largest department store in the world, Hudson's.

So I checked into a large but somewhat shabby downtown hotel. I called the father of one of my colleagues, Bob Sabaroff, and we agreed that he would take

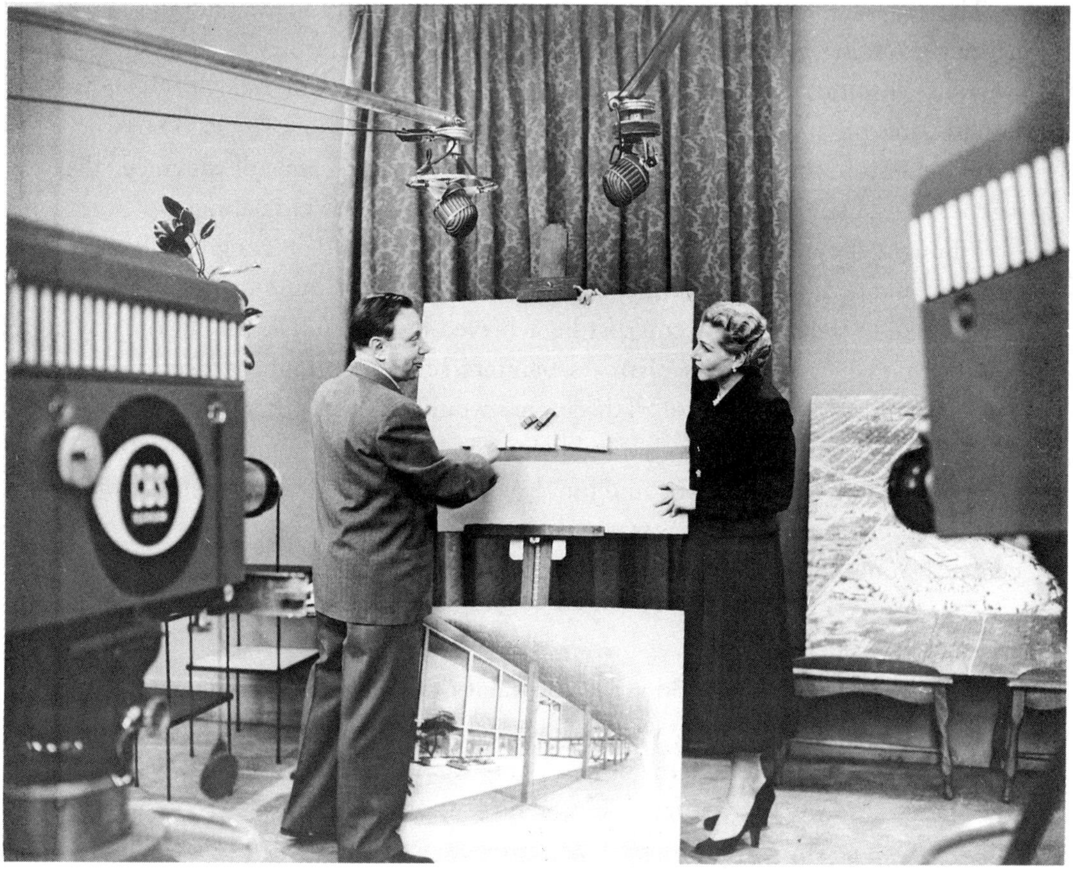

Gruen presents the Shopping Centers of Tomorrow with Margaret Arlen at Studio CBS, Los Angeles, 1953. Library of Congress.

me on a drive through Detroit and the surrounding areas the next day. For the evening, I was invited to dinner with Mr. Ben Goldstein, the managing director of Winkelman's, the women's fashion company.

DESOLATE CITY CORE

Before bedtime, I decided to wander through the very center of the metropolis. The walk did not take much time. There were only two broad main roads: Washington Boulevard, lined mainly with office buildings, and the shopping street, Woodward Avenue, where there were some branch stores, discount shops, and a few closed businesses with "For Rent" signs. Everything seemed outdated, run-down, and lifeless. There was only one dramatic exception. Amid the stagnant desolation, the ten-story block-long J. L. Hudson department store, with its seemingly endless brightly lit windows, was like a bulwark. Its solid, red-brick facade was not marred by any logos or advertising—only on the side entrances did I find small bronze plaques with individual business names. I could find new buildings or businesses nowhere else, though I did see several vacant lots. Every time I took a step away from the main street, I entered desolate slums, from which, smelling danger, I retreated quickly.

TOURING DETROIT

On Sunday morning, Mr. Sabaroff picked me up in his huge car, and we made a thorough reconnaissance tour of the most famous automobile capital in the world. During breakfast, I received information on the city's location and history from this well-informed man. He told me that Detroit was the oldest city in the United States beyond the East Coast. The city was founded in 1701 by French settlers under the leadership of Antoine Laumet, known as Laumet de La Mothe, sieur de Cadillac. As a town on the border with Canada, it originally developed in three directions, forming a semicircle. In 1805 a fire broke out that left the town in ashes, with the exception of one house. As a result, an entirely new town plan was developed in which unusually wide roads were designed like the spokes of a wheel. The hub of the wheel was located on the river bank opposite the much smaller Canadian sister city of Windsor, which could be reached via a road bridge. The authors of this urban plan, it almost seemed, must have anticipated a development that would arrive nearly a hundred years later: the flood of cars.

Detroit had long been the headquarters of the U.S. transportation industry. For example, the Pullman Company's train car works had been established there. In 1903, the city became the center of the new automobile industry, where companies like Ford, Cadillac, and Oldsmobile employed two thousand workers. Some thirty years later, there were five hundred thousand workers in Detroit's car industry, which produced more than 90 percent of all cars made in the United States.

Mr. Sabaroff said we could do without a visit to the city core—with the exception of the Hudson's building, he said, there was nothing happening there. The adjacent residential areas served as the dwelling places of the poorest residents, especially the blacks. Real life, he explained, happened exclusively in the suburban areas. To see this, we had to take an eight-hour drive.

Given Detroit's geographic proximity to two large lakes and a wide river, I had expected the city to have a unique landscape. My expectations were disappointed. All along the shores of Lake Erie and the Detroit River, there were only ugly industries associated with cargo ports and warehouses. Along Lake St. Clair, though, the rich had settled in palatial villas with swimming pools and marinas, even though the neighborhood was intersected by a main traffic artery. The rest of the outlying area that was not covered by industry resembled a patchwork quilt: it was composed of small lots of land with small yards and medium-sized lots with medium yards. On each plot sat a boxy house with a completely useless piece of lawn; this yard was the calling card of the home's inhabitants, and it was constantly edited with a lawn mower. On the road-facing sides of the houses were rarely used living rooms with oversized windows (called picture windows). In passing, it seemed to me that through each of these windows I saw the same floor lamp with plastic shade, the same vase, the same flowers on the same table. This was what lay between the main roads.

The main roads themselves were zoned exclusively for business. Here, a motley collection of small and large companies had settled, a garishly advertised parade of filling stations, hot dog stands, department stores, snack bars, liquor stores, supermarkets, chain stores, used-car lots, and funeral parlors. Most of these enterprises were housed in buildings of only one story and were dependent on roadside parking. In exceptional cases, parking spaces were provided in front of or behind a row of buildings, in which case the block then proudly called itself a "mall." Included were three large department stores, all branch locations of national companies. Although these main streets were extraordinarily wide, they could not accommodate the combined burdens of shopping traffic, parking, the delivery and shipping of goods, and pedestrian needs. To escape the endless traffic jams, one had to park on residential streets. The generously planned major road network had become unusable. In a city where there was no notable public transportation system, an ambitious urban motorway network had ruthlessly torn the residential areas into pieces. Everyone concerned cursed the roads, and there were numerous protest movements against them. But when confronted with the argument that without motorways they could not reach their jobs in the auto industry, the protesters capitulated.

ENLIGHTENING EVENING

That night, I visited Ben and Edna Goldstein. I was already exhausted by the time I reached their elegant villa. Both proved to be charming, educated, and friendly people with whom I immediately developed a close friendship. They planned to give up Edna's ladies' fashion shop in the city to build a row of shops along the main streets of the suburbs. Because of the chaotic conditions prevailing there, they could hardly find suitable locations with respectable neighbors and adequate parking space. I asked why they wanted to escape from the inner city, when Hudson's department store, with over two hundred thousand square meters, obviously persisted with success. At the mention of the name Hudson's, my hosts grew nervous and seemed unsure whether they should express their admiration or aversion to their powerful competitor. Eventually they claimed that nobody within the sickly city center could compete with Hudson's variety of goods and services (including home delivery). A few years before, there had been many major department stores and hundreds of retail stores downtown, but as more residents moved to the suburbs, merchants also fled to the outer edges of the city. Hudson's, they argued, was an exception, a giant rock standing out among the dust and decay around it. Edna admitted that she still shopped at Hudson's, despite the long, tiring journey, because this was the only place in Detroit where all her needs could be met in one place. Ben remarked, however, that even Hudson's was concerned about the increasing competition in business on the periphery.

When I said that I thought I would pay a visit to Hudson's the next day to discuss just these issues with the management, Edna and Ben broke into peals of laughter. When they calmed down, they explained to me that I was the most naive person in America. Hudson's was not a commercial venture but a kind of monarchy. You do not speak with a king—you wait until you are summoned to an audience, then you receive commands. The current reigning king was named Oscar Webber. He was a shy, very conservative man who was considered stubborn and whom they had never seen. Edna and Ben said I could of course visit the J. L. Hudson Company and inspect all its floors—I would probably find them exemplary—but the idea that I would be allowed to enter the hallowed halls of the offices on the eleventh floor seemed to them bizarre. To underline the absurdity of my idea, they declared that the Hudson's people had never had anything to do with people of Jewish descent. The more I heard, the more fascinated I became.

That same evening, I realized something: perhaps Hudson's was the extraordinary client for whom I could accomplish extraordinary tasks with the extraordinary organization I envisioned. Only a few small obstacles had to be overcome. The Hudson's people knew nothing of my existence, and they had no idea that I was the only man in the entire United States who could successfully fulfill their plans—plans that they were not even aware of yet. Finally, I didn't happen to know this king, nor did I know of anyone who had relations with him. Given the conditions in Detroit and its suburbs, I realized that decisive measures were necessary, and only a huge corporation like Hudson's could take them. I knew my goal now. What I needed was a strategy.

ON A HOT TRACK

My first move in this exciting chess game was a thorough inspection of all of Hudson's thirteen floors; their exquisite features and rich range of goods impressed me very much. Then I arranged lunch with the business architect, Fred Wilkins, at the department store's restaurant. Soon it became clear that Mr. Wilkins held a rather subordinate position, which was restricted to the maintenance of the rooms and furniture. He was not interested in anything else. He explained to me that if I wanted to investigate the general business situation in Detroit, I could ask for an interview with the general manager and vice president James B. Webber, but, he shrugged, this was not likely to be granted.

My next move was to ask Lazette and her contacts to make inquiries about Hudson's in New York, but this was not an easy task. Hudson's appeared to be a blank slate. However, some of my contacts believed that Hudson's business had been stagnating for years. All I could find out about Oscar Webber was that he had lived in seclusion on a large farm since the death of his wife. His nephew James, the crown prince, was accessible, but he had far less influence.

A MOMENTOUS LETTER

I decided to write to James Webber and offer my detailed analysis of the Detroit retail scene. In this twelve-page letter, I hinted at my ideas for how Hudson's could counter the current situation, which I portrayed in very bleak terms, and I asked that he grant me an interview in this regard.

Within a few days after returning to Los Angeles I received a short, polite reply. My report, Mr. James Webber wrote, had impressed him very much. And he told me that if I happened to be in Detroit again, I should drop by. Only three days later I happened to arrive "accidentally" in Detroit again. I called and got an appointment. Within ten days I had succeeded at the impossible task of entering Hudson's sacred eleventh floor.

James B. Webber proved to be an interested and interesting conversationalist. He was very impressed by my economic analysis of Detroit. He and some of Hudson's directors had long tried to persuade the president to establish branch operations in the surrounding areas, but they had failed thus far to rebut his strong counterarguments. Oscar Webber's reasoning was that the Hudson's name was connected to the store's size. Small Hudson's stores would be a contradiction in terms, like small giants. He also argued that most of the then-existing shopping centers were of bad quality with regard to their structural foundations and local traffic conditions as well as the goods sold, and therefore, Hudson's participation in such evils had to be avoided.

A PROPOSAL

I explained to Mr. James B. Webber that I shared the views of his uncle entirely. My suggestion would be of an entirely different nature. Hudson's should establish its own center in an area of urban growth, where future development could still be influenced. The center, and thus the Hudson's business, had to be of exceptional size and quality; it should serve as a cultural, social, and service center for the more than five hundred thousand people who lived in its vicinity. I described my vision of a center that would reproduce the standards of the parent company in terms of quality, distinction, and reputation.

James Webber had many detailed questions, which I answered as intuitively and completely as possible. Jim (as he was called) avidly took notes, and I was very satisfied to see that he was interested in my vision. He finally admitted that this concept opened up completely new perspectives, some of which might interest his uncle.

SUMMIT

Once again I returned to Los Angeles. Within a week, I received an invitation to present my ideas to Mr. Oscar Webber and his general staff. This meant I only had a little time to develop and deepen my concept.

Not long afterward, I entered Hudson's large conference room accompanied by a nervously shaking director. I was introduced to Mr. Oscar Webber, a small, unremarkable man dressed entirely in brown. About fourteen respectfully silent directors had placed themselves around the large conference table. Oscar Webber mumbled something, which I took for a friendly greeting, then he told all those gathered to cede the floor to Mr. Gruen. All of them proclaimed, in unison, "Yes, sir." I found out later that Mr. Webber addressed all of his subordinates by their first names, but they addressed him only with "Mr. Webber, sir."

I began with lots of courage. For about an hour, I spoke on my views on the development of retail trade in the Detroit area and Hudson's vulnerable position, as well as my vision for a regional Hudson's center. I went into more detail now compared to the previous conversation I had with James Webber. I then closed my presentation with the suggestion that Hudson's had a social and public responsibility.

Icy silence all around. Oscar Webber kept a straight face. He asked his staff if they had any questions. "No, sir," responded the chorus. "Then I have a very serious question." Webber said. "How do you, Victor, imagine that we could solve all these problems by erecting a single, large-scale center? In my opinion, at least four centers are needed. What do you have to say to that?"

"Oscar, I think you're absolutely right," I said, as the staff reacted in horror at my use of the man's first name. "I just did not dare to make such a far-reaching proposal."

"Nonsense," grumbled Oscar. "You're not usually at a loss for words. If it is okay with the other gentlemen, I want to hire you for a nonbinding research project.

Within three weeks, I want to know how much and what type of land will be needed for each of the four centers and where these lots should be located. I will find people for you who can determine whether it is possible to acquire land with the qualities described. The success of this affair, however, depends on the fact that nothing that has been said in this room will be made public. Everybody present has to commit himself to total secrecy. Victor, you'll work in this room, and, indeed, we will lock you in here. I assure you that all the information you need will be provided. Talking about fees is unnecessary—Hudson's is generous. Do you have any questions?"

"Yes," I said. "I want to do this secret research, but I would like to call in one of my most trusted employees, Mr. Karl Van Leuven. Otherwise, I will be bored to death."

"Granted," said Oscar. "You will stay at the nearest hotel, at our expense, but you are only to enter our building through a side entrance. When do you start?"

"Tomorrow," I said.

"Okay," said Oscar. "I want to talk to you every day at nine o'clock in my private office."

After this memorable meeting, it was clear to me that there were still many obstacles to overcome before Hudson's was to be the one customer that I needed for the extraordinary organization I was working on. However, Oscar Webber had quadrupled my plan to build a giant center. I sensed that this man, once he bought into an idea, did not give up. I also did not have to fear opposition from his choir of yes-men. Finally, by addressing him by his first name, I had distinguished myself from his followers and broken with tradition. I could expect to be treated as an equal by Oscar Webber.

PROPOSALS AND SETBACKS

The work of the prisoners in the conference room proceeded apace—even our meals were served to us there. Karl Van Leuven and I began to calculate the land requirements for seven buildings and space for pedestrian and auto traffic, as well as for wide green lawns around the parking lots.

When we finished these calculations, we were in shock. We needed to gather our courage to report to Oscar Webber that we would need about one hundred acres of land for each center. But we were also of the opinion that an area should be purchased that was two to three times larger than this, because the center would need to protect itself against so-called piracy from competition companies (which could benefit from our large parking lots). Furthermore, we believed the surrounding land would no doubt become more valuable, and that Hudson's should control its development, including that of homes, offices, hotels, and shops, because these should be planned and designed in harmony with the center.

Oscar did not bat an eyelid and said that it sounded very reasonable. We would have to deal with the planning of the surrounding land later, though. Our secret project "X" was on a fast track. Although Oscar was our only contact person, obviously there had to be dozens of little people at work who could provide us with maps, land-use data, traffic statistics, and other information. When we requested demographic data such as population counts and income levels for different regions, we received these with surprising speed.

Based on our studies, we now added a number of possible zones, marked as red rings, to the map of Detroit and its surrounding areas. Through middlemen, who did not know who the client was, Oscar set in motion an army of agents to inquire whether land could be purchased within the large red zones we had chosen.

The first proposals were examined theoretically, and most were discarded as unsuitable. But it became possible to conceive of four central areas, which we named Northland, Eastland, Westland, and Southland.

I must confess that it was a little unsettling to see our proposals, which we had worked out largely intuitively, put into action with such striking speed.

When we had at last made our decisions on the approximate locations of the centers, Oscar told us we had fulfilled the research project. He freed us from our house arrest. It would now probably take several months until all the formalities and negotiations were completed over the land acquisition. He didn't want to start planning any single center before he had finally acquired the land for all four; otherwise, property values would increase rapidly.

Over the next ten months, Karl and I were only called in from time to time to inspect properties. We rejected many of them, which impressed Oscar, and encouraged him to believe that, for us, quality was more important than speed.

PREPARATIONS

It was high time that I returned to my office in Los Angeles, which had been carrying on successfully without me. It was also time to make serious preparations to create an extraordinary organization. I met with my best employees. These included Karl Van Leuven, my first employee at the Kings Road studio; the Italian, Edgardo Contini, who had distinguished himself as an excellent static engineer; and my old school friend Rudolf L. Baumfeld, my ally at the State Vocational School in Vienna.[3] After he had made an adventure-filled escape to America many months after me, Baumfeld joined me in California. He had been on my staff since the end of the war.

I invited these three men to be my partners on the Hudson's project. They had one thing in common: they all were strong personalities, and I respected their opinions. I always experienced discussions with them as enriching experiences. On the other hand, I knew that they had enough respect for me to defer to me if that was in the interest of the overall organization.

Karl and I broke the news that if everything went well, we could have a monster of a commission in Detroit within the year. Our office was satisfactory, but we didn't believe we were ready for such a colossal job. I proposed to my three friends that we establish a stock corporation in which they would be partners with me. I would be founder and senior partner, with veto rights in the event of any disagreements. In return, I asked that the new stock corporation would assume all costs resulting from my divorce from Elsie. My intention was that the new organization would not be limited to architecture but would produce everything from graphic and interior design to engineering, transport and economic planning, and landscape design. For this purpose it would be necessary to look inside and outside our office's current staff for qualified personalities to form a leadership cadre. We could later promote these people as associates, who would be entitled to profit sharing to ensure their complete loyalty. Van Leuven, Contini, and Baumfeld were all enthusiastic about the proposal.

From now on, each partner had his own field of responsibility. Rudolf Baumfeld was responsible for design, Karl Van Leuven for client contacts, and Edgardo Contini for all engineering disciplines. Ben Southland, who joined us in 1956, was responsible for planning.

All these men had gained considerable experience in different parts of the world. They were ready to take on their tasks, and, in addition, they all possessed a quality that seemed essential to the success of a universal organization: they saw architecture, engineering, design, and planning as parts of an indivisible whole. Everybody mingled in all aspects of the project. This led to time-consuming discussions, but each project benefited from the diversity of our views.

I went to Detroit now and then to inspect land with Oscar Webber. He insisted he would not complete any purchase without my agreement, since I had final responsibility for the success of the projects.

Difficulties arose only in the acquisition of part of the land for Northland Center: an eighty-year-old farmer was willing to sell, but he insisted on keeping the right to use his land until his death. This farmer was an interesting opponent for Oscar Webber. He was narrow-minded and resisted all financial inducements. I advised Oscar to give in—at the worst, we would have to postpone the construction of Northland or try to find a temporary solution that would address this obstacle.

CONTRACT NEGOTIATIONS

In 1949, Oscar informed us that the land purchases were completed, and that it was time to come to a contractual agreement. He told us we should bring our corporate lawyer to Detroit, where he was to negotiate the contract with the Hudson's attorney. The problem was that we had no corporate lawyer. But Karl did have a friend, a Mr. Griffith, who was an attorney. Karl asked him by telephone to appear as soon as possible in Detroit. We informed him in detail about our desire to negotiate an overall contract for the planning of all aspects of the four centers. We wanted our fee in the form of a complete expense reimbursement and the payment of our entire technical staff with an appropriate amount for profit and controls.

The two lawyers seemed to understand each other excellently, and after about two weeks they reported that they had agreed on all points. One afternoon, we had a meeting with Oscar at which both lawyers handed out a forty-page contract. They assured Webber that he could sign it with no qualms, because the interests of both parties were protected in every way.

Oscar weighed the extensive document in his hand, then said, "I will not sign this." Both lawyers protested that he hadn't even read the document yet, and Oscar replied that something of this length was obviously too complicated and, thus, not suitable as an arrangement.

With these words, he angrily left the room. Karl and I were thunderstruck. Our hopes had been shattered in an instant.

THE HOTEL STATIONERY

After a dismal dinner, Karl and I sat down at a desk back in our hotel and wrote a short contract on a piece of hotel stationery. It read something like this:

1. The two parties will pursue a shared goal, which is to be carried out over a period of fifteen years.
2. They are committed to close cooperation, especially between Victor Gruen and Oscar Webber personally, with no step taken unless there is agreement from both.
3. Hudson's shall reimburse the Gruen Company for all the cash expenses that prove to be necessary for the project.
4. The Gruen Company will present, at monthly intervals, a bill for all of their costs for technical staff, and this will be multiplied by 2.5 and paid by the Hudson Company.
5. In the event that this contract must be dissolved for any reason, the Hudson Company will not hold the Gruen Company liable for expenses and damages arising therefrom.

The next morning I called Oscar Webber, who said he had been expecting to hear from me. I should come to see him immediately. I said that I had a concept of a short contract with me, and he said that was a funny coincidence, because he had written a short contract as well. I asked him to show me his proposal, but he said he wanted to see mine first. I gave him the handwritten hotel contract. He read it attentively, then took a pen and signed it. I said that I would have liked to hear his proposal. He said that was not necessary, and that my contract was better.

Then he expressed some extra wishes. The main work should be done in a Detroit office. He also wanted Karl Van Leuven, for whom he had developed a deep affection, to head the work office and to settle in Detroit. That was a problem, since Karl had a wife and six children. Oscar would provide us with consultants, highly qualified people who would act on our instructions. We should build our organization, make the necessary relocations, rent suitable office space, and then begin as soon as possible with the plan of the first center. When I told him that it would be necessary to bring in some of our employees from Los Angeles over the short and long term, he agreed and said that he would leave this completely to us, and that Hudson's would of course pay all travel and other expenses.

In this unorthodox manner, a contract for one of the largest construction projects in America in the 1950s was written within half an hour. With this piece of paper in my pocket, I had won an extraordinary client. The question of whether I should build an extraordinary organization was no longer relevant: we now had to establish it as quickly as possible in order to meet an all-encompassing task in an all-encompassing way.

But we were still in for a few surprises. When we made suggestions to Oscar regarding both the establishment of our office and the accommodation of the Van Leuven family, he found them all completely inappropriate. He said that our organization was now a part of the Hudson family, and that we should meet their standards. He decreed that Hudson's would buy the Van Leuven family a large house in the most elegant residential area, near Lake St. Clair, and that it would be furnished appropriately at the expense of Hudson's. Our office premises on nearby Washington Boulevard would also be equally appropriate, and twice as large as we had estimated, because he intended to build the four centers at intervals of about three and a half years, and therefore we would probably have to work simultaneously on multiple projects. He smirked and added that it would be wrong to save money on our gigantic project at the expense of those who had created the project.

I was also accused of false frugality in regard to my appearance. Immediately after signing the contract, I was taken to the Hudson's men's department and redressed from head to toe, with new shoes, coat, underwear, hats, and more (and in many different combinations). In the process, I discarded the last remnants of my European wardrobe. I had finally slipped out of my European skin.

SETBACKS

There was a second, more serious, setback. During the preparation of the Eastland project, the Korean War broke out, and all construction activities were required to stop, as they had during World War II. We feared that Oscar was going to stop our project. Our fears were groundless. Oscar thought that we could use the time delay to complete land negotiations for the Northland Center. In that case, it was his wish to build Northland first, because it had potentially the best location.

Since we were directed to begin the planning for Northland immediately, I took the opportunity to confess to Oscar that I had come to the conviction that our first approach and design for Eastland were not satisfactory. I now had a much better idea, which I described to him. He excitedly agreed to the new concept (which was what we actually built later). He said that the expenses we had incurred thus far for the old approach could be written off as a lesson learned.

A third serious setback concerned the question of cost-effectiveness and financing of Northland. Hudson's had appointed two economists to assess profitability. I had recommended Larry Smith, with whom I had worked previously and with whom I later wrote the book *Shopping Towns USA*.[4] The other was Homer Hoyt, the chosen expert of Hudson's. Larry submitted a long report, equipped with many statistics, that drew on the experience of existing shopping centers and came to extremely pessimistic conclusions. According to Larry, the center would be much too large and too expensive to build, with a total estimated cost of one hundred million U.S. dollars. Profitability would therefore be out of the question. He estimated the highest revenues after five years of operation would be about fifty million dollars. On the other hand, Homer Hoyt submitted a brief report that was based more on intuition than on statistics. He said the project was so unique that it would be a success from the very start.

Oscar was unimpressed by both reports. By contrast, the large finance companies were discouraged by Smith's report, and none of them were ready to commit to the project. I thought that this meant the end, but I was wrong again. Oscar was personally so convinced of the success of the center that he decided that, if nothing else, the Hudson's Corporation itself would finance it.

Oscar's reasoning seemed to be proved sound when all of the commercial space in Northland was rented out to prominent tenants on favorable terms before construction had even begun. The same finance companies that had previously passed on the deal now fell all over themselves to offer favorable loans. The construction of Northland was now obstructed only by the restrictions in place owing to the Korean War.

FROM VISION TO REALITY

Before we look at the way Northland was designed, from its conception in 1948 until its opening in 1954, it is important to be clear about its historical significance. It was recognized as the first large and successful experiment to have created, in an environmentally conscious way, an oasis of community, culture, and shopping in the endless desert of suburban America. Its importance was underlined by coverage in the national mass media and architecture magazines in an unusual show of unanimity.

For instance, a few months after the center's opening, the well-known urban planning critic Jane Jacobs wrote in *Architectural Forum,* "This is a classic in shopping center planning, in the sense that Rockefeller Center is a classic in urban skyscraper group planning, or Radburn, New Jersey, in suburban residential planning."

Model for Northland. Courtesy of Gruen Associates.

Jacobs described Northland as a rewarding object of study for urban planners: the flexible use of open spaces, similar to a market town, offered a very cost-efficient way of rehabilitating existing neighborhoods threatened by decline. According to her view, Northland also provided a model because of its sophisticated graphic design and its casual and refreshing inclusion of works of art.[5]

Many illustrated magazines, most notably *Life,* published feature stories about Northland, usually accompanied by color photographs. Eleanor Roosevelt paid a long visit to Northland and wrote an enthusiastic article for a women's magazine. Northland became a pilgrimage site for journalists, urban planners, merchants, and contractors.

Authorities and professional associations showered us with honorary certificates and prizes. The federal government took a huge color photo of the project, which was later shown at an exhibition of American architecture in many parts of the world, including in Moscow.

This extraordinarily positive reaction was vital for our future as a new interdisciplinary organization. Without this confirmation of our success, our working principle of universal activity would have been regarded a failure. As it happened, we found support for the future of our work, our understanding of environmental architecture, and our idea of working together as a partnership, as we had with Hudson's.

In retrospect, I must say that Oscar Webber deserved most of the credit for the project and the praise with which we were showered. Without his ethical attitude and his entrepreneurship restrained by conservatism, we never could have breached the prevailing practice of focusing on short-term profit motives. Since this breach proved to be a path to economic benefits, we were later able to convince other clients of the advantages of long-term planning, thinking, and acting.

At the end of the first year of Northland's operation, with total sales of more than one hundred million dollars, Oscar sarcastically asked Larry Smith how he could have so seriously underestimated the center's success. Smith replied, "Sir, I assumed that you intended to build a conventional shopping center. I could not include in my evaluation the fact that you would build something entirely different and never seen before. But if you were to ask me again in the future, I would be able to create realistic forecasts." Oscar asked him to do so for the three next centers.

Why was a project of commercial nature considered by the general public to be an architectural "mighty deed"? Was this work the result of a brilliant flash of inspiration, or was it just the logical result of circumstances and constraints? Northland was actually free from many of the usual constraints, with the exception of building regulations. By sticking to our building ethos, the constraints we encountered were self-imposed.

The Detroit Times
Tues., Oct. 12, 1954

International Sound Photo

Northland in New York. A New Rochelle (N. Y.) housewife, Mrs. Laura Finn, getting a detailed explanation of Northland Shopping Center from Karl Van Leuven, an architect with the firm that designed the center. Northland was featured in an exhibit, "Shopping Centers of Tomorrow" presented by the New York Museum of Natural History. Shopping comfort was stressed.

Newspaper clipping from the *Detroit Times,* October 12, 1954. Library of Congress.

Our team, composed chiefly of Oscar Webber, Karl Van Leuven, and myself, also included, in a broader sense, the partners of our company in Los Angeles, some persons of leadership within the Hudson Company, and a number of our consultants. Within the management team there was a simple agreement: Oscar would not undertake anything on the four planned projects without our consent. On the other hand, we would discuss all important steps with him. If we were in doubt, we would try to convince him of our opinion, and if this failed, we would make new proposals.

In short, we proposed and Oscar paid for an arrangement that created an unheard-of situation. We generally advised thriftiness, but Oscar insisted on the finest quality in materials and execution, which caused high additional costs. He demanded, for example, that in the construction of the first phase, accommodations should be made to allow for the expansion of every building, its foundation and basement, so that we could later create additional rentable buildings.

The planning was easy in one important sense, in that our views and objectives coincided. We all wanted to create regional, multifunctional town centers that would improve the quality of life in the surrounding residential areas. Therefore, precautions had to be taken to protect the adjoining areas from noise, traffic, and pollution. Disturbing views of loading operations were as undesirable as glaring signs of commercialism.

COOPERATION

Oscar Webber may have subliminally desired an additional monument to Hudson's. (The downtown department store was to Detroit as the Eiffel Tower is to Paris. I recently learned from U.S. newspapers that due to the progressive decay of the inner city, this landmark would be demolished.)[6] It was his wish that all Northland tenants would design their storefronts and interiors with the same high quality standards set by Hudson's. Since it could not be expected that this would be achieved by persuasion alone, it was determined that each tenant would be given a considerable grant for the design of its business and would in turn submit to the supervision of the center's architects.

These and other arrangements seemed insane to finance and real estate experts. The conventional view was that a shopping center should be a cheaply produced shopping machine that should never distract customers from exchanging their money for commodities as quickly as possible.

We thought economically, but in an unconventionally broader sense. It was our opinion that only centers of outstanding quality would discourage any future competition. We took the view that a central place that offered more than just shopping venues would become an unusual attraction, and this would ultimately benefit business. The subsidies to the tenants, said Oscar, could be viewed as a bond.

We dealt with things that didn't have much to do with architecture in the strictest sense. For example, we developed a kind of legislation for the future community that would consist of many thousands of employees and hundreds of thousands of visitors. We provided lawyers who drafted leases and regulations on the conditions that seemed important for a functioning shopping center. For example, there were prohibitions against the spillover of commercial activities into the public pedestrian areas and rules on the maximum size of the lettering of logos; there was a ban on neon signs and on paper signs glued to windows. There were rules against outside signs, against spoiling roofs with any individual structures or television or radio antennas. Shop opening and closing times had to be uniform; there was an obligation to illuminate the showcases daily from dawn until 10:00 p.m., including Sundays and public holidays.

We framed statutes for a tenant parliament that would address issues affecting the center. We also had a strong influence on the strategy of renting by creating a prerental plan wherein the sizes and locations of companies in all sectors were registered. This plan also indicated that only one supermarket should be allowed. All those businesses that needed a lot of floor space, such as furniture, hardware, building materials, and similar businesses, would have ground floors that consisted solely of entrance halls with escalators and would have to accommodate their sales and exhibition spaces elsewhere.

With all these constraints and limitations, we complicated the work of Mr. Horace Carpenter, the man who had been entrusted with leasing and tenant relations. We had chosen him because he was not tainted by previous experience in the rental business. Renters initially could not understand that there was no space available for them at all or that there was far less than they demanded, and this only in a predetermined place.

The Northland project offered us the opportunity to test our opinions about the task and nature of architecture. Architecture is meaningful only when it is a synthesis of art, technology, science, politics, economics, philosophy, planning, and design. In this sense, architecture is a challenge that requires the use of complex thinking.

This concept ran throughout all our projects until their completion. For instance, we were politically active, attending citizens' assemblies and informing the public with photographs and lectures about the unusual nature of our projects, trying to convince people not to submit any objections to our receiving building permits. In these discussions, we faced a good deal of skepticism. We negotiated with authorities of all kinds to achieve exemptions, such as mixed land use for various functions. We persuaded the traffic authorities to carry out certain improvements; one of these was to set up public bus service for the region.

THE DRAFT

The planning and architectural design of the center took place in parallel to these efforts and originated in the same spirit of architectural thinking. As the German word *Entwurf* aptly expresses it, a fundamental idea is "thrown" onto a piece of paper in a moment of inspiration. This throw is based on intuition, which subconsciously includes long-term experience and knowledge of the building site and its environment, as well as knowledge of the client. The human brain of a creative person seems capable of storing myriad information, like a computer, and then giving birth to a concept in a single moment of inspiration.

In the case of Northland, the sketch of the idea that I initially presented to Oscar Webber looked something like this: in the center of a vast space, remote from all public roads, was a sharply defined complex that consisted of building structures and open spaces. All other parts of the overall composition were arranged around this central core of irregular form. The first ring consisted of landscaped public spaces of various shapes and sizes. On the edge of these green spaces, which were to serve pedestrians only, lay a crown of five rental properties. The gaps that resulted from the large distances between these objects became pedestrian promenades, which established connections to another broad ring that provided parking for cars. On one side of the central nucleus, the crown of rental properties was interrupted to give a full view of the Hudson's building to the main road. A generously proportioned pedestrian walkway led to the central building, where major events could take place.

The sketch also showed how different modes of transportation could be separate from one another. The public spaces in the center were exclusively for pedestrians, as were the elevated sidewalks that divided the parking area into nine sectors. A separate road was provided for auto traffic. Another road loop exclusively for bus and taxi traffic was planned. For private cars, there was a ring-shaped connecting road on the outskirts of the parking lot with connections to the five surrounding public streets. As a final concentric ring, there was a wide greenbelt, which was intended to serve as a protection zone between residential areas and the car parking area. The technical facilities, including central heating, air-conditioning, repair stations, a firehouse, and a police station, did not take up valuable space in the central building but were housed in a remote corner of the site.

This design prevented access to the large department store from the car parking area. Oscar Webber accepted it nonetheless because he thought that Hudson's would attract shoppers as a main destination anyway. He believed the design would be beneficial to the interests of the whole center. Hudson's abstained from placing its company logo on the department store building and was satisfied with small bronze plaques at the entrances, which spoke to the company's self-confidence as a business. Oscar Webber thought a logo was unnecessary, since everyone in Detroit and the surrounding area already knew that a building of such significant size could only be a Hudson's store.

The result of a flash of inspiration, of course, must be tested. I had already done a draft for Eastland that didn't match my true ambitions. I had wanted the businesses to form a ring around a large parking lot. Additional car parking was provided on the outside of this ring. This scheme would have created optimal accessibility to all the shops, but there would have been no separation of pedestrians from car traffic. Also, the distances between the shops had become too large. Afterward, I told myself that this car-friendly design was the biggest egg I'd ever laid. But the construction delay caused by the Korean War saved us from acting on this bad plan.

Instead, we tried to apply our new knowledge to Northland. In architects' language, this process of examination is referred to as a preliminary drawing, in which we work from the inside out. But even construction of the Hudson's building itself proceeded concentrically. This nucleus—the inner core of Northland—needed to accommodate various mechanical functions. To determine the size of this inner core, engineers of all fields had to calculate the amount of space required for things such as freight and passenger elevators. Only after the size and shape of this mechanical core were clear would we be able to deal with the dimensioning of the core shell, which would in turn provide the form for the rest of the premises. In this phase, all of Hudson's department heads would need to collaborate with the people in our organization who had experience with the furnishing of businesses.

THE DESIGN OF THE INTERIOR

On any sales floor, a passage should allow customers to view all of the sales departments, and customers should be able to find small boutiques on the sides or near to the mechanical core. They should see opulent goods from the individual departments on the outer walls. The exact size, shape, and number of the floor levels of the Hudson's building could be determined only after such interior details were worked out. And after this set of designs and calculations was completed, it would be possible to determine the locations of the rental units and the dimensions of the five different garden courtyards.

A practical collaboration between engineers and architects was required to find the optimal solution for a construction that would allow the greatest flexibility for subdivision of Northland's space into individual shops. We decided that all of the buildings, even Hudson's, should be surrounded by colonnades, which would offer protection from the summer sun as well as from rain and snow. We erected wooden models in various parts of the buildings to determine the height of these colonnades and the optimal proportions of the support pillars.

To distinguish the five public places from each other, we used covered walkways, some of which had solid sidewalls. Within the walkways themselves, these solid walls were used to display mounted maps and announcements; the outsides of the walkways were designed as backdrops for artistic works, such as mosaics and sculptures.

The design of the center's exterior came last. To emphasize identification with Hudson's, the walls were covered with red brick and structured so that the pillars were visible from a distance, appearing as columns. The recessed walls of the ground floor were glassed in to be used as window displays and to open up sight lines to the sales departments. The style of the facades of the rental stores was dictated by the colonnades. It was supplemented by vertical stone strips that separated the various businesses clearly from each other. Emergency telephones were mounted on the walls, as were letter slots that fed directly into mailboxes in the underground supply areas.

The average visitor to a shopping center cares less about the facade than about the character and atmosphere of the public spaces, where one might stroll or sit on benches. These public areas fulfill their function only when they provide extraordinary experiences. That is why so much attention, love, and money are devoted to the arrangement of trees, shrubs, and flower beds in these areas.

We invited a group of about ten young artists to submit proposals for sculptures, murals, and mosaics with which we hoped to merge architecture and landscape design. We gave them the following guidance for their work: We wanted to create an atmosphere of untroubled joy. Dramatic or tragic topics would be out of place. We didn't want art with old-fashioned realism, but we didn't want total abstraction either, because shoppers might not identify with it. We wanted to encourage visitors to reflect on the art, but not if their inability to understand it might lead to frustration.

The artists had a lot of relevant ideas. They proposed mobiles, reliefs, and fountains that pictured animals and children at play. But it turned out that these artists, some of whom had created small sculptures for galleries, simply had no clue as to how to create very large works that would have to survive wind and weather. This problem was solved only through artists' collaborations with engineers and architects. In the end, the artworks created for Northland proved to be so effective that a major New York gallery organized an exhibition of models and photographs of them.

PLANNING ERRORS

I should also mention the environmental planning opportunities we did not utilize. On our advice, Hudson's had purchased, in addition to the approximately fifty acres of land necessary for the center, about 150 hectares. We succeeded in using this reserve land partly for a greenbelt and partly for other functions, such as hotels, residential buildings, laboratories, and a theater with fourteen hundred seats. But we did not really integrate these facilities with the Northland Center. The development of this land was eventually transferred to a Hudson's-related real estate company. The planning and management team of the center became so occupied with other tasks that control over the additional land slipped away.

The exploitation of the land was given to individual enterprises. This benefited Hudson's financially in that the company recouped some of the total construction costs of the center. But each of the individual enterprises on the periphery built its own center—a hotel center, a business center, a residential center, each of which was surrounded with the necessary parking area. In this way, an agglomeration that could be described as a scattered center developed, and it was actually not possible to reach Northland without a car. Thus, the need for traffic areas grew.

DIFFERENT PATHS

Around the same time Northland opened, the new General Motors Technical Center, a very large and ambitious management center in Detroit, was finished. It was designed by the famous Finnish architect Eero Saarinen. During a visit to his idyllic studio in the suburbs, I noticed that Eero had mastered his task with a relatively small staff of architects. Given the intimate atmosphere that prevailed in the studio, I asked myself whether our way of working with a large staff really was the right method. I expressed to Eero that maybe in the future it would be better to follow his example. He laughed heartily and said that he had just come to the opposite conclusion, that only our way of uniting design and completing execution within an organization could provide satisfactory results. He had left the process of making preliminary drawings and working drawings to a large engineering company. Convincingly, he argued that if he hadn't been working with a client like General Motors, for which money spent for the project did not play a role, he would not have been able to produce all the documents several times over, and the project could not have been executed. He also said that his energy and usually strong nerves were worn out by confrontations with people who didn't want to understand his ideas. He decided that he did not want to go through this a second time. This statement encouraged me to continue to expand our great organization.

AN INVENTION

Inventions sometimes are based on coincidences. In this way, the invention of the indoor, air-conditioned shopping center took root in my observations of the weather conditions in Minneapolis, Minnesota. In this city, the Dayton's department store was run by five young brothers. Although they were all engaged in academic professions, they had promised their father, who died prematurely, that they would continue the family business together.

Because Oscar Webber was close friends with the Dayton family, he took the Dayton brothers aside to give them some fatherly advice—namely, that they should hire our organization to realize their plans. The first project was a branch department store that was to be built in Rochester, Minnesota. The successful interior and exterior design, which was in large part done by my partner Rudolf Baumfeld, encouraged them to discuss plans for a large shopping center in the Minneapolis suburb of Edina.

While working for the branch business in Rochester and during preliminary discussions for the shopping center, I had occasion to visit Minneapolis repeatedly. During those visits, the city was either buried in snow and bitter cold in winter, or scorching hot in summer, or rained out in spring and autumn. The Dayton brothers greatly admired the plans for Northland, but under these circumstances, the proposal to duplicate Northland and create landscaped pedestrian areas under the open sky did not seem very promising.

Inspired by the Oriental bazaar and by European galleries and passages, especially the Galleria Vittorio Emanuele in Milan, I wanted to create a modern center with indoor and air-conditioned pedestrian areas. This inspiration was expressed in a draft: a large, covered public space with skylights surrounded by a ring of two department stores and many smaller shops.

In principle, this draft found general agreement. But questions remained as to how certain technical and economic problems, mostly involving the additional cost of a roof, could be solved. Here the multidisciplinary structure of our organization proved to be extremely useful. Once the objectives had been set up in discussions among all partners and heads of departments and had been accepted, we focused together on finding the means and ways by which it would be possible to produce an indoor center for approximately the same cost as a so-called open center. From a planning and architectural point of view, it was clear that the vast extent of the public spaces, as they existed in Northland, should be restricted. The site density was to be enlarged, and instead of one shopping level, there had to be two. In addition, the basement would have to be used to an even greater extent than in Northland for profitability purposes. The question of how both sales floors could receive the same share of shopper flow was resolved by having half of the parking areas start from street level, connecting directly via an inclination to the upper sales floor, while the other half would have direct access to the lower sales floor via a downward inclination.

The operating costs for heating and cooling large pedestrian areas were kept low through the use of a heat exchange pump for the first time in a large project; now, in times of energy saving, this method has come back in favor. The large courtyard would be the central air reservoir.

Such a system would produce springlike temperatures regardless of the outdoor climate and could work only if individual store entrances from the parking areas were eliminated. Instead, it was necessary to create three main entrances with double doors for the upper and lower sales levels. Through these six entrances, one could pass through pedestrian promenades alongside the shops to the large central courtyard.

This arrangement opened a new set of possibilities. By eliminating signs and displays on the outer side, large savings would be achieved. Each individual business could use its rented space, which would be directed at only one internal entrance,

Public announcement for Southdale Center, Edina, Minnesota, circa 1956. Library of Congress.

more efficiently, and the exterior of the two-story building complex could be designed in a uniform manner without any corporate branding. Southdale was the first indoor, air-conditioned, "introverted" shopping center in the world.

Since the entire complex of buildings enjoyed the same climatic conditions, there were further savings. Double doors to the shops, necessary for an open center, could be totally eliminated. You could even go one step further and establish so-called open glass fronts, which were closed only at night with glass sliding doors or grates. Due to these and many other special measures, the roofed, air-conditioned center could compete economically very well with the open center.

UTOPIA

Our working relationship with Dayton's, in matters of compensation and partnership, resembled the method we had established with Hudson's. Only in this way could we persuade Dayton's to perform the lengthy studies needed to confirm the concept. Because the Dayton brothers were convinced of the rightness of the design and technical proposals established in the preliminary stage, they had the courage to resist the warnings of business and real estate professionals claiming special knowledge about shopping centers. The unanimous opinion of all these so-called experts was that the idea of an indoor, air-conditioned center as a single utopia could never be achieved technically or economically.

In terms of rental conditions, controls on trademarks, the tenants' parliament, and prerental contracts, we again followed the pattern we had worked out for Northland. Creatively, however, we were faced with a completely new situation. Because the public spaces were covered, there was great concern that visitors might have the perception that no difference existed in the atmospheres of the public spaces versus the commercial ones. In order to dispel this impression, we gave special attention to the design of the covered pedestrian area. We wanted to create a kind of outdoor atmosphere, so we shaped the garden courtyard as a three-story space and introduced a continuous glass surface on the north side of the third floor. This glass surface generated a visual link with the outside world: visitors could see the sky and the clouds at different times of day. With this direct exposure to daylight, it was possible even to plant trees and flowers on the floor, as well as along the balconies of the upper sales floors. A birdhouse, goldfish pond, and garden café enhanced this artificial outdoor character.

The Daytons—especially Bruce Dayton, who was an art collector—were extremely interested in artworks. For example, the eminent sculptor Harry Bertoia was hired to build two three-story abstract sculptures, which people soon called "golden trees."

In the case of Southdale, our task area was comprehensive. We designed the interiors of the Dayton's department store and a number of retail stores. We planned the construction of the surrounding plots, which were owned by the Dayton Company, with residential buildings, office buildings, and so on, that conformed to the center and its surroundings. The main workload was borne by the Los Angeles office. In Minneapolis, there was only a small coordination and supervision office, which was led by an employee, Herman Guttman. For his contribution he was made a full partner in 1956.

A small adjustment was necessary because of the springlike climate at the center. Near the entrances, a large number of lockers were set up so that visitors could store their raincoats, umbrellas, and galoshes.

It turned out that the large courtyard, which permitted strolling, resting, drinking coffee, and viewing artworks, as well as the orchestration of evening symphony

Herman Guttman, Victor Gruen, and Rudi Baumfeld in Southdale Center, Edina, Minnesota, circa 1956. Courtesy of Gruen Associates.

concerts and balls, exerted a surprising attraction, which further benefited business sales.

When Southdale opened in 1956, the reaction in the mass media and in the architectural press was as extensive and positive as in the case of Northland. After it was completed, the center was enlarged repeatedly, until it had expanded from an initial 60,000 square feet to 110,000 square feet of retail space.

Despite the apparent success of this indoor, air-conditioned shopping mall, nearly ten years passed before anyone else dared to reproduce this new building type. Then suddenly air-conditioned shopping malls became common worldwide, even in climates where open centers would have been possible or even superior options.

Fashion show, Southdale Center, 1957. Courtesy of Gruen Associates. Photograph by Anthony Lane.

5

Development of the Storm

THE SPIRITS THAT I CALLED

"The malling of America" was the topic of the May 1, 1978, issue of the American weekly magazine *New Times*.[1] *Malling* is a newly coined word for a new phenomenon. The term *mall* was originally used in England in reference to a broad promenade; it was borrowed in America for the pedestrian shopping street and later for indoor, air-conditioned shopping malls. As the word is used in America, you don't say, "Let's go to the shopping center" but "Let's go to the mall."

According to the twenty-two-page feature article in this issue of *New Times*, since the opening of Southdale Center in 1956, *malling* has become a term in American life. According to *U.S. News & World Report*, the average person spends more time in malls than anywhere else outside the workplace and home. Shopping centers make about three hundred billion dollars in annual sales, or about half of total U.S. retail sales. Sixty billion dollars are invested in these ventures, primarily by large insurance companies. About eighteen thousand shopping centers exist in the United States, of which one thousand are very large and hundreds are gigantic. Together they comprise two hundred million square feet of retail space. They require about five times the retail space (one billion square feet) for parking space and traffic areas. They occupy a total of almost thirteen billion square feet of floor space, plus a similarly large area of public access and exit roads.

Malls provide jobs for a half million employees (which is almost twice the number of employees of the Republic of Austria); in some cases, malls are visited by customers from as far away as twenty to twenty-five miles.

The construction of shopping centers has become an aggressive and complex industry organized by the International Council of Shopping Centers, an association

Cherry Hill Mall, New Jersey. Courtesy of Gruen Associates. Photograph by Joseph Molitor.

that has an annual budget of one million dollars.[2] In the United States there is an influential mall lobby in Washington, D.C., and in addition to the official ICSC magazine, *Shopping Centers Today,* three other magazines are devoted to the shopping center.

Malls have changed the scenery, the cities, and the habits of America dramatically. Gigantic shopping malls on the outskirts of cities have made the city centers into empty shells that are at risk of becoming economically and culturally desolate. This is especially the case in the West and Midwest. Shopping malls did not cause the great exodus of residents, commerce, and industry from their original settlements in urban areas after 1940, but they provided additional momentum.

So Ralph Keyes writes in his sociological study *We, the Lonely People*: "Malls aren't *part* of the community. They *are* the community."[3] In his dystopian film *Dawn of the Dead,* George Romero has the four sole survivors of a man-made disaster search by helicopter for a place of safety and security. They find it in the form of a huge indoor shopping center, but they are totally confused by the excess supply of consumer goods.

The absolutely latest in malls is allegedly already in the process of being designed as a spaceship for tens of thousands of people. The astrophysicist Gerard O'Neill, in collaboration with NASA, has drawn up a project and baptized it "Iceland No. 1."[4] The drawing shows a structure that is similar to a covered shopping mall, with campers above the shops and a garden courtyard between the buildings. O'Neill has called it "Southdale of the Stars."

The flood of shopping centers has overwhelmed not just the United States. In Canada there are thirty-five hundred shopping centers. The development has also caught on in Australia, Japan, South Africa, and other parts of the world. In Europe there are, according to the Institut für Gewerbezentren (Institute for Business Centers, Starnberg, Munich), in Germany alone, six hundred shopping centers, of which only sixty-five are regional shopping centers, with a combined sales area of two million square meters. In France, there are twenty-five regional shopping centers, in the United Kingdom seventeen, in Switzerland eleven, in the Netherlands twenty-nine, in Denmark nine, in Sweden nine, in Belgium four, and in Austria two.

Even the Communist countries are interested in the development of shopping centers. I was invited to the Comecon Conference in Brno, Czechoslovakia, in 1975, to give a lecture on this subject.[5] I explained that the American shopping center model is not transferable to European conditions, because the city centers would be disturbed. Whether my criticisms had some deterrent effect, I cannot judge now.

Nor I can estimate what kind of influence my lectures had at meetings of the International Council of Shopping Centers and at the Institute for Commercial

Centres in London in 1978, and earlier, in Munich in 1974. In both cases, I was invited, as the so-called Father of the Shopping Center, to be a keynote speaker, to lecture on the theme "the future of the mall."[6] The audiences were shocked to hear that the monofunctional suburban or "greenfield" shopping center is completely dependent on individual traffic and stands or falls by the car.

Originally, these centers were created to counteract the desolation of the vast American suburbs. The aforementioned *New Times* article states that the visionaries of the centers said they would create community facilities in the middle of the suburbs.[7] But the original objective, to eliminate existing abuses, has disappeared and been replaced by a selfish pursuit of profit, which has created new evils: traffic avalanches, energy waste, and runoff from these centers of increased purchasing power. Cesar Pelli, a former Gruen Associates partner, now dean of the School of Architecture at Yale University, once observed that the mall has become a great machine. Shopping centers were initially successful because they were designed on the basis of idealistic motives. But now they have simply become too successful, in the same way the car has become too successful. They are so overwhelming that nothing is able to restore the balance. Settlements and even cities simply disappear. Even the president of the International Council of Shopping Centers, Albert Sussman, has admitted that some centers have raped the landscape, created ugliness and chaotic traffic conditions, and destroyed local community life.

The book *Shopping Towns USA,* which I coauthored with economist Larry Smith in 1960, is still regarded as the bible of the shopping center industry, but only for those parts that deal with technical and management issues.

For example, the book insists that the new urban planning ideas that were carried out most easily in the territory of the suburban areas should be considered only as pilot projects, which would become significant if they could be transferred to the densely populated urban areas. It argues that within the next twenty years, the importance of environmentally conscious planning will be identified for urban areas, and the will and the knowledge to vitalize the core cities will develop from the present desperate situation.[8]

Yet, in spite of the proliferation of malls, resistance to them has grown. For example, a California center was subjected to 140 public hearings before it could be approved after significant changes. The period between completed planning and opening of a center, which formerly amounted to one to three years, has extended to an average of four to six years.

In Europe, a distinct departure is noticeable. During the period 1972–73, ten to twelve large centers were opened annually, but there are now only about three to four. Also, the size of the centers has decreased. The first European centers had approximately sixty-four thousand square feet of retail space; the average now is about thirty-one thousand square feet.

The Institut für Gewerbezentren notes, in a 1978 report, that the sites are moving from the periphery into urban areas and that a trend toward smaller centers is noticeable. This is also true in the United States, where the largest and most successful new centers are often planned as part of the revitalization of downtown areas. One resounding success was the restoration of the historic Faneuil Hall in Boston as an urban focal point.

ENVIRONMENTAL INFLUENCES

The deeper reasons for this shift are rooted in the global environmental and energy crisis. The peripherally located single-purpose center is agriculture and energy depleting and contributes to the endless usuriousness of urban structure. In 1973 in the United States, the birthplace of the shopping center, before the so-called oil crisis, the federal Environmental Protection Agency issued regulations that required each application for a building permit to be complemented by an application to the EPA. Those applying for building permits had to prove that their construction would not have negative environmental impacts.

These regulations naturally arouse the violent opposition of all those affected, including car manufacturers, road contractors, and planners of shopping malls. Since loopholes and corruption also exist in America, it will probably take quite some time before these provisions can be fully implemented. But clear signs of a turnaround are already visible.

Both in America and in Europe, moribund city centers are blooming again. It is significant that in recent years, 340 inner-city pedestrian areas have been created in Europe, mostly with the active support of merchants.

The suburban and peripheral shopping center is a child of the oil age. We know that this nonrenewable raw material will be exhausted at some time in the future, and before that, it will become steadily more expensive.

The worldwide, almost fetishistic love of the car will always demand increasing financial sacrifice, so that a growing part of the family budget must be allocated to operating this beloved status symbol. But this is obviously not in the interest of business: enormous centers located far outside the city limits seduce citizens at the cost of long, increasingly expensive car trips, and, as a result, they have less money at their disposal for shopping.

The growing environmental consciousness of the population has resulted in many legal measures against the construction of shopping centers. If, as it seems, the Shopping Center Age is ending, the fault lies largely with the irresponsible behavior and the shortsightedness of those entrepreneurs and speculators who have engaged in ruthless business practices. There are many indications that we will experience a change in attitude toward city planning in general; this is expressed in the slogan "Urban renewal instead of urban expansion."

FROM THE SUBURBS TO DOWNTOWN

The great economic success of the shopping center in the United States had two effects. First, it mobilized the opposition of those who had made significant investments in urban centers and who then, with horror, perceived the value of their land and buildings as melting away. Second, because the suburban centers owed their success to more targeted planning activities, the term *to plan,* which previously was frowned upon as un-American and Communist, became socially acceptable. As a result, the most zealous defenders of individual liberty, banks, insurance companies, property owners, and public authorities undertook or supported interventionist planned projects.

"Save downtown!" became a battle cry. First the municipalities tried with legislative measures; when this did not help, the state governments intervened. Finally, the federal government in Washington took action. Remarkably, the so-called urban renewal legislation was adopted under the conservative administration of President Eisenhower.

Individual measures were taken. In the belief that suburban shopping malls succeeded only because they offered plenty of parking places for cars, downtown businesses received government subsidies for the construction of large garages. Billions were invested for this purpose, but without success—the garages stayed empty. White Anglo-Saxon Protestants could not be lured back into muddy, clogged, minority-inhabited and unsafe city centers just because of plentiful parking.

Then, big "slum clearance" policies were attempted; these were made possible by state expropriation renewal legislation. Slums were leveled. Gigantic public housing projects were built, and spaces within them were given only to the poorest of the poor. Although they looked clean from the outside and were equipped with better toilets, these new sterile complexes improved neither the downtown business climate nor public safety. The overcrowding and misery in large complexes led to new problems. In the case of one major project in St. Louis, designed by a famous architect, the problems became so dire (robbery, murder, juvenile delinquency, rape), the entire vast complex was demolished in one afternoon.[9]

The acquisition, demolition, and redevelopment of slum areas was generally undertaken by a local agency known as the Urban Renewal Authority, but then the land was handed over to the highest-bidding contractor, with the effect that the

Urban Renewal Authority ran large deficits due to uncovered costs of this transfer. Following the goal of generating returns on their investment, contractors replaced the slums with homes for wealthy tenants. But since these new tenants were difficult to find, the new homes stayed vacant for a long time. Meanwhile, those in the displaced population settled down again as close as possible to their previous residences. So, ultimately, the slum was not removed but simply relocated.

The seemingly intractable problems of the American inner cities, exacerbated by ethnic and religious prejudices, distress us as environmental architects. We have come to the conclusion that measures against individual symptoms cannot be useful. A concerted effort is needed to push forward with a package of measures to root out the evil. It is obvious that many of these problems cannot be solved only by the arts of architects or planners. Without political and sociological intervention, neither the provision of decent shelter nor the integration of populations of different incomes, ethnicities, and religions is possible.

But such intervention is difficult in the United States, where an overwhelming majority of "haves" outweighs a 20 percent minority of "have-nots." With such a population structure, the rules of democracy work against the disadvantaged minority. This is evident not only in the composition of public bodies but also in popular votes. When, for example, the state of California held a vote, at the behest of a citizen initiative in 1978, on whether property taxes, the revenues from which constitute the backbone of all public expenditures, should be radically reduced, the public expressed two-thirds approval. This proved that two-thirds of the California population are land and house owners and/or do not sympathize with the task of balancing economic inequities in their communities. The predicament of inner cities is mainly due to the fact that they have become the homes of the "have-not" minority. A majority of affluent citizens have settled in areas that are often outside the political city limits. This may explain why in many U.S. cities, mayors who belong to ethnic minorities are elected and are on the whole unable, with the limited budgetary resources available, to carry out major improvements.

THE CRUCIBLE

This "practice" of apartheid is being fought by government at all levels, but progress is slow, especially in the field of human habitation. In the workplace, economic and ethnic integration moves faster. Among the approximately three hundred employees of Victor Gruen Associates, for example, were people with all sorts of skin colors and ethnic origins. The doors of the restrooms were inscribed with "Men" and "Ladies" in twenty-six languages. Overcoming prejudice in the workplace offers the hope that similar things can be achieved in housing in the foreseeable future. Only universalist planning measures will make a difference for the revitalization of the cities. It is necessary that planners recognize their professional and disciplinary boundaries but also devote their attention to social and political tasks.

REBIRTH OF URBANITY (THREE EXAMPLES)

Fort Worth

Immediately after the completion of the Northland Center in Detroit in 1954, *Harvard Business Review,* the business magazine of Harvard University, published an article of mine in which I said that the new planning principles applied to suburban projects were transferable to inner-city areas. I argued that the technique of integrating planning, which we could test at the malls for the first time, could be used even more reasonably and meaningfully for recovery of the inner cities.[10]

A direct consequence of this article was an invitation to the city of Fort Worth, Texas, from J. B. Thomas, president of the Texas Electric Service Company. In our first interview, he proved to be one of those rare captains of industry who is able to convert idealistic and deeply felt motives (like a love for his hometown as well as concern about its decline) into cool business reasoning. He explained that his company, which supplied the city and the region of Fort Worth with electricity and gas, was finding it increasingly difficult to do this successfully. The city's downtown district was in steep decline, while the suburbs would soon require enormous investments in new plants and distribution networks. If it was true, as I had alleged in the *Harvard Business Review,* that it was possible to achieve a marked revival of downtown and thereby increase the utilization of existing capital values of his company and, at the same time, to slow down the centrifugal expansion of the pipeline network to the outlying areas of the city, then this would be of great financial importance to the city. If Victor Gruen Associates was able to develop such a plan, then his company would pay for it in the most generous way.

This offer was enticing, so our team in Los Angeles dedicated itself to the eighteen-month intensive development of a general plan for the core area of Fort Worth. J. B. Thomas insisted that in order to preserve the integrity of the plan, it should be kept completely confidential until the public presentation; he personally served as the coordinator between Texas and Los Angeles.

In this way, the first urban revitalization plan in the United States, and probably even in the world, occurred. That the client was not a city agency but a private company that promoted urban environmental planning because of commercial reasons is provocative. The details of the Fort Worth plan are described and graphically demonstrated in my books *The Heart of Our Cities* and *Survival of the Cities.*[11] Here I will note only the main points of the plan:

- The entire area of downtown, with the exception of small electric buses, is cleared of traffic. All of the traffic is carried into underground streets.
- The resulting vacant land, all currently used for "noncore" functions such as parking lots, warehouses, gas stations, repair shops, and vacant building lots, is then repurposed for worthwhile uses such as residential buildings, offices, shops, cultural and social institutions, and public parks.
- There is a varied sequence of promenades, smaller and larger squares, and these public spaces are beautified by greenery and art, similar to arrangements in Northland Center.
- A bypass ring surrounds the central area as a multilane road—like the medieval defensive wall—in order to keep the core area free of car traffic. Six large parking garages are attached and serve as a collecting pond for vehicles. Pedestrians enter and leave the garage from the side that is closest to the center of the city. On the roofs of the parking garages are gardens, tennis courts, and other sports facilities.
- This ring is also accessible by a new local and express bus system, whose routes radiate out from the center of the region in all directions.

We provided a cost analysis and a brochure that explained the planning strategy. The city would enjoy better air quality, safer traffic conditions, and less noise, and would become a preferred place of residence. At the same time, the environmental conditions, richness of experience, and easy access of downtown would make it a favorite place to work and visit. New commercial ventures and new sites of cultural and social life would arise. All this would bring the city administration a significant increase in tax revenues.

When the plan was formally presented and discussed in detail in the presence of the mayor, the city council, and representatives of the national press, trade, and industry, the reaction was unconditionally enthusiastic. But the project was ill-fated. After the initial enthusiasm, the city council approved the general plan in principle, but voices of doubt and opposition were soon heard. Organized resistance arose from the owners of inner-city parking lots, who were concerned about their continuing existence, even though they were told that they could use the future large garages on the ring.

Then there were the problems involved in gaining federal funding for urban renewal. In addition, the great and proud state of Texas defended with obstinacy its "autonomous" status and was suspicious of any aid from Washington. Self-financing perhaps would have been possible in this rich state, but the city council, which felt patronized in this matter, was not willing to make extraordinary efforts in this direction. The construction of only one part of the proposed ring road was begun.

Drawing from the brochure *The Greater Fort Worth Tomorrow.* Library of the City of Vienna, City Hall.

Further Fate

Somehow, the concept remained in the consciousness of the population. In March 1978, *AIA Journal*, the official magazine of the American Institute of Architects, published a long article about the twin cities of Dallas and Fort Worth in which the remains of a nineteenth-century urbanity were praised. It stated that these qualities were first recognized in Victor Gruen's classic inner-city plan—the first project in the nation that promoted the vision of a car-free city center. The fact that this influential vision was not executed at that time prompted Edmund Bacon (a former city planner from Philadelphia) to state that the Fort Worth plan was the only unborn child that had produced hundreds of grandchildren, and one of those grandchildren had now returned home. Together with Lawrence Halprin, the city planning board had now introduced a plan that included some—in most instances, scaled-down—elements of Gruen's original proposal.[12]

But the plan also brought tangible results for Victor Gruen Associates. Its full significance for city fathers and the public was illustrated in the popular book *The Exploding Metropolis*:

> The 1956 Plan for Fort Worth, Texas, was the inspiration of Victor Gruen, a successful designer of shopping malls. . . .
>
> . . . Gruen's plan proposed a car-free office and retail downtown. A circumferential highway punctuated with six huge parking garages with spaces for 60,000 cars . . . was to make it possible for the downtown streets to be limited to pedestrians and reworked as two-story retail plazas. The drawings of kiosks, banners, tasteful coordinated signage, raised planters, and interesting street furniture and paving patterns suggested an exciting alternative to a car-clogged street.[13]

The central point was that the streets should be diversified, more intimate and at the same time more lively than before—this mental-spiritual dimension of the plan was something that many imitators did not understand.

This last point was particularly important to the copycats in an era when hundreds of cities and towns believed that they could awaken inner-city shopping streets to new life simply by setting up stoplights for automobiles on both ends. All these experiments, including some that put small flowerpots in the middle of the pavement, were doomed to failure from the outset. A road cannot be revived only by a subtraction (of automobiles); the addition of new functions and activities is needed as well.

As a result of the Fort Worth plan, we were asked to participate as planners or advisers on approximately fifty urban renewal projects, which often concerned the revitalization of inner cities. In the older cities of the East Coast, such as Philadelphia and Boston, the projects primarily concerned the preservation and conservation of valuable building stock and the improvement of the existing traffic. Due to our general plan, both in Boston and in Philadelphia, the subway systems were extended. In the newer cities of the Midwest, such as Cincinnati, Ohio, and Kalamazoo, Michigan, the projects focused on the protection of historic buildings. In the youngest cities on the West Coast, like San Bernardino and Sacramento in California, public transport systems had to be introduced at first. In addition to the rehabilitation of transport systems, our proposals aimed at bringing residents and cultural activities back into the city centers.

Gruenization

This method of integrated urban planning was dubbed "Gruenization" by the mass media, who are always eager to provide an activity with a label. Eventually, I was awarded the title "Father of the Pedestrian Street," which soon became as embarrassing as "Father of the Shopping Center."

From the Fort Worth project, we had learned that planning activities without the consent of the authorities was fruitless. But we soon found out that projects that come about only in cooperation with official authorities can also be viewed suspiciously by the people, hindered by citizen initiatives, and criticized by the mass media. We were successful with projects where we had cooperation from the responsible federal agency, a representative citizens' committee, and the city council.

Altering environmental planning requires political and public commitment and a complete response to the needs and aspirations of the citizens concerned. I can illustrate how the collaboration with government agencies and private interests in the core area of cities goes from design to implementation in the shortest time possible with two examples from the United States, one in the East and one in the West. But first, I will compare American cities with European ones.

Anatomy of the Cities

City center is not a common phrase in English. A certain part of town, mostly near the railway station or the port and marked by a variety of skyscrapers, is generally known as downtown. In the language of planners and the business world, it is called a CBD, or central business district. These areas have historically been dedicated to business and marked by a modest level of urban management.

In the streetcar era, employees settled down in the CBD, mostly in nice little wooden houses within walking distance of tram stations, while the wealthy, who possessed carriages, lived a little farther from downtown. Then the automobile age ascended in America, much earlier and more intensely than in Europe. When the majority of CBD employees could afford cars, they followed the example of the wealthy and moved to surrounding areas, steadily increasing their distance from downtown. Their former homes were emptied, but the vacuum was quickly filled by the mass immigration of those who had lost their jobs due to the mechanization of agriculture, as well as by members of ethnic minorities who had emigrated from their homelands. In economic boom times, they found employment in subordinate positions, similar to today's guest workers in Europe's industrialized countries. The run-down neighborhoods became the so-called gray rings that finally threatened to strangle the CBD.

That the major business cities of America did not also became centers of government had something to do with the puritanical attitude of the "Fathers of the Republic," such as George Washington and Thomas Jefferson. They regarded all European capitals as dens of iniquity. Because of this reasoning, they made sure that governments were established in insignificant rural communities, which became the capitals of the individual states. In this way, any potential influence of the corrupting business world on the people's representatives could be minimized. Also, the federal capital of Washington, D.C., had to be as distant as possible from the trade centers of the East. President Jefferson, an architect, predicted at that time that Washington would never have more than one hundred thousand inhabitants.[14] (In 1980, Washington's population was more than three million.)

By contrast, the seats of emperors, kings, and princes of the church in European cities formed cores around which rallied the members of the courts. Only a few of the privileged built palatial summer residences outside the fortified cities. Then the onset of the Industrial Revolution in Europe brought profound changes to the structure of cities. Heavy industry attracted hundreds of thousands who sought employment. This mass influx required mass accommodations that could be built only outside the city walls. Industrial development also brought new weapon systems, so that the old fortifications became useless. A numerically and economically powerful middle class evolved on the edges of the formerly fortified cities and forced the rulers to make democratic concessions. But the elite also increased their prestige with representative buildings and boulevards in their immediate vicinity. The population increase fused these "inner-city" areas with new suburbs.

At the beginning of World War II, there were fundamental contrasts between the anatomies of American and European cities. The mass use of the car had not yet begun in Europe. The inner cities and adjacent areas in Europe remained the homes of the materially better-off, but they were also the locations of all government agencies and almost all the cultural sites. In the U.S. suburbs, the "haves" settled in, whereas the suburbs of most European cities were vast fields of proletarian quarters with the lowest standards of living. In addition, the gardens and hunting grounds of former feudal lords were converted to public parks and recreation areas, so in this respect, the old European cities are superior to American cities.

If one disregards the destruction caused by World War II, this structural difference remained until the era of the so-called great economic miracle. But then came the outbreak of the European automotive age and, with it, incorrect or incomplete planning, which brought an equalization between European and American inner cities in terms of the problems afflicting them.

The central-city areas lost their populations, which bled away. Many historic city centers became central business districts, garnished with tourist attractions. In European cities, gray zones of neglect emerged, to be partly filled with a new type of proletariat, the guest workers.

The endless sprawl of cities resulting from the automobile age is a serious problem in the United States. But the problem is much more serious in densely populated Western and Central Europe, as one can see by comparing population density. The irony is that many American cities are trying vigorously to transform their anatomies based on the example of European cities (as they once existed), while many European cities eagerly and blindly rush to imitate the American destruction of the city, which has caused a crisis in the United States. In San Francisco's Central Market neighborhood, Market Street was narrowed and reinvented as a tree-lined avenue, while in European cities, existing avenues are being destroyed to make way for traffic. The United States is experiencing a renaissance of urbanity, while Europeans are engaged in the obliteration of their historic centers.

Midtown Plaza

In the city of Rochester, New York, which is the home of the Kodak photo company, the Midtown Plaza project represents an early example of how new life was given to the inner city in the years 1956 to 1961. Two great department stores, McCurdy's and Forman, which were friendly competitors, asked me for advice. McCurdy's had had a location on the main road for a long time, while Forman, having been very successful for about ten years, had invested all its capital in a store on the only lively side street in the central business district. But now, both stores were negatively affected by the general decline of the CBD. They had both opened branch stores in small shopping centers, but these did not produce the hoped-for profits. In 1956, they were faced with the choice of whether to build a large regional suburban shopping center like Southdale, and then completely withdraw from the CBD, or to support the very vague revitalization efforts of the city.

The regional population of the surrounding area was not sufficiently dense to justify a big center, so only the second choice was logical. As a result of my advice, McCurdy's and Forman first purchased a large area of land near to their stores, in the so-called gray ring. The land was acquired relatively cheaply from a multitude of small owners and extended up to a road running parallel to the main traffic artery.

This project proved to be extremely time-consuming. It wasn't possible to speak with the mayor about building a multifunctional ensemble in the middle of the CBD until 1958. He was sympathetic to the idea, but thought that the city council would want to know whether the proposed construction project fit harmoniously into a general plan that was already being developed. This general plan, it turned out, resembled the Fort Worth plan: it allowed for the establishment of an outer highway-type ring road and for an inner ring with parking garages.

For the city council, we worked out a plan that envisioned a widening of the inner ring road and demonstrated the possibility that this could transform the entire central district into a pedestrian area. Midtown Plaza would be an integral piece of the overall project. But its feasibility depended on three measures to be decided on by the city administration:

- First: A three-story parking garage with two thousand parking spaces had to be built, instead of the smaller one which had been previously proposed.
- Second: Part of the inner ring road, which formed the rear boundary of the project area, would need to be built soon.
- Third: The public bus system to the outskirts and to the inside of the city limits would need to be strengthened and improved.

It took several meetings with the entire council before these three conditions were accepted. To ensure close cooperation between public authorities and private enterprise, we were entrusted by the city council with the design of the garage.

The project was essentially a translation of our work in the suburbs to the city center. It was similar to Southdale in that all the key sites were grouped around a three-story air-conditioned room, though this room was significantly larger than the garden courtyard at Southdale. Since it would be frequented mostly by pedestrians and bus users, it differed from a peripheral shopping center in that an extensive parking area with thousands of spaces would be replaced with an underground parking area.

Besides the two stores, both of which were considerably enlarged, the center contained about seventy shops and a wide range of other urban functions, such as a central bus station, administrative centers, schools and offices, a hotel, a panoramic

Model of Midtown Plaza, Rochester, New York. Courtesy of Gruen Associates.

restaurant, and medical offices. In striking contrast to peripheral shopping centers, where the so-called public spaces remained in private ownership, the city would own the large covered space and its arcades.

The pessimists who had predicted it would be impossible to win stakeholders for an inner-city project were surprised that the entire center was rented at the time of the opening in 1961. The opening ceremony took place in front of more than ten thousand people in the central square. The two department store companies very much enjoyed the fact that Midtown Plaza proved to be a big success. Consequences were inevitable: a significant number of offices, shops, and hotels were built in the vast area around Midtown Plaza. Kodak changed its plans for an office building located outside the city and built at Midtown Plaza instead. Restoration activity throughout the downtown area took off, while projects for shopping centers outside the city limits were buried in silence. The city council noted these developments with great satisfaction.

Midtown Plaza, Rochester, New York, 2008. Photograph by Anette Baldauf.

A soulless central business district had been transformed into a real town center. It was especially great to be able to visit this "main square" in any kind of weather and at any time of day. Visitors could stroll, gather in coffeehouses, hold political rallies, see exhibitions or concerts, or attend ceremonies and high school proms.[15]

In the middle of this main square was a European-style clock, two and a half stories high, known as the Clock of Nations. It was basically a musical clock with chimes, and soon became a landmark of Rochester. It was designed by Rudolf L. Baumfeld in a baroque style. Puppets representing the many ethnic groups in Rochester danced around a central clock tower, which rang with chimes and music. At noon each day, when it displayed the most activity, the clock was admired by many onlookers.[16]

This toy cost our clients a lot of money, but it became popular to an unexpected extent. When it had to be shut down for repair, its subsequent start-up was the subject of newspaper headlines. This cheerful clock was merely an eyesore for purist architects. To me, it confirmed the view that architecture should be not only serious but also humorous, emotional, and imaginative.

Fresno

A second urban development project was the revitalization of the core area of the city of Fresno, California. This project went from planning to implementation between 1958 and 1964. Fresno has about two hundred thousand inhabitants; it is the market center of the fertile San Joaquin Valley and is located halfway between Los Angeles and San Francisco.

The plan, which followed the principles of Gruenization, is described and illustrated in my books *The Heart of Our Cities* and *Survival of the Cities.* In this case, the central pedestrian area was connected by passages to the neighboring administrative center, the town's great park, and a new conference center and hotel.

The project was undertaken by Victor Gruen Associates together with the landscape architecture firm of Eckbo, Dean, Austin and Williams (EDAW). Again, it was important not only to solve the most challenging planning and traffic problems but also to create an urban and diverse atmosphere in a traffic-free area. The writer Bernard Taper testified to the project's success in *McCall's* magazine in April 1966. He reported that while writing the piece, he was sitting in the middle of Fulton Street, the main street at Fresno's center. Only a few years ago he would have been run over, arrested, or unceremoniously packed off to a psychiatrist for doing this, but now sitting on the street was simply part of a new lifestyle—a lifestyle that assumed that the city center was there for the people. Instead of traffic congestion, exhaust gases, and the usual ugliness of an American city, he was now surrounded by gardens, fountains, ponds, and many beautiful sculptures. For children there were imaginatively stimulating playgrounds. And for the elderly or those seeking quietness there were benches shaded by vines.[17]

The secret behind the rapid implementation of this project was that we had to solve the same task for three clients. These were the federal authority, the Urban Development Corporation, as well as the city council and a committee of merchants called the Hundred Percent. It required some diplomacy to reconcile the interests of all three, which at first seemed to be at odds with one other. The best thanks for our efforts occurred when the merchants, who did not initially believe they could do any business without car traffic, presented us with the sum of $150,000 for the purchase of artworks in the pedestrian areas.

Nevertheless, it should be noted that this project was not a complete success. It later proved impossible to lure larger commercial enterprises into this lively new city center. Attracted by the economic potential of the city fully reflected in our project, speculators built a large shopping center just outside the city limits. Because of low land prices and the nearly complete lack of regional planning, the authorities could not prevent this act of piracy.

The failure to protect the outskirts of cities as recreation sites has caused immeasurable damage around the world. Expensive urban renewal, such as that in Fresno, is deprived of much of its value, and the tax revenues of the cities also suffer.

In 1976, for example, a lack of effective regional planning prevented the authorities of the city of Vienna from averting the opening of a gigantic shopping mall five hundred meters outside the city limits. The center, whose major commercial tenants were French, Swedish, and Swiss companies, went on to attract a considerable part of the purchasing power of Viennese residents.[18]

GROWTH

In the late sixties, Victor Gruen Associates was one of the twenty largest architectural firms in the United States. In 1967, we employed about three hundred people in three offices in Los Angeles, New York, and Washington, D.C.

Our scope had grown enormously. Along with the design of individual buildings, such as shops, homes, banks, department stores, office buildings, apartment buildings, and religious and cultural monuments, we were increasingly winning long-term contracts for projects such as shopping centers within and outside cities, satellite towns, regional plans, and general plans for the future development of large cities.

We took on projects in Canada, South America, Australia, Europe, and Iran. We began to recognize that large-scale projects took many years, even decades, to complete and usually required political commitment and compromise. My partners and I had to become active in the political arena at the levels of city, state, and federal government. Our political commitment should be mentioned here: I contributed to the urban planning elements of the electoral program of John F. Kennedy, and during the presidency of Lyndon B. Johnson I collaborated with the secretary of housing and urban development, Robert Weaver, and the secretary of the interior, Stewart Udall, in a study on how to develop new cities on yet-undeveloped terrain. This last project involved the very feasible goal of curbing excess population growth in existing urban areas while making model improvements to existing city cores.

Our growth also led to financial difficulties, particularly with the rise in production and overhead costs. An increasing proportion of the partners' time and energy had to be devoted to administrative and organizational tasks, so the time for creative activities decreased. Nevertheless, we were barely able to resist this urge for growth.

PUBLIC PLANNING AND THE PRIVATE SECTOR

With the exception of projects such as Midtown Plaza and Fresno, large-area city planning is rather frustrating in a free market economy. The U.S. federal government introduced the Urban Development Corporation as a way of ensuring that city planning remained independent of political changes in city governments; this created the possibility that many projects in the general public interest could be completed. But difficulties almost always arose in the transition between public planning and private, entrepreneurial execution. The Urban Development Corporation controls proved too weak in preventing planning in the interest of profit. The discrepancy between public planning ideals and profit-driven execution seriously called into question the degree to which the taxpayer should pay for the planning and improvement of urban environment.

I was confronted with this problem again in France in the seventies, and solving it seemed to require a shift in the demarcation between public and private activities.

In the interest of public welfare, public agencies should go beyond merely providing a concept. They should also be responsible for generating all construction documents, and only then should they assign the physical construction to private entrepreneurs. In such a case, the public should remain the owner of the project because it has paid the costs, and the public should also be eligible to benefit from the revenues generated by the project.

The public agency should invite a limited number of private companies to bid for the job according to public guidelines. An appropriately assembled jury would choose a plan that serves the interests of the common good and could therefore be executed. In this case, appeals would be possible, which would induce the chosen entrepreneur to follow his own plan faithfully.

In this way, it seems right and proper that the responsible entrepreneur who bears the costs of land acquisition and planning, and is the owner of the new facility, would profit from it. For all these reasons, forward-looking planning in democratic countries with free market economies can be a very tedious and often unsuccessful business.

GENERAL PLAN FOR TEHRAN

In the hopes that planning under an authoritarian regime would be simpler, we accepted an invitation from the Iranian government to prepare a general plan for Tehran. We had worked very hard to win this project. Through the mediation of the Iranian architect Abdol-Aziz Farmanfarmaian, who had excellent connections with the shah's regime, we managed to get the job without even having to pay the usual local commissions.

We established a work space in Tehran and placed it under the management of one of our associates, Fereydoon Ghaffari, who was of Iranian origin and spoke Farsi. Coordination with Farmanfarmaian's Tehran studio was facilitated by the fact that his office chief was a native of Innsbruck and spoke the best Tyrolean German with me.

To coordinate the overall project planning, His Majesty Reza Shah Pahlavi appointed a planning director: his wife, Her Majesty Farah Pahlavi Shahbanou. I was instructed to discuss all the important planning issues with Her Majesty personally.

Due to a number of formalities—referring to her as Your Majesty, leaving the room by moving away backward—our first meeting was rather stiff, and we didn't accomplish much more than getting to know each other a bit. She seemed like an attractive, very educated, and intelligent woman. For our second visit, I tried to create a more informal atmosphere. I knew that she had studied architecture in Paris. I told Her Majesty that we would actually be working together, and therefore we could regard each other as colleagues, and she was flattered. Now it seemed like nothing would get in the way of an insightful exchange of ideas.

Some of the problems and objectives that we discussed and decided upon together were as follows:

- That the plan should be prepared for implementation over a twenty-year period.
- That the then-current large annual population growth would lead to serious problems over the next twenty years, and that it could not be absorbed by any urban planning. Therefore, sociopolitical actions at the national level would be necessary to stop a rural exodus and to create employment opportunities in other parts of the country.
- That measures to improve public health were a priority. A public water supply and sewage system would improve unsanitary conditions in which wells and septic tanks were so close together that drinking water was contaminated.
- That a modern mass transportation system in the form of a subway would be necessary to prevent the destruction of the city by car traffic.
- That the housing shortage would need to be addressed with new construction, and that this housing would need to take into account local living traditions. (During the summer months, many people live in courtyards and sleep on their rooftops.)
- That in terms of urban structure, a polycentric system with one main center and numerous neighborhood and district centers should be created as a way of maintaining a tradition of bazaars and open markets.

In our many conferences, Her Majesty proved well suited to her post as director of planning. She was socially and environmentally conscious. Our planning was making good progress. But we soon realized that His Majesty the shah, whom I never had the honor to meet, was in the meantime expressing his own plans to our Iranian partner Farmanfarmaian. These plans were focused on prestige and on representative buildings, boulevards, and monuments. Some of these wishes seemed manageable, albeit undesirable, but others were actually commands from His Majesty, and we were confronted with a crisis of conscience because of this.

One command was to create a giant pedestrian square in the city center, with the dimensions of the famous historic square of Isfahan. His Majesty believed that this place should be surrounded by magnificent buildings such as an opera house. But the largest and tallest structures should help to express the source of Iranian wealth: skyscrapers as administrative buildings of the oil industry. I explained as tactfully as possible that this command of His Majesty would make me very unhappy for planning reasons. This was on a Thursday.

Her Majesty tried to calm me. She said I would be completely in error if I interpreted this proposal as a command. His Majesty was not an authoritarian man, and he would have put forth these ideas only as a way to find out what experts would say on the matter. So if substantial arguments against his ideas were possible, I should explain so in writing. I said I didn't have enough time to do this. His Majesty had scheduled a meeting for Monday, at which a final decision about the big square would be made. So Her Majesty said I should try to explain my concerns to her. If she came to agree with me, then she would have the long weekend (Friday, Saturday, and Sunday) to persuade His Majesty of our viewpoint.

I put forward the following arguments: A place of such gigantic dimensions could not be crossed by Tehran's pedestrians in the blazing sun. The beautiful historical square of Isfahan had been designed for specific functions, none of which exist in modern Iran. In Isfahan, for example, jousting tournaments were held, and the surrounding buildings had been used as viewing stands. That square was a place of religious ceremonies, dominated by a great mosque. The site also served as a regional trading center, where merchants pitched tents each month. Today, jousting tournaments are no longer common. For major sporting events there are stadiums. Trade is conducted in shops and department stores, and mosques are available in sufficient number.

Using some books I had brought, I showed Her Majesty pictures of the Italian Renaissance cities, with their densely woven urban patterns, in which a permanent shift to close, shady lanes and medium-sized places with colonnades achieved a high degree of urbanity. I said that considering the similarity of climatic conditions, a similar design would be suitable for the car-free downtown area of Tehran. Her Majesty was completely persuaded by these arguments and told me that I could look forward to the Monday meeting with confidence.

But it turned out that she was too optimistic. On Monday, His Majesty said that the place would have to be planned and built based on his proposals. He added that since Her Majesty had been entrusted with the coordination of planning, he as shah would make all the decisions. He went on to say that if certain people he did not want to mention by name continued to put crazy ideas into Her Majesty's head, those people would not be welcome in Iran anymore.

I paid a farewell visit to Her Majesty, where I found her a bit depressed. She regretted that she could not achieve anything, but His Majesty had broken off his discussion with her by threatening that he would not enact the law of succession (through which she would continue the regency for their minor son in the event of the shah's premature death).

The general plan influenced by the imperialist desires of His Majesty was completed, with a minimum of my personal participation, by our partners and associates. While under way, it had to be modified repeatedly because of the inexorable population growth of the city. The award of the contract for subway construction also complicated completion of the general plan. Originally, the Soviet Union had offered to build the subway. But when the Soviets asked for a huge supply of oil, the contract was awarded to the owner company of the Paris Metro, which was tasked with conforming to our general plan. Whether these problems were ever solved successfully, and how they may have contributed to the exploding metropolis of Tehran, is beyond my knowledge.

Later, after our consulting on urban planning issues for the military regime of Venezuela proved to be equally fruitless, our belief that planning would be easier under dictatorships than in market democracies was thoroughly vanquished.

RUSSIA

What happens to city planning in a Communist state, which is indeed dedicated to a planned economy and in which the profit motive is eliminated, since everything belongs to the state? We hoped to get an answer to this question in 1963, when a delegation of fourteen Russian colleagues visited our offices in Los Angeles as part of a tour sponsored by the U.S. State Department. Two interpreters were present because the State Department thought that a second one should monitor the Russian translator, to make sure he translated everything accurately.

We presented some of our architectural and planning projects to provide our guests with an overview of the activities of a privately run business. The men showed mild interest and asked only a few questions; the atmosphere was fairly stiff. Therefore, I proposed that the entire group should join me for dinner. It was already five o'clock in the afternoon when I informed my wife of an impending invasion of about twenty Russians, but she responded coolly. She prepared an excellent meal and laid in a considerable stock of vodka.

The Russians were very civilized guests; they brought us gifts of art and architecture books, one of which was on old Russian churches. My wife received caviar and small folk art objects, which were obviously mass-produced.

During the cocktail hour the Russians drank American whiskey, while the Americans preferred Russian vodka. When the tongues began to loosen, a lively debate developed. But it was not about the pros and cons of professional activity in one or the other economic system; rather, it was about the rivalry between city planners and architects. Soon two parties formed: one of Russian and American planners, the other of Russian and American architects. During the meal, I made a toast to the friendship of both peoples. But when I proposed a second toast to the fruitful cooperation of planners and architects, the head of the Russian delegation, a planner, stood up and shouted, "Nyet!" He explained that such a thing would be impossible, and the American planners agreed. Despite this exchange, the evening proceeded in high spirits. We made acquaintances that proved helpful when we took a study trip to Russia in autumn that year.

In Moscow, we were accompanied by the inevitable Intourist tour guide.[19] We admired the official tourist attractions in Moscow and were impressed by the exemplary maintenance, especially of the churches. The subway, whose "neobaroque" design shocked me a little, was great. On rides through newer parts of town, we saw main streets of enormous breadth lined with sterile apartment buildings of low quality. Here and there was a modern department store with sparsely stocked shelves. One got the impression that the planners of the new Moscow had had a mixture of Paris and New York in mind: the broad boulevards were Parisian, and the skyscrapers, where public institutions were housed, represented New York. Our expectation that neon signs would not exist in a Communist country was disappointed. The names of state enterprises and political slogans were all announced with impressive neon lights.

During a visit to Moscow's central planning agency, an institution with sixteen thousand employees, I was kindly received by one of the directors and invited to present a lecture to a larger group of city planners the next day. When I declined by explaining that my officially established itinerary required a visit to Leningrad the next day, arrangements were immediately made for me to present a lecture at the central planning office there.

Leningrad, formerly St. Petersburg, is far superior to Moscow. Founded in 1703 by Czar Peter the Great, who wanted to open Russia to Western Europe, it was planned and built in swampy terrain, which caused great difficulties and necessitated human sacrifice. Situated at the Gulf of Finland, in the delta estuary of the Neva River, and crossed by dozens of channels, Leningrad is reminiscent of Venice. As in that city, most of the houses are built on wooden pillars. The major construction activity took place between 1801 and 1825, when huge complexes were created with planning and architectural unity.

In Leningrad, named Petrograd after the outbreak of World War I, the contrast between the wealth of the rulers and the impoverished plight of the citizens was most visible. Riots were frequent there, and these climaxed with the storming of the Winter Palace in 1917.

Leningrad natives—as we learned from our charming tour guide, who was an architect—are very proud of the preserved beauty and history of their city. In comparison, they say, Moscow is a large village without any culture. In fact, after the mustiness of Moscow, we felt that the atmosphere in Leningrad was more cultured and liberal.

The Leningrad planning office was already prepared for my visit. About forty senior members of a planning collective had gathered in a large room—these were the people who had been entrusted with the design of new towns in many parts of Russia. At the request of the chairman, I talked about the problems of American cities, about attempts to solve them, and about my own thoughts on this topic. Our tour guide served as an interpreter, and he translated fluently, with great intensity and enthusiasm. After a round of applause subsided, I was asked to critically evaluate one of the town planning projects exhibited on the walls of the room. I attempted to avoid this potentially dangerous request by explaining my principle of practicing no criticism abroad. This did not work: to duck out of this task would have been an unfriendly gesture.

After a brief review, I focused on a project for the satellite city of Novosibirsk. The city, I thought, would not be worth living in, because nothing was planned to shield the population from the environmental effects of the major industrial companies. The road system, which was a strictly geometric grid, seemed boring and sterile. The endless rows of identical residential buildings and the lack of city squares and parks would make any identification with either the housing or the environment impossible. In summary, I said that the project reminded me of the worst examples of capitalist speculation, in which all human needs are sacrificed at the altar of profit.

After this, I received frenetic applause. Since I had condemned the project so harshly, I was somewhat surprised, and I asked if the translation had been accurate. The chairman assured me that my criticism had been understood correctly. Explaining the planning process in a planning collective, he pointed out that each team leader was responsible for a particular job, but that all projects would then be judged by all the leaders of the collective. The project that I had discussed was scheduled for such a review the next day. The collective member Mr. Y. (here he pointed to a man) had been a thorn in his side for quite some time. So I had done the whole collective a big favor by pointing out the shortcomings of his project. In addition, he said that in some respects, the planner could not be held fully responsible. As for the location of industries, he explained that it would be extremely difficult to exert an influence on this. Planning, he said with a sigh, has its limits, unfortunately. He asked if there were similar problems in America, a question to which I could answer yes with full conviction. But I thought to myself, in a democratic system it would probably be easier to make private industrial enterprises follow environmental protections. And for the author of such an unfortunate plan in the United States, the consequences would be considerably less damaging than those that I had just unintentionally incurred for Mr. Y.

AT THE WHITE HOUSE

At about the same time we were working on the master plan for Tehran, I was visiting the White House every month, and this was how I came to understand the vast differences between authoritarian and democratic systems.

After a stay in Hawaii, where I had been working on the design of the core area of Honolulu, I decided to visit one of the nearly uninhabited islands of the Hawaiian archipelago, just for relaxation. I instructed my secretary to hold my mail for two weeks. She asked jokingly if this applied to letters from the White House, and I told her that in that case, she could make an exception. The hotel was an ideal place for resting. It consisted of a small central building and a number of widely spaced bungalows right on a sandy beach. We were unpacking when we received a telegram. I was told that I had been nominated as a member of a White House committee to beautify the capital, and that the chairman would expect me to be at the opening session in two days.

This is how the vacation ended, and I was able to be at the meeting in D.C. in time. The committee consisted of about a dozen members, including the mayor of Washington, D.C., who was named George Washington and who was a black man; Stewart Udall, the U.S. secretary of the interior; Lawrence Rockefeller; and other important personalities of the city.

The chairmanship was held by the First Lady, Mrs. Lady Bird Johnson, who seemed a bit insecure in her new role. She opened the meeting by reading a prepared statement: millions of people visited the nation's capital annually, she said, and as the symbol of the country, Washington should therefore be beautiful. The beautification of Washington with flower beds was a national task, and the committee should realize this task.

The discussion that followed focused merely on cosmetic beauty. One wealthy lady offered a donation of hundreds of blooming azalea bushes, which was gratefully accepted. Finally, I interrupted the discussion. The objective of beautifying the national capital was highly commendable, I said. But it was unclear whether azalea bushes would improve street scenes in the slums or whether they would merely accentuate the urban misery even more. Beautification should intervene more deeply than simply removing "ugliness."

I asked for permission to ask Mrs. Johnson a personal question: "When you get up in the morning, do you wash your face first and then put on your makeup, or vice versa?" Mrs. Johnson blushed and said, "I wash myself first, of course. In addition, I understand your question. Before our next meeting I'll consider the slums thoroughly."

After the meeting, I offered the secretary of the interior my resignation, since I believed I had embarrassed or even offended Mrs. Johnson. Mr. Udall laughed and said I should simply continue acting in this way, because this was exactly what he had hoped I would do. Later, the committee's work began to change because of the insights Mrs. Johnson gained on a series of walks through the city. Issues of urban renewal and the housing shortage came to the fore.

The entire committee took bus tours out into some of the more troubled areas of the city. When we visited one of the black ghettos, the committee group was surrounded by hundreds of women (their men were working). After several appeals to her, Mrs. Johnson decided to deliver a short speech on the porch of one family's home. In a warm, easy manner, she spoke of the problems that were common to all women: concerns about their husbands, their finances, and especially their children. A wave of sympathy washed over her. To the dismay of her security detail, she went into the crowd, where the women hugged and kissed the First Lady. When she returned to us, Mrs. Johnson seemed deeply moved.

I began to feel more respect and admiration for this extraordinarily clever woman. A relationship of mutual trust and friendship began. The complete lack of any formality in the White House, where work spaces and private rooms were mixed up, was a striking contrast to the court manners in Tehran. Once, while I was in search of a bathroom, I walked into the bedroom of one of the president's daughters, who was reading on her bed. She said hello, then jumped up and showed me the right way to the lavatory.

Farah Pahlavi Shahbanou and Lady Bird Johnson actually knew each other, and corresponded frequently. Once, when Her Majesty asked me to send a message to the First Lady of the United States, Mrs. Johnson received me for tea in her boudoir. When I suddenly saw a tape recorder in front of the fireplace, I inquired about its purpose, whereupon Mrs. Johnson confessed that she had thought I had brought it. When I said I hadn't, she averred that it probably belonged to one of her daughters, who had the habit of leaving things lying around.

The collaboration with Mrs. Johnson was also important because she had a great influence on her husband, the president. The newspapers reported that she had encouraged him to read *The Heart of Our Cities* by putting it on his bedside table every night.

Mrs. Johnson's interest in the work of the committee did not lessen with time. Even after her husband's term in office ended, she spent much of her energy on the topic of environmental planning.

After these experiences working with both authoritarian and democratic systems, I have come to believe that in all economic systems, even those that have committed themselves to substantive growth, environmentally friendly planning is an extremely difficult, long-term affair. But in democratic societies, there are at least opportunities for it.

TURBULENCE

These professional developments were also influenced by personal experiences—both joyful and tragic. I had a happy marriage with Lazette van Houten, whom I had married after divorcing Elsie in 1952. Lazette and I lived in our New York apartment and sometimes shared a small house in Brentwood, a western suburb of Los Angeles. We traveled a lot and spent our vacations in different European countries every year. Lazette, who was originally from Ohio, particularly loved the Austrian countryside. So it happened that every year we spent at least one week at the Hotel Weißes Rößl on the Wolfgangsee.

It was there that we met a charming girl named Kemija Salihefendic in 1959. She worked in the hotel business. From friendly discussions, we learned that Kemija had been only eight years old when she had fled from the Yugoslav war and partisan turmoil of 1945, in which her father was killed and her siblings were lost. She had arrived all alone in the south of Carinthia, where a peasant family took her in. We offered to adopt this extremely lovable and capable young girl. She rejected this idea and said that she would like to continue her independent life, but she offered us her friendship. From that moment, we maintained a lively correspondence and met her regularly during our summer vacations.

VIENNA

During these vacations, we regularly spent several days in Vienna. I needed these visits to my hometown, and they touched me deeply. My first return to Vienna took place in 1948: I wanted to deal with the nostalgia that haunted my dreams. This first visit was dramatic. Even arriving at the station that had once been the Westbahnhof was a shock. Nothing was left of the building but rubble. You got out of the train and you were on the street. An old taxi in poor condition took me to the Hotel Astoria, and we passed the ruins of the ring road; piles of brick and stone were distributed throughout the city. I wandered through this scene of horror for several days, riding the old trams, whose windows were boarded up, all the way up into the Vienna Woods. I finished my return visit in profound grief over the state of this city and its inhabitants.

Many of my friends and acquaintances, because of their persecution in Austria, hated the country, particularly Vienna, and they never returned. I did not share this feeling. I was convinced that every generalization, judgment, and prejudice expressed in national or racial terms was ethically irresponsible.

Based on my experience with mass hysteria and terror, I was able to understand that hundreds of thousands had not dared to defy the Nazis. Furthermore, I perceived that the true friends of my youth, many of whom I met on my return visits to Vienna, felt they had to do the right thing in that time of terror. Many of them had emigrated temporarily, others had fought in the resistance movement at great personal risk. Even among those who were in the army or were party members were many who had behaved decently. This knowledge always prevented me from being hostile to my hometown.

In 1960, Lazette suggested that we should buy a home in Vienna for our old age, and I agreed enthusiastically. In the Fourth District, at Schwarzenbergplatz, we acquired an apartment that had been reduced to a pile of rubble.[20] As we inspected the devastation—parquet floors burned by fire, plaster knocked from the walls and ceilings, sinks and toilets ripped out—Lazette broke into tears. We could never build an apartment from these ruins, she cried. But for me, the task of setting up a modern apartment in a building built in 1890 was alluring. Recalling the experience I had gained remodeling old apartments from 1933 to 1938, I zealously began to create a comfortable home. By 1974, it would be my main residence in Europe.

After the contracts were awarded for the reconstruction of the apartment, we asked Kemija to monitor the work in our absence. She accomplished this with such skill that on our next holiday, in the summer of 1961, we could have an informal housewarming party for some old friends in our "new" Vienna apartment. Lazette and Kemija worked together to cater the event.

LAZETTE'S DEATH

In 1962, I traveled to Austria with my artistically talented daughter Peggy, who planned to attend artist Oskar Kokoschka's summer academy in Salzburg. I stayed briefly in Vienna to visit Kemija and to see our finished apartment, and one evening,

I had a long telephone conversation with Lazette. A few hours later, at 3:00 a.m., I received a phone message that my wife had suffered a stroke and died in our home in Los Angeles.

Completely bewildered, I returned to Los Angeles. It was only the loving care of my son Michael that prevented me from having a nervous breakdown. The meetings with the greedy undertakers were disgusting. I took care of Lazette's will and estate and arranged for the future care of her elderly mother. After that, it was impossible for me to continue living in Los Angeles and New York, in the homes where I had lived with my wife. Likewise, it seemed to me impossible to take up my work in the studio again.

KEMIJA

So I returned to Vienna to immerse myself in work. In order to forget my pain, I worked from early morning until late at night on the English manuscript for *The Heart of Our Cities.*

Kemija ran the household, and one night during supper, she told me suddenly that she did not want to call me "papa" anymore. She told me she had discovered quite a different feeling for me. In my grief, I took note of this remark only superficially, and I reflected on its full meaning only much later. I left Vienna after a few months. Kemija, who had become a beautician, remained in the apartment there.

In Los Angeles, I took up my work again, but I was overwhelmed with invitations to social events. Soon I noticed that these were well-intentioned attempts to set me up with a new female companion. But these temptations left me cold, and my thoughts wandered back to Vienna, to that girl who did not want to call me papa anymore. Telling her that one of my friends, who resembled me in character and appearance, needed a housekeeper, I invited her to come to America. Her response was prompt. She accepted, but only on the condition that the aforesaid friend not only resembled me but was identical to me.

At Christmas of 1962, I met Kemija in New York; from there, we traveled to Los Angeles. The happy ending of this story is that, in spite of the frowns of many friends and acquaintances about our age difference of thirty-three years, Kemija and I were married on February 28, 1963.

Besides love, a "Pygmalion-like" idea on my part may have also played a role; perhaps I wanted to show the world to an orphan from Bosnia, and to shape her. But I soon discovered that a shaping occurred in the opposite direction. With her incredible adaptability and great wisdom, her love and youthful enthusiasm, I was inspired with new energy to undertake new adventures, new work, and a new way of life.

We agreed that we needed a new home in Los Angeles, to overcome our grief over Lazette. But it was Kemija who, with unerring instinct, found that unique house among many offers. She insisted we buy it, despite my financial concerns. Afterward, I immediately felt at home there.[21] It suited my aesthetic demands completely—and we didn't even have to rebuild it!

The advantages of this house were its spaciousness, the favorable arrangement of the rooms to each other, a big garden with old trees, and its perfect fit with the climatic conditions of Southern California. It was a faithful copy of a Spanish hacienda. With its thick, Mexican-style walls of adobe, its shady colonnade, its red-tile four-layered roof, it very much stood out from typical California homes, including the ultramodern ones. It refuted the myth that one could not live without air-conditioning in Southern California: because of its energy-conscious design, its interior remained cool during heat waves.

We did not take possession of the house until December 14, 1963. After we removed a few external decorative elements, we painted two rooms and moved in modern furniture, mostly of Scandinavian origin. We opened our door on New Year's Eve 1963 to one hundred guests. Our astonished friends admired how swiftly we'd settled in, and some of them told us they had the impression that we had already lived in this cozy place for a long time.

We lived in this house until 1974. It was the first time since I had fled Vienna in 1938 that I felt I was living in a private environment that was appropriate for me. I had more or less just inhabited my many other homes in the United States. But we would also have beautiful homes in various other countries later, thanks to Kemija's talent and versatility.

After this, though, we always tried to create a connection between the old and the new. In 1970, we established an apartment and office in Paris in a nineteenth-century building. In Austria, we transformed a manor house from 1900 that had been neglected for several decades into a little paradise. It was at the foot of a two-thousand-meter mountain called Rax, and it became our weekend and holiday retreat. And we were moved to settle down in Bergholtzgut, partly because of childhood memories I had of holidays with my parents in the area. Here my environmental planning efforts would find practical expression.

My colleagues may find it strange that I've never tried to build a new house for myself. But breathing new life into something old, something existing, has always been much more interesting to me.

Kemija Salihefendic, Prein, Austria, 1970. Courtesy of Peggy Gruen.

UNFINISHED SYMPHONIES

Our growing field of responsibility forced us to streamline the organization after 1960. It was becoming impossible for all seven partners to devote their full attention to all of the projects that were in progress simultaneously. If our overall performance was already satisfactory, it was only because of a loyal management team of associates and department heads, which had been built over many years of cooperation. A reorganization of the firm resulted in a more precise division of work space and responsibility.

This delegation of responsibility did not lessen my involvement in all of our work, despite the trust I placed in my employees. I frequently walked through the drafting rooms, settled myself at some of the desks, gave advice on individual projects, expressed criticism or suggestions with quick sketches. I did this with the best of intentions and all due courtesy. But this habit was resented by those who took care of our finances. "Each of your walks," they said, "costs the firm thirty to fifty thousand dollars." I did not ignore this argument, but I also did not want to be a figurehead.

Finally we agreed that in addition to my organizational obligations, I could personally oversee one or two projects, from design to completion, every year. Although I dedicated myself to these projects with all my energy, and they mostly had strong public support, many of them did not come to pass, were only completed much later, or were modified substantially by other designers and architects. Three of these "unfinished symphonies" seem important enough to describe. These three projects were dream projects, desired by every architect. They were realistic, despite their fantastic nature, but also taken seriously by the authorities and the media.

World's Fair 1964

The first dream project concerned the international world exhibition proposed for 1964 in America. Since many cities in the United States were competing to be the site of this world exhibition, President Eisenhower appointed a three-member commission that was to consider the candidate cities' proposals. Then the commission would prepare a recommendation to the president.

In the early 1960s, we were asked by the Chamber of Commerce of the city of Washington, D.C., to prepare a project that would be financially supported by the Broadway producer Roger Stevens, with whom I had become acquainted through my theatrical activities in 1939. The choice of Washington—a federal capital with monuments, spacious avenues, and national cultural sites—as the site of the world's fair was not an obvious one. We therefore developed a plan, drawings, and a detailed report that stressed the mission and the origins of the world exhibitions—the first one had taken place in London's Crystal Palace more than a hundred years ago. In the recent past, world exhibitions had devolved into propaganda events for industry and tourism. We also suggested that it was unfortunate that in the past, the vast resources invested by organizers, exhibitors, and city government were typically abandoned after the exhibition period of six months. My concept contained two fundamentally new ideas: first, the exhibition should have as its theme the question of how urban life could be improved; second, it should be planned and constructed in such a way that it could be converted into a model satellite town after the period of the exhibition proper. An undeveloped, scenic plot of land would be secured in the Washington area. After the end of the fair—which was expected to be attended by about fifty million people—significant urban services that had been created for the exhibition would remain to be used by the new satellite city. Express train lines and highways would establish connections between Washington and Baltimore; an entire technical infrastructure and pipeline network for water, electricity, heating, cooling, and disposal facilities would be in place; and pedestrian areas, parks, and an electric vehicle network would have been established, all to support foot traffic in the new city. Furthermore, this future city would swiftly have major urban institutions after the rededication of the exhibition halls and administrative buildings as opera houses, theaters, town halls, museums, amusement parks, shopping bazaars, and hotels.

A few weeks after we had presented our project to the commission, my partner Edgardo Contini and I were attending a meeting of the Architectural League of New York when we were informed that radio and television broadcasts were reporting that the commission had chosen our design for the world exhibition in Washington. We embraced each other joyfully, and we cheered.

But our jubilation ended with the morning papers. These reported that Nelson Rockefeller, then governor of New York, had visited the ailing President Eisenhower in the hospital to tell him that the American financial world would not contribute a cent for any world exhibition outside New York City. Under this pressure, Eisenhower had no choice but to ignore the commission's advice and decide in favor of a world's fair in New York.

In the spring of 1960, the cultural magazine *Horizon* published an eight-page article in which the Washington world exhibition concept was extensively illustrated, analyzed, and praised. The author of the article, the architecture critic of the *New York Times,* Ada Louise Huxtable, appealed to the organizers of the world's fair to follow some of the basic ideas of our concept. She wrote that Victor Gruen had proposed a plan for a 1964 fair that could be converted into a permanent community—a full-scale demonstration of what the city of the future could be, as the site would be turned into a new satellite city after the fair ended.[22] Nothing like that happened. After eighteen months, the New York World's Fair was abandoned—leaving behind the usual mountain of debt and unusable buildings.

Valencia

My second unfinished symphony was a plan for a city of 250,000 inhabitants on two hundred acres of land that had previously been used as farmland. The unusual thing about this project was not only its size but also that we were dealing with an idealistic principle.

The project arose from a group that consisted of about thirty people. I got to know them all at one of the excellent old clubs in San Francisco. The head, Scott Newhall (editor of the liberal newspaper the *San Francisco Chronicle*), explained that I would reside with the Newhall family—the grandchildren and great grandchildren of the first Mr. Newhall—who had acquired, in an earlier time, when Los Angeles was still an inconsequential village, the land for a large ranch forty miles outside the town.

In the meantime, much had changed. The Los Angeles basin and the adjacent hills and valleys had become the living and working space for about seven million people. Los Angeles had pushed to within two miles of the Newhall Ranch. Two highways and a railway line crossed through the area now. A connection to the California water system had been established. Finally, an oil company had struck oil on the property in 1937, but, according to geological reports, the oil would last for only another ten years.

The family, whose members were no longer economically dependent on the ranch, had decided to honor the memory of its founder by building a model city that would conform to optimum environmental requirements and be free of the usual urban ills. They intended the planning and implementation to extend over a period of twenty to thirty years and hoped that the project would be free from the usual pressure for rapid profitability. The current use of the land for agriculture and oil production could be continued during the early stages of development, ensuring that there would also be no financial problems.

We went to work with great enthusiasm. The city was to be called Valencia. We conceived of it as an economically autonomous entity, with its own industrial and commercial sector, which would be in the desert in the far north and would have direct connections to the railroad and highway networks. Moreover, the city would be a federation of ten semiautonomous districts, each of which would have its own center and be divided into several neighborhoods. The arrangement of the urban sectors rhythmically echoed the contours of the hilly landscape. The residential density of each district would be significantly higher than standard within the Los Angeles region. This could be achieved through the building of townhouses, atriums, and family apartment buildings, but it was especially important that each of the districts would be free of internal roads. For car traffic, there would be only bypass roads with community garages. Otherwise, each district and neighborhood would be a quiet pedestrian oasis, and the usual waste of land for roads could be avoided.

Neighborhood and district centers, easily accessible for pedestrians, would include not only shopping but also community and care facilities. The proposed higher residential density allowed us to separate the urban units from one another with greenbelts, and also to leave large, charming areas completely untouched: these were nature reserves and parks for hiking, horseback riding, and other sports activities.

Once the settlement of the districts had progressed enough, the construction of a very compact city core would be initiated between the industrial zone and the city districts. The model of this central core is illustrated in my book *Centers for the Urban Environment: Survival of the Cities.*[23] There would have been apartments for about fifteen thousand people as well as offices, administrative buildings, cultural and entertainment venues, hotels, and service establishments, with a total floor area of one million square feet.

High-speed trains would connect the districts, the industrial zone, and the center; several federal government agencies had pledged subsidies for the construction and operation of this transportation network. Furthermore, there would be a system of pedestrian and bicycle paths within and between neighborhoods; these paths would be separated from highways and automobile traffic by pedestrian overpasses.

The conceptual plan was approved by the Newhall family. But no one in the family was able to devote themselves completely to such a large project, so they founded a management company that was run by experienced banking and real estate professionals. Our idealistic motives were soon lost in conventional business practices. Plans that focus on the common good are difficult to achieve in a profit-driven market economy.

One difficulty was the laws of the United States, which tax capital gains lightly and tax income more heavily. In the traditional real estate market, the landowner took care of only the most important preliminary tasks, such as roads and pipelines, then sold land parcels of various sizes to "dividers." It was then extremely difficult, if not impossible, to require the many dividers to follow the guidance of a single overall plan. If the original landowners had themselves erected the buildings according to plan, then they would have been classified by tax authorities as contractors and would have had to pay high income taxes on the sale or rental of the property. In addition, most California banking and real estate professionals, and many other Californians, were skeptical about a public rapid transit system, despite the proposed government subsidies. They could not believe that a Californian would take a train instead of a car.

Parts of our plan for the city did survive, including the general arrangement of the districts, a portion of the separated pedestrian network, and the concept of a polycentric organization. In 1978, Valencia was still under construction. The population growth of the entire region had come to a standstill because of smog and traffic problems.

Welfare Island

One of our clients, Fred Richmond, had invited me to his apartment, which was on the twentieth floor of a skyscraper on the East River in Manhattan.[24] From high above, we looked down on the sea of lights that was the boroughs of Queens and Brooklyn. In the middle of the river, we saw a dark, narrow strip of land, known as Welfare Island, just across from one of the busiest areas of Manhattan. It was bizarre to see completely unused land in the middle of one of the largest metropolises in the world. We had an idea.

The next morning, we endeavored to inspect Welfare Island in daylight. Getting there was complicated because the island was not reachable from Manhattan. It was necessary to cross the bridge to Queens first, then take another bridge to the island.

Though it had appeared empty from high up, once on the island we saw impressive ruins, rubble, garbage dumps, and thousands of rats. The island had originally served as a prison for dangerous criminals. When the notorious Capone gang killed the guards and took over the place, Welfare Island had to be recaptured by the military. The criminals who survived this battle were taken into custody on the mainland, and the sprawling, demolished prison buildings of Welfare Island were deserted. Of the original "welfare facilities," only a home for fallen girls remained (whose occupants had in the meantime become elderly ladies), as well as two medium-sized hospitals, which were little used by doctors, nurses, and visitors because of their restricted accessibility. It seemed to us that this island was simply forgotten.

We decided to put together the necessary planning documents and presented a design for the use of the island to the mayor, then Mr. Robert Wagner. The design would comprise a new urban district in which up to four thousand people of all income levels and ethnicities could reside. The area would be equipped with educational, cultural, health, shopping, and entertainment facilities. Instead of a main road, a two-story, covered, air-conditioned promenade would serve as the heart of the district. On a balcony-like intermediate level, a conveyor belt would circulate with fix-mounted cars, each of which could hold two people. The New York City subway, two lines of which already crossed the East River underneath the island, would establish a new station on Welfare. In addition, ferries and cable cars could bring commuters from Manhattan and Queens. On the island, there would be no car traffic. Residents who owned cars could park these in garages in Queens. Promenades on both sides of the island would be designed as gardens.

The mayor took on the project with great enthusiasm and made sure that it was announced to the public by the mass media, which greeted it favorably. But then came the mayoral elections. Robert Wagner lost the election, and his successor, John Lindsay, entrusted the project to the esteemed architect Philip Johnson.[25] The project was downsized in magnitude, and its character changed completely. At present it is still under construction.[26] A cable car connects Manhattan to the place, which has been renamed Roosevelt Island.[27]

In my view, the later development of the island completely lacked social engagement. I once expressed this to Philip Johnson. Our long correspondence about the matter ended when Philip wrote, "As an artist, I design what I like personally!"

6

Architectura

WHAT IS ARCHITECTURE?

I have been busy for half a century, creating those artifacts that form and influence the human environment. During that time, one question has turned up again and again: "What exactly is architecture?" I have also frequently been asked, "Would you identify yourself as an architect?" My work has included tasks of different sizes and importance, from the design of a table lamp to the design of groups of buildings and neighborhoods to landscape and regional planning, so the question is meant to address whether one term can capture all these activities.

Discussions with my colleagues in the profession have given me some answers. Some describe architecture as art and try to equate it with music, painting, and poetry. Others reject this definition and argue persuasively that buildings are indeed articles of daily use. Many believe that architecture is a profession, like that of lawyer, physician, or veterinarian, and should therefore be practiced only by those who have completed the required studies and training. These chosen few should be protected by licensing against competition from "quacks." Representatives of the economy, also known as clients, consider architecture to be a service that should be judged by how it contributes to the maximization of returns. The industry expects customer service from architects, meaning their unconditional subordination to economic goals at the lowest possible prices; the client does not care whether the architect feels like an artist or an academic professional.

None of this describes the work that I have done. I start to doubt whether I really am an architect, and I often see evidence that my doubts are justified. Whether I'm an architect or not depends, for example, on the country in which I am located. In twenty-six of the fifty U.S. states, I am an authorized and licensed architect. In some

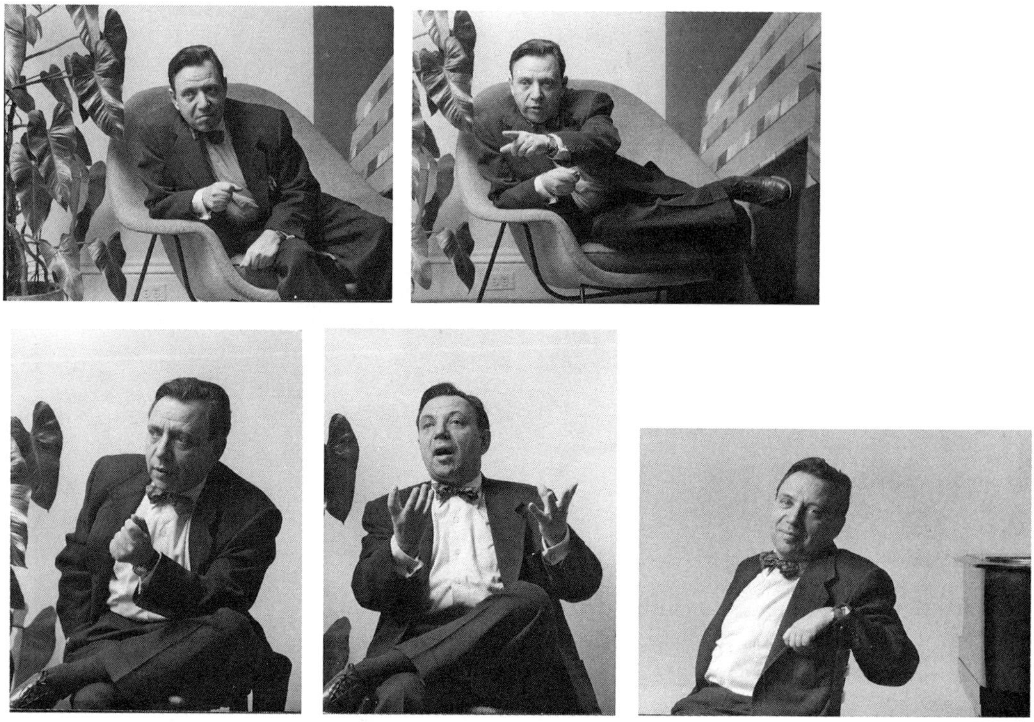

Victor Gruen, Los Angeles, circa 1960. Courtesy of Peggy Gruen.

of the other twenty-four states, only individuals who have graduated from one of the local universities with a technical degree are entitled to pursue an architectural license. In Switzerland, I am an architect simply because I sign plans; in Austria, I am forbidden from calling myself an "Architekt," or even letting other people call me one.

In 1967 I was brought to court in Vienna because I had been addressed in public, in speeches, newspaper articles, and radio and television broadcasts, as an "architect." Charges were brought against me by a group of Austrian architects at the instigation of Mr. Herbert Müller-Hartburg, who aspired to become president of the Federal Chambers of Architects and Engineers.[1] He hoped to gain popularity through this action. It was a memorable trial, which happened to take place in the same hall of the inner-city district court where I had once watched my father working.

Mr. Müller-Hartburg and the other plaintiffs, all of whom were not present in person, were represented by the law firm of Dr. Guertler. I decided to appear in my own defense, without an attorney.

In his opening remarks, the judge criticized the plaintiffs' absence and contrasted it with the defendant's presence, noting that I had come all the way from New York to attend the trial. Then the lawyer for the opposing party argued that, in Austria, only people who had completed their studies, held internships, and passed the civil engineer exam could be referred to as architects. He stated that only such people are entitled to display the federal coat of arms next to the title of architect. He argued that I could not meet these requirements because I was an American citizen. He said that my crime was especially significant because "Arch." was printed next to my name in the phone book. I replied that this surely could not be mistaken for a title and was merely meant to provide information about my occupation.

Now the judge turned to me and asked, "What is your profession, Mr. Gruen?" I refused to answer this question, explaining that I didn't want to incriminate myself. The judge smiled. "As a defendant you have every right to refuse to answer this," he said. "I will question you as a witness under oath."

I was then asked the questions, "What do you do for a living, and what profession is written in your passport?" I had to answer that I was working as an architect, and that this professional designation was noted in my documents. Under further questioning, I admitted that I was licensed to practice the profession of architect in twenty-six states in the United States.

Then, the judge turned back to the plaintiffs' lawyer. He asked, "Do the plaintiffs know that Mr. Gruen is actually an important architect in America?" The lawyer admitted they did, but added that the same was not true for Austria. The judge asked, "When the archbishop of Boston comes to visit Vienna, is he still an archbishop or is he suddenly something else?" The plaintiffs' lawyer admitted that in Vienna, such a person would most likely also be considered an archbishop.

"Ergo ipso," the judge said. "Mr. Gruen is also an architect in Vienna. If the law says otherwise, then such provisions are ridiculous and need to be changed. I advise you to come to a reasonable agreement with Mr. Gruen. Should you not be able to do so, I will make a decision in another trial in favor of Mr. Gruen. This hearing is closed."

In the hallway, the plaintiffs' lawyer drew me into a conversation. "Mr. Architect," he said, "how can we resolve this case?" "It's fine with me if you address me as Mr. Gruen," I corrected him. Then he suggested the following settlement: I could use the professional title without further ado if I spelled the word with a *c* and not with a *k* (*architect,* not the German *Architekt*). He added that he would advise his client to let the matter go if I would also make a donation of ten thousand schillings to the Federal Chambers of Architects and Engineers. I smiled and agreed to this rotten compromise.

Shortly thereafter, it became known that our firm, Victor Gruen Associates, had won the first prize in the international competition to design the headquarters of the United Nations in Vienna. Some Austrian architects turned to me, hoping that they might be appointed to the staff of our Austrian office. One such letter came from Herbert Müller-Hartburg, who had in the meantime become president of the chambers. His letter was addressed to "Herr Architekt Diplomingenieur Victor Gruen," and it began with the salutation, "Dear colleague."

When the city administration of Vienna hired me to create an urban design concept for the downtown, core area of Vienna, the contract bore the name of one of my employees, who did have a professional architect's license. The first condition was that the contractor was required to perform all work under the direction of Mr. Victor Gruen. The project impressed the architectural community of Vienna so much that I was awarded the Architecture Prize of the City of Vienna, on the recommendation of the Federal Chambers of Architects and Engineers.[2] Since then, all doubts about whether I am an architect in Vienna have vanished.

On the other hand, it has been proved in Switzerland, in a trial that has lasted six years, that what I have created there is not architecture. In this case, I went to court to confront the shopping center developer Glatt AG, because the company had used a different architect to completely distort a plan for a multifunctional community center that I had initially designed.[3] The project was eventually stripped of its intellectual content and built purely as a commercial center.

My complaint against the theft of my intellectual property in this case was dismissed on the grounds that architectural works are protected by law only insofar as they may be understood as works of art. But since the complex of buildings I had designed satisfied human needs, in contrast to Saint Peter's Cathedral, the court ruled that it could not be described as architecture in an artistic sense. In the court's view, it was my obligation to give in to all of the client's desires, even if I believed that doing so would be harmful for ethical reasons, or to withdraw from the contract without making any further claim to the work.

So in Switzerland, the architect was a completely subordinated executive assistant who must set aside an interest in public welfare and environmental protection and concentrate on enhancing the profits of the client. The negative outcome of this legal proceeding, which was later confirmed by the Swiss Federal Court, was a big disappointment for me and my lawyers. The case strained both my financial and my intellectual resources, and it demonstrated to the entire architectural community of Switzerland their complete dependence. The appeals I addressed to international professional associations went nowhere, perhaps because these associations had long ago abandoned their goal of preserving the reputation of their profession. Their actions were confined to protecting themselves as representative unions against competitors.

I have not become too involved in American professional organizations despite the great honors bestowed on me by the American Institute of Architects, which appointed me a fellow of the institute and awarded me many diplomas and medals. However, I wasn't able to avoid one big national convention in Hershey, Pennsylvania, in the 1960s, because, together with Philip Johnson, I was chosen to give a celebratory speech at the final event. That night, along with special guests from politics and business, Johnson and I waited patiently through a long and culinarily mediocre banquet. With great difficulty, we stayed awake during endless speeches on the rules of procedure. Meanwhile, a thousand of our colleagues consoled themselves with great amounts of alcohol. When at last the chairman began a long-winded introduction of two famous architects, we realized that it would be futile to talk about architecture. Instead of presenting our lectures, we stood up simultaneously, put our arms around each other, and loudly sang a German folk song: "You, you, lie to my heart / You, you, lie to my mind / You, you give me much pain / You do not know how good I am to you." And so, typically for this profession, the great national congress of the American Institute of Architects ended in a chaos.

ARCHITECTURE IN CHAOS

The tragedy of the architectural profession lies in the deep gap between myth and reality. In the popular mind, there is a belief in the almost godlike omnipotence of the architect. He is therefore to blame for everything that is uncomfortable and ugly in our housing and our cities. The public holds the architect responsible for traffic jams, parking problems, the sterility of new neighborhoods, and the decay of old ones, for inadequacies of technology and small apartments with thin walls and low ceilings. Naturally, the architect is also to blame for the damage caused by natural disasters such as earthquakes.

The reality is somewhat different. In our materialistic society, the architect is usually a service slave who must create a concept that matches the financial planning of his private or public employer.

Architecture is a profession that has not overcome its past and has never seriously sought its present. The architect has forfeited his responsibility to shape the human environment to those who are less interested in design than in disfigurement. In most cases, such as the construction of prefabricated houses, the design of cities and neighborhoods, and the planning of transport and production facilities, an architect is not used at all.

When an architect is consulted, the important parameters for his work have already been set, including the building location, use, size, and height, as well as the project budget. The free movement of the architect is further constricted by building inspections, planning bureaucrats, and the construction industry. Against his "client," who is actually his superior and commander, the architect is defenseless, because his training has not given him the ability to question shortsighted, harmful, environmentally irresponsible instructions.

The architect who lives in the past dreams of the "legendary times" when patrons of the arts built proud monuments to themselves, and both the mood of the builder and the ideas of the architect were taken into account.

This dream can rarely be fulfilled. After the "industrial explosion," a market-oriented, pluralistic society emerged. It replaced the time when monuments reflected feudal prestige, whether they were palaces, domes, cathedrals, museums, or temples. Even in the mid-nineteenth century it was possible for Emperor Franz Joseph I of Austria to order, with one stroke of a pen, both the construction of the Viennese Ringstrasse and the demolition of thousands of structures (which would today be protected as monuments) because of his "God-given omnipotence." Such an act would be conceivable only in a dictatorship nowadays.

So the more realistic and ambitious contemporary architect who dreams of creating monuments sets his sights on Arab sheiks, dictators, tribal chiefs in developing countries, and billionaires who are desperate for admiration. The supply of this "ideal client" is too small to employ the whole profession. Since Stalin's death, even the Soviet Union requires little monumentality.

There is also no longer a market for representative and splendid architecture. Ironically, the training of the architect, if it is not purely technical, is based on learning historical forms. I was educated and drilled in such a way, and I still know enough about Doric, Ionic, and Corinthian capitals, architraves, pilaster strips, risalites, pedestals, vaults, and domes to take over the construction of a Greek temple at a moment's notice. Unfortunately, I've never had the opportunity.

Things are probably similar for most other architects. The projects for which we have been trained are not available, and the countless problems that we must solve in the service of human society were never mentioned in our years of study. So when architects leave school, they are unprepared to become independent in a materialistic market economy, let alone to find social, human, and ecological solutions in their work.

It is estimated that for every thousand graduates with an architecture degree, nine hundred are employed by construction companies, industrial groups, or architecture supermarkets. After frustrating attempts to practice as architects, approximately five survive as journalists, critics, or historians. About forty are active in small studios, usually without much success. Perhaps four become the heads of large architectural firms and gain great reputations as businessmen. Perhaps one in a thousand succeeds in finding one of those rare patrons who allows him to do his own thing in relative freedom and become a so-called style shaper.

These numbers are probably just as unreliable as those recorded by pollsters and computers. But if they are even approximately correct, they prove that in the architectural profession there is an unbridgeable gap between the supply and the demand for architects. The amount of construction activity may be impressive, but most of it is focused on the ruthless exploitation of land and rarely meets any demands for greater quality.

The scope of the architect is further limited by the fact that he is forced to obey the dictates of the specialists his client consults about structure, heating, ventilation, lighting, air-conditioning, transport, and finance. Since the average architect knows little or nothing about these fields, he is served up to an army of so-called experts who know much about their own fields but nothing about anything else. Since these various specialists occasionally have rumpuses with one another, rotten compromises result.

When it comes to the execution of a project, the architect is often a helpless bystander. Building contracts are usually awarded by the client, and usually to those who provide the lowest bids or maintain good personal, business, or political relations with him. Construction companies are naturally less interested in satisfying architects than they are in satisfying those from whom they receive payments. They will propose project changes, often in matters related to their material storage and equipment. They persuade the client that such changes will save money or time.

So the architect's ability to work creatively as an artist is limited in most cases. The opportunity to be an effective architect with a private practice, like that of a doctor or lawyer, does not exist, given this system of rewards. It transforms the architect into something more like a representative of the real estate business.

In this payment system, the architect receives a certain percentage of the construction costs. Professional considerations determine this percentage, usually in reverse relation to the construction costs. (For a small building, an architect receives about 15 percent, but for a larger one, he might get as little as 2 percent of construction costs.) This system is shameful, unjust, and demoralizing, because it tends to punish great achievements and reward small ones.

Since the architect is rewarded not for his achievements but for his accommodations to the costs of a building, he finds himself in a bizarre dilemma. The more conscientiously he provides his services, the more time he must spend, but due to the quality of his plans, the costs of the building are reduced, which reduces his fee.

If the architect recommends better, more durable, and energy-saving measures, his client may suspect he is trying to raise the building costs and therefore also his fee. The good architect is also a lousy businessman.

The situation is different with the bad architect. He strives to create his own work as cheaply as possible. For instance, he uses a large card index of advertising and detail information, all collected from architectural magazines. Whenever necessary, he passes these cards to his draftsmen to copy. In his planning and building specifications, he adds factory-made items from the construction industries. These industries show him their gratitude by delivering the finished drawings to him at his house. He does not care for accuracy of construction documents, and so he causes construction companies to calculate with reserves for inaccuracies, and therefore the total price of the building increases.

In this way, this good businessman, who must necessarily be a bad architect, creates low quality in his own product but receives a large fee. Thanks to these higher profits, the enterprising architect can spend more on promotional activities and equipment for his offices, and with some luck and skill, he will become an architecture-superman with a hundred or more employees. His firm isn't a delicatessen, it's a supermarket.

The percentage reward system is also of questionable use in unstable economic times. If the architect has the good fortune to plan in a time of recession with relatively low wages for his employees, and then construction takes place in a time of inflation, when construction costs increase, he collects a huge, undeserved bonus. But in opposite economic conditions—when his plans are made during periods of inflation and the execution of the project occurs in a recession—this can mean his financial ruin.

In the United States, otherwise powerless architects retain one obligation: they are responsible for all defects and infirmities of each building they design. These architects try to protect themselves with liability insurance, for which they pay high premiums. But this has a shady side. The client, who knows (and insists) that his architect has liability insurance, will nonetheless blame the architect for everything that goes wrong in the building or its surroundings.

In one of the shopping centers we designed, for example, a lady broke her leg when she stumbled over a wooden threshold that separated two parking spaces. The owners of the shopping center paid her a substantial compensation, then withdrew this amount from our fees. They argued that our liability insurance would not hold us liable anyway. The insurance company indeed paid, but it also immediately increased our premiums and threatened to cancel our policy if something like this happened again.

For an aspiring young architect, if he has a liberal client, the only way to work is as a decorator of facades or interiors. His client will allow him a playful streak if the decoration does not cost too much and it increases the income of the business. This means that many architects are competing to work as decorators!

In the majority of all buildings in urban areas, such surface embellishments are futile. In our chaotic cities, when architectural expressions can no longer be perceived, they become invisible.

INVISIBLE ARCHITECTURE

The overestimation of the achievements of technology at the expense of important human values upset me even in my early youth. At the time, I wrote a few satires that I intended as weapons against so-called technological progress.

This deep-rooted feeling that the excessive use of technology conjures up the appearance of prosperity but endangers the welfare of mankind deepened even more when I moved to Los Angeles in 1941. There I discovered that instead of being useful, one technological achievement in particular—the automobile—was terrorizing an entire city.

In Vienna and Manhattan, like most citizens, I was relatively independent of automobiles, because my home was only a few minutes' walk from my place of work, and all my other destinations—building sites, friends' homes, restaurants, and theaters—either were within walking distance or could be reached by public transport. But in Los Angeles, I could see that without a car, we would be cut off from professional activities, shopping, and social and cultural activities. When my children were growing up and we needed to separate our living and working spaces, second, third, and fourth cars became necessary to keep our household, education, work, and social lives on track.

During my tour of American cities, I found out that this way of life had transformed them all. A personal vehicle that can be used at any time makes it possible to live a greater distance from one's place of work, but it also brings irritation and danger. There is a continual urge to move away from the city center.

URBANITY

In Los Angeles, the proliferation of fragmented settlement areas has proceeded to such a degree that urban structure has completely disintegrated, the city has become a noncity, and all activities that may be considered part of "urbanity" have become impossible. Defined as the quality that made cities the cradles of civilization, science, and art, urbanity is based on the idea that the burden of each single person is taken over by the community, the "commune," or the "municipality." It is the nature of "urbs" to provide collective facilities—water, sewage, energy supply, and security—for their citizens. The mass use of individual transport machines within a collective is an absurdity, a life-endangering breach of all values of the city. It means that all citizens may also insist on possessing their own wells, septic tanks, and rifles.

Although other technical innovations, such as air conditioners, affect the natural way of life, the car is the misuse of technology that manifests itself most clearly. The culture-conscious architect must realize that any effort to make the exterior of a building visually appealing is pointless, because in a noncity, where all the houses and buildings border rivers of rushing traffic, architecture becomes as invisible as paintings in a darkened gallery. The full attention of any citizen who is driving is necessarily focused on the thousands of drivers behind him, in front of him, to the right and to the left, and on traffic lights, warning signs, and arrows. Here and there, garish billboards and neon signs may succeed in gaining his attention for a few seconds. The buildings along the edges of this traffic stream sink into utter insignificance. In his automotive container, the citizen becomes architecture illiterate.

We experienced this hopelessness in 1964, when we designed a building complex that included our own large office. After the complex opened, both the carefully crafted facade and the entrance hall, which were designed with a lot of talent and money, became examples of "invisible architecture." After the opening of the building, the beautiful ground-floor entrance was unused by anyone other than the postman. Even a carefully landscaped pedestrian promenade between the two parts of the building remained deserted and neglected in this place where people have forgotten how to walk. In fact, our building, like all modern office buildings in Los Angeles, had no entrances, only driveways. You didn't enter on foot—you drove into one of three parking garages in the basement and from there took an elevator to the offices.

In the planning stages, it was necessary for all human needs to be subordinated to traffic requirements. At the beginning of each town planning project we undertook, one of our first steps was planning roads and parking facilities. As part of my architectural philosophy, I declared war on the automobile as a misunderstood means of mass transportation. One aim of this war, which I have conducted throughout my career, has been to reduce forced mobility. In contrast to the Athens Charter, coauthored by Le Corbusier, my efforts to restructure cities attempted to avoid large-scale separation of different areas of life, such as working, learning, and leisure. Le Corbusier preached "unbundling," but I advocated "fine-grained integration." As additional tools to free cities from the terror of mass car traffic, I argued for the generous expansion of collective transport (buses, streetcars, rapid transit, subway trains) and the opening of completely car-free urban living areas. These objectives were expressed in my writing, but also in my projects, in pedestrian zones in suburban and urban centers that I planned in new neighborhoods and towns.

In this fight, I always tried to demonstrate plainly to the public the dangers of air pollution and traffic fatalities. Another of the sins of mass automobile traffic is the egregious consumption of land by such traffic. Car travel requires much more land than that required for all other human activities. This insatiable appetite for land means, for example, that in downtown Los Angeles, two-thirds of the land is used for transportation and only one-third for buildings. It also means that in the areas surrounding some cities, land that is vital for agriculture and recreation is sacrificed for highways and roads.

SUPERSTITION

But the mistaken belief in a permanent increase of the automobile stock is only part of the larger myth that unrestrained material growth will continue in all areas. Besides this superstitious belief in constant growth, affluent citizens have two unrealistic dreams that are closely related. They are based on a widespread desire to transfer the customs and traditions of a feudal society to a democratic welfare society. In feudal societies, the upper ten-thousandth of the population retained an excess of privilege, which included the privilege of individual mobility through the use of riding horses and coaches. This then created a sufficient amount of envy and annoyance in the underprivileged to produce changes that terminated a large part of the privilege. But this mobility privilege of the rich, while it lasted, did not result in traffic jams or require superhighways or traffic lights. It was satisfied by tree-shaded avenues.

Furthermore, an exceptionally privileged member of the feudal population could afford both a town palace and a country estate, which often took the form of a pleasure palace, grand hunting lodge, or villa. This also created annoyance among the underprivileged, but it in no way led to a significant loss of agricultural land or natural landscape.

THE "UPPER MILLIONS"

But in an affluent society, if the privileges initially enjoyed by the "upper ten thousand" are claimed by the "upper millions," and those millions wish to drive their own coaches and live in their own pleasure palaces (or second homes with gardens), then the dream of an affluent citizen becomes a nightmare. Everyone must be angry at everyone else, because everyone finds that everyone else is getting in their way. On top of this, the feudal behavior of the upper millions causes irreparable environmental damage. In our own bitter experience, we can already see today that the promise of individual mobility for millions ultimately results in collective immobility.

The fight is not against the individual transport vehicle itself (though it could be improved by the use of other fuels) but against its abuse. There is no doubt that in the city, when it comes to rapid deployment, such as that needed in fire, rescue, or medical emergency situations, the automobile is of great value.

My steady campaign against the misuse of the automobile, which I waged in books, articles, and speeches, was only modestly successful. It also provoked vicious counterattacks, anonymous letters, and death threats. It was, thanks to the power of the international automobile lobby, generally unpopular. This isn't surprising: as a toy that has made technology available to individuals, the automobile has become a status symbol and won the hearts of the people.

GRAVEDIGGERS OF MANHATTAN

In the 1960s, Manhattan business interests created a detailed plan for the construction of high-rise garages with ten thousand parking spaces in the Midtown area, the commercial and cultural center of New York. I publicly criticized this plan because it would have brought not more business but only more vehicles into these already crowded streets, and because these warehouse buildings would occupy urban land that would then be lost to any other productive use.

I received the usual number of threatening letters. One such letter was noteworthy because it had been written by the president of New York's largest department store, Mr. Jack Straus, with whom I had a professional relationship. He called me Manhattan's gravedigger. I answered him politely and returned the compliment by pointing out that as an apologist for this monstrous garage project, he could be called the same thing. There followed a lengthy personal correspondence, during which I presented Mr. Straus with a few questions, including "What percentage of the hundreds of thousands of customers who visit Macy's every day are currently coming in their own cars?" Mr. Straus called in his statistician, who told him that the number fluctuated between 1 and 2 percent. Nevertheless, Mr. Straus said that if it became possible to park a car in a nearby garage or in front of one of the entrances to his department store, this number would probably increase significantly. I pointed out that even if five cars were parked in front of each entrance, this would amount to only 210 additional customers. Even a medium-sized garage could contribute only a few thousand customers. This small profit would be erased by the fact that the resulting traffic jams and safety hazards would deter tens of thousands of the store's current customers from coming on foot or by bus. Jack Straus responded with a sly smile and the suggestion that one could demolish the building across from Macy's and create a garage there. Thus he hoped to kill two birds with one stone: the building across the street was Gimbels department store, Macy's largest competitor.

My opposition to the Midtown garage project was successful, and it disappeared from the scene. Shortly thereafter, in the Sunday magazine of the *New York Times,* I suggested a plan for a counterproject that would make the core of Manhattan more humane, more attractive, and, in the end, even more profitable for business. According to my plan, the long, narrow island of Manhattan would be largely freed from surface automobile traffic and transformed into an environmental oasis, with only pedestrian traffic and transportation such as electric buses. Car traffic to the city via numerous bridges and tunnels would be collected by a peripheral road system with integrated underground parking garages. This plan attracted widespread attention and, in the next few years, resulted in temporary closures of Fifth Avenue and Madison Avenue to car traffic. However, these experiments were halfhearted, and they soon fell victim to pressure from the automobile industry lobby.[4]

IN THE LION'S DEN

My second adventure in the battle against the car took place in Detroit, the world capital of automobile production. The state of the inner city there was completely desolate and almost sadder than that of Los Angeles. The conditions were so alarming that the Chamber of Commerce invited me to speak at the largest hall in town about ways to revitalize the city center. This great hall was filled to bursting with representatives of city government, commerce, and industry (particularly the automotive industry). I understood that the obliteration of Detroit's city center was a result of the flight of some of the population and the business community into the ever-expanding suburbs. This flight was made possible by the efficient motorway network and the mass car market. In other words, the desolate state of the city, its disastrous financial situation, and its complete cultural disrepair were the direct result of something Detroit revered: the automobile.

I was anxious to hear a response to my speech from the automotive industry, and it arrived promptly the next morning. I received a phone call from the General Motors Company in which I was politely but firmly invited to visit their headquarters. I prepared myself for the worst. In the lion's den, I was surprised to be received warmly. My hosts told me they wanted to show me a film that would interest me. This well-done film was the most explicit condemnation of the car I have ever seen. Compared to this movie, all my arguments seemed polite and reserved. The second part of the film detailed the obvious benefits of mass transit. When the lights came up again, I wondered where I was. My smiling hosts assured me I was in the headquarters of General Motors, but in the subdivision for bus production. I asked if General Motors management would tolerate an attack on its main product, the private car. I learned that GM management would not interfere, because the task of this subdivision was to sell buses, and they were expected to fulfill this task optimally.

THE AUTOMOTIVE INDUSTRY

The American automobile industry took my concerns quite seriously. A meeting was convened with the presidents of all the car companies, where I was asked for advice on how we should plan for the future. This all happened, incidentally, at a time when no one foresaw an oil crisis. But even then, in the early sixties, the leaders of the automotive industry were very concerned that the problems of smog, traffic congestion, and recklessly built roads were creating an increasingly negative image of the industry in the popular consciousness. The senior men felt that if conditions did not improve, a crisis would develop for the automobile industry within the next twenty years, and they wanted to be prepared for this. My recommendation to the industry to upgrade and accelerate the production of buses and other means of mass transportation seemed to be taken quite seriously.

The automobile manufacturers' association commissioned us to undertake a scientific study on the traffic-friendly city. We were asked to prove whether it was possible to accommodate a growing number of automobiles in cities, eradicate traffic problems, and, at the same time, create a satisfactory arrangement of housing and other urban facilities. Our traffic department went to work with great seriousness. They designed a hypothetical city with a system of streets of first, second, and third order and an arrangement of underpasses and overpasses that kept intersections to a minimum. In the open squares of the grid, we tried to accommodate the homes, workplaces, and urban facilities required for this hypothetical town. Our first experiment showed that if we assumed a fairly reasonable population density, our road network would not be sufficient for the traffic. It had to be enlarged, and since this required more land, the space to be colonized had to be expanded, too. This expansion of the settlement area led to a greater burden on the roads, which meant that the road network needed to be extended again. It was a vicious circle from which we could find no way out. We had to tell our clients that we could fulfill only part of the contract—the design of a perfectly functioning road system. We could not also accomplish the second part of the task—namely, accommodating the users of the cars on the rest of the land.

Solving this problem was indeed impossible, and this was confirmed a few years later when the Los Angeles County attempted to use a computer to validate its twenty-year program for the gradual extension of the existing highway network. The computer evaluation was devastating. It said that the traffic problems of the day would double in twenty years. The authorities were surprised, and then they made the only logical choice. Since it now seemed hopeless to simply enlarge the road system to accommodate an increased number of cars, throwing away the whole plan for a future highway system was the best thing to do. Further highway construction was discontinued, and many existing highways added a lane for express buses in the hopes of increasing traffic capacity. This was done in 1973, and since that time, the use of buses and the number of passengers on them have increased noticeably.

RAPID TRANSIT SYSTEM

But these steps were not enough to satisfy the insatiable need for mobility in the Los Angeles basin. Some came to the conclusion that Los Angeles required a modern rapid transit and subway system. This revelation arrived rather late, especially if one considers that Los Angeles had had a good electric train network with a central station until the end of World War II but gave it up under pressure from the automobile industry (the system was also in debt). At that time, all the tracks were ripped up and the plots of land were sold to real estate brokers.[5]

Our organization and several others worked on a succession of projects for a new public rapid transit system. But whenever we tried to plan transit lines, we came to the disappointing conclusion that there were not enough starting points or destinations of sufficient density in Los Angeles to justify a rail transit system. We became convinced that on one hand, without such a mass transit system, Los Angeles was in jeopardy, but on the other hand, because of the city's shapeless territorial expansion, construction of such a system was impossible. There seemed to be no other choice but to plan Los Angeles all over again, from scratch. After years of work, the city planning commission created a plan that envisioned a city composed of large, multifunctional, compact districts that could be efficiently connected with each other and a central part of city. The implementation of this ambitious plan was halted by huge financial problems that have never been solved.

TRANSPORT PLANNING IN MOSCOW

Another episode involved the situation in the Soviet Union. Several years ago, the city planning director of Moscow, Mikhail Posokhin, visited me in my Vienna offices. The main purpose of his trip to the city was to buy crystal chandeliers for a representative building in Moscow. However, he did not want to leave Vienna without having seen me to report on his work on a new general plan for Moscow.

The objectives of the general plan were laudable. The plan was intended to stop further growth of the population, prevent the geographic spread of the urbanized area, increase green areas and recreational areas significantly, create a greenbelt around the capital, and increase the average size of city apartments. Posokhin verified the details of the plan with statistical materials. I congratulated him on the general concept, which would have prevented the sprawl that was occurring in Western cities. He was pleased, but he said that I had not yet heard the best part of the plan. The number of automobiles in the city, which was then relatively small (approximately 150,000), would be increased to 1.5 million. I was quite surprised, since I knew that the Russian capital was well equipped with public transportation, including an exemplary subway. I reminded him that the Soviet chairman, Nikita Khrushchev, had seen traffic jams during his visit to America and scoffed that such nonsense could only happen in capitalist countries.

I explained that this one aspect of his plan would erase all its other laudable intentions. The land requirements for the use of 1.5 million automobiles would be so great that limiting the urban area, increasing the green areas, and increasing the residential units would become impossible. He couldn't believe this, because many of the streets of Moscow were very broad. So I worked out for him how much space each car would need for parking and moving between three points (home, work, and at least one additional stop), as well as the space required for gas stations and garages. This need resulted in a requirement of approximately three hundred square feet per vehicle.

He checked my calculations and asked in consternation, "Why didn't anyone tell me this? This is a disaster!" I suggested that he should revise his plan and leave out the proposed increase of the number of registered automobiles. "You imagine that being so easy," he said. "The proposed number of cars is based on the wishes of Comrade Leonid Brezhnev, and is part of the national plan for the expansion of the automotive industry." I then realized there was no difference between the profit-oriented growth of the capitalist auto industry and the power-oriented growth of the Soviet car industry. I later heard that the planned quota for cars in Moscow had been somewhat reduced.

AUTO AND ARCHITECTURE

My efforts, and those of many like-minded individuals, to take action against the misuse of the automobile have achieved only sporadic success, partly because the fragmentation of the cities forces people to drive, and partly because of the prestige of this beloved vehicle itself. Even the great shock of the oil crisis of 1973 had only temporary influence on current events. Strangely enough, though, there have been some strong efforts to overcome traffic problems in the birthplace of the automobile. Speed limits have been introduced, even for highways (about eighty miles an hour). Fuel taxes in the United States are used for the construction and improvement of public transport, and in a number of American cities, new underground rail networks are being planned and built. In the interest of cleaner air, the U.S. Environmental Protection Agency has declared that construction permits can be denied to planned supermarkets and shopping centers if those facilities may become producers of excessive automobile traffic, as well as to any peripherally located residential projects that are not accessible by public transport. Given the opposition of the auto and construction industries, of course, it remains to be seen to what degree these provisions will be effective.

Despite the disappointing results of the fight against the terror of the car, I am confident about the foreseeable future. I believe that the pressure from a growing scarcity of raw materials will bring about important changes for us. Also, the population has a growing understanding of environmental protection, so the efforts to make cities people-friendly rather than car-friendly are destined for success. Until then, architecture will remain invisible as it is now, and since it is not noticed, it is not respected. The denser the car traffic, the lower the architectural quality.

Modern architects' reactions to this unpleasant but undeniable truth vary. Many resign themselves to it and give up trying to design the exteriors of their buildings. Others hope to attract the attention of the automobile driver by designing buildings that appear to be more prominent than others. However, in the car traffic environment, it is difficult for buildings to compete with pop art billboards, hot dog stands shaped like large sausages, and giant roadside pinups.

A third group of architects avoid the dilemma by escaping from an inhospitable reality to a few remaining "islands of the blessed." These include university, trade union, and insurance company buildings and the isolated mansions of millionaires. As for buildings in urban districts, these may become visible, noticeable, and respectable only if people use their feet to walk again.

The possibilities that this would open up became clear to us in February 1978, when we spent three weeks in the car-free village of Mürren, in the Bernese Oberland of Switzerland. There my wife and I wandered small, snow-covered alleys that were neither marked by tire tracks nor sullied by oil stains. We "refueled" ourselves in the clear, pure atmosphere, which was completely free of engine noise, and let everything around us—the majestic peaks of the surrounding mountains, the snow-covered trees and shrubs, and the old farmhouses, residential buildings, and hotels that had been built by human hands—affect us gently. Architecture was in no way "invisible" in this village, and one could easily recognize good, mediocre, and bad forms of it.

ARCHITECTURAL ATTITUDE

Perhaps because of the chaotic state of my profession, I have become uncertain about the meaning of the terms *architecture* and *architect.* So I have searched for definitions of these words, because I've always regarded this profession as important and fulfilling. Then I remembered something that I had heard in class about the history of architecture. Like much other wisdom, it is very old. It is from *De architectura libri decem (Ten Books on Architecture),* which was written by the Roman state architect Marcus Vitruvius Pollio between 33 and 22 B.C.

According to his definition, architecture should exhibit *firmitas, utilitas,* and *venustas.* Langenscheidt translates these three conditions as *strength, practicality,* and *beauty.*[6] I would translate them as *durability, comfort,* and *amusement.*

In German architecture schools, the term *usability* is substituted for *convenience* or *comfort.* This translation of Vitruvius is dangerous because we might take *usability* to mean something that is materially beneficial to the client. It becomes clear that Vitruvius does not intend to say this when he states that strength must be achieved "sine avaritia" (without greed).

It is also significant that Vitruvius refers to the environmental aspects of architecture. He writes that it is important to choose a very healthy place. It should be exposed to neither fog nor rime, and buildings should be aligned at the right cardinal directions. He warns that one should not build near a swamp, because fog and poisonous fumes may make the place unhealthy. He then describes exactly which rooms must be oriented in different cardinal directions: sleeping quarters and libraries should have windows to the east; baths and winter quarters to the south; artists' studios and any rooms that require uniform illumination to the north.

Even Vitruvius's thoughts on the use of materials seem relevant to our times. The Langenscheidt translation reads: "The use is but the appropriate distribution of the material and space and a thrifty and calculated moderation of expense for the buildings. This is so important that if the builder does not accomplish it, it will not be found or obtained later, except at a high price." Vitruvius devotes an entire chapter to the various materials that may be suitable, depending on the location and use of a building.

After studying the original text, I have given Vitruvius's terms a different ranking: comfort, durability, amusement. The quality of comfort is essential for both a viewer outside and a user inside the structure. Furthermore, the building should fit comfortably into the environment, with other buildings, public spaces, the landscape, and the natural environment.

Durability is a better translation of the term *firmitas* than *strength.* Strength could indeed mean that a building doesn't collapse with every gust of wind. This type of strength is now guaranteed by building regulations. But durability also implies the functionality of all the systems required by a contemporary building: heating, cooling, ventilation, water supply, waste disposal, electricity. In addition, sustainability is required, and is best achieved through methods of energy conservation. All the features that ensure the building's durability and sustainability should do so in an elegant manner and conflict with neither comfort nor amusement. Sustainability should not dominate the building or bully its other components, but instead should serve the structure unobtrusively.

Finally, it seems to me that the Langenscheidt translation of the third term as *beauty* is too vague. I believe Vitruvius means to express that architecture should go far beyond the mere satisfaction of human senses. It should provide warmth in the cold months, and a shady coolness in the hot. The word *amusement* implies that the emotional life of man must be considered. Boredom and monotony are to be avoided. This would mean an end to vast repetitions of the same types of buildings, like those found in social housing, which is often more reminiscent of an endless array of filing cabinets for people. The German concept of *Ergötzlichtkeit* is relevant; it can mean mental stimulation through visual variety, which can be achieved through surprising design, artwork, ponds and aquariums, and millions of other ideas inspired by fantasy.

The three conditions of Vitruvius need to be expanded with two more requirements to suit the contemporary situation—namely, flexibility and removability.

Flexibility is important because the contemporary architect usually does not meet the final owner or user of a building, but instead must follow orders from an as-yet-unknown user. Even when owners and users, as in the case of a family home, are known, one must assume that their needs will change significantly in the future. The family may increase or decrease in size after the children leave home. The needs of the owners may change depending on their financial position or health. With flexible partitions and a clever arrangement of the rooms, an architect may make it possible to redivide the building later.

In large residential complexes, using the walls between individual units as load-bearing structural elements has become a disadvantage because this makes it impossible to increase or decrease the size of individual flats later. In contrast, a construction method that uses only pillars as supports will make it possible for the architect to create different sizes of apartments and to accommodate later requests for space division, enlargement, or reduction.

If designed on the basis of profitability, an apartment for a married couple in a contemporary social housing complex may become too small for the couple to use when a new generation arrives. A joke illustrates this problem: "Two old people find an apartment, but it's too small. The landlord assures them that the apartment has been scientifically designed to meet the needs of exactly two people. The couple tell him, 'That's the problem, we want to have a goldfish.'"

Some architects have tried to achieve a maximum of flexibility in the single-family home by forgoing all divisions in the home's interior (except one for the bathroom). They combine all the various functions of the space, from cooking to sleeping, eating, watching TV, and studying, into one open room without any partitions.

Navigating such a single-room house can be quite an adventure. A few years ago, I visited the home of my ultramodern colleague Ray Kappe, who is also the director of a school of architecture.[7] Apparently, he felt obliged to live in the sort of house he has been teaching his students to build. (This is unusual—most glass-and-steel architects actually live in romantic old barns, mills, and farms, with oversized wood fireplaces and lots of candles.) The interior of Kappe's place was shrouded in confusing half darkness. The various areas of life were separated not by walls but by platforms of differing heights. Some platforms were one to two meters higher than others. For aesthetic reasons, the platforms were reached by barely visible glass steps and had no outside railings.

After our hiking tour of the house, I felt relieved when we sat down to an excellent supper on the highest platform. From there, the view of the mountains and valleys was quite impressive, but the thought of stumbling off our perch prevented me from drinking any of the superb wine.

Modern department store interiors are designed for flexibility, with partitions between departments and even product shelves that are movable, like the backdrops in a theater. This flexibility is aided by grid systems of power outlets on the ceilings and floors. In large office buildings, the sizes of rentable units and their internal subdivisions can be adjusted at any time through the shifting of strategically placed dividing walls.

I saw a stunning example of flexibility at a dinner we gave for our French clients in the restaurant Ledoyen in Paris. To change the size of the dining rooms in the restaurant, one simply presses a button, and partition walls, along with their lights and mirrors, emerge from the basement or disappear into it.

The criterion of removability has become important because the constant change in contemporary life may cause us to question the comfort and convenience of a building, despite its flexibility. It is not my opinion that we should build throwaway buildings, or obey the instructions written on the foundation of one New York skyscraper, which read, "Built in 1966, to be demolished in 1986." But in a developing society, the removability of buildings must be taken into consideration. The antiaircraft towers built during World War II in Vienna constitute one argument for this perspective: they were constructed by the Germans in urban parks and have been preserved solely because it would be impossible to demolish them without destroying the surrounding neighborhoods.

After the automotive age, we will wonder how to get rid of the reinforced concrete structures of urban freeways. In San Francisco, one section of a city highway was never opened due to violent public protests, and eventually it had to be removed. Its removal cost more than its construction. The incident was memorialized by an abstract sculpture that resembles the rubble of a demolished freeway. The locals call this sculpture the "Monument of Human Stupidity."

Nuclear power plants also violate the criterion of removability. They have a functional life of just thirty years, but after this period, they may not be removed for hundreds of years, and in fact must be carefully guarded, since the accumulated radioactivity in such sites is life threatening for every visitor.

The three conditions of Vitruvius and my proposed additions have been important principles for me. I also confess to admiring something the American architect Frank Lloyd Wright once said: "The architect should not give the client what he wants, but what he should want!" The premise is that the architect has beliefs and knowledge that allow him to know what the client should want. Somewhat expanded, Wright's motto could read: "The architect should not give the client what he wants, but what he should want in his own interest and in the interest of the community."

Nowadays, if one attempts to use such principles to create architectural works, one must confront some questions. The first question: Is there a demand for true architecture in our profit-oriented, market economy and society? Obviously, those clients who wish to make lots of profit, those who could be called speculators, are not interested in comfort or durability or amusement. In many cases, however, I have found that there are also clients who wish to be successful in the long term and therefore think it wise to respect the common welfare.

Perhaps I could be described as a dreamer, but I believe I am a realistic one. I don't believe that one can influence clients with beautiful words and phrases. But I am convinced that reason can persuade an open-minded and farsighted client that a building that takes the common welfare into consideration will be economically successful as well.

So if an architect brings to bear far-reaching knowledge and experience beyond his particular field, he puts himself and his clients in a position to ensure the long-term health of a building. He becomes something more like a doctor who practices preventive medicine.

What kind of knowledge, experience, and skill does an architect need? Most major construction projects require the deployment of a multidisciplinary, integrated team. Such a team may be compared with an orchestra, within which each musician knows his instrument but needs a score and a particularly sensitive conductor. If all of these elements are present, the orchestra can play a symphony.

How can the architect sell his architectural conception? There is no formula for success. It is not enough to be convinced of the strength of your own ideas—you must be able to convince others. This will depend on the personality of the architect. To compete in the market successfully, the architect needs a rich knowledge of economics. He must be able to effectively counter the erroneous evaluations of clients and financial institutions.

Selling ideas and concepts requires the use of psychological methods. It is important to involve the client in the creative process, or at least give him the feeling of participation. Once, I was too successful with a client in this regard. On completion of the project, the client expressed his total satisfaction, then told me, "Why should I actually pay you a fee? All the good ideas came from me!"

TYPES AND ANOMALIES IN ARCHITECTURE

Nonpracticing architectural outsiders, such as critics, journalists, and historians, exert a significant influence on the development of contemporary architecture. Because they are above the miseries of everyday business, they may have larger perspectives

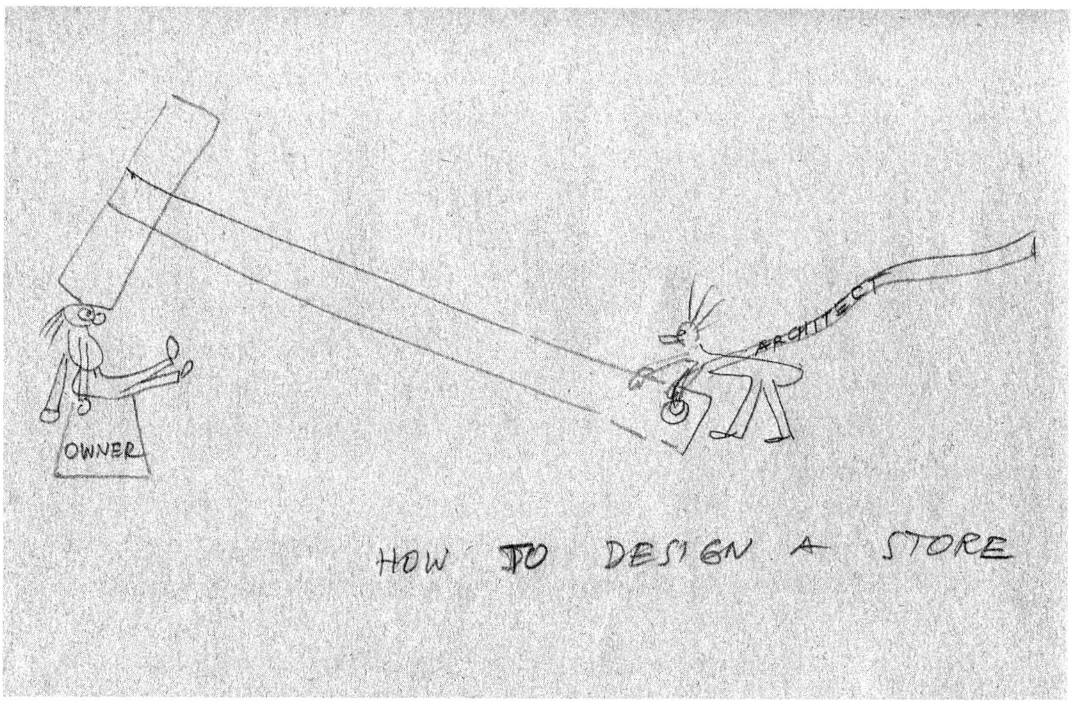

Victor Gruen, "How to Design a Store," Los Angeles, 1959. Courtesy of Peggy Gruen.

and deeper insights, as is the case with the architectural philosopher Lewis Mumford and the great architecture writer Wolf von Eckardt.[8] But the vast majority do not see the forest for the trees. Many regard journalism as a means of transmitting thrills to the reader instead of information. Just as some irresponsible mass media outlets put murder and scandal in the spotlight, some architecture journalists strive to offer the public sensations while disregarding solid, conscientious work. On the other hand, some architects simply attempt to attract attention and may do so even at the risk of wrongdoing. The task of the journalist should therefore not be underestimated.

Architects who deliver sensations now have extraordinary opportunities to become famous. In this way, they may acquire a sort of immortality and, as a by-product, interesting clients. So, to be "in" as an architect, you can either create something really meaningful or just be sensational, in much the same way that a movie actress can become a star through her acting skills or her love affairs, or (better yet) a combination of both.

In the United States, some architectural historians have created a list of the fifty most important international architects, to be used as a study aid by anyone trying to get an architectural license. Each architect on the list has been assigned a particular style, such as classicism, humanism, expressionism, functionalism, or technologism. Although my name is on this list, I am highly doubtful of its utility.

The list is a mixture of legitimately famous and merely notorious architects. It is by no means comprehensive. It doesn't include many who satisfy both the needs of their clients and those of society. Such architects are recognized in the serious trade press because their works promise a better environment, but they are neglected by other, more sensational media because their work isn't ostentatious.

It's also doubtful that the styles of architecture identified in this document can really be regarded as such. You might as well add styles such as Hitlerite, Mussoliniesque, and Stalinist. Efforts to define the styles of our time are futile, because the style of an era can be defined only retrospectively, after a hundred years or more.

In the past, architectural styles were determined by the construction period, geographic region, technical features (round arch, pointed arch, dome), materials (stone, clay, brick, timber, iron), and climatic conditions. In two hundred years, if anybody has the time and leisure to look back on the creations of our era, they will discover that there wasn't a uniform architectural style in the twentieth century. Due to our sophisticated communication systems, myriad materials and techniques may be used all over the world. Perhaps, once they have become as worthless as the Egyptian pyramids are today, our highways and their daring bridges will be regarded as the true expressions of our time.

Today, many architects aspire to create new styles, and eager journalists work their fingers to the bone to champion and catalog these styles, but they have confused the terms *style* and *fashion*. Architectural fashions change, perhaps not quite as fast as women's fashions, but fairly rapidly. In the past seventy years, we have witnessed the following fashions in architecture: eclecticism, Secessionism, functionalism, monumentalism, puritanism, Brutalism, abstractionism, and nostalgia. But this bears a resemblance to the fashion industry, where there are designers of haute couture and then there are garment manufacturers who spread fashion through mass production.

The difference between the fashionable architect and the serious one is that the latter begins by considering the content, purpose, and outer form of the building. These he tries to adapt to the landscape and the environment. The fashionable architect conjures up an external form and then tries (or leaves to others to try) to stuff the contents of the building into his "brilliant" form. The harmony between his work of art and its surroundings does not interest him. On the contrary, he knows that the greatest dissonance will attract the most attention.

Since some fashionable architects become famous, it seems appropriate to ask if they practice architecture as defined by Vitruvius, or if they are more or less imaginative people who just happen to design buildings rather than paint pictures.

Contrary to standard industry practice, I personally admire many living architects, some of them famous and many more not yet famous. I have been lucky enough to meet several great architects.

Frank Lloyd Wright is unique, in that he cannot be assigned to a so-called style. He drew from his rich imagination, based on the principle that architecture should be organic. Structure and nature would thus merge into one work. Each of his buildings exudes personality, and rarely that of its owner or user, but that of its builder.

One of his clients once described her suffering. She had made only a single personal request of the architect: namely, that he provide an open view from the kitchen into the garden. When she moved into the house, she discovered that since Wright conceived of the kitchen as the center of organic life, he had built a circular, windowless kitchen in the center of the house. It was lit with a skylight.

Celebrating Wright's creative work requires an appreciation of ingenuity. He founded two schools in the United States, one in the West and another in the East. He called them Taliesin West and Taliesin East. Tourists and disciples flocked to these sanctuaries, but once there, they all had to serve in the studio or work in the local economy without pay. My late friend the graphic artist Alvin Lustig once escaped from this servitude, but he was recaptured and made to stay until the end of his "educational obligation."

I was lucky to see two houses by the Master, one in the hills of Los Angeles, the other in a forest in Pennsylvania. These homes had an almost magical power, particularly Fallingwater, which we visited for a few weekends at the invitation of its owner, Edgar Kaufmann.[9] The house was like an exciting, romantic landscape—it seemed to have grown out of the forest and the rock formations that surrounded a rushing waterfall. Through a constant alternation between low, narrow spaces and overwhelming height and size, and without any reference to historical styles, the place stimulates visitors as much as a grand old castle.

Our host complained about the high maintenance costs. The living room featured a large glass skylight that opened out to a view of majestic treetops. It was unfortunately not watertight and in need of constant repair. The plaster of the facades was also not quite weather resistant. Kaufmann grouched that one needed to be a multimillionaire to own such a house. I told him, "Since you are a multimillionaire, it is custom-made for you."

I met Frank Lloyd Wright himself twice, once during a lecture that was organized by our client Dayton's. He used this opportunity to criticize the recently completed Southdale Center and its creator. He spoke of the desecration of nature. He was right in some ways, because the complex was intended for people's amusement.

After the lecture, a shy student approached and asked the Master his opinion about studying engineering. He responded: "Do you see these little warts on my left hand? These are engineers! I use them like an encyclopedia. When I find the appropriate answer, I shut the book again."

Frank Lloyd Wright hated not only engineers and modern architects but also cities. Nevertheless, he designed a futuristic community, and he gave it the name Broadacre City. In this city, every home was adjacent to an open field. He was obviously trying to find a way to get back to nature.

Wright's single famous building within a city is the Guggenheim Museum on Fifth Avenue in New York City. Wright had intended it to be a freestanding temple of art amid the romantic landscape of Central Park, which one could approach only on foot. Then city officials were seized with a sudden fever for environmental protection, and they prohibited any structural disturbance of the parkland. So the museum administrators acquired a property opposite the park. Wright refused to change anything in his plan, so this temple was inserted, like a small drawer, into a series of skyscrapers.

This extraordinary man could express his creative power only in places where rich people made it possible. Wright is also the only architect who is said to have continued to work after his death. His office is run by his widow, who says that for each new project she is able, thanks to her spiritual powers, to consult with the deceased.

Richard Neutra was also a gifted and creative architect. He and I were personal friends. He was the first to recognize the connections between architecture and biology, then study them and write about them. His works were mostly houses for educated and affluent members of the upper-middle class. His favorite building material was wood—he understood it well—and without borrowing from the past, he created architecture that was integrated naturally and comfortably in the hills and canyons of Southern California.

As with Wright, Neutra had only a casual interest in dense urban areas. The Los Angeles County Hall of Records, which he designed with Robert Alexander, displays decent ideas about architecture, but it is in no way exceptional.

In his later years, he dreamed of undertaking major projects, such as an opera house, university, or museum in one of the Arab states of the Middle East. Since he didn't have his own organization, he offered to make us his partners and architectural inheritors. But our further discussions revealed that Richard wanted to do all the design work himself and use us only for technical and graphic services. So, unfortunately, we turned down his offer. He shone in his writings and in his informed and witty speeches. He was undoubtedly one of the great men of architecture.

Unlike the two aforementioned architects, Le Corbusier had a keen interest in the fate of cities. Two phenomena impressed him most: the scandalous hygienic and social situation of European cities at the beginning of the twentieth century, where lightless, noisy, and polluted streets contributed to the spread of diseases such as tuberculosis; and the prevailing belief in the omnipotence of modern technology. In 1920–21, Le Corbusier wrote a dozen articles for the Paris magazine *Esprit Nouveau* that were republished in the book *Vers une architecture* in 1923 (the German translation was *Kommende Baukunst,* 1926).

As mentioned in chapter 4, I was deeply impressed by this universalist social reformer. Le Corbusier thought engineering should be "advised by the law of parsimony and governed by mathematical calculation and harmony," and he believed it was the great hope of architecture. He was a great admirer of ocean liners, airplanes, and cars, and he preached the development of a housing machine and the serial construction of residential homes. He regarded architecture as a pure creation of the mind.

By 1920, Le Corbusier had produced plans for tower cities wherein sixty-story, uniformly designed buildings, spaced at intervals of 250 and 300 meters, would be located amid large green areas, which, in turn, would be cut by powerful, nonintersecting motorways. The tower city, which he wanted to build at the center of Paris, would serve the city as a work hub. In his vision of the Ville Radieuse, subways and highways radiated from the center into greener residential areas. In the years since, his essays from 1921 and 1922 have had a lasting influence on the planning and building of all cities.

Le Corbusier later became a romantic. He created the beautiful chapel at Ronchamp, France, and the plan for the Indian city of Chandigarh, which included an irregular street pattern and a romantic headquarters building. In this spirit, he wrote in the German preface to a 1958 edition of his book *Ausblick auf eine Architektur*: "The gourmet of the salons (in Paris or in the United States) calls me today a 'baroque' architect. This is the most cruel name you can call me. I started as a 'dirty' engineer in 1920 (that I had accepted), but now I obviously arrived at the opposite end of hell—long live the extremes! But maybe it's not even that bad, to be slandered at seventy!"[10]

I admire architects who deal successfully with the difficult tasks of urban conservation, regeneration, and housing construction, with the relationship between architecture and environmental problems, and, against all odds, with the enhancement of the quality of life of cities and other settlements. This group includes some of my closest associates, such as Rudolf L. Baumfeld, Edgardo Contini, and Ben Southland.

On the other hand, I count many of the most famous shapers of form as friends and acquaintances, but I am critical of them. The German Bauhaus school provides one example: the Bauhaus cleared away all the characteristics of past styles with a chrome steel brush, and then it began to search for a new design language. I was a close friend of Walter Gropius, the school's founder, and I had great sympathy for his creations, because his deep humanism broke all formalistic chains.

Ludwig Mies van der Rohe was different. He understood the phrase "Form follows function" solely as a reference to the structural skeleton of a building. He threw out the baby with the bathwater by abandoning ornamentation and everything else that unites architecture with humanity, traditions, and feelings.

He was hailed as a classicist by architecture critics because he developed a very specific language of form and then deployed it everywhere, regardless of the purposes of his buildings. The lecture halls, power plant, and church of the Illinois Institute of Technology in Chicago (built after his design) all look the same. The power plant could be mistaken for a church—its high chimney even looks like a bell tower.

Mies concentrated on the external appearance of buildings. He used simple grids of vertical and horizontal lines. This resulted in a need for horizontal roofs. Philip Johnson was a student who later turned away from him, but he initially called Mies his "guru." He claimed that Mies didn't leave Germany because he had an objection to the Third Reich, but because he thought Adolf Hitler was a bad architect who wouldn't allow him to build buildings with flat roofs.

I saw Mies (his many followers called themselves Miesianer) as a humorless, hardheaded man. He also seemed to be a Puritan, as implied by his motto "Less is more," as well as by the fact that he limited his vocabulary of building materials to glass, metal, and polished marble. Two other precepts were important to him: first, the architect is a sort of sculptor whose task is to put large sculptures into space; second, the sculptor should not engage with any problems, such as town planning, that lie outside the architect's art.

In Chicago, a contractor named Grunewald gave Mies the chance to execute his first two "sculptures" in the United States. The building site was in the most beautiful location on the shore of Lake Michigan. Through friends who were collectors of modern art and had lived in one of his sculptures, I met Mies at his home in Los Angeles. He was surrounded by many admirers. My dialogue with him was resented by both the Master and his disciples. I reported that my friends were very proud to live in a building by a famous architect, but that this pleasure was muted, because in winter, they froze behind the huge glass areas on the northwest side, and in summer, they burned on the southwest side. To this, Mies dryly remarked, "For the arts, one must be willing to make sacrifices."

I stated my objection that the function of the structure was not fully expressed because some elements, particularly the steel columns, were not visible. They had had to be covered with concrete because of fire regulations. Therefore, I continued, the aluminum grid in the facade that framed those large windows was, in my opinion, nothing more than ornamentation. Mies replied angrily that he was not responsible for idiotic fire regulations, and that the aluminum grid was to be understood as symbolizing the construction and was therefore perfectly legitimate.

My friends had complained of the lack of air-conditioning and the very poor interior layout of the building. Mies pushed aside these concerns and proclaimed that such things are the responsibility of the building owner and do not concern him as an architect. His job was to take care of the aesthetic appearance of the sculpture at any time of the day. To do this, he explained, he had provided all the windows with the same silver-gray shades, which were meant to be lowered by all the tenants at the same time.

I joked that the motto "Less is more" could, if taken to its logical conclusion, mean "At best, nothing." Mies was visibly annoyed, and he ended our discussion.

In the glass houses he built later, all rooms were air-conditioned. I must concede that Mies gave a lot of loving attention to the proportions of his sculptures and the design of his metal grids, which made them very costly.

I encountered Mies again in the sixties in Detroit. A working group consisting of architects Oscar Stonorov (Philadelphia) and Minoru Yamasaki (Detroit) and my organization had designed a large new residential building in that city for a redevelopment agency. It was located in a slum in the city center and was meant to be inhabited by minorities.

According to the rules of the redevelopment agency, bids were now being accepted for the building's construction. One bid was from the Chicago company Grunewald. This bid was subject to the condition that a new project by an architect of Mr. Grunewald's choosing would replace our design. The new project was conceived by Mies and the city planner Ludwig Hildesheimer. It was presented to the building committee with a large, exquisitely executed model. The model depicted a group of similar residential towers in strict geometrical order. The chairman of the building committee, Walter Reuther (president of the United Automobile Workers labor union), remarked, "The problem with you Germans is that you never understood the difference between military discipline and harmonious order."

Despite the general unease around their plan, however, the Mies/Grunewald project bid was accepted. At a luncheon sometime afterward, I had a conversation with the successful contractor. I asked him how their plan could be economically feasible, given Mies's expensive facade design. At first, he explained that as a patron of the arts, he was an admirer of the great master Mies. When I demonstrated that I was not satisfied with this answer, he explained to me that the exterior design would be more expensive than usual, but that it would constitute only a fraction of the total cost of the building. "I can build cheaper with Mies per square foot than any other architects, because Mies shows no interest for anything within the building. Therefore, I use my own discretion inside, and achieve great savings. Since intelligent people are willing to pay higher rents for the privilege of living in a building designed by the Master, I get an excellent return on my investment."

The motivations of the owner of Mies's most famous creation, the Seagram Building in New York, were quite different. The building was set far back from the street, so much of the property remained undeveloped, and this slim tower had an elaborate facade of bronze and glass. In fact, the Seagram Building was the most expensive office tower in the city.

The contractor, Mr. Bronfman, had two objectives. The building was meant to be a three-dimensional advertising poster for Seagram's whiskey—the more sensational and expensive this poster looked, the greater would be the advertising effect. Mr. Bronfman was also anxious to polish up his role as a patron of the arts, because he had been battered by suspicions that he was a rumrunner during Prohibition.

Mies worked with Philip Johnson to design the Seagram Building, and while it was still in the planning stages, I praised their design to Philip. By setting the building back from the street, I said, they would create a public square in the rocky desert of New York. With trees, flowers, and benches, this might become an inviting space for recreation. Philip looked at me aghast and said that this was certainly not Mies's intent. The space would serve to increase the monumental impact of the building and encourage people to note their own insignificance compared with the majesty of the building. There would be no trees or benches. On the contrary, Johnson and Mies were designing symmetrically arranged fountains so that it would be impossible to sit anywhere in this square.

The Seagram Building demonstrated the kinds of sacrifices that must be made in the quest for monumentality. During construction, the engineers insisted that for stability reasons the entire north facade would have to be built as a solid reinforced concrete wall. Another group of engineers claimed parts of the west and east facades for ventilation shafts. Mies would not allow his sculpture to be spoiled by these considerations. So the north facade was clad in marble and then masked with the same glass-and-bronze grid used on the rest of the facade. Because of this, important sections of the interior became dark and unusable. The masking of glass was an obvious hoax, but Mies asserted that it was justified in the interest of monumentality.

Mies's grid system of glass and metal was advantageous because it could be cleaned easily by workers on small gondolas lowered from the roof. It was also easily imitated and proved to be a good source of income for producers of metal grids. These "curtain facades" were soon mass-produced, albeit with significantly less sensitivity to proportionality, and sold at low prices per square foot. The result was what is called the International Style, which owes its existence to cheap mass production and was indeed used around the world, without regard to climatic conditions and local architectural traditions. Mies himself probably disliked this development, which had nothing to do with art anymore.

As these glass towers sprouted everywhere, users revolted against the *Neue Sachlichkeit* (New Objectivity) of these futuristic facades. Interior spaces were decorated in various historical styles. Air-conditioning and electric lighting made the inside totally independent of the exterior, and the glass surfaces, which had been meant to deliver light and great views, did neither. Any correlation between facade and interior design disappeared. This is why I ask whether Ludwig Mies van der Rohe should be regarded as an architect or as a dedicated creator of gigantic sculptures.

Philip Johnson, on the other hand, has become an excellent example of a highly talented author of architectural haute couture. In 1978, he was honored with the highest distinction bestowed by the American Institute of Architects.

Because of our personal acquaintance—Philip once offered to be my partner—I have been able to follow his changing affiliations with various architectural fashions. When I first met him, he was devoted to glass houses and the *Neue Sachlichkeit.* At that time, he built himself a glass house in a park, where he still lives. "I just look at architecture as art, it can therefore not be combined with functionality and humanity; otherwise it is not free," he once said. But he later became an expressionist, because the puritanism bored him and had started to seem like a hoax, the sole purpose of which was artistic self-realization.

Other quotes from him include the following:

> We modern architects are all swindlers.
>
> I'm just an aestheticist.
>
> I'm against all that is working, I want to annoy people.

And:

> I know that I'm arrogant, but it is better to be honestly arrogant than to be honestly modest.

Since he was not afraid of these arrogant comments circulating in public, he published them in some of his books. His spectacular quotes, and the buildings resulting from his attitude, earned him an unusual amount of publicity and business. His actual way of thinking became clearer in an interview he gave. He said, "Victor has the opinion that if we talk about design, we neglect the big picture: his architecture is clean, he makes no attempt to be witty. If you are in one of his creations, one gets the impression that this is more than design. You could say, there is no one like him. Architecture may be lucky to have him as an architect."

A European example of Brutalism is the Centre Pompidou in Paris, which the Parisians ironically call "refinery Pompidou." This building is meant to bring culture and art closer to the population, but as designed by architects Renzo Piano and Richard Rogers, it is like a terrorist attack on a lovingly restored old ensemble. A naive observer might believe that it is not yet finished and still surrounded by scaffolding. In fact, that steel-frame scaffolding is part of the load-bearing structure.

Because this sleek, unprotected structure might bend under the influence of heat, and the whole building could collapse upon thousands of visitors, the support structure is purely symbolic, like some of the elements in Mies's creations.

Merely revealing the construction elements on the outside seemed unsatisfactory to the designers. An entire system of intestines and digestive organs, which is protected in a natural organism by skin, flesh, and bones, appears as a facade here, painted in bright colors, an "artistic" design. Ventilation shafts, water lines, sanitary drainage lines, pipes of all kinds serve as decorative exterior elements. (One must be grateful that the artists did not add toilet bowls.)

Even the escalator is not what would be convenient for the numerous visitors to the center, but instead runs like a snake along one of the outer edges. It is wrapped in a clear plastic tube and requires very powerful heating, ventilation, and cooling systems, which consume a great deal of energy. (In fact, it resembles the plastic tubes visitors to Charles de Gaulle Airport must ride like some sort of roller coaster.)

This obsession with exposing the structure's "guts" on its luxurious exterior required so much attention and money that little of either was left over for the interior of this temple of art. As a consequence, the building is already showing signs of wear that give it a shabby appearance. Despite everything, because of the publicity and the sensational appearance of the building, it will certainly win a place in the history of architecture in the twentieth century.

The abstract architect is a packaging artist who tries to find a very uniform geometric shape for all of his buildings, even if they serve different functions. Perhaps he adorns his buildings with colorful mirrors. Architecture photographers are fascinated by such buildings because they create interesting reflections of the surroundings, of turrets, domes, and steep roofs. If heaven allows, they also reflect the sunrise or sunset, cloud formations, and brilliant azure skies. One can imagine a city consisting of nothing but such mirrored buildings. They would reflect only each other, and the city would become an enormous carnivalesque hall of mirrors.

Architectural expressionists seem to address any problem with the question "Why not?" They ask: "Instead of the usual rectangle for this structure, why not choose a triangle, a pentagon, a hexagon, an octagon, a circle, an egg shape, a kidney shape, or a blend of all the above? Why should the exterior walls be vertical? Why not develop pyramids, cones, etc.? Let the house resemble a snail shell, a cone, a tent, or an igloo! Let's do something unprecedented to impress or shock or annoy the world, but especially the critics."

At the risk of being called a heretic, I suggest that those who merely focus on the form and shape of the outer shell of a building should not be considered architects in the tradition of Vitruvius.

Public indignation over the many fashions in architecture was inevitable. Therefore, many architects are now riding a wave of nostalgia. Different "home styles" and other folk art motifs are imitated. But that seems hopeless. Naïveté is like virginity: once it is lost, it cannot be found again.

Nevertheless, it seems promising to study anonymous architecture, and to investigate the reasons for slow-growing traditions, for certain usages of materials, for selection of certain forms, and perhaps then to bring them to an environmentally conscious humanity in the form of contemporary architecture meant for enjoyment.

7

Environmental Planning

AN END AND A NEW BEGINNING

In March 1938, there were external circumstances—a fascist regime and my escape from it—that changed the course of my life. But thirty years later, in July 1968, it was internal forces that changed my life again. These forces, subconscious or otherwise, had worked on me since my youth. It became more and more difficult from year to year to calm a certain restlessness I felt by staying busy, hunting for professional success, and searching for domestic bliss.

I took many steps to avoid this danger. Working on my dream projects, teaching at Columbia University and the University of California, and participating with humanitarian organizations were escape attempts. The turning point was, as so often in my life, brought about by accident: in 1950, we had drafted a set of bylaws for Victor Gruen Associates that stipulated that at the age of sixty-five, partners should retire to make way for their children.

Since I would be celebrating my sixty-fifth birthday in July 1968, my resignation was now within sight. I had made my decision long before that. By as early as 1966, I was already expressing this to my partners. I rejected well-intentioned proposals about the abolition of the age clause or a continuing role for me as a senior consultant. I wanted to devote myself to consulting work in the areas of urban and environmental planning. I declared that I would begin as soon as possible and would use the time before my official retirement to facilitate the transition of the organization and gradually transfer my areas of responsibility to others.

My decision caused problems for everyone. It became a question of how we could prevent a conflict between my consulting work and the work of the organization.

We made an agreement of geographical nature. I concentrated my work in Europe, and the rest of the world was open to the organization founded by me.

During the transition period, from 1966 to 1968, I helped to find new partners. We managed to retain the extremely talented Cesar Pelli for creative design (a few years later he left the company and became dean of Yale University's School of Architecture). Some of the associates were promoted to partner. "Victor" was dropped, and we became simply Gruen Associates. My friend Rudi Baumfeld, who was about my age, decided to remain with the firm as a consultant.

The initial concern that my exit would lead to the ruin of the firm proved to be unfounded because of the ability of the partners and staff. Old clients stayed loyal, new ones were added. Even after I had withdrawn completely from its activities in 1968, the firm continued to prosper.

For me personally, the break was accompanied by heavy sacrifice. I could cope with the loss of my offices in Los Angeles, New York, and Washington, D.C., and the prestige I had enjoyed as president of a large organization because of my newfound personal freedom. But it was much more difficult to lose close personal contact with my partners and many of the staff, especially our secretary Hortense Hockett, executive director Helen Michaelis, and many of the associates, who had also become personal friends. I saw them all during my trips to America, which I made almost every year until 1976. On these occasions, meetings were held with all the partners and associates.

AN INTERNATIONAL COMPETITION

In 1969, I was in Vienna when Cesar Pelli asked my advice on participating in an international architectural competition to design a center for the United Nations in the Austrian capital. I advised him to avoid the competition. In general, because of my experience as a member of juries, I consider architectural competitions to be an improper means of finding optimal solutions for projects. Decisions are often made not based on the quality of the designs but because of a particularly effective graphic presentation or because of the overwhelming eloquence of one of the jurors.

In the case of this U.N. competition, my concerns were also related to urban development. The office buildings of the United Nations had previously been scattered all over the city, and their planned centralization appeared problematic to me because of the amount of traffic and the danger of ghettoization such a project might produce. I also feared that politics would play an important role in the selection of the architect.

But Pelli and his team found the task so attractive that they worked very hard to apply for participation in this gigantic project. The jury's decision was a big surprise.

The first prize was awarded to Gruen Associates; fourth prize went to an Austrian architect. Now in a euphoric mood, Pelli and his team went to Vienna to accept the prize. I agreed to act as an interpreter in the negotiations with authorities. Some journalists in the mass media even suspected that I had opened an office in Vienna several years earlier for the express purpose of taking part in this competition.

But a minor paragraph of the jury's ruling called for an additional competition. This paragraph indicated that none of the winning projects were regarded as ready for execution. From this the Austrian authorities deduced that the four winners should give details about their projects. It was further clarified that this "second stage of the competition" would not affect the initial ranking of the judges.

So a commission of experts compared the feasibility of the four projects. They came to the conclusion that the project by the Austrian architect, Johann Staber, would be by far the cheapest to build, while the prize-winning American project would be the most expensive.

For patriotic reasons, the Austrian authorities favored the winner of the fourth prize. The experts had calculated the costs of the projects by using a simple but entirely inappropriate method. They had carefully calculated the cubic contents of each of the four projects with the help of a computer, then multiplied the results by a fixed unit price per cubic meter, without consideration of different construction methods. Since the project of the Austrian architect provided far less space than the competition rules had called for, his design required the smallest number of cubic meters and therefore had the lowest projected price. The other three architects in the competition and representatives of the United Nations all protested this method of calculating the project costs.

I personally drew the Austrian authorities' attention to the experts' blunder and finally contacted the man I knew would make the final decision, my old friend Chancellor Bruno Kreisky. There followed an extensive correspondence, some of which Kreisky allowed to be published in the media. Eventually, Kreisky announced his decision in parliament and explained that he didn't want to be accused of favoring his friends. The project by the English architect was supported by Kreisky's good friend the prime minister of Great Britain, Harold Wilson; the project by the German architect was supported by his good friend German chancellor Willy Brandt; and the American project was supported by his old friend Victor Gruen. If Kreisky wanted to avoid charges of favoritism, he had no alternative but to make a decision in favor of the previously unknown Austrian architect, Johann Staber.

This impressive project was completed in the summer of 1979 and opened with great fanfare. The cost exceeded all estimates. This was quite understandable: during the planning, Staber had to increase the amount of space in the complex in deference to the demands of the U.N. agencies. The curved facade of the building was also much more expensive per cubic meter of construction then it would have been in the much simpler project proposed by our first prize-winning plan.

The gigantic U.N. complex is today a false landmark of Vienna. Even the basic idea that this was necessary to accommodate the various agencies and to increase the efficiency of four thousand U.N. employees was wrong. In this age of telecommunications, a decentralized system is just as efficient and, from the perspective of users and visitors, more humane and comfortable. At the time, I also suspected that a public transportation connection to the complex would be enormously expensive.

NEW GOALS

With the exception of my contribution to the U.N. project competition, I spent most of my time from 1966 to 1968 preparing for my official retirement in July 1968. Strangely enough, I didn't consider it a reasonable idea that as a sixty-five-year-old one should not begin a new life and creative period. With a young, dynamic woman at my side, it was tempting to end a successful career in the United States after thirty years and start all over again.

I took two challenges at the threshold of this new chapter of my life: I wanted to make a contribution to improving the human condition in general, and I wanted to warn Europe to take heed of the American example.

To achieve the first, I had already set up a nonprofit organization in Los Angeles called the Victor Gruen Foundation for Environmental Planning (later renamed the Victor Gruen Center for Environmental Planning). I did this out of personal beliefs that I have long cherished. In 1966, the *Los Angeles Times* wrote: "Long before anyone dealt with environmental problems, there was a man named Victor Gruen who preached environmental planning."[1]

This was an era when the concept of the environment was familiar only to a few visionaries. It required the most intensive efforts to convince the public of the meaning and importance of "environmental activity." This seemed so urgent to me that I sacrificed a great deal of money to this dream of making the world better.

VICTOR GRUEN INTERNATIONAL

Our spacious home in Bel Air now became the headquarters of our environmental efforts. We established an environmental library in one of the wings of the house, while other rooms were converted to administrative offices and meeting rooms; in good weather, meetings and seminars were held in the garden as well. For our personal use, we kept only the bedrooms, bathrooms, and guest room, in which we placed the family of my brother-in-law, Kemal Salihefendic, who had moved with his wife and son from Yugoslavia to the United States. Our relatives proved to be extremely helpful with the maintenance of the house and garden, but also with their work for the center.

A bathhouse and changing room in our garden was rebuilt and became my second work area. It was a study room with a desk and a drawing board, and it would serve as the headquarters of the newly established company Victor Gruen International.

This metamorphosis of our home into a place of work meant heavy sacrifices, particularly for Kemija. Until then, our house and garden had given her ample opportunities to exercise her various talents. She had transformed the garden into a paradise of flowers. Because of her parties, our house had become a center of social life in Los Angeles.

Kemija was also very inspired by an oil painting called *Schloss Kammer,* by Gustav Klimt, which Lazette and I had acquired in 1959, and she had become a painter. She did a large number of oil paintings, which triggered both surprise and admiration in me. Her paintings, which she created in the garage of our house, would later shape the character of our apartment in Vienna. But all of these activities that brought Kemija's personality to full development had to move to the background because of the new obligations she took on in 1968. From then on, she was my closest colleague—perhaps the most crucial partner in my life.

Whether our sacrifices of money, time, and work on other cherished projects have paid off is a question that I dare not answer. Efforts at environmental planning of course cannot provide any immediate visible or tangible results. An echo, or even an aftereffect, can be expected only in the long run. We continued our efforts anyway: in 1973, we founded a similar organization in Europe called the Zentrum für Umweltplanung.

I had a mission: I wanted Victor Gruen International to bring all the experience and insight I had collected in the field of architecture and urban and environmental planning to Europe. I hoped that I could impart some knowledge to my home continent and prevent it from repeating the urban planning mistakes of the United States. My motto was, "America must not be imitated, it must be understood."

A MISSIONARY IN EUROPE

The question of how to attract prospects for my consulting work was completely open, because we had no clients in Europe. I optimistically assumed that my return to Europe would be similar to my arrival in America in 1939, when the seeds I had sown in five years of work as an architect in Vienna bore fruit in the United States. This hope was based in the fact that I had prepared the ground well in Europe. During my annual summer trips since 1948, I had given lectures, attended conferences and meetings, and held talks with influential architects, planners, government officials, politicians, economists, and scientists across the continent.[2] Many of my American projects had been featured in the leading European architectural journals, such as *Architectural Record* in London, *L'Architecture d'Aujourd'hui* in Paris, and *Baumeister* in Germany, and in the newspapers of many countries.

Even the times seemed to favor the project. Twenty years had passed since the end of World War II, enough time to heal the wounds of destruction almost everywhere, overcome the horrors, and undertake something new. At the same time, the United States had reached the peak of its prestige. Everything that was American was admired or envied in Europe. I hoped that my status as a successful American architect with a European upbringing and state of mind would help me.

Initially, I expected a slow evolution and a leisurely pace of work. I was wrong. Although I insisted on high hourly and daily fees and remuneration for all travel and accommodation expenses, I was overwhelmed with challenging jobs. Accordingly, we had to adapt to a new kind of nomadic life. We found out that we both needed additional language skills. Kemija and I spoke German and English (Kemija also knew Slovenian and Serbo-Croatian), but what we both lacked was a thorough knowledge of French. We subjected ourselves to intensive instruction. We found an excellent French teacher in Los Angeles, with whom we worked a few hours daily for three months. To our amazement, it turned out that he originally was from Wiener Neustadt, a small town south of Vienna. We soon mastered the new language so well that I could write papers and reports in French, while Kemija improved her linguistic skills so much that in Paris she was soon mistaken for a Frenchwoman—albeit one from Marseilles.

One of my consulting activities, for the housing company Neue Heimat in Hamburg, gave me an opportunity to revisit my childhood times in the town of Eutin. With pleasure, I discovered that the romantic little town appeared to be intact and unchanged. Everything was much as it had been at the time of our annual visits there before World War I. However, the family house and the beautiful garden were gone. In their place was—what irony of fate!—a modern shopping center. Inquiries revealed that the house was seized and demolished during Nazi times, as it was owned by Jews. I felt melancholy about this.

From 1966 to 1972, we commuted almost without respite between Los Angeles, New York, France, Belgium, Germany, Italy, Switzerland, Austria, Spain, the Netherlands, Denmark, Sweden, and Norway, with side trips to Russia, Czechoslovakia, Hungary, and Yugoslavia. We tried to combine work and pleasure.

Unforgettable feasts were arranged for us. The biggest impression was made by a feast arranged by the architectural community in Bergen, which had hired a line of torchbearers for the occasion. At a gala dinner in Paris, we gathered together about sixty representatives from government, business, culture, and politics in the restaurant Ledoyen. We created a small sensation by inviting our guests' wives, which was actually not a common practice in France.

We weren't able to do all of the work ourselves. To make my ideas understandable, I needed highly qualified draftsmen. Even as Kemija became an excellent travel marshal, we needed the help of lawyers, accountants, and tax consultants. But above all, we needed to have our extensive correspondence in various languages clearly organized. Wherever possible, we improvised with the help of secretaries provided by the hotels, but in some cases, this was not enough.

In Paris, for example, we established a branch office called the Société Civile de Recherches sur l'Urbanisme in spacious quarters that took up one full floor of the building at 4 Avenue Marceau. There we combined an apartment with work and conference space, a drawing room, and several guest rooms for the temporarily hired technicians. Other work spaces, such as those for Victor Gruen International in Vienna, began as the garden of the house at Goldeggasse 7; we later founded Victor Gruen Planning and Architecture AG, based in Cham in Switzerland, and also rented work space at Traungasse 7 in Vienna. Still other work spaces emerged temporarily in Louvain and Brussels in Belgium, and in Milan. We employed multilingual secretaries in all of these studios and also at the birthplace of the society in Los Angeles.

Seven years passed this way, during which we were at home everywhere and nowhere. During one boring flight, we counted the number of toilets we had in our various homes in Los Angeles, New York, Paris, Vienna, and Bergholtzgut: twenty-seven.

I became a city doctor, an urbanologist, and I was asked to diagnose various symptoms. Occasionally, the diagnoses of various other specialists were already available, and the nature of the disease and potential cures were already known. I identified the following symptoms in sick cities: circulatory disorders, aging, poisoning from overdoses of foreign substances, vitamin deficiencies, anemia, constipation, malnutrition, oversaturation, and heart failure.

As a city physician, I used a first aid kit full of the remedies that I had developed in my long years of experience and finally presented in my books *The Heart of Our Cities* and *The Livable City.*[3] I argued that even a large city should not be a pompous caricature; rather, it should be a structured federation of independent city units that fit together, each of which should have a population of forty to eighty thousand people. To avoid sterility, each of these city units should be divided into subunits that fit together. These subunits might include counties, districts, neighborhoods, communities, or family organizations. Each element of the structure and substructure should include different sociological groups and city facilities (dwellings, workplaces, cultural centers, training centers, entertainment centers, health centers, and so on).

This can be achieved only if each individual function of the livable city is a spatial city, which means it is planned using the three dimensions of length, width, and height. Small-grained integration is achieved through both horizontal and vertical integration. Although close integration is desirable in the field of human relations, in the relationship between technical facilities and human spaces the greatest possible separation is desirable. Using multidimensional planning principles, it is possible to locate technical facilities and main lines (distribution substations, gas mains, and operational traffic) in those areas that are less desirable for human housing and activities. Such arrangements can be built underground or under artificial platforms, while respecting the basic principle that technical support facilities should be seen and heard as little as possible.

As the outer shape of the city units and their subdivisions, the circle is the ideal form because it establishes equal distances to the center and has the largest surface in relation to its circumference. This is not to imply that a mechanical use of the circle is recommended, but only that under consideration of topography, geography, climate conditions, and traditions, irregular shapes should arise with round rather than oval forms. Also, the population density of a city (population per unit) is a question that causes quite a stir. The density and sprawl of Los Angeles make urbanity impossible and waste natural assets such as land, water, air, flora, fauna, and other resources unnecessarily. Excessive density leads to supersaturation and the strangulation of urbanity. An acceptable density is 150 to 400 people per hectare, which amounts to the crowding of neither people nor infrastructure.

Freedom of individual expression can be achieved in a structured city that is composed of smaller units, because the individual buildings and installations can be designed through interaction between the users and tens of thousands of creative forces. Sterile superprojects should not be present in a livable city. Due to the livable city's structural composition, which consists of autonomous and semiautonomous divisions and subdivisions, and following from the principle of small-grained integration, the opportunity for direct human communication increases. At the same time, the demand on transportation facilities shrinks. The need for mobility can be met easily by community vehicles (e.g., taxis) and collective vehicles (buses, underground trains, trams).

The livable city does not have to be an exceptional case, or the result of the planning and construction of a new town. Each of our existing cities can gradually be brought closer to the vision of the livable city. Since quality of life derives partly from an interweaving of the old and the new, there is great promise in the gradual transformation of existing cities.

In response to the ideas developed by Le Corbusier in his Athens Charter, I published the Charter of Vienna in 1973.[4] Basically, I countered the key themes of the Athens Charter—including traffic-based city designs—with a call for high-density, carefully integrated, pedestrian-friendly, and people-friendly cities. I declared my belief that city planning that gives transportation planning the highest priority is wrong. I recommended planning against traffic to achieve a maximum of communication on foot and a minimum measure of mechanized traffic.

My urban medical work was complicated by various national "spleens" (which I had not come across in the United States). For example, the architects and planners of France held certain perceptions of monumentality and representation. One repeatedly proposed idea there was to establish a "Place de la Prestige" in the city center; however, usually no one knew what kinds of buildings should frame this square. Reasoning that "animation" would be essential, many colleagues wanted to allow cars even in areas where this was not necessary. The young architects who belonged to the extreme political left argued for so-called agoras as places for student demonstrations and barricade fights. Older colleagues, however, were inspired by Haussmann to create impressive buildings along wide promenades. Among my Russian colleagues I discovered a preference for bureaucratic and military order; the Italians changed their preferences according to either futurism or nostalgia.

The histories of about sixty cases for which I served as an urbanologist are documented in the archives of the city of Vienna and also in the Library of Congress in Washington, D.C. Many of these case studies are described and illustrated in my book *Centers for the Urban Environment: Survival of the Cities*.[5] I will mention one of the projects here in brief.

CORE AREA OF VIENNA

During my many trips to Vienna between 1948 and 1968, I met with mayors, planning directors, and other leaders to discuss the design of my hometown. In 1969, I finally received an order from the city council to undertake a study on the redevelopment and revitalization of the core area. The order also applied to all measures that had been deemed necessary for the improvement of the downtown district and the surrounding area.

The core area of Vienna, the First District, is the oldest part of town, and until 1860 it was surrounded with ramparts and city gates. The original population of the district was more than one hundred thousand, but the number had fallen to

Report cover, Victor Gruen International, *Kerngebiet Wien* (Vienna, 1969/70). Library of the City of Vienna, City Hall.

twenty-five thousand. The vacant residential space was taken over by commercial businesses and offices. The core area is also home to the most important public buildings, including many museums, concert halls, cathedrals, ministries, the Burgtheater, the State Opera, and the main building of the university. Shoppers and visitors have access to hundreds of small and medium-size shops as well as to a large number of restaurants. Their use, however, had suffered from the fact that the tight, irregular, weblike system of streets, alleys, and squares was overloaded with passenger cars and trucks. Traffic jams were permanent, and pedestrians were severely endangered. The traffic noise and exhaust fumes harassed and threatened to expel the last residents of the district and deterred shoppers and tourists.

Our study, which was concluded in 1971, articulated methods by which the entire inner city (within the Ringstrasse and the ring roads Franz-Josefs-Kai and Lastenstrasse) could be transformed into an environmental oasis.[6] Furthermore, the study suggested how this area could be made more accessible through the improvement of public transportation, and how electrically powered small vehicles could be introduced for intraurban travel. For transport of commercial goods and waste, we proposed the use of the subway lines during the late night and early morning hours, as well as a system of underground conveyor belts and even electric freight vehicles, which would also operate only during the early morning.

The annoying side effects of personal auto traffic could be contained by concentric rings. Each of these rings would consist of a bypass road, associated garages, and goods relocation sites. The ultimate ring would be outside the city limits and would serve as a retention basin for most of the incoming individual traffic to the region. Another concentric circle would be comprised of the Ringstrasse, Franz-Josefs-Kai, and Lastenstrasse. Underground garages could be built along this ring, and private vehicles would not be allowed in the inner city.

The aim of the concept was that the First District would again become the most appealing, livable part of the city, with the air kept clean, the noise reduced, and the environmental conditions improved through additional green zones. My suggestions: the development of new subway lines downtown, the complete exclusion of gasoline-powered vehicle traffic, and the replacement of conventional, single-home heating systems with remote heating. I also suggested the relocation of noncore functions, such as warehouses, trucking companies, and certain industrial facilities, to other parts of the city. Any areas made vacant through this relocation could be used for residential development.

This attempt to make my hometown a better place was a labor of love to which I devoted energy, experience, and considerable sums of money (about twice as much as I received in fees). I had to conduct this task in cooperation with various departments of the city government. Unfortunately, this requirement proved an obstacle rather than an aid. It turned out that here, as in most cities of the world, the planning bureaucracy consisted of specialists who were unable to think or plan universally. Specifically, I had to deal with traffic experts who suffered from the very common disease of "autoneurosis." The planning ethos of this kind of traffic fetishist attempts to adjust the city to cars and regards trams, buses, and especially trees as annoying obstacles. First, I had to teach them what a pedestrian is.

All of the measures that I proposed, which were meant to make the city more human oriented, were met with the total ignorance and open resistance of the planning bureaucracy. I was forced, for example, to eliminate an entire chapter of my report because in it I recommended that a previously planned motorway network should be abandoned. It was made clear to me that if I did not submit to this censorship, I would receive no fee.[7]

Drawing of Luegerplatz. Victor Gruen International, *Kerngebiet Wien* (Vienna, 1969/70). Library of the City of Vienna, City Hall.

Nevertheless, the city management refused to publish the planning report and even refused the offer of a large private publisher (Fritz Molden) to publish the report in the form of a book.

It is worth noting that some of this overall plan eventually came to fruition. By 1979, a few lines of the subway were finished, and some underground garages had been built and put into operation. A number of streets in the inner city have been turned into pedestrian zones, and a limited number of diesel minibuses, for travel within the core area, have been put into operation.

I repeatedly remarked that the plan would work only if put into effect in its totality. I was answered by one of the senior officials of the municipal department in the following way: "We know, Mr. Architect, that what you have suggested may be necessary in its entirety, but we are afraid to frighten the voters and therefore we are going forward with salami tactics" (so named because salami can be eaten one thin slice at a time).

Despite all odds and obstacles, I was officially honored in connection with this project. I received not only the architecture prize of the city of Vienna in 1972 but

Victor Gruen, Peggy Gruen, and Herta Firnberg at the award ceremony for the Great Golden Medal for Merit to the Republic of Austria (Großes Goldenes Ehrenkreuz), Vienna, 1978. Courtesy of Peggy Gruen.

also the Golden Medal for services to the county of Vienna in 1978. Ultimately, even the partial realization of this plan yielded a strong improvement in the business, social, and cultural life of downtown Vienna.

Looking back over this period of intense activity as a missionary in Europe, I believe it was very instructive for me and fruitful for many people with whom I worked. If results lagged behind expectations, this was due to obstacles and constraints that occurred between social and economic systems.

In my view, one set of circumstances was the main cause of the disappointments. The decisive factor was the lack of personalities who were willing or able to act as universalists, to consider town planning issues from different perspectives. I found that highly trained specialists were available everywhere—for example, in transport planning and in the design of individual systems—but what couldn't be found were people who were willing to look beyond the limits of their specialized fields. For example, in the planning of satellite towns in the region of Paris, I had to deal either with graduates of the École Nationale des Ponts et Chaussées (National School of Bridges and Roads) or with the more aesthetically oriented graduates of the École des Beaux-Arts. The employees who were made available by the planning office of the city of Vienna were all underground engineering technicians.

It also seemed to me that politicians have little interest in planning activities. Nevertheless, they usually insist on exercising decisive influence, particularly with regard to popular implementation measures. For planning projects, which require periods of twenty to thirty years for their realization, it is particularly damaging if politicians want clearly perceptible results on key dates—such as before elections. It often comes to pass that essential measures that are less sensational or audience-grabbing are postponed or not executed at all.

Moreover, even if a large project is created through a planning organization that works independently from the politics of the day and stresses the long-term interests of the community, when it comes to the execution of the project, at least some of it will be outsourced to private companies. It usually turns out that it is impossible to reconcile the interests of the private firms with those of the project planners. Any interest in a project's benefits to the community will become transformed by private entrepreneurs into the pursuit of high returns. As long as this dichotomy continues, the money that is spent on public, nonprofit municipal or regional planning is not fully justified.

Despite these barriers and constraints, some of the ideas I put forward in my consulting work had implications for both the cities with which I worked directly and cities elsewhere. The idea of introducing car-free areas was taken up by nearly four hundred European cities. In addition, the setbacks and obstacles that I faced taught me and thousands of others that serious problems that are common to all human settlements can be solved not only through conventional means of architectural planning but also through fundamental changes in human behavior in regard to sociological and ecological conditions. These tasks cannot be accomplished by politicians, planners, engineers, and architects alone. They require the closest of cooperation among scientists of all disciplines.

As proof that my missionary work was understood by some, I quote from an article written by the Swiss author Rudolph Schilling that appeared in the *Tagesanzeiger* in July 1978: "Victor Gruen pioneered a new definition of the role of the architect. In his view, this role is not so much that of building monuments as it is of representing the social conscience against that of the client. The architect as an environmental planner and modifier of the environment is primarily responsible to society and nature, and today he must always stand up for self-restraint and respect for the social and natural environment."

ENVIRONMENTAL CENTERS

The aim of the Victor Gruen Center for Environmental Planning was to act on the basis of knowledge of human ecology. This was to be done through the study and expansion of research results in the natural and social sciences, the sharing of knowledge and findings with students and the mass media, efforts to influence legislative bodies and individuals, and practical work in the field of urban, regional, and energy planning.

We tried to do justice to the program by publishing books, brochures, and pamphlets; by organizing conferences, seminars, and radio and television programs; and by leading courses for teachers in public schools. In addition, we founded and continually expanded a freely accessible library of books, brochures, and magazines as well as an international collection of newspaper clippings. We also maintained a lively correspondence and exchange of information with other domestic and foreign organizations, scientists, and politicians.

To direct the institute, I appointed Dr. Claudia Moholy-Nagy, daughter of the Bauhaus artist László Moholy-Nagy. She devoted herself to her job with the greatest personal and idealistic dedication. It was all the more admirable that, despite having hands that were completely disfigured by gout, she was a rapid typist. She eventually became severely ill and died of her disease in 1971, at the age of thirty-five.

One of her friends, Mrs. Tracy Susman, then took over the direction of the center. Her deputy and librarian was Mrs. Rose-Marie Rabin-Epstein. She was particularly interested in the problems of humanistic education as well as the environment and had acquired a master's degree in urban issues and urban planning from Antioch

University in Los Angeles. Otherwise, the center's staff were partly paid and partly volunteers.

We considered it our duty to awaken an environmental "conscience" in an otherwise materialistic, goal-oriented, faith-based society. We wanted to sound a warning against the mindless exploitation of natural resources such as clean air, pure water, and fertile soil. At the same time, we warned against the exploitation of human beings, particularly the populations of the Third and Fourth Worlds and ethnic minorities, and finally those who rush through life, putting their physical and mental health at risk while striving for increased production and consumption. We tried to show that a continuation of the current behavior inevitably would lead to global catastrophes, to famine, environmental pollution, energy and resource crises, and then to revolutions and eventually to disastrous wars.

In our efforts we were supported by a slowly growing group of scientists, planners, architects, and public representatives who worked as a consulting team. However, it was difficult to know how to awaken an environmental conscience. Should and could one try to achieve that from top to bottom—that is, by influencing policy makers, administrations, government members, and elected representatives? Should one seek to exercise a moderating influence on the business community? Or, on the contrary, should one work from the bottom up? In that case, one would have to reach a broad public—especially the youth—by means of enlightenment and education, raising awareness of the threats and possible responses to them, all in the hope that an increase in environmental consciousness in the population will reverberate with the representatives of the people and the government in the democratic process.

We tried all these ways to get ahead, and we were disappointed. Mass mailings, through which we sought contributions, cost us a lot of work and considerable financial resources but remained ineffective. From decision makers we received encouraging words, but there followed no deeds. Especially in the first three years, while Kemija and I were still in Los Angeles, it seemed to me that our meager successes did not justify the work and money invested in any way. In an era of affluence and an expansive economy, our message seemingly fell on deaf ears.

Finally we understood that an effort to win something besides profit, power, honor, or achievement would not be successful quickly. It would succeed, if at all, only after decades. In the meantime, our funds were running low. We could no longer maintain our big house on Beverly Glen Boulevard, which served as headquarters of the organization, and we sold it in 1974. At the same time, we were surprised to learn that the reputation of the center was already such that one of the great private universities, Pepperdine University in Los Angeles, gave us space in one of its campus buildings to use for free.

We gained financial support slowly, most notably from the private Leshay Foundation, the California Council for the Humanities, the National Endowment for the Arts, the radio station K-100, and others. The willingness to donate in America comes partly from the fact that all payments to nonprofit groups can be deducted from an organization's taxes. In addition, some public authorities agree to match any amount that a nonprofit corporation receives from private donations.

Through these grants, we were able to maintain the center's staff and the library. We organized numerous events in Los Angeles and the surrounding area. For example, in 1972, the science fiction author Ray Bradbury gave a lecture titled "Life on Our Planet in 2025"; we also organized a symposium on the projected legislation known as the Environmental Quality Act. We provided a study program for five students from developing countries. In 1973, we granted a scholarship to a student from the Third World: Emesiobi Benson is now a town planner in Nigeria. In the same year, the center awarded its first prize for planning to William D. Ruckelshaus, the first administrator of the U.S. Environmental Protection Agency. In 1974, the center presented a lecture on the energy crisis by Stewart Udall, secretary of the interior under Presidents Kennedy and Johnson. John Hirten, director of the American Institute of Urban Planning and federal commissioner of public transport, gave a lecture titled "Transport and City" in 1975. During 1975 and 1976, the center offered training programs for hundreds of teachers across the entire Southern California area; among those who gave lectures were environmental expert Jean-Michel Cousteau, planning director Calvin Hamilton, and history professor (and later U.S. ambassador to Mexico) Julian Nava. In 1978, the center held a conference on quantitative and qualitative water problems in California. In 1979, we presented a discussion of the nuclear crisis that included physicists Henry W. Kendall and John Gofman; Charles Warren, chairman of the Presidential Council on Environmental Quality; and California governor Jerry Brown. In that same year, we offered seminars on legal issues concerning environmental protection.

The permanent working staff, still led by Tracy Susman and Rose-Marie Rabin-Epstein, was small and modestly paid, but it was effectively supplemented by a group of enthusiastic volunteers and consultants. The latter included scientists, urban planners, members of environmental councils, representatives of state environmental quality agencies, city planners, architects, designers, business experts, lawyers, writers, educators, and other environmentally conscious personalities.

When my "missionary" activity began to require me to spend more time in various European countries, I left the management of the center to its directors and continued our cooperation through correspondence and visits at intervals of about eighteen months. The last of these visits took place in the summer of 1976 and was very labor-intensive. I gave a series of talks and lectures at several universities. I was awarded an honorary doctorate from Pepperdine University and gave a speech there on the equilibrium of the urban system through economic, ethical, and environmental planning. I worked on a film about urban planning for the U.S. State Department and negotiated with California television stations about participating in an environmental television series. In addition to all these obligations, I joyfully met with old friends in many cities, visited with my daughter in Spokane, Washington, and my son and his family in New York, as well as with Kemija's brother and his family in Van Nuys, California, and with the daughter of Fritz Jahnel in Seattle.

For Kemija and me, this was an enjoyable but exhausting tour de force. Obviously, I had somewhat overextended myself. Shortly after our return to Vienna, on the same day that the Viennese Reichsbrücke collapsed, I also suffered a breakdown and had to spend a few days in the hospital because of a heart attack. Though the event had no other serious consequences, my doctors advised me to refrain from any further trips to the United States.

Several years before that, after long preparations, I had founded a European center, the Zentrum für Umweltplanung, with headquarters in Vienna. The reason for this was the same as that which led me to create the center in Los Angeles: the tools that are available for city planners and architects are not sufficient to solve global environmental problems. The constraints of the market economy become obstacles on the path to human ecology.

The pragmatic experience I had gained in my fifty years of work as an architect and planner seemed sufficient to put into an attempt to increase the quality of human life. Finally, I hoped that the material fruit of my career would be sufficient to make us financially independent enough to have some time to work on environmental planning.

When my work on the Glatt Center in Zurich, which was then the largest-ever project for a multifunctional secondary city center, ended because of a breach of contract, I decided that I wouldn't waste my energy with customers anymore. Kemija and I decided to concentrate our work entirely on the charitable mission of the Zentrum für Umweltplanung.

The material and staff expenses that had been necessary for our varied activities for an international clientele now decreased. Most of the technical and administrative staff were dismissed, travel activities were severely restricted, and the branch offices were closed. In 1975, with a heavy heart, I finally also gave up the garden wing of the house at Goldeggasse 7, because it was too big and expensive. We moved the center to the significantly smaller premises at Traungasse 7.

The Zentrum für Umweltplanung, or ZUP for short, was briskly active. Today, our influence stretches much further through the many employees who pursue scientific and economic professions. This group of employees came together informally and includes men and women with special skills and knowledge in design, all of whom are convinced of the need for interdisciplinary work.[8] Our "employees" are neither paid nor obligated. They take part in discussions and events only to foster the exchange of views, with the intent to convey something of their own knowledge to others and to enrich their own knowledge with the knowledge of others. There are no bylaws and no voting. We respect only one rule: for the internal group meetings, held about every five to six weeks, reporters of the mass media are not invited. Thus, we achieve a climate of complete candor in conversation. Whenever we announce findings to the public, we are invited to press conferences, which get a lot of attention.

Because participation is entirely voluntary, the number of participants at these meetings varies considerably. Usually between fifteen and twenty-five people gather

Drawing from the brochure *Grundlagen für die Schaffung von Leitlinien für die Stadtentwicklung.* Zentrum für Umweltplanung, Library of the City of Vienna, City Hall.

around our long conference table. Political party affiliation plays no role. What's important is that each participant has a sound knowledge of a scientific or artistic field and a conscience in relation to the human and nonhuman environment. The job titles of these "employees" illustrate the multidisciplinary nature of the group: they are biologists, physicists, sociologists, behavioral scientists, chemists, engineers, environmentalists, doctors, lawyers, urban planners, architects, statisticians, psychologists, historians, zoologists, geologists, landscape architects, geographers, economists, agricultural economists, political scientists, tax advisers, construction experts, writers, and publishers.

The center has published books, brochures, and some fifty articles in various national and international journals. Examples of our publications include the brochure *Leitlinien für die Stadtentwicklung Wiens* (Guidelines for the urban development of Vienna), the Charter of Vienna, and my book *Ist Fortschritt ein Verbrechen?*[9] Center employees have participated in twenty-seven radio and television programs. In 1973, we organized the conference "Science and Research as a Basis for Regional and Urban Planning" at the University of Vienna. We hosted an international seminar titled "City and Traffic" in the Amerika Haus in Vienna in 1974. In 1975, we organized the international scientific colloquium "Environmental Aspects of Nuclear Energy," and in 1976 we gave a seminar on future aspects of Vienna based on the example of Vienna's inner city at the Palais Palffy.

The center has also conducted detailed scientific work. In 1974, we produced the study "Correlation between Settlements and Infrastructure" on behalf of the Chancellery of the Republic of Austria; in 1975, we wrote the research proposal "Energy Housekeeping in Urban Areas" for the Jubilee Fund of the Austrian National Bank; in the same year, we also authored a report on the colloquium "Environmental Aspects of Nuclear Energy" for the Federal Ministry of Science and Research. In 1977, we wrote the resolution "Faster Dispersion of the Use of Solar Energy in Austria."

My twelve years of experience with these environmental centers in Los Angeles and Vienna have led to spiritual enrichment and an expansion of my knowledge and understanding. This applies particularly to areas outside my own field of architecture and city planning. I owe this to the intensive exchange of ideas within a large group of inspiring men and women from all parts of the world.

As of this writing, the center's most active period has come to an end because of my weakened state of health. In addition, the financial resources I have been using to maintain the operation have run out. I had originally hoped that I would find people who would financially support a charitable society in Austria, but this proved to be an illusion. Donations to charitable and nonprofit organizations are not tax deductible in Austria as they are in the United States. We did not win support from the private sector. On the other hand, state and municipal organizations expressed great interest in our work, and we were awarded the Great Golden Medal for Merit to the Republic of Austria on the occasion of my seventy-fifth birthday in 1978. This meant financial aid from three grants, each for thirty-five thousand Austrian schillings, from the Federal Ministry of Science and Research. This amount covered almost all of the cost of stamps for the mailings of statements by the employees. Despite all efforts, my hope that I would find someone who would utilize the considerable physical and spiritual value of the center has yet to be fulfilled.

According to conventional methods of management, and considering the commitment of time, energy, and capital it has required, my work in environmental planning would have to be regarded as a bad investment. Other criteria, however, indicate that our efforts to awaken environmental awareness have had a global impact. When I founded the Center for Environmental Planning in Los Angeles in 1968, we were called a small group of "hecklers in the desert." The same can be said for Europe and other continents. In the past twelve years, however, the word *environment* has entered the public consciousness to such a degree that it runs the risk of being misused as a catchphrase. Environmental ministries, agencies, and departments have been established in almost every country and city. In many countries, attempts have been made to found environmental political parties. This is somewhat problematic, because it requires getting a diverse group of political actors to agree on a single platform.

Ten years ago, one could barely find anything about the existence of environmental problems in the mass media; today it is almost impossible to avoid information on this issue. Political parties of almost all persuasions have incorporated environmental issues within their programs. Many are just following fashion by using the terms *environment, environmental protection,* and *environmental planning,* and others don't know what they're talking about. But there is a growing worldwide recognition that profound changes are needed in human behavior. For the future of humanity, the most important kind of détente that may now be achieved is situated in the cold war between *Homo sapiens* and nature. I believe that the efforts of the Center for Environmental Planning and the Zentrum für Umweltplanung have contributed to this détente, and in that sense, they have been worth every effort.

Portrait of Victor Gruen. Courtesy of Peggy Gruen. Photograph by Peggy Gruen.

Epilogue

"Growth of knowledge is increase of concern," said Goethe. This was my motto for July 18, my birthday.

I recently received two letters in one day, both of which provoked a deep ambivalence in me. Both letters were related to work I had finished some twenty years ago. The first letter came from the city council of the city of Kalamazoo, Michigan. It congratulated me on the twentieth anniversary of the revival of the city center, which I had planned in 1958 (and completed in 1960). The city council was now preparing a comprehensive honorary publication and asked if I wanted to submit an article on my planning concepts regarding the renewal of inner cities, plus a photograph of myself. The letter explained how beneficial the plan had been to the social, cultural, and business life of Kalamazoo, and it expressed the gratitude of the citizens of Kalamazoo.

The second letter was from the Dayton Hudson Corporation. These former clients, originally two separate family-owned businesses, had joined forces and now represented America's largest retail trade organization. Twenty years after the opening of the Northland Center in Detroit and the Southdale Center in Minneapolis, the company's management still felt thankful toward me, especially since these pioneering complexes had been reproduced by a large number of new shopping centers. In fact, this happened to many of the projects of Gruen Associates, which I headed until 1968.

Both letters were written in such a way that they complimented me for my work. Still, I was greatly concerned, especially about the second one. In this letter, the Dayton Hudson Corporation mentioned that they were planning their next big shopping center about six miles away from downtown Kalamazoo.

My experience has taught me that if such a project comes to pass, the citizens of Kalamazoo can forget about their celebration of the rebirth of their city center. A shopping complex with department stores, air-conditioned pedestrian areas, and ample parking will compete with the city core. Merchants and traders, as well as their customers, will eventually leave downtown. Urban desolation and bankruptcy of the city's finances will follow.

I planned the Dayton's and Hudson's shopping centers, as well as the revitalization of Kalamazoo, more than twenty years ago based on the knowledge and beliefs I had back then. Now I was torn: How could I answer these two letters? If I wished Dayton Hudson success in the company's new venture, it would be like signing a death warrant for downtown Kalamazoo. If I congratulated Kalamazoo, I would have to warn my friends at the Dayton Hudson Corporation and then encourage Kalamazoo to take all steps to block this project.

I could have tried to convince Dayton Hudson to abandon the shopping center near Kalamazoo. But I knew that my advice would be rejected on the grounds that the corporation was bound to represent the interests of its shareholders and to act accordingly. Also, I would have left myself open to accusations from my colleagues at Gruen Associates that I had deprived them of an important contract.

Today, I know that the "conservative" project of the Kalamazoo city council to improve and continue to renew the downtown area is preferable. It contributes to a better quality of life for the city's residents, and it maintains and increases community values. It does not cause additional traffic. I know now that the "progressive" project of the big shopping center would be the destructive one. It would not only mean paving agricultural land, but it would also cause additional sprawl and waste energy because of the use of air-conditioning and automobiles. Ultimately, it would suck the life out of an organically grown city center.

I experienced my own personal dilemma. It confused me, because it shed light on an ambivalence in me and because I realized that despite all my knowledge, I could not escape this ambivalence. What was happening in Kalamazoo was also happening in hundreds of other cities in the United States and in other countries of the world. The most bizarre cases involve urban renewal that is promoted by state funds (i.e., taxpayers' money) and then undermined by entrepreneurs who establish peripheral shopping or office centers.

This struggle between private interests and the interests of society is taking place in the prototypical free market economy. At present, U.S. laws are being drafted to protect communities from any competing commercial construction activity when they plan or carry out urban renewal with the help of public funds. I hope that these provisions come into force in time to solve my personal dilemma regarding Kalamazoo.

But even if the field of city planning experiences a happy-ending phase, I will remain concerned, because the world at large is facing a dilemma. We continue to exploit natural resources, as well as human physical and mental health, without replacing these resources with anything durable.

One phenomenon explains both my own ambivalence and this utterly nonsensical behavior by our society. The medical term for this phenomenon is *schizophrenia.*

Afterword

MICHAEL GRUEN

My father wrote me in 1978 that he had embarked upon this work, a combined autobiography and statement of his beliefs concerning architecture, planning, and ecology.

Not surprisingly, he would begin it with the autobiographical portion, narrating life-altering events of 1938, when the Anschluss of Austria forced his departure from a land he loved dearly, his arrival in New York, and finding a way not only to work as an architect but also to produce two Broadway revues, and then flashing back to his birth and childhood.

Autobiography is an introspective subject. My father preferred to devote his time to the social good through politics, theater, architecture, and environmental planning—to look outward toward the needs of others. And so the reader would soon discover that the great adventure of his professional career and his philosophy of architecture and planning take priority over the personal details of his life.

It is also evident that, had he lived longer, he would likely have provided more details of the phenomenally productive professional career of a phenomenally persuasive man. I undertake this afterword both to express my appreciation and love of my father and in the hope that I can flesh out his story to some modest extent. I particularly hope to provide a sense of the human being behind the career by relating some details of my life with him.

In doing this, I rely primarily on the fact that he and I talked together a great deal. Fortunately, at least for purposes of this essay, he did most of the talking, and I most of the listening. Our talks were mostly over meals at the adult table at which I, in my childhood, was always seated as long as I can remember, from highchair-hood onward. They also occurred while we were sitting at the pool, or in a corner of a garden that he had set up as an outdoor study, or on long walks in the mountains close to the city of Vienna, on evening dog walks, and in countless other locales.

I have no direct knowledge of my father's life in Vienna before his emigration in 1938, his earliest work there as a designer and architect, or his vigorous ability in young adulthood to pursue his nascent profession while simultaneously devoting himself to his role as leader of a political cabaret and, at least in his spare time, to his first wife, Alice (Lizzie) Kardos. Nor have I any direct knowledge of his life in New York from 1938 until 1941, his acquaintance with my mother, Elsie Krummeck, soon after he arrived in New York and their rapidly burgeoning romantic relationship, or their venture as partners in architectural design in New York and then, starting in 1941, in Los Angeles. I am told, however, that by the time of my birth in 1942, they had a quite successful architectural design practice under the name Gruenbaum & Krummeck.

My birth was a firm project. A well-designed photograph taken before the event juxtaposes what was often affectionately described as my father's barrel chest with my mother's voluminously pregnant belly, in sinuous interrelationship. Not long after that photograph was taken, a drawing, or what might better be called a "rendering" (the lavish sort of pastel an architect produces to make a design look better

Belly to belly: Victor Gruen and Elsie Krummeck, Los Angeles, 1942. Courtesy of Peggy Gruen.

than the ultimately constructed building might turn out to be), was distributed depicting me as a project of the Gruenbaum & Krummeck office. Clearly, the drawing was my mother's. She had the more outstanding artistic talent; he the conceptual. The idea might well have come from either of them, as it reflects a playful sense of humor they shared. I later was called Mikey, but first I was known as Bürscherl, or "Baby Boy," in the manner of an untitled project for an as-yet-uncommissioned design for an imagined ideal storefront. The idealized rendering seemed to collide with reality in the usual way; I was often told later that the nurse who first brought me to my mother after I had been suitably cleaned peeled the blanket from my face and recoiled in horror, exclaiming, "My God, if I had a face like that I'd hang a bag over it."

Perhaps my earliest memory is of my father singing lullabies when I was presumably still in a crib. I can still hear clearly in my mind his tender rendition of a German lullaby with music by Brahms:

Guten Abend, gute Nacht,	Good night and sleep well,
Mit Rosen bedacht,	Under roses about you,
Mit Nelken besteckt,[1]	And carnations interspersed,
Schlupf unter die Deck:	To keep you warm for the night.
Morgen früh, wenn Gott will,	In the morn, if God wills,
Wirst du wieder geweckt,	You will wake up again,
Morgen früh, wenn Gott will,	In the morn, if God wills,
Wirst du wieder geweckt.	You will wake up again.

He generally sang it in German. This translation approximates his translation into English.

Another early memory repeats like a bad dream, but the repetition was all too real. We are at the dinner table. Dessert is served, a pastry, and I get a nice big portion. Before I can take more than a mouthful, my father shouts, "Look, the dog is on the stove." I glance away, see nothing at all of concern in the kitchen, and, before I can lift my fork again, discover that my dessert has been snatched away and my father is wearing a quite satisfied demi-smile. He loved a practical joke almost as much as he loved pastry.

My sister, Peggy, was born almost two years to the day after me. She and I loved the smoke ring game. Daddy would take a puff from the ever-present pipe or cigarette, then tap his cheeks and send a perfect ring of smoke wafting into the air. Then we would tap his cheeks to somewhat less perfect effect. He smoked much too much. The first instrument of what seemed both a pleasure and an affectation

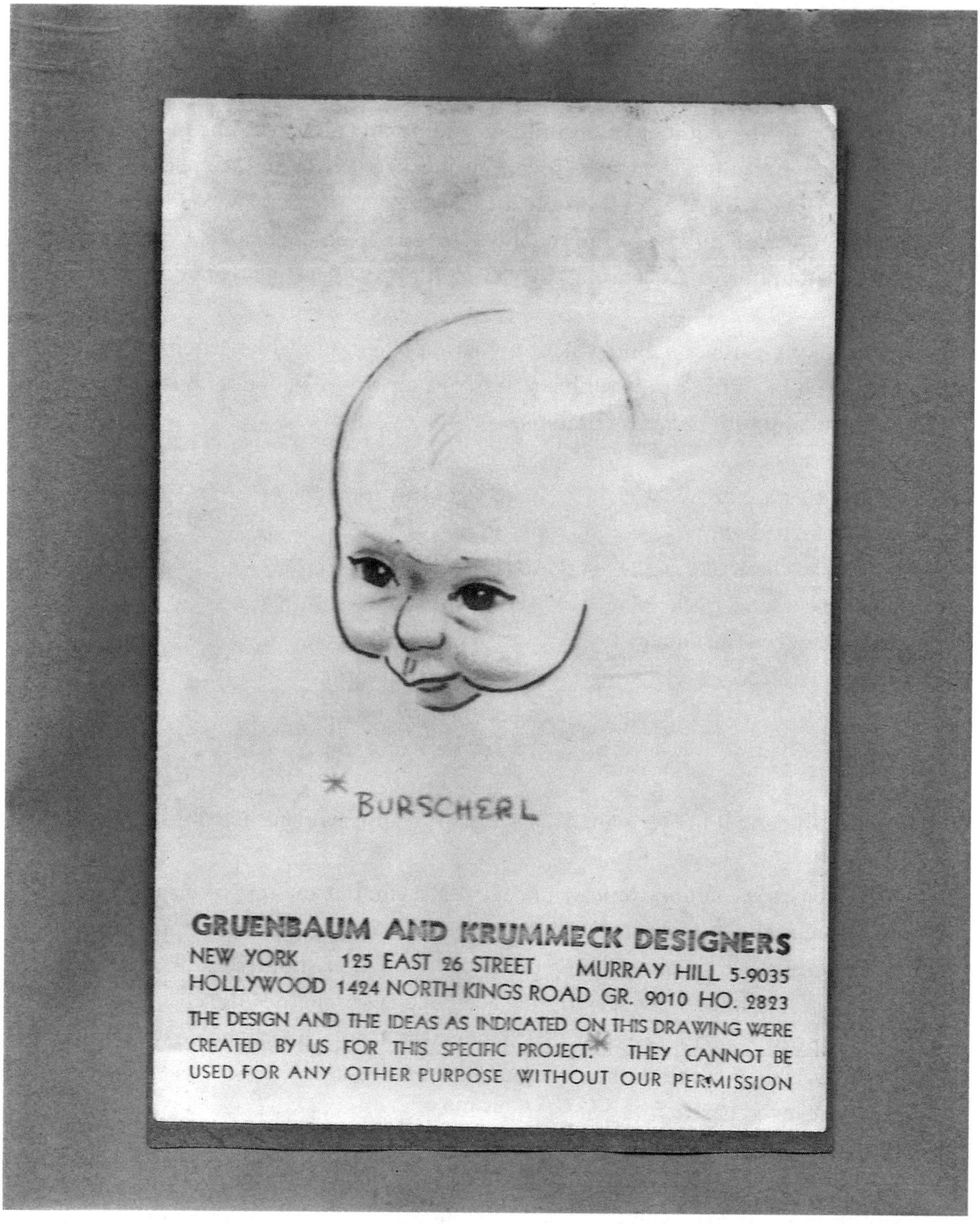

Elsie Krummeck, *Bürscherl* (Michael Gruen), Los Angeles, 1942. Courtesy of Michael Gruen.

Victor Gruen in the garden, Los Angeles, 1947. Courtesy of Peggy Gruen.

was a pipe. He moved on to cigarettes, then cigarettes in a Franklin Roosevelt sort of cigarette holder containing a little cylinder with fibrous fill to filter out the most damaging elements.

We had a friend and neighbor in New York in the 1950s who drank a certain herbal tea every morning to get herself going and urged that we all do the same. She assured us that it was not addictive—that, indeed, she had taken it every morning for many decades. Daddy said he understood entirely: he had smoked for decades and had successfully quit any number of times. Ultimately, he did permanently quit, I suspect on emphatic doctor's orders.

From my earliest childhood, he found time to do special things with me. We went together to pick up flowers from Benny Franco, the florist on Sunset Boulevard. We got our haircuts together from George, whose shop was next to Benny Franco's. I watched as he got a manicure and George kneaded his scalp with the fingers of each hand motivated by an electric vibrator. Despite George's assurance

Peggy, Michael, and Victor Gruen, Coronado Hotel, San Diego, circa 1947. Courtesy of Peggy Gruen.

that my hair was so thick that I would never lose it, I did, while my father, thanks presumably to the massages, kept all of his.

He taught me chess and let me beat him for the first time when I was six, though not often after that until, in junior high school, I took up the game relatively seriously. He also liked Parcheesi and, later, backgammon. As a good American citizen (which he became at the earliest opportunity) and a good father, he bought fireworks and presented a show of them every Fourth of July.

Once I got old enough to wear a gray flannel suit and tie (probably about six years old), he took me to construction sites to supervise. The site I remember best is the Milliron's store in Westchester, Los Angeles. We spent a good deal of time on the roof there because he was very proud of the use of the roof for customer parking. As I recollect, he considered roof parking a significant innovation, a view that is somewhat ambiguously supported by the book *Design for Modern Merchandising*.[2]

I also often visited the office, no doubt making a pest of myself with the draftsmen. Once I could see over the edge of the drafting tables, I got to tour the drafting room with my father and listen to his design comments. I acquired a taste for architecture and made plans for a motel; I also constructed a stick-and-string model of a house with lichen landscaping, which Daddy patiently and sympathetically critiqued.

Daddy keenly observed Peggy's efforts to seek attention and do whatever I did. When she was around two or three, he wrote a poem for her called "Little Miss Me Too" that I think has been lost. I remember only that "me too" occupied a prominent position in each refrain. Writing poetry (some call it doggerel) was something he did often.

Each Christmas, the task of buying a Christmas tree fell to Daddy, with the assistance of Peggy and me. Large vacant lots in Los Angeles had thousands of trees for sale. Most were spray-painted white, light blue, or pink. Some were sprayed green, a bit like natural trees. Only a few were unpainted, and we had to hunt hard to find one of those of the right height (about eight feet), circumference, freshness, and well-balanced fullness. It was as full a course in Christmas tree appreciation as our little minds could handle. Once the tree had reached home and gotten dressed, we gathered around it and sang "O Tannenbaum."

On Christmas Eve, Peggy and I were told earlier than usual to go upstairs to bed. Shortly later, Daddy would call upstairs in a panic, "Come quickly! Run!" We would find him standing at the window, pointing upward toward the sky. As we ran toward him, it was impossible not to notice that the formerly empty space around the Christmas tree was now piled high with wrapped packages. He insisted we look out the window, fast. But when we got to the window, we saw nothing, and he would describe in awestruck tones the spectacle of Santa sledding off into the sky, which we had just missed by the whisker's breadth of a split second. He never explained how Santa got down the chimney, something we did not have.

I mention these childhood experiences because my father says very little in this book about the details of his family life as a child. Somewhere, however, he learned to excel in the art of fatherhood, and I have to think that his own father, whom he greatly admired, must have set the example.

As my father reports, his mother, Elly, and Mom's mother, Katherine or Katie, lived together in a house about two miles from ours. Katie (whom Peggy and I called Nanny) came out from New York when our parents moved to Los Angeles; she had lived in the New York area since emigrating from the Rhineland, where she was born. Elly must have lived for a short while in New York, having left Vienna soon after my father. My father describes her as actively involved in social life in Vienna, so she must have felt quite uprooted. I cannot imagine that living with Nanny gave her much comfort. Nanny was a rather domineering hausfrau whose character and disposition seemed to go little beyond the conventions of that description. What I remember of her was her sternness, her lack of humor, her very long white hair (which was braided and wrapped into a crown around her head), her seeming disinterest in children other than as to their orifices (she inspected each expulsion of stool and treated all manner of perceived illnesses by inserting globs of Vaseline into our nostrils with the rounded end of a hairpin), and her nurturing of a garden full of geraniums, the extensive variety of which stemmed from her going about the neighborhood surreptitiously cutting sprigs from other people's bushes to replant in her own garden.

Almost by imperceptible degrees, my father spent more and more time traveling in the later 1940s. The office had moved out of our house, where it had occupied three or four rooms on the second floor, into a much larger space on Santa Monica Boulevard in Hollywood, probably around 1948. At some point, he began using a former office upstairs in our house as a bedroom. All of this went over my naive head. At Christmastime in 1952 (I think), our parents sat Peggy and me by the Christmas tree and explained that their marriage was not working out and they would be getting a divorce. Peggy, or it might have been either of us, asked, "Will you still be our father?" a question that seemed to inquire with childlike innocence and fear as to what this meant for our identities and welfare, but implicitly recognized the meaning of all the previous absence. It was, of course, explained that he would still be our father, and that we would visit him on certain weekends and holidays. It was a devastating blow that has affected my enthusiasm for the Christmas season ever since.

My parents must have agreed on a further explanation for the breakup of the marriage that would be given to Peggy and me over time: the architectural practice was rapidly expanding, and Mom was more interested in hands-on design, while Daddy was intent on pursuing larger projects; their professional lives, which had been at the heart of their relationship, had grown apart. That was about all either of them told us.

Of course, there had to be more. Mom was, as Daddy writes about his first impression of her, a stunningly beautiful woman. She had the looks of Ingrid Bergman, but less vulnerable and even more open and unaffected. She was generous in her dealings with others, not only in providing help but also in the giving of her unrestrained emotions. She had many good friends to whom she was intensely loyal. She also expected, even demanded, equal intensity in return, and on her terms. Those included, as to her children, "heart-to-heart talks" about the most intimate matters. As an adolescent boy, or earlier, I don't think I was abnormal in pulling away from such talks and feeling unwelcomingly smothered. I can well imagine that my father, who was not given to introversion, might have had a similar reaction. It was also true that their interests differed. Mom was utterly devoted to artistic creativity and emotional life. She loved to draw, paint, cut shapes in paper, mold clay. Her work was hands-on. It was not her style to delegate creative activity to someone else, or to think about architecture in terms of grand projects for the improvement of humankind rather than as a matter of very personal artistic design. I do not doubt that Mom resisted the transformation of their firm from a small design studio to a behemoth institution for the output of major projects.

That is not to say that she did not admire my father's talents, among them his charm and persuasive ability. A favorite story of hers was of something that happened more than once. The two of them would walk into a roomful of people. My father would say to her, "You see that man over on the far side of the room? I intend to get him as a client." Before they left the party, my father had succeeded.

Once the legalities of the defunct marriage had been settled, Peggy and I were invited to come east to meet our father's new wife, Lazette. Lazette was not experienced with children but had definite ideas about how they should be brought up. She made it clear from the start that she expected proper dress, proper behavior, and proper manners. Peggy, who was much more of a free spirit than I, totally resisted Lazette's efforts to tame her, and the two remained pretty much at odds as time went on. I felt I could adapt to Lazette's requirements with no great loss of selfhood, and I also found her very engaging. She had enormous charm, emanating from her avid interest in everything and (almost) everyone she encountered, and strong, vividly expressed opinions. She delighted in literature, politics, art, design, theater, and travel. She clearly admired and adored my father and greatly inspired him in his career. Plus she loved me and demanded nothing in return but good company and civility.

I felt the sharp edge of Lazette's strong opinions in the summer of 1955 when Mom took Peggy and me on what was intended to be a tour of Europe. We went by ship and landed in Southampton, England, where we picked up the Hillman station wagon Mom had bought. After a couple of weeks, Peggy decided that she had had enough of traveling and wanted to stay in England for the remainder of the summer. She was left at a "riding establishment" (from which she emerged several months later with considerable equestrian skills and an English accent), and Mom and I crossed the channel for the grand tour. The first day on the Continent, we drove from Cherbourg to a small town in Belgium near the French border. I wrote to Daddy and Lazette about my few hours' worth of impressions of France versus my by then supposedly deep knowledge of England, focusing on a contrast in tidiness that immediately caused me to take a dim view of France. Given what I knew of Lazette's hygienic standards, I thought my letter would meet with her approval. In some way, she knew of our itinerary for the next week or so, and I received a return letter from her that severely chastised me for the superficiality and lack of openness to other cultures reflected in my letter. Her letter had a galvanizing effect on my attitude toward the world and other peoples and dramatically increased my already great respect for her.

In this small town in Belgium, we made some inquiries at a public house of some sort on a main square to find lodging. A man who had been sitting on the plaza took an interest in helping us, which led to our having supper with him, followed by a ride, separately for each of us, over the cobbled streets in his three-wheeled Messerschmitt minicar, driver in front, single passenger behind. By no coincidence, he was Gerhard Messerschmitt of the industrial family that built warplanes for the German Reich. Mom seemed not to feel too much discomfort regarding his background, and some weeks later we visited him at his cabin in the Bavarian mountains.

Here again was a contrast with Lazette. Her strongly held opinions included one or two implacable prejudices, most notably against the Germans on account of Nazi atrocities. She absolutely refused to set foot in Germany. Oddly enough, this prejudice did not extend to Austrians despite the well-known collaboration of many Austrians with the Nazis. She may have bent on this issue because of my father's love for Austria and his willingness to forgive those he had inveighed against as a young man, satirized when he was a leader of the socialist political cabaret, and suffered from in the loss of his property and forcible eviction from his homeland. She may also have been seduced by Austria's charm and gemütlichkeit, both of which she quite openly admired.

Lazette was also prejudiced against airplanes. She did not fly. Period. This was just fine with me because it meant that my trips with my father and her were always by Super Chief or 20th Century Limited when we traveled across the United States or on the *Queen Elizabeth* or *Ile de France* when we crossed the Atlantic. On the Continent, the preferred mode was the Orient Express.

In politics, Lazette was totally liberal. She owned a leftist-oriented bookstore in Greenwich Village in the 1930s. She deplored racial discrimination to the extent that in the face of prejudiced comments from anyone at a social gathering she would announce that she was herself partly Negro (the enlightened term of choice in the fifties), then watch the chagrined backpedaling.

As my father writes, he and Lazette bought a house in Los Angeles and also had an apartment in New York on West Twelfth Street. He describes the Los Angeles house as modest, which it was in terms of size. Yet it was in Brentwood, a rather plush part of the city. He installed a pool but did relatively little in the way of remodeling.

Lazette had a cocker spaniel named Reddy, a finicky dog of considerable discrimination. Just as Lazette would not travel by plane, Reddy chose not to move his bowels anywhere except in three places in the entire United States: Washington Square Park in New York, the Albuquerque railroad station where the Super Chief stopped, and a certain front yard in Brentwood that I will identify further in a moment. Daddy and I were generally responsible for walking Reddy in the morning and, especially, in the evening. This was a good time for talking, and the talk often turned to politics. Reddy evidently absorbed some of our opinions, as the front yard he chose to perform in belonged to Richard Nixon. I can assure you that this was Reddy's choice. We did not lead him to it, and no amount of encouragement would prompt him to make any different choice.

Reddy's opinions lead me to my father's. As he notes, he had been a socialist in Austria. He points out that the Social Democratic Party was the only one that welcomed Jews, and it occupied his preferred portion of the political spectrum. In America, he was a fervent Democrat. He supported liberal positions on such issues as government involvement in economic planning, government support for the poor, racial integration, and civil liberties. I was always interested in political doctrine (at least from around age nine), and we talked often about socialism, communism, and capitalism as economic and political systems. While he had some sympathy for the idea of public ownership of vaguely defined key economic resources, such as sources of energy, he did not advocate for that in America and had nothing against private enterprise in general. He was a planner by nature and sympathized with the view that regulation should be used to control the excesses of capitalism. He admired Franklin Roosevelt. He enthusiastically supported Adlai Stevenson; we listened for hours to the precinct-by-precinct election returns on the radio when Stevenson ran for the presidency. He backed John Kennedy. He was particularly impressed with Lyndon Johnson's political skill in putting Kennedy's programs into effect and achieving significant advances in civil rights.

A journalist asked me recently how my father, as a socialist, could have done so much to promote the financial interests of capitalist businessmen. I really did not see much of an issue there, and I doubt my father would have. His great interest was in bettering the lives of the general populace, regardless of individual wealth or lack of it. That some would make a buck off his ideas was not, I believe, of any consequence to him (so long as he was fairly compensated for his professional services). Aside from being a visionary, he was a practical man and would not have let such an incidental matter as who would build a shopping center get in the way of its getting built. What bothered him much more was the shortsightedness of some of the businessmen he dealt with in failing to develop the land around shopping centers into communities that would not only provide profits in themselves but also support the shopping centers as focal points for local populaces and diminish the prospect of competitive magnetic centers. As he writes in this book, he thought governmental planning would do better, but later experience with governmental bureaucracy made him doubt that view.

The apartment in New York was in a thirteen-story building built at the end of the nineteenth century and the beginning of the twentieth; it was taller and wider than most buildings in the area. We had half of the twelfth floor, half of the thirteenth, and the roof, on which my father erected a platform for a patio and garden. He made some renovations, primarily adding cabinetry. He created an office on the thirteenth floor in which his working space had a distinctly Viennese early twentieth-century modern flavor. Bathrooms, kitchen, and Lazette's mother's bedroom and sitting room (Lazette brought her mother to live in the apartment for several months each year) were left substantially as built.

This was where my father and Lazette preferred to be and spent the greatest proportion of their time (perhaps a third to half of the year). We had company for dinner most evenings—friends, clients, or both. Often, singing around the piano followed dinner. Lazette played the piano quite well. She favored American standards, especially the songs of Cole Porter and Harold Arlen. My father loved singing Viennese songs, which Lazette played from an old songbook Daddy had salvaged from his home in Vienna.

We spent much of one summer in the mid-1950s in Detroit. I was employed some of the time at the Gruen office, running the switchboard, a Medusa's head of entangled cords with adorning lights and buzzers. To connect calls, I had to plug the male ends of the cords into female receptors on the panel; disconnecting them reversed the process. Activity could get hectic, with many lights flashing, attention-getting buzzers buzzing, and cords snaking about the board and around one another so that identification of the beginnings and ends became all but impossible. Unfortunately, I was prone to premature disconnection, invariably affecting Karl Van Leuven, the head of the Detroit office. The call I cut off was always an extremely important one, and he would storm out of his office screaming at me.

I spent quite a few summers in Vienna. With Lazette, we always stayed at the Hotel Sacher, an imposing Beaux-Arts edifice behind the State Opera. The personnel there punctiliously observed the Austrian custom of addressing people by title, such as Herr Architekt, but always one title higher than the one the addressee had actually earned. Thus Daddy was addressed as Herr Professor, I (not old enough to be called Mr. at home) as Herr Gruen. I usually had a garret room at the back side of the hotel, generally reserved for the personal servants accompanying some of the guests. It looked onto a dimly lit street that met the Kärntnerstrasse. The better view was in front toward the Opera and the Ringstrasse, but Lazette was quite envious of my view because the little street I overlooked was a meeting point for prostitutes. It fascinated her.

Vienna had a population well exceeding one million at the time. But it was also a small town. We frequently encountered people on the street whom Daddy had known before he left Austria. Once, as I was driving Daddy and Lazette in their car, going out the Währingerstrasse toward Grinzing in the early evening, we came to an intersection where I saw that another car was stopped on the cross street to the right. As I crossed the intersection, the other car suddenly lurched into us. I was about eighteen years old and did not have vast driving experience; this was my first accident, and I was kind of shaken. Daddy got out of the car to deal with the other driver. I noticed that another man who had been passing by stopped and talked with him and then with the young woman driving the other car. After a few minutes, Daddy got back into our car and said everything had been worked out, and we continued on our way. He added that the other man, who had evidently been instrumental in resolving the matter, was an old friend from the socialist youth movement. Felix Slavik was now the mayor of Vienna.

For Daddy, visiting Vienna was a very emotional experience. It was not only that he came from Vienna. To him, the city was the paragon of civilized and joyful life. It was, to begin with, a cosmopolitan center, a status stemming not only from its prestige as capital of the Austro-Hungarian Empire and its situation on the Danube, a main trading route, but also from its role over centuries as bulwark against a Turkish invasion of Europe. It was, like New York, a melting pot of cultures, a place where being Viennese often meant coming from Hungary, Czechoslovakia (where my grandfather came from), or, as in the case of my father's mother, Germany. While the Turks were held at bay, they nevertheless had a strong influence on the city, not least on its coffee.

The coffeehouses, which were everywhere, served as social centers. As my father told me, everyone had his own coffeehouse—that is to say, a favorite where he had a *Stammtisch,* or regular table, at which he could sit for hours after ordering a single small cup of coffee and read the racks of newspapers representing every political persuasion. Your colleagues knew where to find you, as the coffeehouse was the equivalent of your office. You conducted your business there.

One ate small meals frequently, and the experience was intercultural. A full regimen of daily meals in Vienna included not only breakfast, lunch, and dinner but also a midmorning *Gabelfrühstück* (fork breakfast) and an afternoon *Jause* (snack) of coffee and pastry. When I visited Vienna with Daddy and Lazette, we might well, on one day, have eaten a light lunch of open-faced sandwiches and small glasses of beer or apple juice at Trzesniewski, had *Apfelstrudel* at Demel's or the Sacher in the afternoon, then had dinner at the *Griechenbeisl* (Greek bistro) or the Drei Husaren (Three Hussars, named for the Hungarian cavalry officers who founded the restaurant). And these examples of ethnic variety were within easy walking distance of one another.

The grandeur of the former empire is visible everywhere in the palaces of the kaiser, the many smaller scattered palaces of the aristocracy, and government buildings. In the nineteenth century, Emperor Franz Joseph I created a degree of connectedness between the people and the royalty by opening to the people elegant parks and public buildings along the Ringstrasse, which replaced the fortified city walls. The parks served the usual functions of green spaces, but they also drew the common people into a realm of elegance and reverence for the magnificence of their empire, where they could attend outdoor concerts in beautiful pavilions and eat in attractive surroundings. One could walk along the Ringstrasse and experience one magnificent edifice after another, many open to the public: the Votivkirche, the university, the National Museum, the city hall, the Burgtheater, the Opera, the Karlskirche.

My father loved the intimacy of the narrow winding streets in the inner city, many barely wide enough to accommodate any traffic, and the contrast they presented to the wide Ringstrasse encircling the so-called First District and providing a means of reaching any part of the city center by traveling relatively quickly on the periphery rather than very slowly through the middle. But, then, an excellent tram system along the Ringstrasse and along radial roads toward the outer edges of the city made a choice between driving routes rather unnecessary. In the inner city there was even a small version of the indoor shopping mall, an arcade of stores on the Michaelerplatz. I do not recall that my father ever referred to that as a precedent, but he often referred to the much larger and grander Vittorio Emanuele arcade in the center of Milan. In short, when my father writes that metropolitan planning should be devoted to satisfying the needs of people, not cars, that what makes a good shopping environment is that it is integrated with opportunities for leisurely enjoyment of a social environment, that motorized vehicles do not mix well with pedestrian life and are best consigned to periphery roads, not the center, that artistic culture and varied social cultures are essential elements of the successful city—somewhere in the back of his mind, he is always writing about Vienna.

It was probably in 1959 that we spent several weeks in St. Wolfgang, a beautiful lakeside village in the Salzkammergut, about fifty kilometers from Salzburg. It has enough charm to have earned its own song, indeed a whole operetta called *The White Horse Inn,* after the leading hotel of the area. We stayed in an annex to the White Horse between the village and the base of the cog railway that climbs to the top of the Schafberg, twelve hundred meters above the lake. There is plenty to describe in St. Wolfgang, but what is important for present purposes is that one of our chambermaids was a young woman named Kemija Salihefendic. She made great efforts to serve us well, and we learned from her something of her life story, the key elements of which were early childhood in Bosnia, abandonment by her parents in Carinthia, and the poor state of her health. Daddy and Lazette became quite friendly with her. We took her a couple of times to see a local doctor. After we left St. Wolfgang, Daddy and Lazette stayed in touch with her and may have helped her in studying to become a cosmetician. I tutored her in English one summer. After a while, I was encouraged to think of her as a member of the family. It did not cross my mind at the time that she would eventually become an actual member of the family as my father's fourth wife.

In the summer of 1962, Daddy escorted Peggy to Vienna, where she was to take a course on painting with Oskar Kokoschka and he intended to start renovations on the apartment he and Lazette had recently bought on the Schwarzenbergplatz. Kemija was to stay in the apartment and watch over it. Daddy seldom traveled without Lazette, but this was intended as a very short trip, by air. Lazette, as I have said, did not fly, so she remained in Los Angeles. One night after I had gone to bed, I got a call from Daddy's old friend and partner Rudi Baumfeld, who told me that Lazette had just died very suddenly of what appeared to be a stroke. This was surely the saddest event of my young life. It was so sudden, unexpected, and pointless. She was young, not over fifty-eight and probably younger. Her only ailment of which I was aware was an agonizing case of psoriasis. Most of all, she had lived a life of generous love, for which death was mean compensation.

I arranged to fly to Los Angeles the next morning. Daddy arrived soon after me, tired and bereft. We drove together to their house. We went into the bedroom, and Daddy sat down at Lazette's vanity table, lay his head against the assemblage of perfumes that she dabbed behind her ears and sprayed beneath her blouse, and cried, it seemed interminably. Behind him on the wall opposite the dressing table hung her ten or so favorite belongings—the birthday poems Daddy wrote and embellished with romantic and amusing drawings for her, which she had framed identically in red wood frames. I wish I knew where they are now. I do remember the text of one, given for her fiftieth birthday:

Half a cent' you represent,
And the fact that I resent
Is that, of all this, I have spent
With you only ten percent.

We did what we could to console each other, but consolation seemed futile.

Gruen and Lazette van Houten on a cruise to Hawaii, March 1962. Courtesy of Peggy Gruen.

Peggy later told me of the scene in Vienna when Friedl and Herta Scheu, close friends of Daddy's from the thirties, came over at Rudi's request to tell him of Lazette's death.[3] Peggy and Kemija were both present in the apartment. As Peggy told me, she sat against Daddy on one side and said, "Don't worry, Daddy, I'll take care of you." And Kemija sat against him on the other and echoed, "Don't worry, Daddy, I'll take care of you."

Perhaps six months later, Daddy visited me at Harvard, where I was a student. He asked me what I would think of his marrying Kemija. Somewhat stunned, I could only think of saying that she seemed very young, and was it not a little incestuous, what with her being so much treated as a member of the family? I think, though, that we were talking about a decision that had already been made. My blessing was a formality, and I assured him that I would support his decision. The wedding did occur soon after, a private affair without guests, as far as I am aware.

Daddy's relationship with Kemija was always somewhat of an enigma to me. His marriage to her lasted some fifteen years, five years longer than any other—although the marriage to Lazette was surely prematurely cut off by her death. Kemija certainly had qualities one could admire: she was smart, ambitious, and artistically gifted, and she worked energetically. She was capable of being ingratiating but could be abrasive too. I do not think I know of anyone, other than Daddy, who professed to like her as a person during the marriage. She was uneducated, and conversation with her never seemed particularly interesting. Daddy writes that she was very helpful to him in his work. I do not know exactly how, but I have to assume that he honestly believed that. His history with previous wives suggests that this would be a strongly cohesive factor. I would expect that he was flattered by the combination of her attention and relative youth. A curious mélange of chemicals, but apparently they worked.

For obvious reasons, Daddy wanted a new home in Los Angeles after Lazette died. The search led him to a spacious Spanish hacienda-style house on a large, very beautifully landscaped lot on Beverly Glen Boulevard in Bel Air. It had one bedroom but a large living room and large dining room. It also had substantial servants' quarters in an outbuilding across the driveway from the kitchen. Kemija's brother Kemal and his wife, Ramsa, soon arrived from Bosnia to live in that space. He did the gardening and she the cooking for the Gruen household. The seeming awkwardness of their functioning as servants was presumably alleviated by the opportunity this situation provided for them to come to America as sponsored immigrants.

The house was very handsome and livable. Daddy did little to improve it beyond adding lighting and a built-in buffet in the dining room and decorating a den in the style of Kemija's origins. In the "Bosnian room," both floor and furniture were covered in vivid Caucasian carpets, which also wrapped the many pillows. There were, as I remember, a hookah and a samovar. Adjoining the room was a modest Occidental-style bar—of little avail to my father, as he drank only modest amounts of wine and occasionally beer.

In early 1964, I met Susie Lloyd, an actress who supplemented her income from movies and television shows with work as a saleswoman in various department stores and with political office work, primarily for Jesse Unruh, a Democratic Party leader and legislator at the time. Susie was very charming, and we quickly decided to get married. Daddy had a private interview with Susie in the Bosnian room—the substance of which I never learned—before condoning the marriage and offering to hold the wedding at the Beverly Glen house. It was a lavish affair, with about a hundred guests. Kemija, with Ramsa's help, did a magnificent job of setting the whole thing up and cooking. At the end of dinner, a many-tiered "cake" was presented, carried with poles like a sedan chair. In keeping with my political dreams, and Daddy's own dreams of how high they should reach, the "cake" was a cardboard replica of the White House, the details drawn by Daddy on a construction produced by his office. The bridesmaids paraded it through the garden, after which it was opened up to reveal real cakes baked by Kemija and Ramsa.

In 1968, my father retired from his U.S. firm and established his primary home in Vienna. It has been suggested that, faced with American cities in turmoil that included racially charged rioting, my father "retreated back across the Atlantic to live in Vienna."[4] The implication that the move was involuntary and somehow shameful may stem simply from an unfortunate choice of words. In any event, I think it is quite inconsistent with the evidence as I know it. My father had told me years before that he had a long-standing agreement with his partners that he would retire at age sixty-five. Along the way, steps were taken to reorganize the firm. After 1966, a tier of vice presidents was established between the level of partners and that of associates. Later, the name of the firm was changed to drop his first name, thereby somewhat diminishing any implication that this was an organization dependent on one person. His agreement allowed him to continue practicing, but only outside the United States. Vienna was the logical place to go. He had returned to visit there in 1948, apparently as soon as it was possible for him to do so. It was a favorite vacation spot. He and Lazette had bought the Vienna apartment in anticipation of moving there when he retired, and in the expectation that he would continue working. Already before that, he had begun building up some international business, most notably with his plan for Tehran, a project that terminated with the shah of Iran's overthrow years later.

Gruen's apartment on the Schwarzenbergplatz, Vienna. Courtesy of Peggy Gruen. Photographs by Peggy Gruen.

He made this transformation in a spirit of enthusiasm and hopefulness. The phenomenal success of his new international firm demonstrates that that typically optimistic spirit was fully justified. Not only did jobs flow in, but many major planning jobs also provided the satisfaction of actually being executed, something that had not happened with the key American urban planning projects of Fort Worth and Roosevelt Island.

My own transition from student to career, and acquisition of my little family, reduced the frequency of visits with my father. One of the more memorable was on the occasion of his seventieth birthday in 1973. In the meantime, I had separated from Susie and established a relationship with Vanessa Ahlfors, a woman so charming and intriguing that we have remained together for some forty years now. She came with two children from her former marriage, Stefan and Sebastian Keneas, and I with one, Madeleine. We had met in connection with the planning and preservation work we both did with the Municipal Art Society, an organization dedicated to improvement of the urban environment of New York City. We have both maintained that interest for decades. In the summer of 1973, Stefan and Sebastian went to spend the summer with Vanessa's parents at their summer cabin in Boothbay Harbor, Maine, as was their custom. Vanessa, Madeleine (then age six), and I drove through Austria and visited my father and Kemija in Vienna and at the country house they had purchased about an hour's drive south of Vienna.

The house is halfway up a mountain between the village of Prein-an-der-Rax and the Preiner Gscheid Pass, on a narrow tortuous road of switchbacks. It sits on mountain meadows and overlooks a valley and the rocky mountains framing the valley on one side—a spectacular view. I think the house had been built around 1900. My father remodeled it, with Kemija's help, to make it more reminiscent of a farmhouse, with a built-in bench nearly surrounding the dining table and a large stucco heating stove in the shape of a quarter of a dome-like beehive in the corner of the main living space. He added an indoor swimming pool and a terrace overlooking the valley and protected by a glass screen. Kemija was responsible for creating the very attractive landscaping and for populating the meadows with Icelandic ponies and some cows and sheep.

Quite a few people made the trip from Vienna and elsewhere to attend the birthday celebration, including several of the "girls" from the chorus line of the political cabaret of the 1930s and others of my father's friends from that period. Kemija suggested that I take a ride on one of the Icelandic ponies, and the company enjoyed seeing the little brute toss me off. As daylight waned, a brass band arrived to provide rustic dance music. Guests who knew about such things said that the band was from near the border between two particular provinces. The music of one province is lively and upbeat; the music of the other is dirgelike. This band—half a dozen men in lederhosen and green felt hats with long feathers—came, it seems, from just over the wrong side of the provincial border. And so the evening was spent under the spell of tubas wailing a cadence suitable only for trudging under the weight of a coffin.

Daddy was in great spirits. While we were there, we went on an excursion, hiking around a relatively flat area at the top of the Rax mountain near the house. He also took us for a hike on a hillock on the property that he had named Mount Victor and was very proud of.

Victor Gruen on his seventieth birthday. Courtesy of Peggy Gruen.

In January 1976, after a long wait for divorces to come through on both sides, Vanessa and I got married. Our first child together, Alexis, was born a month later, quite prematurely by conventional standards. Viveca came about eighteen months after that.

In February 1978, my father gave a speech in London complaining of the failures of shopping center development. M. Jeffrey Hardwick construes the speech as a bitter self-denunciation and a renunciation of the entire intellectual patrimony my father had created in siring the shopping mall.[5] Gruen "looked at what he had built and despised what he saw," Hardwick writes, adding, as proof of the bitter spirit of repudiation of his life's work, that my father pronounced from the podium, "I refuse to pay alimony for those bastard developments."[6]

I suppose that pithy phrases are their own worst enemy: they invite easy recollection and equally easy forgetting of the context that defined their meaning. In this instance, Hardwick hangs a whole concluding chapter describing end-of-life dejection and rejection on the "no alimony for bastard developments" quote. But, in fact, the phrase does not appear in the speech. Rather, it appears ten months later in a journalist's syndicated column, a venue that doubtless gave my father little to no control over the bon mot's context or construction.[7] My father mentioned the phrase to me and seemed pleased by its clever summation of his feeling about being dubbed "father of the shopping mall" and thereby being implicitly held responsible for the multitudinous errors of other architects, other planners, other developers, and absence of governmental oversight in allowing a good idea to get out of hand.

The speech reflects that he distinguished between the shopping centers he had designed and lesser imitations. He was disappointed that others had extracted the most superficial formulaic aspects of his shopping center concept without also inserting the soul. Yes, they imitated the enclosed malls, but they made them nothing more than shopping machines, removing all the social and cultural characteristics that made a Gruen shopping mall a center of social activity that people visited even when all the stores were closed. They omitted the careful planning for diversity in leasing and chose to lease overwhelmingly to chain establishments with name brands rather than to a variety of stores, including mom-and-pop businesses offering unique products. Far from reflecting the despair of a man approaching death and repenting for the sins of a lifetime—as Hardwick paints the picture—the London speech is a hardheaded assessment of undisciplined abuse (by others) of the Gruen shopping mall formula and of dramatically changed circumstances, coupled with a prescription by a self-described "incurable optimist" for creating better ecological and human environments by promoting urban clusters with "small-grained intermingling of social and usage categories." The speech defends the original purpose of introducing multifaceted urbanity to the then wasteland of suburban life in America. It condemns the average shopping center builder for ignoring all the cultural facets that would make a shopping center urbane and focusing exclusively on making the biggest buck with the smallest investment. It criticizes government's laxity in the planning process and its inability to transcend arbitrary political boundaries, thereby enabling developers to evade sensible control simply by building just outside municipal boundaries. And it recognizes that, as oil depletes, centralization of urban life will become increasingly essential in order to reduce reliance on gasoline. The speech is full of hope, not despair. It ends with my father's affirmation of his confidence that the urban pattern of the future he foresees—one, incidentally, quite reminiscent of Vienna—"will evolve."

We talked about these very issues. He was not discontent or self-critical about the concept of the shopping center. To the contrary, he believed that, properly implemented, his concept of creating centers not just for shopping but for obtaining routine medical services, engaging in formal social and political activities such as town meetings, and passing leisure time in an environment that appeals to the sense of beauty was an important contribution toward creating urbane environments and manageable and functioning satellite communities while preserving surrounding open space.

His objection was, in substantial part, that his ideas had not been properly implemented. Where he had advised client developers to acquire substantial acreage surrounding a new shopping center to facilitate the orderly formation of a working community anchored by the shopping center, and perhaps incidentally to prevent the self-destructive construction of competing centers nearby, the clients routinely took the shorter-range approach of maximizing near-term profits without worrying about how the center would fare twenty years later, surrounded by undisciplined development and competition.

A second major problem, closely related, was the reaction of competitors, each seeking to cash in on the success of a predecessor without recognizing that, at some point, supply will exceed demand and all will fail. Thus the success of Southdale Center in Edina, Minnesota, inspired another developer to build the Mall of America just a little more than six miles away. Today almost any small city has its peripheral roadways speckled with mile after mile of repetitious sequencing, like strands of DNA with their GACT segments: shopping center, drive-up bank, fast-food restaurant, gas station, automobile dealer; shopping center, drive-up bank, fast-food restaurant, gas station, automobile dealer; over and over and over. At some point, the supply exceeds demand, and the businesses start to fail.

Vanessa and I tried to arrange several times to bring our little girls to Austria to meet Daddy and Kemija. Kemija was, by that time, quite concerned about Daddy's declining health and discouraged a visit as overly taxing. Daddy, on the other hand, was very eager to see his granddaughters. He finally prevailed, and it was arranged that we would come to Vienna for a few days around October 1979. We arrived and Kemija spared no effort to ensure that the girls saw everything in Vienna that two- and three-year-old girls would want to see, other than their grandfather. So, she very kindly hired a full-time nanny to take care of the girls while we visited with Daddy. It was all very thoughtful, but when we saw him, Daddy kept asking why we had not brought the girls with us. Finally, he insisted that they come and we brought them for a visit and dinner.

He was delighted and could not have had a better time, crawling about on the floor with the two little girls. It was much like he had been with Peggy and me thirty-five years earlier. It came time for dinner, which Kemija presented with more formality than might have been ideal. But, then, she had little to no experience dealing with children and could not have known better. The adults all sat on leather dining chairs. For the girls, Kemija selected very beautiful silk-upholstered Biedermeier chairs. A maid with a white apron and white gloves served a consommé with noodles. Vanessa and I worried about how much of it would end up on the Biedermeier chairs. But the girls handled the challenge extremely well, dipping their hands into the bowls to delicately move the noodles to their mouths. The next course arrived on a large platter under a silver cover. Before the cover was removed, Kemija stage-whispered to Vanessa and me, "Don't tell them. It's Bambi!" Whereupon the girls decided that they had eaten enough and Kemija said to Daddy, "You see, Victor, how badly American children behave." In fact, he seemed not only uncritical but extremely pleased by them.

He was in good spirits on that visit and showed no overt physical signs of illness. He did complain that his diet was sharply restricted. The one thing he could eat as much of as he might wish was pastry, but his desire for it had diminished. Given his love of pastry, one had to assume that his health was indeed failing.

The following February 14, with nothing of note having been communicated in the interim, I received a telegram from Kemija at my office. It read, in German, "Your father is dying in the hospital." About twenty minutes later, a second telegram from her arrived: "Your father is dead." Even as telegrams go, the curtness took my breath away. In a way, it presented the fact in so abstract and detached a manner that it took some time for an emotional response to register. It hit me a few days later as I collapsed on our front stairway at home and cried on end.

So there it is. At one moment life is a heartbeat, a brain wave, a quick body and mind. At the next, an ultimately banal thud.

The physicality of it is one view. Another, as it appears in a written life—a biography or autobiography—presents the meaning, the purpose, the impact, the inspiration. *Time* magazine enshrined my father's life as one of the ten most influential of the twentieth century. Such lists are risky, as they lead the gentlest cynic to ask, ten? Maybe twenty? Or some other number? But no one would doubt his importance as a leading thinker and doer in a field that, since Babylon, Alexandria, Athens, and Rome, has lain at the heart of civilization: the city.

Victor Gruen lived in an age when the city had been wrenched apart by the advent of a means of transportation, the automobile, which made it possible to live on one's own half acre, insulated from others by an expanse of lawn and a fence that made one's neighbors tolerable if not good, yet find employment within driving distance. The highway works of the 1950s only exacerbated the urban exodus, as did the resultant social upheaval as it came to appear that suburbs were for middle-class white people, cities for poor black people.

Victor Gruen reminded America and the world that people actually enjoy communal life. He brought a humanitarian emphasis to the planning profession, an emphasis on improving communities for the enjoyment of people, not just for the passage and parking of motor vehicles. The impact was mind-boggling. Not only do we see shopping centers, perhaps too many, everywhere, but we also see dedicated pedestrian zones (his answer to the deadening tyranny of the automobile) in virtually every significant city, and they are commonly the most popular attractions of these cities. We see zoning that rests on integration of activities rather than their segregation. We see increasing variety. We see, at least in larger cities, and sometimes in the smallest villages, artisanal bakeries and small specialty stores among the brand chains.

Most of all, despite the urban decline of the 1950s, and despite even the common wisdom of more recent times that people can live secluded lives, many miles from one another, and communicate exclusively through cyberspace, city life is resurging. So, Victor Gruen's life lives on and thrives. And thanks to him, there is a little bit of Vienna almost everywhere.

More about My Mother

PEGGY GRUEN

Though I have been in possession of a copy of my father's manuscript for this book since shortly after his death in 1980, my German-language skills are far too limited for me to have been able to read more than one-third of every sentence. With great appreciation I thank Anette Baldauf for translating the entire manuscript into English so that I could finally read the words he penned so many years ago.

What a joy it has been to read about his life experiences, his insights, his thoughts and ideas, his process and the history leading to various projects, and the psychology he used in communicating with people to be sure to reach his goals. Many of the stories are familiar but have been wonderful to hear again, and in even more detail. So much of what he has written concerns things he had not shared with me. I found reading about these thoroughly fascinating and entertaining.

Yet with all the details describing his life, there is much, especially of a personal nature, that he skips over. I would like to add some information about his life with my mother, Elsie Krummeck, later Elsie Gruen, and then Elsie Crawford.

Though he mentions her, almost incidentally, several times, somehow the essence of that relationship and its importance to my father's career and life is lost and so seems unimportant. She was a very creative and talented designer in her own right and had already accrued many accolades and much recognition for her work before my father met her (and this was at a time when women were not often recognized and rewarded for their accomplishments). As my father does mention, when he got his first job in America at Ivel in 1938, she was the most highly regarded designer there. She was earning one hundred dollars per week, compared to my father's thirty dollars, and as he points out, he was fired when he asked that his salary be raised to fifty dollars. Their romantic involvement began at Ivel, and their design and architectural

Elsie Krummeck, New York, 1940. Courtesy of Peggy Gruen.

collaboration began soon afterward (in 1939, I believe) as they formed the firm of Gruenbaum & Krummeck. He describes how he declined business partnerships with several people who made him offers early in his career. The fact that he turned them down yet chose to go into partnership with my mother suggests that he must have been very impressed with her on a professional level as well as a personal one.

The characteristics of her design style are evident in all of those small boutique stores in New York that they created together. My father was without a doubt full of brilliant ideas. He was also charming and persuasive, and he knew how to land a job. But his success in securing jobs was surely aided by my mother's ability to put ideas to paper visually. She was an excellent artist and made beautiful pastel and airbrushed renderings of proposed designs to show the clients. Besides being an enthusiastic and capable design partner, with many ideas of her own, she was extremely beautiful, personable, and fun loving. I imagine they were a duo hard to resist. Their professional partnership lasted approximately ten years; she dropped out after giving birth to my brother and me, recognizing that the demands of child rearing needed to take precedence.

They shared much excitement and giddiness as their architectural practice took off, taking them to California, where the jobs became larger and larger. I have delighted in reading the notes, letters, and telegrams that they sent back and forth while my father was traveling to different jobs. The excitement of the task at hand is so clear, and at the same time it is also clear how much in love they were.

I find it somewhat puzzling that he was surprised at my mother's response when he told her that he was already in love with another woman. My mother had believed that his frequent trips away from home were necessary because of business. I think his bitterness surrounding that experience clouded his recollections of the fabulous collaboration they had.

Since he has made the claim that she tried to ruin him financially, I will come to her defense. First, she was an extremely generous person, and I cannot imagine

Elsie Krummeck and Victor Gruen, Kings Road, Los Angeles, circa 1941. Courtesy of Peggy Gruen.

that ruining him or making him a pauper would have even been in her vocabulary. Even without the fact that he was secretly having a relationship with another woman and was away from home and our family quite often, I think she was rightly entitled to a large portion of his earnings, primarily because she had launched his business with him. In many cases, just being someone's wife is enough to make a claim on property and funds, but my mother had also been an active participant in establishing the value of that business, which laid the foundation for his future. He was never a pauper, and whatever she ended up getting from that settlement did not make her rich. We lived comfortably but never extravagantly.

My mother continued her career as a designer for the rest of her life. After the divorce, she worked at home while raising my brother and me. She worked beyond the limits of conventional architectural and interior design, creating designs for a multitude of projects, including fabrics, toys, interiors, murals, and large sculptures.

Among her greater successes were her designs for large concrete and fiberglass planters used in shopping centers, airports, and parking lots. She also developed a series of sculptural paper lamps, the most well known being her "zipper" lamp, which had an ingenious patented interlocking system to hold two sections of the lamp together, forming a zipper-like seam that became part of the design.

My mother was widely recognized as an important California designer, and many of her pieces were published in books and journals. She is today considered to have been one of the top women designers in the United States. Her work is in the permanent collections of both the Los Angeles County Museum of Art and the Oakland Museum of California.

Consumed?

The Heritage and Legacy of Victor Gruen

ANETTE BALDAUF

Nearing the end of this long journey through Victor Gruen's life and work, I am struck by a paradox: Gruen seemingly succeeded in achieving his central goal of responding to shoppers' longing for imaginary escape and mobilization and at the same time failed in materializing what he cherished as the central virtues of a city: intimacy, diversity, and variety.[1] I will take this opportunity to once again unpack the convoluted history of the mall, first tracing this tension back to Gruen's early urban experiences in the city of Vienna. It was prewar Vienna, with its class antagonism, rigid politics of representation, and growing anti-Semitism, that taught Gruen how to materialize moments of distraction and disconnection in space. Years later, just outside the city of Detroit, Gruen translated these spatial devices into the segregated landscape of U.S. suburbia, allowing for Vienna's social tensions to reappear in a new and rearticulated manner. The effect was a spatial quality that enabled shoppers to claim the place as public space in spite of itself. But the public space created was not public because of an existing physical site or an innate quality of purity and openness; instead, it was public because of a precious, unstable moment that shoppers around the globe have produced against and as a result of a multiplicity of constraints.

IN-BETWEEN SPACE

In 1936, a small store opened in the center of Vienna. For the renovation of the textile outfitter Singer, the store owner had commissioned a fairly unknown architect with no formal degree and no office. Viktor David Grünbaum moved the doorway several feet back from the sidewalk and created a small, publicly accessible arcade between the street and the store. Framed by shopwindows and centered on

Stoff Singer, Vienna, 1936. Library of Congress.

a theatrically lit showcase, the space in between invited pedestrians to steal away from the flow of the street to gaze momentarily upon newly arrived products as well as the vivid urban life rushing by them.

Two years after the opening of the Singer store, magazines including *Glas: Österreichs Glaserzeitung, Architectural Review,* and *L'Architecture d'Aujourd'hui* published articles on Grünbaum's work in Vienna. The photographs of the Bristol-Parfumerie (1935), the men's fashion boutique Deutsch (1936), the perfumery Guerlain (1936), the above-mentioned textile provider Singer (1936), and the women's fashion shop Richard Löwenfeld (1937) illustrated a striking continuity in Grünbaum's interventions: all of them transformed small boutiques into elaborate exhibition spaces within which shoppers could reenact the dramas of urban life.[2]

Creating work that was firmly embedded in the principles of Vienna's modernism in general and Adolf Loos's concept of the theatricality of space in particular, Grünbaum made use of a simple but distinct device of spatial intervention: he inserted windows and showcases that playfully challenged the identity of the space, and, extending the concept of the shopwindow into the entire store, with pedestrians walking by and peeking in, he defined retail space as performance space.[3] As Gruen elaborates in chapter 2 of this book, at this point, theatricality was a key element of his life. In the late 1920s and the first half of the 1930s, he redesigned apartments and stores during the day, and at night he appeared onstage as a member of the Political Cabaret, a Jewish antifascist performance group. Together with writers, dancers, and other performers, including Robert Ehrenzweig (Robert Lucas), Karl Bittman, Jura Soyfer, Edmund Reismann, and Illa Raudnitz (Illa Raudnitz-Roden), Gruen walked a mortally precarious line between political activism and popular entertainment.[4]

During the interwar period, theatricality was also a constitutive feature of everyday life in Vienna. The city exposed urban dwellers, intellectually and physically, to painful discrepancies between image and everyday life. Elegant facades hid dilapidated courtyards; rigid impression management masked inner turmoil. The daily experience of these discrepancies—between abstract ideals and social and spatial fragmentation, between overt conservatism and radical innovation—fueled the perception of the city as a stage.[5] The writings of many authors of the time testify to this. In 1914, Robert Musil wrote about the city of Vienna: "Street images: curvature of the Favoriten[straße]: the Theresianum in evening as if covered with pale paint. When one looks at the Rasumovskygasse . . . onto the small road: the church with its light clock like a stage."[6]

While Grünbaum mused over how to transform the city into a series of seductively illuminated stage sets, the social and physical fabric of the city lapsed into ruins, denunciation, and murder. In a 1924 novella, Arthur Schnitzler evokes the tension inherent in keeping up the standards of representation. Rigid social conventions dictate the lives of his female characters, their attempts to free themselves almost always ending in isolation, embitterment, or suicide.[7] Against this backdrop, Grünbaum defined the store as a performance stage that invited shoppers, mostly women, to become lost temporarily in the script of the store and to act collectively upon what Jacques Le Rider has described as the paradoxical tension between identity crisis and the new cult of the I.[8] Grünbaum's designs perforated the boundaries between life and theater, street and store, private and public space. In this intermediary zone, shoppers could be present and absent at the same time, right there as well as at a distance from the constraints of their everyday existence. Here, time and space could be forced to shift; women's performative shopping acts could obey the oppressive regime while at the same time subtly undermining it. Shoppers could assert the conventions of consumerism and gender roles and also mimic, ridicule, and exaggerate the order of things.

In 1938, two months after the Anschluss, Grünbaum and his first wife, Lizzie Kardos, barely managed to escape Nazi Austria. After the Gestapo confiscated their luggage, a friend of Grünbaum dressed up in a stolen *Sturmtruppler* uniform, fetched the suitcases, and drove the couple to the airport. They fled to Switzerland first, before continuing on to the United States. Within a year of his arrival in New York, Grünbaum was hired to redesign the Fifth Avenue boutique of Ludwig Lederer, a businessman who had also fled Vienna. As he recalls in chapter 3, Grünbaum presented Lederer the following vision for the store: Along Fifth Avenue, he would introduce an atrium that would open up to the sidewalk and allow racing pedestrians to stop and linger. On the two sides and the back wall of the atrium, six small glass cabinets would jut out, and at the back wall a glass entrance door would offer a view into the store. The ceiling of the atrium would be made of diaphanous glass; hidden light sources would illuminate the open forecourt evenly. In the middle of the new outside space, he envisioned a glass exhibit case; the commodities on display in this case would be lit by hidden, very strong spotlights like those used in the theater.

Eventually Grünbaum made use of the architectural license of an acquaintance, Morris Ketchum, and the dazzling designs of a well-known interior designer, Elsie Krummeck, who became his second wife soon after his arrival in New York. Together with Krummeck, Grünbaum realized the concept of a quintessential space in between street and store. In 1939, architectural magazines, trade journals, and newspapers hailed the Lederer store as a new inspiration in retail architecture and celebrated "the highly novel arcade store front."[9] The New York Museum of Modern Art published images of the Lederer store in its guide to modern architecture.[10]

In many ways, the store on Fifth Avenue anticipated what eventually became the signature device of many Gruen interventions. He treated commercial space as a performative stage and addressed shoppers as performers of city life, and while operating within the constraints of a confined space, he tried to take advantage of shopping's potential for imaginary mobilization. His interventions were driven by an intuitive understanding of the city as a showroom and an unquestioned faith in the integrative power of commerce. The urbanist Lewis Mumford recognized this tension in the Lederer store. In his review in the *New Yorker,* he described the entrance area as a peep show for lusting consumers.[11]

Fifteen years after the opening of the Lederer boutique on Fifth Avenue in New York, Grünbaum, now a naturalized U.S. citizen going by the name Victor D. Gruen, expanded the idea and the scale of the in-between space of the Vienna Singer store by more than a thousandfold and introduced the concept of the regional shopping center as a social experiment. On Northland Center's opening day, March 22, 1954, Gruen enthused that his creation was the "first shopping center of the future."[12] Whereas in Vienna and New York bright display cases had marked the centers of Gruen's boutiques, in Southfield, Michigan, the prominent Hudson's department store anchored the 44,000-square-meter complex. In chapter 4, Gruen recalls at length how he, in collaboration with the owner of the J. L. Hudson Company, the ominous Oscar Webber, developed a new retail architecture that enhanced the concept of the arcade by introducing a large courtyard dotted with fountains, benches, whimsical sculptures, and colorful mosaics. The courtyard was framed by the large windows of the shops surrounding it, and at the interface between the courtyard and the shopwindows, a colonnaded arcade provided what Gruen called an "essentially urban ambience." One hundred stores of various kinds were combined with noncommercial spaces, such as a conference room, a child-care facility, and a zoo, all of which asserted the urban identity of the thirty-million-dollar complex.

Soon after his arrival in the United States, Gruen started to claim that his vision of the "shopping town" could provide structure for the amorphous, monofunctional agglomerations of living spaces that started to spread to the urban peripheries after World War II. Arguing that all European cities were built on a solid combination of civic and commercial spaces, he suggested re-creating the basic coordinates of cities like Vienna in postwar suburbia, hoping to strengthen civic life in an otherwise atomized society. But like the memories of many emigrants who were forced to flee Austria during the Holocaust, Gruen's memories of the city of Vienna emerged in the context of the collective trauma within a dialectic of remembering and forgetting.[13] When Gruen translated key features of Vienna's urbanity into U.S. suburbs, what he had in mind was the bourgeois inner-city culture, with its distinguished boutiques, sophisticated coffeehouses, and high-culture concert halls and theaters, situated along and within the Ringstrasse that encircles the First District. Many historians have since interpreted the so-called *via triumphalis* as the spatial figure of Vienna's liberalism and also the dictum of visual appearance.[14] By translating this organizational device into an American context, Gruen introduced not only the concept of a dense center and an enclosing ring but also a series of tensions that included, among others, the spatialization of an inside–outside dialectic. While the emerging middle class settled along the circle, the Ringstrasse in Vienna aggravated the focus on the inside and foreclosed the recognition of an outside—in other words, the poor and rejected popular classes residing in Vienna's suburbs.[15] These tensions unfolded in a slightly twisted manner once they met with the forces driving the expansion of postwar U.S. suburbia.

CONTAINMENT AND SOCIAL ANTAGONISM

In 1943, the U.S.-based journal *Architectural Forum* invited Gruen and Krummeck to participate in an exchange of grand visions for postwar city planning. The editors of the special issue "New Buildings for 194X" called on acclaimed modernists such as William Lescaze, Ludwig Mies van der Rohe, and Charles Eames to design parts of a model modernist city for the year 194X, the unknown year when World War II would end.[16] In chapter 3 Gruen recalls how they also approached Gruen and Krummeck to submit a prototype for a postwar shopping center, anticipating that it would be located at the city's periphery. They envisioned the center, situated between two major highways, as complementing the existing downtown pedestrian shopping strip. "How can shopping be made more inviting?" the editors asked Gruen and Krummeck, who at that point were known mainly as New York–based store designers.[17]

With Krummeck focusing on design and Gruen on writing, the pair responded to the initial call for the design of a "small neighborhood shopping center" by proposing a center that far exceeded the scheme laid out by the editors in both size and functionality. The proposal, Gruen muses later in his writing, reflected their own frustration with Los Angeles shopping strips, where long distances between stores, traffic jams, and a lack of pedestrian spaces made shopping a painful chore. Convinced that Los Angeles was the blueprint for postwar U.S. development, Gruen and Krummeck modeled their proposal on the main squares of older cities, or, rather, Gruen's memories of the city of Vienna. Following this scheme, Gruen and Krummeck suggested introducing two key innovations: first, the separation of parking from shopping areas; and second, the uniting of commercial and civic functions. In the afterword to this book, Victor Gruen's son, Michael Gruen, reminds the reader that the Vienna at the time of his father's upbringing was a tight-knit labyrinth of small-scale streets and narrow alleys. Encircled by the pompous Ringstrasse, this dense urban fabric served as the political, commercial, and cultural center of the old aristocracy and the emerging bourgeoisie. In the mid-nineteenth century, the Ringstrasse had been introduced as part of the city's refortification, and, according to Carl Schorske, the emperor's intention had not been basic urban restructuring but mere beautification.[18] While the densely built inner city offered spaces to get lost in, the boulevard provided a circular walking promenade along which the newly empowered middle class followed the dictum of visual representation. Walking along the Ringstrasse, the flaneurs and flaneuses enjoyed the pleasures of seeing and being seen. Inspired by this spatial device, Gruen and Krummeck proposed creating a dense and tightly woven center surrounded by a green plaza, which would allow visitors to stroll and relax in garden restaurants, at milk bars, and in front of music stands. The complex encompassed twenty-eight stores and thirteen public facilities, which included a library, a nursing school, a post office, a game room, a theater, a clubhouse, an auditorium, and stables for ponies.[19]

The editors of *Architectural Forum* rejected the proposal based on its unprecedented scale, pointing out that they had called for a design for a neighborhood shopping center. Asked to downscale the project significantly, Gruen and Krummeck responded with what would later turn out to be a momentous adjustment: they discarded the idea of the courtyard and proposed a circular building made of glass. In their proposal, the fully enclosed complex was surrounded first by a pedestrian path and then by a parking ring. Again the editors refused to accept the proposal. George Nelson, *Architectural Forum*'s associate editor, asserted that without a courtyard, shoppers would have no place to linger and stroll.[20] In the end, Gruen and Krummeck submitted a design for a more conventional shopping center that was organized around a U-shaped green courtyard. The forces that led to the enthusiastic appraisal of the fully enclosed, self-contained shopping environment a few years later were not yet in place.

Eight years later, in 1951, Victor Gruen gave a lecture at the national convention of the American Institute of Architects in Chicago. At this point in his career, Gruen's presentations followed a predictable pattern: He first painted a dark picture of suburbia's anomalies, highlighting its social isolation, unhappiness, and boredom. He then identified the sources of the problems—that is, sprawl and spatial compartmentalization. Finally, he presented his solution, the regional shopping center. But for this occasion Gruen took a different turn. "Modern warfare has erased the boundaries between the fighting front and the hinterland," he stressed in his lecture. He asserted that large industrial centers were the main targets for enemy air attacks, and, as a result, urban peripheries had to provide emergency shelters.[21]

Gruen's lecture was seemingly catalyzed by a speech given three weeks earlier by President Harry Truman, in which Truman announced the creation of the Federal Civil Defense Administration and introduced a national dispersion policy that encouraged citizens to build shelters into their homes and asked municipalities to establish fallout shelters at the peripheries of urban centers.[22] "As far as new buildings are concerned, it would, of course, be foolishness to assume that public funds would be available to build new emergency centers," Gruen asserted at the convention. "However, there seems to be one ideal way in which private capital can be encouraged to build structures which are well suited for the purpose. I am referring to regional shopping centers, if they fulfill certain basic requirements." Regional shopping centers located five miles outside city centers, Gruen argued, could be of "great value in peace—and of tremendous effectiveness as emergency shelter should this peace, against all hopes, be interrupted."[23]

It is hardly a coincidence that Gruen realized his vision for a regional shopping center in Southfield, just outside the city of Detroit. In the 1950s, Detroit was home to two million residents and three of the world's largest automobile companies: Chrysler, Ford, and General Motors. In Detroit, the auto industry had enabled the rise of a prosperous middle class with significant purchasing power. Detroit was thought of as an economic paradise and a potential military target for Cold War attacks. The Ford Motor Company provided employees with their own company bunker, and local civil defense organizations offered training sessions in preparation for nuclear emergencies. In addition, the city pursued an aggressive decentralization plan.

The cumulative effect of these forces turned Detroit into a pioneer of suburbanization. Affluent, mostly white residents moved to the suburbs, where they settled into safe—that is, racially segregated—neighborhoods. The roads necessary for building much of this new housing often cut through African American working-class areas: new city planning was used to destroy old problem zones as much as to create new enclaves.[24] In 2004, on the occasion of the fiftieth anniversary of Northland Center, the *Detroit Free Press* reported that certain mayors and real estate agents had actively prevented African Americans and other minorities from moving into the new suburbs. When people of color nonetheless succeeded, their homes were often attacked by neighbors.[25]

As described in chapter 3, in 1956 Gruen convinced the family owners of a leading department store in Minnesota to commission his firm for the development of a retail complex that would meet the needs of suburbanites. Gruen and his team suggested building an "entire new community," that is, a city unto itself. The Dayton family acquired 463 acres of land in Edina, southwest of Minneapolis, and Gruen and his team realized a project that comprised houses, apartment buildings, a park, a medical center, a lake, highways, schools, and, finally, a fully enclosed shopping mall.[26]

Inspired by the Galleria Vittorio Emanuele in Milan, Gruen designed the first enclosed, temperature-controlled shopping environment. It was organized around a fully covered and brightly lit two-level central court. The complex housed two major department stores and seventy-two additional stores, and for all intents and purposes, the Southdale Center was considered the first shopping mall. Even though other, similar projects were introduced near the time of its completion, Southdale Center established Gruen's reputation as the father of the shopping mall.[27] "It is the best answer that imaginative and thoughtful people have been able to design to the urgent problem of how people live together more happily, more comfortably, more prosperously, in the metropolitan areas of modern America," enthused the *Minneapolis Tribune* when the plans were presented to the public on June 18, 1952.[28] It was the beginning of a lasting tradition in which shopping malls emphasized the difference between the world outside and the world inside. Large malls, in the words of Margaret Crawford, started "to reproduce the single element missing in suburbia—the city."[29]

When the fully enclosed Southdale Center opened its doors in 1956, the twenty-million-dollar project was considered an immediate success. The local press celebrated the creation of a "complete living environment," and *Architectural Record* praised it as "a better outdoors indoors."[30] An article titled "Suburb or Loop? Which Direction Is Mrs. Shopper Going?" in the *Minneapolis Tribune* observed that with the introduction of the shopping center, "Mrs. Minneapolis Housewife" had more retail choices. She could dress up and go downtown, or if she was in a hurry, she could "pile the children in the car and go shopping—with her hair still in curlers" in the suburbs. Because suburbia's shopping center was "conventional, casual," the article concluded that the "future belongs to the shopping center."[31]

This account, put forth a few months after the center's opening, called into question one of Gruen's central premises—that the suburban and inner-city shopping areas could coexist in a competitive but productive relationship. Eventually, the regional shopping center provided the spatial as well as the social conditions for white, middle-class suburbanites to withdraw fully from the economically and ethnically mixed downtown shopping streets. With its flamboyant bunker-style iconography, the shopping center translated the political strategy of containment into space, and thereby established the material condition for further, subtler forms of social and cultural containment. As the shopping center offered mostly white, middle-class suburbanites a guarded safety zone that simulated urbanism while also assuring social homogeneity, the history of the shopping center is inextricably entangled in the history of containment of African Americans in economically neglected city centers.

CONSUMERISM

Between 1943, when Gruen and Krummeck first presented their idea of an enclosed shopping center to the editors of *Architectural Forum*, and 1956, the moment when Gruen was able to realize his vision of a self-contained shopping town, the American cultural and political landscape had changed fundamentally. The amorphous group called consumers had first been addressed during the Great Depression. During World War II, President Franklin Roosevelt repeatedly mobilized the consumer home front for military ends. But it was not until after the war that the ideology of consumerism came to provide the central ingredient of an American way of life. For ideal postwar citizens, and especially for women, consumption became a civic duty.[32] By the time Southdale Center opened in the mid-fifties, the role of consumerism had changed fundamentally: consumerism was no longer *a* driving force but *the* driving force in the postwar era.

In her book *Fast Cars, Clean Bodies: Decolonization and the Reordering of French Culture,* Kristin Ross reconstructs how in the 1960s in France the politics of consumerism successively absorbed the forces of social unrest and student rebellion, establishing the foundation of what she terms the "democracy of consumption."[33] During that same period in the United States, where various powerful social movements coalesced, all of them calling for a radical reorganization of everyday life, these transfers played a key role while the country shifted its economic foundation from a primacy of production to a primacy of consumption. In the mid-sixties, U.S. corporations started to relocate industrial production first to the national borders and then abroad. For outsourcing to become the dominant mode of industrial production one decade later, a profound social restructuring along the lines of neoliberal paradigms was necessary. Large-scale deindustrialization and the vast displacement of the working class had enormous implications for U.S. society. These changes resulted in a reorganization of the nation's social structure, its everyday culture and politics. When consumerism moved to the center, it promised to make experiences meaningful, identifications significant, and relationships valid, and to make cities anew.

In the 1960s, as deindustrialization proceeded and the power of consumption started to drive the U.S. economy, shopping prepared the path for postindustrialism. The shopping mall became an engine of the postindustrial economy, integrating living into shopping. And while neoliberal ideologies called upon individuals to remake themselves according to values of efficiency, flexibility, and self-reliance, shopping turned into a key technology of the self, blurring the lines between consumption and production.

Gruen's writing does not make clear when he himself started to grasp the power of consumerism and its relation to the mall. In a speech in 1978, he announced that he now "disclaimed paternity once and for all," and a few months later he stated that he refused to "pay alimony for those bastard developments."[34] Two years later, when he was writing this memoir, he stressed that contemporary malls were not "shopping towns" but "selling machines." In 1978, filmmaker George Romero poignantly expressed this view in his *Dawn of the Dead,* in which a shopping mall provides the setting for a gruesome battle involving zombies, "normal" humans, and a gang of violent bikers. In the tradition of horror, the movie draws connections between zombies, racial oppression, and social abjection.[35] Zombies return to the mall because, as a character explains, they feel a residual connection to the place: "They remember that they want to be here." In one scene, the central female character remarks, "It's so bright and neatly wrapped, you don't see that it's a prison." Soon, she too is absorbed by the dream of owning a well-furnished home and fur coats.

CONTROL AND ESCAPE

In addition to its role in the history of the containment of African Americans in economically neglected downtowns, the shopping center is entwined with the history of the containment of women. On numerous occasions, Gruen stressed that he had envisioned his shopping center with a female shopper in mind, claiming that shopping centers would ease women's lives and integrate shopping into living. The center was supposed to provide the social and cultural infrastructure in an otherwise isolated life in suburbia; it was supposed to provide relief in the life of a woman who had no access to public transportation or child-care facilities—a woman who had the feeling, according to Gruen, "that her life was empty and boring" because "there was nothing to do in the suburbs."[36] The center was supposed to provide women with a so-called third place—neither home nor work, but a site in between production and reproduction. "The housewife spends an awful lot of time shopping," Gruen argued in an appearance on a 1953 radio show; he promised that, since his complex was situated in a peaceful park, it would be a relaxing place for women. He then went on to illustrate how "our little Mrs. Shopper" would find tranquility and comfort in a shopping center.[37]

A few decades earlier, the German philosopher Walter Benjamin had painted a radically different picture while excavating the "original form of commodity capitalism" in Paris for an article provisionally titled "Das Passagen-Werk."[38] Formally, he too described the arcade as a space in between; it connected the noisy street with a spectacular interior. Aesthetically and politically, Benjamin asserted, the arcade was a place of seduction. In his dialectical fairy tale, he argued that it combined the visual spectacle of light and glass with the dreamworld of commodity goods. This constellation, he claimed, gave rise to a phenomenon he called "phantasmagoria."

According to Benjamin, the arcade was laid out like a church, following the form of a cross. Within this form, the new magic of glass and steel found its material expression. In the shopwindows, goods were placed like icons in a sacred shrine. Arcades, wrote Benjamin in retrospect, "beamed out onto the Paris of the Second Empire like fairy grottoes."[39] Following Benjamin, these "dream-houses of the collective" were home to two types of urban dwellers: the flaneur and the prostitute. The flaneur—

here considered a literary motif as well as the embodiment of a particular urban experience—is a loiterer. Wasting time is the passion of this lonely stranger, who rebels against the division of labor and the culture of industriousness. As he "goes botanizing on the asphalt," he recognizes the city as a landscape—and women as part of the array of seductive objects of consumption composing this landscape.[40]

Moving aimlessly through the space in between defined males as heroic, semi-tragic figures associated with modern subjectivity, but it turned women into street women—that is, prostitutes. Like many of his counterparts, Benjamin was fascinated by women, whom he called "seller and sold at once." "The love for the prostitute is the apotheosis of *Einfühlung* onto the commodity," he stated, and he defined the prostitute as an allegory for the transformation of objects, the world of things.[41]

As Elizabeth Wilson writes, "The prostitute was a 'public woman,' but the problem in nineteenth-century urban life was whether every woman in the new, disordered world of the city . . . was not a public woman and thus a prostitute."[42] Benjamin's appraisal of the "street girl" was not shared by most city officials, at least not publicly. In many European cities, the mere presence of women in the streets was considered a threat to the dominant patriarchal order. Some cities tried to arrest moral decay by introducing curfews, which were meant to keep women from roaming the streets at night. Nevertheless, even though it endangered their reputations, young women often chose to experience what Susanne Frank calls the "Abendteuer Stadt," that is, the "adventures of the night."[43] What drove this undisguised attempt to force women to disappear from the streets, to put them in their place? Wilson believes it was the fear of the "new woman," who often worked in a factory and enjoyed an independent urban lifestyle.[44]

This situation changed fundamentally with the introduction of the department store in the mid-nineteenth century. Unlike the arcade, the department store explicitly addressed a female clientele, incorporating conveniences like child care, custom tailoring, and music rooms. As a mercantile space of goods and a production space of desires, the department store embedded the objects on display in collective imaginaries and popular narratives of longing and desire. It dangled signs of luxury in front of the customer. The department store was safe and clean; *flânerie* was transformed into a commodity, and the flaneur and the prostitute expelled. According to Anne Friedberg, out of the ashes of the flaneur arose the flaneuse, who strolled through the aisles of the department store, enjoying the intoxicating, visual resonance of the commodities surrounding her.[45]

But the flaneuse's liberty of movement through public space came with a certain price. Women were regarded as delicate objects, vulnerable to the spell of commodity culture. Looking into court cases that involved Macy's department store in New

York in the late nineteenth century, Elaine Abelson has reconstructed how kleptomania came to be considered "a natural, if eccentric, inclination firmly rooted in female life."[46] The association of women with mass culture and manipulation, consumerism, and contamination—established at the time of the introduction of the department store—also served a political purpose: At the beginning of the twentieth century, socialist and feminist movements were rattling the doors of the dominant high culture, demanding participation. As women were addressed as consuming subjects, the irrational and easy targets of mass culture, their status as responsible citizens was called into question.[47]

Years later, after women had acquired the rights to vote, attend universities, and walk the street after dark, a slightly transformed version of this battle resurfaced in the postwar United States. After World War II, with male veterans returning to the labor market, there was a strong effort to reassociate the concept of femininity with child rearing and homemaking, at least on the level of representation. Women were asked to retreat from the labor market in order to engage in the so-called labor of love.[48] In the 1950s, while social movements gained momentum, the representation of femininity resembled a battlefield where ideas of women's emancipation, empowerment, and self-determination clashed with ideas of conformity and the "orgy of domesticity."[49] Framed by these tensions, the shopping mall became a means as much as a manifestation of the postwar tightening of gender hierarchies. It was the site of women's reproductive labor, and it also provided women with a place where they could temporarily transcend rigid conventions of everyday life and daydream themselves to another time and place.[50] Thus, for many suburban women, the shopping center resembled a vehicle of control as much as one of escape; it was a place of constriction as well as a safe transit to an imaginary elsewhere.

MALL MATRIX

In the context of increasing globalization in the late twentieth century, cities around the world started to undergo radical transformation, much of which exaggerated segregation, displacement, and fear. Cities were torn down, reshuffled, and rebuilt, but the shopping mall often remained a stable feature in the polarized landscape. As powerful dream machine for shoppers and potent vehicle of financial speculation, the mall satisfied both the longing for escape and the capitalist maxim of profit making. After the millennium, megamall structures continued to prosper in many Asian and African countries, but in the United States, where urban gentrification fostered the violent displacement of ethnic minorities and the poor, mall development took a different turn. In the suburbs, "dead malls" started to litter the landscape, and in the city centers, city administrators made use of the space-making devices developed for and in the mall. Private–public partnerships pushed for a privatization of urban territory, where shared marketing strategies, private security guards, and sanitation workers, in conjunction with zero-tolerance policies, provided a solid foundation for neoliberal city experimentation. With predictable sets of transnational corporations and vast control and surveillance apparatuses, the city centers increasingly approached the model of the mall matrix.

Since the shopping mall's introduction, critics have called it the death knell of the city, a textbook example of a space dedicated to the manufacture of profit and dull happiness. As mall spaces gained popularity around the globe, critics blamed "mallification" for the homogenization of urban landscapes. "If space-junk is the human debris that litters the universe, Junk-Space is the residue mankind leaves on the planet," Rem Koolhaas states in his 2002 manifesto "Junkspace," on dominant spatial formation. Junkspace, he argues in a percussive accumulation of metaphors, is "additive, layered, and lightweight, not articulated in different parts but subdivided, quartered the way a carcass is torn apart—individual chunks severed from a universal condition." The composition of these chunks, Koolhaas stresses, signals a provisional existence; it asserts the space's temporary nature, an expectation of demolition, due any time now. In contrast to architecture, which combines a megastructure with various subsystems and creates an overall cohesion, junkspace, Koolhaas claims, consists of "subsystem only, without superstructure, orphaned particles in search of framework or pattern."[51] Modernization's fallout, he asserts, is ugly, ephemeral, and eventually meaningless.

While Koolhaas's polemic entails an irritated critique of fellow architects (and, possibly, his own practice), it provides little insight into what exactly makes the foundation of the mall's popularity. Pausing to consider how shoppers use a sampling of malls around the world may begin to answer this and other important questions: What is it about these excessive control apparatuses that lends itself to such appropriation? How can these supersized commercial machines satisfy both the greed for profit and the longing for sociability? Why do people looking for what Hannah Arendt terms a "space of appearance" turn to the mall as a site for seeing, being seen, and making a scene?[52]

CityWalk, Los Angeles

In the late 1980s, the entertainment giant then known as Universal/MCA commissioned architect Jon Jerde to capitalize on the "behind-the-scenes magic of moviemaking" of Universal Studios in Los Angeles by using the strip of land between Universal's film studios and the studio complex's vast parking lot. When Universal CityWalk Hollywood opened in 1993, this in-between space integrated Hollywood's

This way to the Mall. Dubai, 2005. Photograph by Anette Baldauf.

sign language and corporate consumer culture into an extensive, walk-in movie set. Thousands of visitors, many of them teenagers, have since visited CityWalk to walk around and be dazzled by oversized billboards and neon hyperbole. CityWalk addresses its visitor as a movie star, or at least a character actor, as well as a potential shopper; the curved streetscape is framed as Los Angeles's ultimate movie set and shopping mall.

The Grove, Los Angeles

Nearly one decade later, a private developer who also happened to be, at the time of the opening, the president of the Los Angeles Police Commission, introduced a place called the Grove, a shopping mall inspired by the nostalgic vision of Disney's Main Street, U.S.A. Since its opening in 2002, this dense, Victorian-style streetscape has satisfied a diverse audience in search of an urban experience. Cobblestone streets, an animated fountain, and an old-fashioned trolley system provide the ingredients for a sentimental setting that simulates an old, innocent, European town. At the Grove, transnational corporations sell their brands behind quaint pink and purple two-story facades, and private security guards survey the street. On a Saturday,

CityWalk streetscape, Los Angeles, 2004. Photograph by Anette Baldauf.

CityWalk wedding, Los Angeles, 2004. Photograph by Anette Baldauf.

acrobats sponsored by the MAC Cosmetics company wear bright makeup, disco dresses, and rollerblades as they encircle potential customers, while young and old Los Angelenos make use of the streetscape to stroll, play, and shop.

Dembel Mall, Addis Ababa

While the Grove's design capitalizes on the semiotics of openness and urban *flânerie,* the twelve-story Dembel Mall in the city of Addis Ababa asserts enclosure. Developed by the firm Yencomad, directed by Yemiru Nega who was the uncle of Ethiopia's minister of trade and industry, this upscale shopping mall also opened in 2002, but in contrast to the Grove, it presents itself as an imposing airport terminal. At the entrance, extensive brandscapes celebrate Ethiopian brides in white, Western-style dresses, while guards and metal detectors control the passage of people and goods. Outside, the mall asserts such values as progress, security, and enclosure, but inside, local traditions relentlessly challenge Western concepts. Much of the organization of and movement in Dembel Mall is inspired by the nearby Merkato, Africa's

The Grove, Los Angeles, 2004. Photograph by Dorit Margreiter. Courtesy of Dorit Margreiter.

The Grove fountain, Los Angeles, 2004. Photograph by Dorit Margreiter. Courtesy of Dorit Margreiter.

largest open-air market, where space, time, and social relationships are subject to ongoing negotiation. In effect, at Dembel Mall too, stores spill and borders leak. Here too, the spatial order is permeated by improvisation and the conventions of collaboration. While shoppers take part in a café ceremony, workers at a nearby flower store expand an already extensive arrangement, embedding the café and its customers in an ocean of red flowers. The smells of coffee and flowers blend as the boundaries of the stores bow to satisfy the needs of both shoppers and merchants.

She Zone, Abu Dhabi

In contrast to Dembel Mall, where the developer aspires to a Western language and store owners and shoppers routinely translate these signs into local vernacular, one developing firm in Abu Dhabi aimed at establishing a distinctly local prototype for future shopping mall development. In 1999 the firm introduced a shopping center called the She Zone, where only women were allowed to make use of the stores and religious and entertainment facilities. At first Western media celebrated the space as a sign of women's liberation. "They come, they take their 'abayas' off, and they're happy," enthused the *Los Angeles Times,* but ultimately the experiment in the United Arab Emirates failed.[53] Women were seemingly not interested in gender-segregated shopping spaces, and in 2003 the She Zone closed due to a lack of customers. Shopping malls in the city of Dubai continue to welcome women and men, young and old, tourists, migrants, and locals, all of whom contribute to the making of a shared space in the city. As the city's imaginary landscape of integration, the mall-scape promises to provide a space that allows shoppers to escape the constraints of Dubai's rigid spatial segregation.

Rolezinhos, *São Paulo*

Similar to the women in Abu Dhabi, poor youth in São Paulo have claimed their right to the city by demanding entry to the mall. For several years now, groups of hundreds, sometimes thousands, of teenagers—largely working-class black and brown youth—have met in the shopping malls of upscale neighborhoods, using social media to arrange the gatherings. The protagonists of these so-called *rolezinhos* come to the malls, mill around, and lay claim to them as public spaces. In the context of Brazil's overtly segregated cityscape, this simple gesture evokes a grand effect: when the teens insert their bodies into the existing landscape of segregation, police military teams counter the excursions with rubber bullets and tear gas. The insurgence of the youngsters challenges the dominant rhetoric of inclusion, making visible the hierarchies that sustain the politics of differentiated citizenship, along with the rules and regulations of what is seemingly a ceaseless flow of movement.

Dembel Mall entrance, Addis Ababa, 2014. Photograph by Anette Baldauf.

Dembel Mall interior, Addis Ababa, 2014. Photograph by Anette Baldauf.

She Zone entrance, Abu Dhabi, 2005. Photograph by Anette Baldauf.

Deira City Center, Dubai, 2005. Photograph by Anette Baldauf.

ANY-SPACE-WHATEVER

The malls in Los Angeles, Dubai, Addis Ababa, and São Paulo have not grown organically out of existing urban structures; instead, they have been built from scratch and now flamboyantly exhibit their compartmentalized features, decorated parking garages, partitioned wings, and pasted signage. They clearly respond to calls for containment, control, and consumerism, but they also respond to shoppers' longing for mobilization and the desire to make the body appear in public. Gilles Deleuze's writing on contemporary space formation suggests that these shopping spaces are able to satisfy such contradictory claims mostly because they are in-between spaces—spaces in between store and street, private and public, real and unreal. Studying the features of space produced in cinema, Deleuze tries to grasp vacant and disconnected spaces that have been put forth by nonrational links and can no longer be understood according to the principles of a particular determined space. For the analysis of these spatial formations, Deleuze proposes the term "any-space-whatever," inspired by the anthropologist Marc Augé, who describes places like subway stations, waiting rooms, and airport terminals as "non-places."[54] In Augé's writing, the term designates anonymous and deeply depersonalized spaces, places that may be thought of as homogeneous and desingularized—places much like those Koolhaas calls junkspace. Deleuze makes use of Augé's concept in order to explore the potentialities of these transitional places further, but in contrast to Augé's non-place, Deleuze's any-space-whatever asserts the connective quality of these places. Any-space-whatever is a mediating space in the transition between other spaces, or between chaos and order. It is composed of parts, but this composition does not follow a single determining order. While the spatial composition can be broken down into components and then reassembled in a new way, the basic spatial constituency—that is, its incompleteness—stays the same. This is how the spatial variations are radically contingent. In contrast to Koolhaas, who dismisses this condition as ephemeral and continues to mourn the loss of cohesion, Deleuze emphasizes the potentiality of this condition: "It is a space of virtual conjunction, grasped as pure locus of the possible," he writes. "What in fact manifests the instability, the heterogeneity, the absence of link of such a space, is a richness in potentials or singularities which are, as it were, prior conditions of all actualisation, all determination."[55]

Following Deleuze, it is the incohesive quality of the shopping spaces, their radical incompleteness and spatial instability, that allows for contradictory appropriations. While rigid policies of exclusion, apparatuses of tight surveillance, and codes of conduct govern the flow and interaction of people, the mall's spatial and temporal separation allows shoppers to move one step away from the constraints of everyday life. As this separation is necessarily incomplete, shoppers are neither fully absorbed by the script of the mall nor fully untouched by it; they move in and out of the mall's constriction. As such, the incohesive quality of the mall allows for shoppers to develop a dual state of mind, which in a different context Margaret Morse has called distraction: it allows them to be here and there at the same time, here in the midst of daily life, at the mall, and there, elsewhere, the world of dreams and longings.[56]

While walking along aisles, riding up and down escalators, leaning against railings, and observing the action unfolding in the atrium, shoppers might become absorbed by consumerism's alluring imaginaries and popular narratives of belonging and despair. They might purchase consumer goods or go on temporary excursions to imaginary elsewheres, and they might also come together and engage in encounters across social fault lines. Because of this condition, the space that shoppers momentarily transform into a public space in the course of their assembly is a precarious gain. When women discuss dress codes in the shopping malls of Dubai and thereby passionately negotiate gender roles, the space they create is vital but necessarily encroached upon by matters of mundane commercial concern; it is an unstable by-product of a purchase, an accidental occurrence accompanying an acquisition, rarely intentional. Similarly, when black and brown youth in São Paulo browse the displays of hip-hop gear and engage in conversations on affordability, the space that emerges has the potential to become public, as it allows for a repudiation of the dominant rhetoric of inclusion. And when teenagers in the mall of Addis Ababa contrast the traveling of their goods with the traveling of their bodies, a debate on migration politics might momentarily transform the enclosed terminal into a site of public deliberation. As such, debates on the shopping mall and those on public space take place on shaky ground. Public space, like the mall, resists neat interpretation—an understanding of such space rests on an ability to ground in practice the concrete interaction of people, objects, and finances.[57] Maybe this is what the architect Jon Jerde, a self-declared Gruen impersonator and the mastermind behind places like CityWalk, had in mind when he said, "Everything we learn about the shopping mall applies to the streets, the same struggles, the same fights."[58]

Notes

PREFACE

1. Alex Wall, *Victor Gruen: From Urban Shop to New City* (Barcelona: Actar, 2005).

2. M. Jeffrey Hardwick, *Mall Maker: Victor Gruen, Architect of an American Dream* (Philadelphia: University of Pennsylvania Press, 2004).

3. William Severini Kowinski, *The Malling of America: An Inside Look at the Great Consumer Paradise* (New York: William Morrow, 1985), 25.

4. From 1968 to 1970, Müller-Hartburg was president of the Chambers of Architects of Vienna, Lower Austria, and Burgenland; from 1970 to 1978, he was president of the Federal Chambers of Engineers. In 1999, the Technical University of Graz awarded him an honorary professorship. His architectural achievements include a radar station in Kolomansberg, a Catholic church in Gablitz, and the Florido Tower in Vienna.

1. VIENNA 1938

1. Victor Gruen, *Meine alte Schuhschachtel: Schriften aus den Zwanziger Jahren* (Vienna: Europa Verlag, 1973).

2. Schuschnigg was chancellor of the First Austrian Republic from July 29, 1934, to March 11, 1938.

3. Yorke was born in 1908 in New York and studied at the Max Reinhardt Seminar in Vienna. She then performed on Broadway and in soap operas on U.S. television and radio. She was married to a member of the Viennese Refugee Artists Group.

4. Under the Nazis, immigration to an Anglo-American country required an affidavit from a friend or relative residing in that country.

5. *Sturmtruppler* describes members of the Sturmabteilung, the paramilitary fighting organization of the Nazi Party.

6. During the Habsburg monarchy, the term *Ruthenen* was used to categorize the empire's East Slavs, Ukrainians, and various other peoples (Russinen, Lemken, Bojken, and Huzulen).

7. During the interwar period, Soyfer was one of Austria's most important writers. In 1929, he became a member of the Political Cabaret. He published regularly in the Social Democratic press, and after 1934 he wrote several plays as well as the unfinished novel *So starb eine Partei* (This is how a party died).

8. Until 1934, Jahnel worked at the Museum of Society and Economy and as a freelance journalist. In 1938, he fled to Paris and then to New York.

9. The National Socialist organization Kraft durch Freude (Strength through Joy) was founded in 1933. Its aim was to organize, control, and streamline the leisure activities of the German population. It attempted to integrate the working class into the *Volksgemeinschaft* through cultural and tourist activities.

10. From 1946 to 1950, the "Kleine Hause" on Liliengasse in the city's First District was used by the Josefstädter Ensemble. Today it is known as the Theater im Zentrum.

11. It is likely that Gruen is referring here to L'Exposition Internationale des Arts Décoratifs et Industriels Modernes, which actually took place in Paris in 1925.

12. Raudnitz, later Illa Raudnitz-Roden, was a member of the Political Cabaret in Vienna. Along with Gruen, she fled to the United States in 1938, where she performed, with Gruen's crew, on Broadway. She later founded a children's school in Los Angeles.

13. Danegger, an Austrian actress and explicit communist, fled to Switzerland in 1933. In 1947, she moved back to East Berlin, where she first worked in theater and later in television and the film business.

14. In the 1970s, Friedrich Scheu published his historical account of political cabarets in Austria during the interwar period. It was titled *Humor als Waffe: Politisches Kabarett in der Ersten Republik* (Vienna: Europa Verlag, 1977).

2. FLASHBACK

1. Franz Lehár was born in 1870 in Hungary and worked in Vienna and Bad Ischl mainly as an operetta composer. Emmerich Kálmán left Vienna after the Anschluss in 1938 and went to Paris and then to the United States. The violinist and composer Fritz Kreisler emigrated from Austria in 1935, going to Monte Carlo and then, in 1939, to the United States. The writer and actor Carl Treumann lived in Hamburg and in Vienna; he was director of the Carltheater and the Kaitheater in Vienna. Mizzi Zwerenz was a theater and film actress in Vienna.

2. Fritz Grünbaum was a politically committed cabaret artist, operetta and pop composer, director, actor, and master of ceremonies. He died in 1941 at the Dachau concentration camp.

3. The name Schlaraffia is derived from the Middle High German word *Slur-Affe*; loosely translated, it means an unworried connoisseur.

4. Lindtberg emigrated from Austria to Switzerland, where he worked first as a director at the Schauspielhaus in Zurich. In the 1960s, he returned to Vienna. He was a professor at the Reinhardt Seminar, then director of the film school at the Academy of Music and Performing Arts. In 1968, he again became director of the Schauspielhaus Zurich.

5. At the beginning of the twentieth century, *Scharpie* (lint) was a typical wound dressing material consisting of fibers obtained through the plucking of cotton and linen fabrics.

6. This is probably a reference to Lassallehof at Lassallestrasse 40–44, which was built from 1924 to 1926 by the architects Hubert Gessner, Hans Paar, Fritz Schlossberg, and Fritz Waage.

7. Behrens directed the master school of architecture at the Academy of Fine Arts from 1922 to 1927. He was a successor to Otto Wagner in that position.

8. Of the many council houses on Margaretengürtel, the "ring road of the proletariat," this is probably a reference to the Metzleinstaler Hof at Margaretengürtel 90–98. In the first construction phase of 1920, it was designed by Robert Kalesa; in the second phase of 1924–25, it was built by Hubert Gessner.

9. In 1923, the socialist Wanderbund merged with the Freie Vereinigung Sozialistischer Mittelschüler, which was founded after World War I by Ludwig Wagner and Paul Lazarsfeld.

10. Marie (Mitzi) Jahoda—a committed socialist, social psychologist, and author, with her first husband, Paul Lazarsfeld, of the study *Die Arbeitslosen von Marienthal* (Leipzig: S. Hirzel, 1933)—left Austria in 1936. She and Lazarsfeld immigrated first to London, then to New York in 1945, then back to London in the fifties.

11. Popper-Lynkeus was born in 1938 in Koln, Bohemia; he worked as a social philosopher, inventor, and writer in Vienna.

12. Gruen showed his admiration for Popper-Lynkeus by titling the 1979 manuscript for his memoir "Ein Realistischer Träumer" (A realistic dreamer).

13. In the mid-1920s, the Vereinigung Sozialistischer Mittelschüler and the Sozialistische Arbeiterjugend organized country visits for urban youth. Inspired by the ideas of education reformer Eugenie Schwarzwald and fueled by their affinity with nature and political commitment, participants in these so-called holiday camps also performed ambitious amateur theater works. Of particular note is a reenactment of the sixteenth-century German Peasants' War that took place in Ferlach in the summer of 1925.

14. Kraus was editor of the magazine *Fackel* as well as an author and a fierce critic of the local media landscape.

15. The amateur theater developed in the holiday camp soon took the form of socialist hiking theater, which specialized in stagings of historical and political revues of events such as the Revolution of 1848 and the peasant liberation. This politically motivated and impromptu theater was a forerunner of the Red Players—some of the best-known authors and organizers of the hiking theater were Marie Jahoda, Paul Lazarsfeld, Robert Ehrenzweig (later Robert Lucas), Ludwig Wagner, and Hans Zeisel.

16. Jürgen Doll, in his investigation *Theater im Roten Wien: Vom Sozialdemokratischen Agitprop zum Dialektischen Theater Jura Soyfers* (Vienna: Böhlau Verlag, 1997), describes the historical events somewhat differently. According to Doll, the Socialist Event Group assisted the troupe Die Roten Spielleute (the Red Players), as well as an orchestra, a chamber choir, and a speaking chorus; the SEG also organized courses in rhythm and language education and on issues of the theater.

17. Karl Kraus wrote the Schober song in 1927. Kraus blamed Johann Schober for the bloody suppression of a revolt in July. In the play *Die Unüberwindlichen,* Kraus has the character of Wacker, inspired by Schober, sing the song: "Yes that is my duty, please don't ya

see?! Would be a story, not to do my duty, though!" Kraus wanted the song to be heard as "a hit song from proletarian housing districts." Some nineteen thousand copies of the song were sold at a price of ten pence apiece.

18. The writer and comedian Robert Ehrenzweig, later known as Robert Lucas, immigrated to London in 1943, where he worked at the German service of the BBC. He was known for the radio satire *Hirnschal-Briefe,* which took the form of a letter from a draftee to his wife. It was produced and broadcast by the BBC.

19. Polgar, a writer, critic, and translator, fled to Paris in 1938, then in 1940 moved on to Zurich, then Lisbon, and then the United States.

20. The place is now called Porgy & Bess located at Riemergasse 11.

21. In 1892 Kunschak founded the Christian Social Workers' Association, the chairmanship of which he held until 1934. From 1920 to 1934, he was a deputy in the National Council.

22. *Grüne Heinrich* is a slang term for a police transport van.

23. Weisskopf lived first in Vienna, then in Zurich. In 1938, he fled to the United States and was engaged as a physicist. During World War II, he was involved with the Manhattan Project, the U.S. atomic bomb program. He was director of CERN, in Geneva, from 1961 to 1965.

24. Josef Frank, Oskar Strand, and Oskar Wlach were among the founding members of the New Viennese housing movement and the so-called Viennese School.

25. Karla Suschitzky and her mother, Olga, led a dance school at Favoritenstrasse 76. Her father, Philip Suschitzky, and his brother Wilhelm ran a bookshop that specialized in literature of the labor movement. In 1938 the company was liquidated. Olga and Philip Suschitzky perished in the Holocaust; Karla survived in exile in Paris.

26. In 1912–13, Loos built a terraced house at Larochegasse 3 for the lawyer and Social Democratic municipal deputy Gustav Scheu and his wife, the writer Helene Scheu-Riesz. Their son, Friedrich Scheu, worked as a journalist for the *Arbeiter Zeitung.*

27. *Der Kuckuck,* published from April 1929 to February 1934, was the weekly newsmagazine of the Austrian social democracy.

28. In 1926, the art historian and bookseller Felix Reichmann owned a bookstore on the Wiener Hauptstrasse. In 1939, he immigrated to the United States, where he worked as a librarian and later as a professor of literature.

29. Lehmann, who was both a poet and a publisher, wrote about his experiences in Vienna in his book *The Whispering Gallery* (New York: Harcourt, Brace, 1955).

3. DISCOVERING AMERICA

1. Farkas, a writer, director, and actor, managed to escape Austria via Brno and Paris to New York in 1938. In 1946, he returned to Vienna and subsequently headed the theater Simpl.

2. Beatrice Kaufman launched many modern poets and novelists (including T. S. Eliot, Djuna Barnes, William Faulkner, John Steinbeck, and Eugene O'Neill). She herself wrote short stories, some of which were published in the *New Yorker,* and plays that were

performed on Broadway. Her husband, American playwright, theater director, and producer George S. Kaufman, wrote numerous comedies, political satires, and musicals, and also wrote for the Marx Brothers.

3. Donald Oenslager was an American stage set designer who won a Tony Award for Best Scenic Design in 1959. Irene Sharaff worked as a costume designer for major Broadway productions and for Hollywood. Over the course of her career, she received a total of five Oscars.

4. *Pins and Needles* was a musical revue commissioned by the International Ladies' Garment Workers' Union. It opened on Broadway in 1937 after a year of rehearsals with a cast made up of young industrial workers. With 1,107 performances, *Pins and Needles* was the most successful play on Broadway at the time.

5. Viktor Grünbaum began spelling his name Victor Gruenbaum soon after his arrival in the United States.

6. Stefan (Stephen) Klein founded Barton's Bonbonniere, better known as Barton's Candy, in 1938. The business, which was based in Brooklyn, New York, boomed in the fifties. After sixty years, the family sold the business, though the name was retained until 2009.

7. The company of Altmann & Kühne opened its first store on the Graben in 1932. It specialized in handmade miniature chocolates and other candies, which were sold in packages that were designed by the Wiener Werkstätte.

8. Emrich Nicholson, *Contemporary Shops in the United States* (New York: Architectural Book Publishing, 1945). The name Altmann & Kühne was Americanized and became Altman & Kuhne when the store opened in New York, as can be seen in the photograph of the store that appears in the preface to this book.

9. Julius Hans Weigel, Austrian writer and theater critic, survived the war years in exile in Switzerland and subsequently went back to Vienna.

10. Peter Hammerschlag was an Austrian poet, writer, and comedian. In performing as a so-called flash poet, he made up poems on the spot, often taking requests from the audience. Before the war he was the house author of the Viennese cabaret theater Der Liebe Augustin and also wrote revues for Die Stachelbeere, Literatur am Naschmarkt, and ABC, among others. He died in Auschwitz in 1942.

11. At Disney, Van Leuven was involved in the production of the animated feature films *Dumbo* (1941) and *Bambi* (1942), among others.

4. THE BIG BREAKTHROUGH

1. Victor Gruen, *How to Live with Your Architect* (New York: Store Modernization Institute, 1949).

2. This article, written circa 1930, was titled "Die Großstadt von Morgen: Ein Spaziergang durch die Stadt der Zukunft."

3. In the early 1930s Baumfeld worked as a consultant for the Viennese housing program. He then led a group studio with Norbert Schlesinger and worked as a consultant for the Julius Meinl company. Baumfeld fled to Czechoslovakia in 1938 and then to Italy, where he was arrested and imprisoned in Genoa. In 1940, he managed to escape to the United

States, where he first worked as a draftsman for the U.S. Navy and then as an employee and a partner for Victor Gruen Associates. He died in 1988 in California.

4. Victor Gruen and Larry Smith, *Shopping Towns USA: The Planning of Shopping Centers* (New York: Van Nostrand Reinhold, 1960).

5. [Jane Jacobs], "Northland: A New Yardstick for Shopping Center Planning," *Architectural Forum* 100 (June 1954): 103.

6. Dayton Hudson sold the Hudson's department store in December 1989, and on October 24, 1998, the building was destroyed. Video of this historic moment is available on YouTube; for example, see "J. L. Hudsons Department Store—Guinness World Record!!—Controlled Demolition, Inc.," https://www.youtube.com/watch?v=JP1HJoG-1Pg.

5. DEVELOPMENT OF THE STORM

1. William Severini Kowinski, "The Malling of America," *New Times*, May 1, 1978, 31–55.

2. The International Council of Shopping Centers, an international trade association, was founded in 1957. As of 2016, it had approximately sixty-seven thousand members in more than one hundred countries. Among the members are owners of shopping centers as well as developers, managers of shopping centers, and corporations and government organizations with business interests.

3. Ralph Keyes, *We, the Lonely People: Searching for Community* (New York: Harper & Row, 1973), 118.

4. Gerard K. O'Neill, *The High Frontier: Human Colonies in Space* (New York: William Morrow, 1977).

5. The Council for Mutual Economic Assistance, or Comecon, operated from 1949 to 1991 as a business organization under the hegemony of Soviet Union.

6. Victor Gruen, "Die Zukunft des Einkaufszentrums," *Perspektiven: Der Aufbau* 41, nos. 3/4 (1986): 158–59.

7. Kowinski, "The Malling of America."

8. Gruen and Smith, *Shopping Towns USA.*

9. This is a reference to the Pruitt-Igoe housing project in St. Louis, Missouri. For architectural historian Charles Jencks, the demolition of Pruitt-Igoe marked the end of modern architecture. Charles Jencks, *The Language of Post-modern Architecture* (New York: Rizzoli, 1984). By contrast, in the 2011 documentary film *The Pruitt-Igoe Myth,* director Chad Friedrich asks the residents to reconstruct the history of the complex and points to massive structural problems, strategic undersupply, and neglect.

10. Victor Gruen, "Dynamic Planning for Retail Areas," *Harvard Business Review* 32, no. 6 (November/December 1954): 53–62.

11. Victor Gruen, *The Heart of Our Cities: The Urban Crisis; Diagnosis and Cure* (New York: Simon & Schuster, 1964); Victor Gruen, *Das Überleben der Städte: Wege aus der Umweltkrise* (Vienna: Molden, 1973).

12. John Pastier, "Dallas–Fort Worth: Metroplex and MegaAirport," *AIA Journal,* March 1978, 60–68.

13. Sam Bass Warner Jr., foreword to *The Exploding Metropolis,* ed. William H. Whyte Jr. (New York: Doubleday Anchor Books, 1957), ix.

14. Among Jefferson's architectural projects were his residence at Monticello and the University of Virginia.

15. See the film *Rochester: A City of Quality,* produced by the Handy (Jam) Organization in 1963, available at the Internet Archive, https://archive.org.

16. While Baumfeld was responsible for the technical design of the clock, Geri Kavanaugh developed the concept and artistic design. Midtown Plaza was closed in July 2008, and the clock has since been exhibited in the terminal at the Rochester International Airport.

17. Bernard Taper, "The City That Puts People First: Fresno, California," *McCall's,* April 1966, 62.

18. The center, Shopping City Süd, was founded in 1976 by Hans Dujsik; in 2007, it was sold for 607 million euros to the Dutch property group Unibailrodamco.

19. Intourist was the Soviet state-run travel agency for foreign tourists; it was founded in 1929.

20. The apartment was located at Schwarzenbergplatz 10/11A.

21. The house was located at 315 North Beverly Glen Boulevard.

22. Ada Louise Huxtable, "Out of a Fair, a City," *Horizon,* May 1960, 80–89.

23. Victor Gruen, *Centers for the Urban Environment: Survival of the Cities* (New York: Van Nostrand Reinhold, 1973).

24. Richmond, who later served as a U.S. congressman from New York, was deputy finance chairman of the Democratic National Committee at this time (1958–60).

25. In 1969, the New York State Urban Development Corporation signed a lease for the island and instructed Philip Johnson and John Burgee to design social housing for twenty thousand residents.

26. Johnson and Burgee's master plan involved three stages: Northtown I, Northtown II, and Southtown. The first phase of the project, Northtown I, was completed in 1975 and included more than two thousand publicly subsidized apartments; Northtown II was completed in 1989. The construction of the third unit, Southtown, did not begin until 1998 and has not yet been completed.

27. The island was renamed for Franklin Delano Roosevelt in 1973.

6. ARCHITECTURA

1. As noted in the preface, Müller-Hartburg was president of the Chamber of Architects of Vienna, Lower Austria, and Burgenland from 1968 to 1970 and served as president of the Federal Chamber of Engineers from 1970 to 1978. In 1999, he was given the title of honorary professor at the Technical University of Graz. Müller-Hartburg built the large-capacity radar station on Kolomansberg, a Catholic church in Gablitz, and the Florido Tower in Vienna.

2. The prize was awarded in 1972.

3. The Glatt Einkaufszentrum, usually called just the Glatt, was one of the first shopping centers in Switzerland. It opened in 1975 and is located in Wallisellen at the city's border with Zurich.

4. See "New City," Talk of the Town, *New Yorker,* March 17, 1956; "Merchants Lose Downtown Blues," *New York Times,* February 27, 1955.

5. In the early 1940s, the Los Angeles public transportation system was kept in good condition by two companies, Los Angeles Railway (1,042 trams) and Pacific Electric (437 trams). In 1943, General Motors began to invest in American City Lines, which began to buy shares of Los Angeles Railway. In 1945, 59 percent of Los Angeles Railway shares were owned by American City Lines, and Los Angeles Railway publicly announced the termination of a majority of Los Angeles tram lines. In 1953, Pacific Electric was sold, and Metropolitan Coach Lines announced that, in cooperation with GM, it intended to convert the train system into a bus system. These events became known as "the great American streetcar scandal."

6. Here and below, Gruen refers to a German translation of *De architectura* published early in the twentieth century by the Langenscheidt publishing company.

7. Between 1968 and 1972, Ray Kappe was active as head of the architecture institute at California State Polytechnic University, Pomona. He later teamed up with colleagues and students to found the Southern California Institute of Architecture.

8. The book often referred to as Lewis Mumford's most important, *The City in History: Its Origins, Its Transformations, and Its Prospects* (New York: Harcourt, Brace & World, 1961), was published in German in 1963 as *Die Stadt: Geschichte und Ausblick* (Cologne: Kiepenheuer & Witsch, 1963).

9. Edgar Kaufmann was the owner of Kaufmann's department store. In addition to Fallingwater, he owned the Kaufmann House, built by Richard Neutra in 1946 in Palm Springs, California.

10. Le Corbusier, *Ausblick auf eine Architektur* (Berlin: Bertelsmann, 1969), 10.

7. ENVIRONMENTAL PLANNING

1. Joyce Haber, "Victor Gruen: Architect, Dreamer and Doer," *Los Angeles Times Magazine,* September 18, 1966, 8.

2. Gruen mentions the following examples: working with the Royal Institute of British Architects in London; working with Mayor Urban Hansen in Copenhagen, with whom he discussed the design of the first pedestrian street in Europe (Strøget); so-called Europa Talks in the city of Vienna (1973), where he gave the keynote lecture, "The European City of Light and Ghost Light"; repeated lecture tours in Scandinavia, including talks in Copenhagen, Stockholm, Oslo, Bergen, and Helsinki; meetings with the Dutch architect Jacob Bakema, especially in the context of the Northland Center in Detroit, which inspired reconstruction of the inner city of Rotterdam; participation in several conferences in Vienna together with politicians Franz Jonas (later president of Austria), Bruno Marek, Felix Slavik, and Leopold Gratz; and exchanges of views with city planners in Hamburg (Hans Konwiarz), Stockholm (Goren Sidenbladh), Zurich (Gerhard Sidler), Vienna (Roland Rainer),

Moscow (Mikhail Posokhin), Paris (Paul Delouvrier), and Venice (Giorgio Gentili), as well as with the mayor of Munich (Hans-Jochen Vogel) and the planning council of Munich (Detlef Marx).

3. Gruen, *The Heart of Our Cities*; Victor Gruen, *Die lebenswerte Stadt: Visionen eines Umweltplaners* (Munich: List, 1975).

4. The Athens Charter was adopted at the 1933 conference of the Congrès Internationaux d'Architecture Moderne (CIAM) in Athens. Under the topic "The Functional City," city planners and architects discussed the concept of a city in which planning would center on function-based zones. Le Corbusier published the Athens Charter in 1943; it was translated into German in 1962. For the Charter of Vienna, see Victor Gruen, *Charta von Wien* (Vienna: ZUP, 1973).

5. Gruen, *Centers for the Urban Environment.*

6. See Victor Gruen, "Kerngebiet Wien: Bericht über den Abschluss der ersten Arbeitsphase" (unpublished brochure, 1970), available at the Library of Congress, Washington, D.C., and the Library of the City of Vienna.

7. In the 1960s, the Danube Canal Highway was planned to run diagonally across Vienna. In 1972, after years of political conflict, Felix Slavik, then mayor of Vienna, made a perfunctory statement and dropped the project.

8. The group included Paul Blau, economist and senior official of the Vienna Chamber of Workers and Employees; Erich Bramhas, city planner and architect; Engelbert Broda, professor at the Institute of Physical Chemistry, University of Vienna; Gerhart Bruckmann, coauthor (with P. Dubach) of the book *Sonnenkraft statt Atomenergie* (Vienna: Molden, 1978); Werner Gamerith, pioneer of organic farming; Gernot Graefe, ecologist and head of the Department of Ecosystem Research of the Austrian Academy of Sciences; Werner Katzmann, marine biologist at the Federal Ministry of Health; Helmut Knötig, employee of the Human Ecological Society of Austria; Wilhelm Kühnelt, professor of zoology at the University of Vienna; Rudolf Libiseller, ecologist and expert on biological agriculture; Bernd Loetsch, chairman of the Institute for Environmental Studies and Nature Conservation at the Austrian Academy of Sciences; Egon Matzner, professor of finance at the Polytechnic and senior functionary of the Socialist Party of Austria; Franz Niessler, manufacturer of solar energy systems; Gertrude Pleskot, professor at the Institute for Zoology at the University of Vienna; Robert Reichardt, professor at the Institute of Sociology, University of Vienna; and Peter Weish, employee at the Institute for Environmental Studies and Nature Conservation at the Austrian Academy of Sciences.

9. Victor Gruen, *Leitlinien für die Stadtentwicklung Wiens* (Vienna: ZUP, 1973); Victor Gruen, *Ist Fortschritt ein Verbrechen? Umweltplanung Statt Weltuntergang* (Vienna: ZUP, 1975).

AFTERWORD

1. It appears that the original used the word *Näglein* for carnations, but this is how I remember him singing it.

2. Architectural Record, *Design for Modern Merchandising: Stores, Shopping Centers, Showrooms* (New York: F. W. Dodge, 1954).

3. Much later, Friedl Scheu published the book *Humor als Waffe.*

4. Hardwick, *Mall Maker,* 209.

5. Ibid., 216–18. The speech, titled "Shopping Centers: Why, Where, How?," was delivered at the Third Annual European Conference of the International Council of Shopping Centers, London, February 28, 1978. A shortened version appeared in print under the title "The Sad Story of Shopping Centres," *Town and Country Planning* 46, nos. 7/8 (July/August 1978): 350–53.

6. Hardwick, *Mall Maker,* 216.

7. Neal R. Peirce, "The Shopping Center and One Man's Shame," *Los Angeles Times,* October 22, 1978, D5.

CONSUMED?

1. See Gruen, *The Heart of Our Cities.*

2. Wall, *Victor Gruen.*

3. On Loos's concept of the theatricality of space, see M. Christine Boyer, *The City of Collective Memory: Its Historical Imagery and Architectural Entertainments* (Cambridge: MIT Press, 1996).

4. Victor Gruen, *Shopping Town: Memoiren eines Stadtplaners (1903–1980),* ed. Anette Baldauf (Vienna: Böhlau Verlag, 2014).

5. See Alexandra Seibel, "Vienna, Girls, and Jewish Authorship: Topographies of a Cinematic City, 1920–40" (PhD diss., New York University, 2008); Richard Sennett, *The Fall of Public Man* (1977; repr., London: Penguin, 2002).

6. Robert Musil, *Gesammelte Schriften II* (Hamburg: Rowohlt, 1978), 152.

7. Arthur Schnitzler, *Fräulein Else* (1924; repr., London: Pushkin Press, 1998).

8. Jacques Le Rider, *Modernity and Crises of Identity: Culture and Society in Fin-de-Siècle Vienna,* trans. Rosemary Morris (New York: Continuum, 1993).

9. *Women's Wear Daily,* quoted in Hardwick, *Mall Maker,* 26.

10. John McAndrew, *Guide to Modern Architecture, Northeast States* (New York: Museum of Modern Art, 1940).

11. Lewis Mumford, "The Skyline: New Faces on the Avenue," Talk of the Town, *New Yorker,* September 15, 1939, cited in Wall, *Victor Gruen,* 30.

12. Victor Gruen, speech for the press preview for Northland Center, Speech no. 9, Northland, March 15, 1954, Library of Congress Victor Gruen Collection (hereafter LoCVGC), box 81, vol. A, 1943–56.

13. See Ehrhard Bahr, *Weimar on the Pacific: German Exile Culture in Los Angeles and the Crisis of Modernism* (Los Angeles: University of California Press, 2007).

14. See Wolfgang Maderthaner and Lutz Musner, *Die Anarchie der Vorstadt: Das andere Wien um 1900* (Frankfurt: Campus, 1999); Roman Horak et al., eds., *Metropole Wien: Texturen der Moderne,* vol. 2 (Vienna: WUV, 2000).

15. See Carl E. Schorske, *Fin-de-Siècle Vienna: Politics and Culture* (New York: Alfred A. Knopf, 1980); Andreas Huyssen, "The Disturbance of Vision in Vienna Modernism," in Horak et al., *Metropole Wien,* 134.

16. Hardwick, *Mall Maker,* 125.

17. Gruen, *Centers for the Urban Environment,* 15.

18. Schorske, *Fin-de-Siècle Vienna,* 25.

19. Gruen and Smith, *Shopping Towns USA.*

20. Hardwick, *Mall Maker,* 82.

21. Victor Gruen, "Defense on the Periphery" (lecture, national convention of the American Institute of Architects, Chicago, February 2, 1951), 5, LoCVGC, box 81, vol. A.

22. See Stephen J. Whitfield, *The Culture of the Cold War,* 2nd ed. (Baltimore: Johns Hopkins University Press, 1996); Paul S. Boyer, *By the Bomb's Early Light: American Thought and Culture at the Dawn of the Atomic Age* (Chapel Hill: University of North Carolina Press, 1994).

23. Gruen, "Defense on the Periphery," 5.

24. See Marshall Berman, *All That Is Solid Melts into Air: The Experience of Modernity* (New York: Penguin, 1982).

25. Sheryl James, "Frenzy of Change: How Northland, Now 50, Jumpstarted Suburbs' Growth," *Detroit Free Press,* March 18, 2004.

26. Hardwick, *Mall Maker,* 143.

27. Victor Gruen, "The Northland Story," LoCVGC, box 79.

28. "Southdale—A Complete Living Environment," *Minneapolis Tribune,* June 18, 1952, LoCVGC, box 4.

29. Margaret Crawford, "The World in a Shopping Mall," in *Variations on a Theme Park: The New American City and the End of Public Space,* ed. Michael Sorkin (New York: Hill and Wang, 1992), 22.

30. "Southdale—A Complete Living Environment"; "Design for a Better Outdoors Indoors," *Architectural Record* 131, no. 6 (June 1962): 175–79.

31. "Suburb or Loop? Which Direction Is Mrs. Shopper Going?," *Minneapolis Tribune,* January 6, 1957, LoCVGC, oversized 5.

32. See Lizabeth Cohen, *A Consumer's Republic: The Politics of Mass Consumption in Postwar America* (New York: Alfred A. Knopf, 2003), 119.

33. Kristin Ross, *Fast Cars, Clean Bodies: Decolonization and the Reordering of French Culture* (Cambridge: MIT Press, 1995), 13.

34. Gruen, "Shopping Centers: Why, Where, How?," LoCVGC, box 78; Gruen, quoted in Peirce, "The Shopping Center and One Man's Shame." See also Gruen, *The Heart of Our Cities,* 222.

35. See Stephen Harper, "Zombies, Malls, and the Consumerism Debate: George Romero's *Dawn of the Dead,*" *Americana* 1, no. 2 (2002), http://www.americanpopularculture.com/journal.

36. Victor Gruen, transcript, NBC program, Channel 4, October 9, 1955, LoCVGC, box 81.

37. "Victor Gruen Shows Model Shopping Center of the Future," transcript, Radio Reports, Inc., January 25, 1953, LoCVGC, box 71, folder 2.

38. Walter Benjamin, *The Arcades Project* (Cambridge, Mass.: Harvard University Press, 1999).

39. Ibid., 8.

40. Walter Benjamin, *Charles Baudelaire: A Lyric Poet in the Era of High Capitalism* (London: Verso, 1989), 36; Benjamin, *The Arcades Project*, 417.

41. Benjamin, *The Arcades Project*, 475.

42. Elizabeth Wilson, *The Contradictions of Culture: Cities, Culture, Women* (London: Sage, 2001), 74.

43. Susanne Frank, *Stadtplanung im Geschlechterkampf: Stadt und Geschlecht in der Großstadtentwicklung des 19. und 20. Jahrhunderts* (Opladen: Leske und Budrich, 2003), 89–116.

44. Elizabeth Wilson, *The Sphinx in the City: Urban Life, the Control of Disorder, and Women* (London: Virago Press, 1991), 146–60.

45. Anne Friedberg, *Window Shopping: Cinema and the Postmodern* (Berkeley: University of California Press, 1993), 37.

46. Elaine S. Abelson, *When Ladies Go A-Thieving: Middle-Class Shoplifters in the Victorian Department Store* (New York: Oxford University Press, 1989), 8.

47. See Andreas Huyssen, *After the Great Divide: Modernism, Mass Culture, Postmodernism* (Bloomington: Indiana University Press, 1986).

48. See Elaine Tyler May, *Homeward Bound: American Families in the Cold War Era* (New York: Basic Books, 1988).

49. See Betty Friedan, *The Feminine Mystique* (New York: W. W. Norton, 1963).

50. See Morris Meaghan, "Things to Do with Shopping Centres," in *The Cultural Studies Reader*, ed. Simon During (London: Routledge, 1993), 295–319.

51. Rem Koolhaas, "Junkspace," *October* 100 (Spring 2002): 175, 176, 178.

52. See, for example, Hannah Arendt, *The Human Condition*, 2nd ed. (Chicago: University of Chicago Press, 1958).

53. Megan K. Stack, "Saudi Shopping Mall Offers Women a Bit of Liberation," *Los Angeles Times*, June 15, 2004.

54. Gilles Deleuze, *Cinema 1: The Movement-Image*, trans. Hugh Tomlinson and Barbara Habberjam (Minneapolis: University of Minnesota Press, 1986); Marc Augé, *Non-places: Introduction to an Anthropology of Supermodernity*, trans. John Howe (London: Verso Books, 1995).

55. Deleuze, *Cinema 1*, 109.

56. Margaret Morse, *Virtualities: Television, Media Art, and Cyberculture* (Bloomington: Indiana University Press, 1998).

57. See Margaret Crawford, "Contesting the Public Realm: Struggles over Public Space in Los Angeles," *Journal of Architectural Education* 49, no. 1 (1995): 4–9.

58. Jon Jerde, remarks in Anette Baldauf and Katharina Weingartner, *The Gruen Effect: Victor Gruen and the Shopping Mall*, documentary film (Vienna: ORF/Pooldoks, 2012).

Index

Abelson, Elaine, 277
Abend, Der (newspaper), 48
Academy of Fine Arts Vienna, 5, 36, 39
Ahlfors, Vanessa, 254
Alexander, Robert, 40, 200
Alexandria, 259
Altman & Kühne, xi, 78
American Institute of Architects, 73, 106, 147, 179, 205, 271
Antioch University, 224
Arbeiter Zeitung (newspaper), 48
Architectural Forum (magazine), 97, 98, 101, 122, 270
Architectural League, 170
Architectural Review (magazine), 266
Architecture d'Aujourd'hui, L' (magazine), 266
Arlen, Harold, 246
Arlen, Margaret, 110
Athens (Greece), 259
Athens Charter, 184, 217, 297
Attersee (Austria), 33
Auer, Michael, 27, 85, 87
Austrian National Bank, 228

Bacon, Edmund, 147
Baltimore (Maryland), 170
Barton's Bonbonniere, 77, 175, 176
Bauer, Helene, 45
Bauer, Otto, 45
Bauhaus, 38, 201, 223
Baumeister, 214
Baumfeld, Rudolf "Rudi," 38, 117, 118, 131, 134, 153, 201, 210
BBC, 50
Behrens, Peter, 39, 40
Benjamin, Walter, 275, 276
Bergen, 214
Berghof, Herbert, 68, 82
Bergman, Ingrid, 243
Berlin (Germany), 31, 32
Berlin, Irving, 68
Bertoia, Harry, 133
Boothbay Harbor, 254
Boston (Massachusetts), 141, 148, 177
Bradbury, Ray, 225
Brandt, Willy, 211
Breitner, Hugo, 45
Brentwood, 92, 164, 245
Brezhnev, Leonid, 190
Brisbane, 36
Bristol-Parfumerie, 54, 266
Broadway, ix, 51, 68, 75, 78, 235; producer, 168; show, 80, 82

Broda, Engelbert, 297
Brown, Jerry, 225
Bruckmann, Gerhart, 297
Brussels (Belgium), 215
Buchenwald, 14
Burgee, John, 295
Burgtheater, 30, 218, 248
Bund Deutscher Mädchen, 17

Cadillac, 77, 87, 111
California Council for the Humanities, 225
California Institute of Architecture, 296
California State Polytechnic University, 296
Cantor, Eddie, 68
Carltheater (Vienna), 27, 30, 290
Carpenter, Horace, 126
Center for Environmental Planning, 75, 212, 223, 229
Central Park, 59, 199
Centre Pompidou, 205
Chandigarh (India), 201
Charter of Vienna, 217, 228
Cherbourg, 244
Chicago (Illinois), 85, 202, 203
Christian Social Party, 11, 48
Christian Social Workers' Association, 292
Chrysler, 272
Cincinnati, 148
Columbia University, 209
Contini, Edgardo, 106, 117–18, 170, 201
Council for Mutual Economic Assistance, 294
Cousteau, Jean-Michel, 225
Crawford, Elsie, 261
Crawford, Margaret, xiii, 273
Czar Peter the Great, 160
Czartoryskischlössel, 43

Dachau, 14
Dallas, 147
Danegger, Mathilde, 23, 290
da Vinci, Leonardo, 108
Dayton, Bruce, 133
Dayton Hudson Corporation, 231, 294
Dayton's department store, 131, 133–34, 199
Delouvrier, Paul, 297
Detroit, 109–11, 113–15, 117–18, 120, 125, 128, 130
Detroit Free Press (newspaper), 272
Detroit Times (newspaper), 124
Deutsch, Julius, 45, 48
Deutsche Bank, 31
Doll, Jürgen, 291
Dollfuß, Engelbert, 9
Donnelly, Ignatius, 43
Dubach, Paul, 297
Dujsik, Hans, 295

Eames, Charles, 270
Eastland, 117, 121, 128
École des Beaux-Arts, 222
École Nationale des Ponts et Chaussées, 222
EDAW (Eckbo, Dean, Austin, and Williams), 154
Edina (Minnesota), vi, 131–32, 134, 272
Edlach an der Rax, 33
Ehrenzweig, Robert (Lucas), 47, 50, 54, 267, 291–92
Eibenschütz, Siegmund, 30
Einstein, Albert, 63–65, 68
Eisenhower, Dwight, 142, 169, 170
Eliot, T. S., 292
Emesiobi, Benson, 225
Environmental Protection Agency, 141, 191, 225
Environmental Quality Act, 225
Esprit Nouveau (newspaper), 200
Eutin (Schleswig-Holstein), 31, 32, 214

Fallingwater, 199, 296
Faneuil Hall (Boston), 141
Farkas, Karl, 67, 292
Faulkner, William, 292

Federal Chambers of Architects and Engineers, 176–78
Federal Ministry for Science and Research, 50, 228–29
Federal Ministry of Health, 297
Fehr, Selmar, 31
Ferber, Edna, 68
Ferdinand, Archduke Franz, 29
Ferlach, 291
Florido Tower (Vienna), 289, 295
Ford, 111, 272
Fort Worth (Texas), 144, 146–48, 151, 254
Foundation for Environmental Planning, 212. *See also* Center for Environmental Planning
Franco, Benny, 23, 239
Frank, Josef, 52
Frank, Susanne, 276
Franz Joseph I (emperor), 33, 180, 248
Fresno (California), 154
Friedberg, Anne, 276

Gablitz (Austria), 289, 295
Galleria Vittorio Emanuele (Milan), 131, 272
Gamerith, Werner, 297
Geddes, Norman Bel, 65–66
General Motors, 65–66, 130, 187–88, 272, 296
Gentili, Giorgio, 297
Gessner, Hubert, 291
Gestapo, 16, 20–22, 34, 51, 268
Ghaffari, Fereydoon, 156
Gimbels (store), 187
Glas: Österreichs Glaserzeitung (newspaper), 266
Glass, Annette, 23
Glatt (Einkaufszentrum), x, 226, 296
Glatt AG, 178
Goethe, Johann Wolfgang von, 38, 231
Gofman, John, 225
Goldstein, Ben, 110, 112
Goldstein, Edna, 112
Gosman, Paul, 18, 61
Graefe, Gernot, 297
Gratz, Leopold, 296
Grayson's, 83–85, 87–90, 96–97, 101, 109
Greater Fort Worth Tomorrow, The, 146
Gropius, Walter, 201
Gruen, Alexis, 256
Gruen, Elly (Elizabeth Lea Levi), 25–26
Gruen, Luise, 25–26, 30, 31, 48
Gruen, Madeleine, 82, 254
Gruen, Michael, xiii, 32, 96, 99, 207, 210, 235, 266, 270
Gruen, Peggy, xiii, 2, 26, 39, 44, 60, 76, 79, 86, 89, 93, 95, 99, 105, 107, 165, 168, 176, 196, 221, 231
Gruen, Viveca, 256
Grünbaum, Adolf, 25
Grünbaum, Fritz, 27, 290
Grünbaum, Viktor, ix, 36, 39, 44, 46, 53, 69, 70, 265–68, 293
Grunewald, 203
Guttman, Herman, 134
Györgyfalvay, Adolf, 21–22

Habsburg, Otto, 33
Hagen, Uta, 82
Halpern, Fritz, 51
Halpern, Liese, 51
Halprin, Lawrence, 147
Hamburg (Germany), 27, 31–32, 214, 290
Hamilton, Calvin, 225
Hammerschlag, Peter, 80, 293
Hansen, Urban, 296
Hardwick, M. Jeffrey, vii, 256
Harnisch, Walter, 48, 51
Harris, Phil, 83–84
Hart, Moss, 68
Harvard Business Review, 144
Harvard University, 144, 251
Hamburg, 214
Haussmann, Georges-Eugène, 217

Hershey (Pennsylvania), 197
Hiroshima (Japan), 99
Hirten, John, 225
Hitler, Adolf, 9, 12, 18, 22–23, 36, 47, 49, 65, 82, 96, 202
Hockett, Hortense, 210
Hoffmann, Josef, 78
Hollywood (California), 92, 242, 278, 293
Honolulu (Hawaii), 162
Horizon (magazine), 170
Horner, Harry, 51, 82
Hoyt, Homer, 121
Hudson's, 109, 113–16, 118–21, 123, 125, 127–30, 133, 232, 269
Human Ecological Society of Austria, 297
Huxtable, Ada Louise, 170

Illinois Institute of Technology in Chicago, 201
Inger, Manfred, 51
Innsbruck (Austria), 157
International Council of Shopping Centers, 137, 139–40, 294
Isfahan (Iran), 158
Ithaca (New York), 54
Ivel, 61, 65, 74, 78, 261

Jacobs, Jane, 122–23
Jahnel, Fritz, 15, 226, 290
Jahoda, Edi, 42
Jahoda, Fritz, 42, 47, 50–51
Jahoda, Marie "Mitzi," 291
Jahoda, Rosi, 42
Jarka, Horst, 50
Jefferson, Thomas, 149, 295
Jencks, Charles, 294
Jesus Christ, 29
J. L. Hudson, 110, 113, 269
Jolson, Al (Asa Yoelson), 68
Johnson, Lady Bird, 162–63
Johnson, Lyndon B., 155, 246
Johnson, Philip, 174, 179, 201, 204–5
Jonas, Franz, 296
Joseph Magnin, 102–3
Julius Meinl, 293

Kafka, Richard, 15
Kahn, Albert, 106
Kaitheater, 290
Kalamazoo (Michigan), 148, 231–33
Kalesa, Robert, 291
Kálmán, Emmerich, 27, 290
Kansas City (Missouri), 102
Kappe, Ray, 194, 296
Kardos, Alice "Lizzie," xi, 52–53, 236, 268
Karl (emperor), 33, 42
Katzmann, Werner, 297
Kaufman, Beatrice, 68, 292
Kaufman, George S., 68, 293
Kaufmann, Edgar, 199, 296
Kaufmann House, 296
Kaufmann's, 296
Kavanaugh, Geri, 295
Kendall, Henry W., 225
Keneas, Sebastian, 254
Keneas, Stefan, 254
Kennedy, John F., 155, 225, 245–46
Ketchum, Morris, 70–71, 74, 268
Keyes, Ralph, 139
Kirschner, Walter, 84–85, 87–91, 97
Khrushchev, Nikita, 190
Klein, Stefan, 75–77, 108
Kleines Blatt (newspaper), 48
Klimt, Gustav, 33, 213
Knötig, Helmut, 297
Kodak, 150, 152
Kokoschka, Oskar, 165, 249
Konwiarz, Hans, 297
Koolhaas, Rem, 278, 286
Kornhäusel, Josef, 29
Kouschai, Heiman, 83, 84
Kowinski, William Severini, viii
Kraus, Karl, 43, 291–92
Kreisky, Bruno, 44, 211

Kreisler, Fritz, 27, 290
Krummeck, Elsie, x, xiii, 62, 74, 79, 86–87, 89, 93, 98, 106–8, 118, 136, 236, 238, 261–63, 268, 270–71, 273
Kuckuck, Der (magazine), 48
Kühnelt, Wilhelm, 297
Kunschak, Leopold, 48, 292

Langer, Karl, 36, 38
LaRosa, Ben, 62
Las Vegas (Nevada), 88, 90–91
Latouche, John, 67
Lazarsfeld, Paul, 43, 291
Le Corbusier, 38, 108–9, 184, 200–201, 217, 297
Lederer, 71–73, 78, 268
Lederer, Ludwig, 69, 70, 268
Lehár, Franz, 27, 290
Lehmann, John, 56
Lehmann, Lotte, 54
Lemberger, Hedi, 30
Lemberger, Leopold, 23, 33
Lemberger, Poldi, 30
Lemberger, Vally, 30
Leningrad (Soviet Union), 160–61
Leshay Foundation, 225
Lessack, Arthur, 67
Libiseller, Rudolf, 297
Library of Congress, vii, viii, 297
Lindsay, John, 174
Literatur am Naschmarkt, 293
Lloyd, Susie, 252
London (England), 20, 23, 51, 140, 214, 256, 296, 298
London's Crystal Palace, 170
Loos, Adolf, 266
Los Angeles (California), xii, 30, 31, 51, 77, 85–97, 102–5, 109–10, 114–15, 117, 120, 125, 134, 144, 154, 155, 159, 164, 166–67, 171–72, 176, 183–85, 187–89, 196, 199–200, 202, 210, 212–16, 224–26, 228–29, 236, 238–42, 245, 249–50, 263–64, 270, 278–82, 286, 290; County Museum of Art, 264; hall of records, 200; railway, 296
Los Angeles Times (newspaper), 212, 283
Louvain (Belgium), 215
Löwenfeld, Richard, 266
Lowry, Harry (Herbert Levi), 7, 31, 74
Lustig, Alvin, 77, 198

Macy's, 77, 102, 186–87, 276
Mader, Friedrich Wilhelm, 43
Magnin, Cyril, 102
Mall of America, 257
March, Fredric, 68
Marek, Bruno, 296
Marseilles (France), 214
Marx, Detlef, 297
Marx, Harpo, 68
Marx, Zeppo, 68
Matzner, Egon, 297
Max Reinhardt Seminar, 18, 289–90
Mayerhofer, Mary, 51
McCall's (magazine), 154
McCurdy's, 150–51
Meiselmann, Arnold, 48, 51
Melcher, Edmund, 34, 38, 40–41
Melcher and Steiner, 41
Metropolitan Coach Lines, 296
Metzleinstaler Hof (Vienna), 291
Michaelerplatz (Vienna), 249
Michaelis, Helen, 210
Michel, Werner, 80
Midtown Plaza, 150–53, 185–87, 295
Mid-Wilshire Medical Building, 106
Miklas, Wilhelm, 7
Milliron's, 103–5, 241
Minneapolis (Minnesota), 131, 134, 231, 272–73
Moholy-Nagy, Claudia, 223
Moholy-Nagy, László, 223
Molden, Fritz, 271
Monte Carlo (Monaco), 290
Monticello (Virginia), 295

Moscow (Russia), 123, 160–61, 189–90
Mueller, Theodore, 34
Müller-Hartburg, Herbert, xii, 178, 289, 295
Mumford, Lewis, 197, 268, 296
Munich (Germany), 94, 139–40
Mürren (Switzerland), 191
Music Box Theatre, 80
Musil, Robert, 267

Nagasaki (Japan), 99
NASA, 139
National Endowment for the Arts, 225
National Socialist Party, 9, 15, 21
Neubauer, Evelyn, vii
Neue Heimat, 214
Neumann-Viertel, Liesl, 51
Neunkirchen (Upper Austria), 48
Neutra, Richard, 200, 296
Never Again War Movement, 5
Newark (New Jersey), 88, 90
Newhall, Scott, 171
New Times (magazine), 137, 140
New York, ix, xiii, 7–8, 14–15, 20, 30, 41, 50–52, 54, 59, 61–63, 65, 67–70, 73–74, 77–78, 80, 85, 87–88, 90–91, 93, 101–2, 107–8, 114, 129, 150, 155, 160, 164, 166, 174, 177, 186, 194, 199, 203–4, 210, 214–15, 226, 235–36, 239, 242, 245–47, 254, 262, 268, 269, 270, 289–93
New York Museum of Modern Art, 268
New York State Urban Development Corporation, 295
New York Times (newspaper), 80, 170, 187
New Yorker (magazine), 268, 292
Nicholson, Emrich, 78, 293
Niessler, Franz, 297
Nixon, Richard, 245
North Beverly Glen Boulevard, 295
Northland Center, 117–18, 121–23, 125–31, 133, 135, 144–45, 231, 269, 272, 296

Oakland Museum of California, 264
Oenslager, Donald, 68, 293
Old Denmark, 78
Oldsmobile, 111
Omaha (Nebraska), 85
O'Neill, Eugene, 292
O'Neill, Gerard, 139

Paar, Hans, 291
Pacific Electric, 296
Palm Springs (California), 87, 296
Palo Alto (California), 102
Paris, 15, 18, 20, 23, 32, 57, 125, 157, 160–61, 167, 194, 200–201, 205, 214–15, 222, 275, 290, 292
Pelli, Cesar, 140, 210, 211
Pepperdine University, 224, 226
Philadelphia (Pennsylvania), 147–48, 203
Piano, Renzo, 205
Pleskot, Gertrude, 297
Polgar, Alfred, 47, 292
Political Cabaret, ix, 5–6, 45–46, 48–51, 54, 56, 62, 68, 82, 267, 290
Popper-Lynkeus, Josef, 42, 291
Porgy & Bess, 292
Porter, Cole, 246
Portland (Oregon), 85, 87
Prague (Czech Republic), 28, 50
Prein-an-der-Rax (Austria), 254
Presidential Council on Environmental Quality, 225
Princeton University, 63
Pruitt-Igoe housing project (Missouri), 294
Pullman Company, 111

Qualtinger, Helmut, 15–16

Rabin-Epstein, Rose-Marie, 223, 225
Radburn (New Jersey), 122
Rainer, Ludwig, 32, 33
Rainer, Roland, 32, 296
Raudnitz, Illa, 20, 24, 51, 267, 290

Reichardt, Robert, 297
Reichmann, Felix, 52, 54, 292
Reichmann, Lilly, 52, 54
Retailing Daily (magazine), 102
Reuther, Walter, 203
Richmond, Fred, 173, 295
Ringstrasse (Vienna), 30, 180, 218, 219, 247, 248, 269, 270
Rochester (New York), 150, 153
Rockefeller, Lawrence, 162
Rockefeller, Nelson, 170
Rockefeller Center, 70, 122
Rodgers, Richard, 68, 205
Rome (Italy), 259
Romero, George, 139, 274
Roosevelt, Eleanor, 82, 123
Roosevelt, Franklin, 239, 245, 273
Rotterdam (Netherlands), 296
Ruckelshaus, William D., 225

Saarinen, Eero, 130
Sacramento (California), 148
Salihefendic, Kemal, 112
Salihefendic, Kemija, xii, 164, 249
Salzburg (Austria), 165, 249; Marionette Theater, 80
Salzer, Felix, 30
San Bernardino (California), 148
San Diego (California), 85
San Francisco (California), 62, 77, 85, 88, 90, 102–3, 150, 154, 171, 195
San Francisco Chronicle, 171
Santa Barbara (California), 94
Santa Catalina (Los Angeles County), 91
Santa Monica (California), 85, 242
Scheu, Friedl, 251, 298
Scheu, Gustav, 292
Scheu, Herta, 251
Scheu-Riesz, Helene, 292
Schiele, Egon, 33
Schlesinger, Norbert, 293
Schlossberg, Fritz, 291
Schlosser, Friedrich Christoph, 43
Schnitzler, Arthur, 267
Schober, Johann, 46, 291
Schober, Monette, 51
Schuschnigg, Kurt, 7, 9, 23, 289
Schwab's Drugstore, 93
Schwarzenbergplatz (Vienna), vii, xi, 165, 249, 253
Schwarzwald, Eugenie, 291
Seagram Building, 203–4
Seattle (Washington), 83, 85, 90, 226
Secession, 43, 108
Seeber, Ursula, xiii
Seeboden (Austria), 33
Seibel, Alexandra, 298
Seitz, Karl, 45
Shanghai (China), 51
Sharaff, Irene, 68, 293
Shopping Centers Today (magazine), 139
Shopping City Süd, 295
Sidenbladh, Goren, 296
Sidler, Gerhard, 296
Singer, Betty, 29
Singer, Kurt, 39, 56
Singer, Rudolf, 24
Slavik, Felix, 247, 296, 297
Smith, Larry, 121, 123, 140
Social Christian Party, 9
Social Democratic Party (Austria), 6, 9–11, 44, 245
Socialist Party of Austria, 297
Société Civile de Recherches sur l'Urbanisme, 215
Socony Oil Company, 61
Sorkin, Michael, xiii
Southdale Center, vi, 132–35, 137, 150–51, 199, 231, 257, 272–74
Southern California Institute of Architecture, 296
Southland, Ben, 118, 201
Southland Center, 117

Soyfer, Jura, 14, 47, 49–50, 56, 67, 80, 82, 267, 290–91
Spokane (Washington), 226
Staber, Johann, 211
Stalin, Josef, 180
Stalingrad (Russia), 22
Steinbeck, John, 292
Steiner, Leo, 38, 39, 41
Steiner, Willy, 23, 30
Stevens, Roger, 169
Stevenson, Adlai, 245
Stockholm (Sweden), 296
Stone, Edward, 70–71, 74
St. Wolfgang (Austria), 249
Suschitzky, Karla, 52, 292
Suschitzky, Philip, 292
Susman, Tracy, 223, 225

Tagesanzeiger, 223
Tandler, Julius, 45
Taper, Bernard, 154
Technical University of Graz, 289, 295
Texas Electric Service Company, 144
Theater Simpl, 292
Time (magazine), 259
Tishman Realty, 102
Treumann, Carl, 27, 290
Trinity Church (New York), 73

Udall, Stewart, 155, 162–63, 225
Ulanowsky, Lilian, 54
Ulanowsky, Paul, 54
Unibailrodamco, 295
United Nations (Vienna), 178, 210, 211
University of California, 209
University of Vienna, 228
University of Virginia, 295
Unruh, Jesse, 252
Urban Renewal Authority, 142–43

Valencia (Los Angeles), 171
van der Rohe, Ludwig Mies, 201, 204, 270
van Houten, Lazette, xi, 101, 164, 250
Van Leuven, Karl, 96, 102–3, 116–18, 120, 125, 247, 293
Van Nuys (California), 226
Venice (Italy), 160, 297
Verne, Jules, 43
Victor Gruen Associates, xii, 143, 146–47, 154–55, 177, 209, 294
Victor Gruen International, xi, 213, 215, 218, 220
Victor Gruen Planning and Architecture, 215
Vienna, vii, ix, xi, xii, xiii, xiv, 2, 4–20, 22–23, 25–26, 29–30, 32, 34, 36, 39, 43, 45–47, 51–52, 55, 61–67, 69, 71, 74–75, 78, 80, 82, 94, 108, 117, 146, 155, 164–67, 176–78, 183, 189, 194, 210–15, 217–18, 220–22, 226–28, 236, 242, 246–49, 251–54, 257–59, 265–70, 289–91
Viennese Refugee Artists Group, 67, 289
Viennese Theatre Group, 66, 80, 82
Vitruvius Pollio, Marcus, 192–93, 195, 198, 206
Vogel, Hans-Jochen, 297

Waage, Fritz, 291
Wagner, Louis, 43
Wagner, Ludwig, 291
Wagner, Otto, 38, 108–9, 291
Wagner, Robert, 173–74
Wallisellen (Switzerland), 296
Walt Disney Studios, 96
Warren, Charles, 225
Washington, D.C., vii, 139, 149, 155, 162, 169, 210, 217, 297
Washington, George, 149
Washington, George (mayor), 162
Washington Square Park (New York), 245
Weaver, Robert, 155
Webber, James B., 114, 115
Webber, Oscar, 113–16, 118–20, 123, 125, 127–28, 131, 269

Wehrmacht, 12, 18
Weidling-Wurzbachtal an der Stadtbahn, 33
Weigel, Julius Hans, 80, 293
Weingartner, Katharina, xiii
Weish, Peter, 297
Weisskopf, Victor, 50, 292
Welfare Island, 173
Westchester (California), 103, 241
Weys, Rudolf, 50
Wilkins, Fred, 113
Wilson, Elizabeth, 276
Wilson, Harold, 211
Windsor (Canada), 111
Winston, Selig, 61
Wittgenstein, Ludwig, 30
Wlach, Oskar, 52
Wright, Frank Lloyd, 195, 198–99

Yale University's School of Architecture, 143, 210
Yamasaki, Minoru, 203
Yorke, Ruth, 68
Yorkville (New York), 67

Zeisel, Hans, 291
Zimbelius, Hermann, 47, 50
Zita (empress), 33
Zobel, Karl, 51
Zurich, 6, 20, 23, 226
Zwerenz, Mizzi, 27, 30, 290

VICTOR GRUEN (1903–1980) was one of the most influential architects of the twentieth century. He is widely considered the inventor of the shopping mall and was an innovative urban designer throughout his life.

ANETTE BALDAUF is professor at the Academy of Fine Arts Vienna in Austria. Her projects include *Entertainment City* and the documentary film *The Gruen Effect: Victor Gruen and the Shopping Mall.*

MICHAEL GRUEN is a lawyer with a special interest in land-use law and related constitutional issues. He is president of The City Club of New York, a tax-exempt organization that focuses on improving the urban environment. He lives and works in New York City.

PEGGY GRUEN is a fine art photographer. She lives in Belchertown, Massachusetts.